William McBrien is a professor of English at Hofstra University. His other books include *Stevie: A Biography of Stevie Smith*; *Me Again: Uncollected Writings of Stevie Smith* and *Stevie Smith: A Bibliography*. He lives in Forest Hills, New York.

COLE PORTER

The Definitive Biography

WILLIAM McBRIEN

HarperCollins*Publishers*

HarperCollins*Publishers*
77–85 Fulham Palace Road,
Hammersmith, London W6 8JB

www.**fire**and**water**.com

This paperback edition 1999
1 3 5 7 9 8 6 4 2

First published in Great Britain by
HarperCollins*Publishers* 1998

Owing to a limitation of space, all
acknowledgements for permission to
quote previously published material
may be found on page 460.

ISBN 0 00 637536 7

Set in Adobe Garamond

Printed and bound in Great Britain by
Clays Ltd, St Ives plc

For Andrew J. Kappel

(1951–1992)

Contents

Acknowledgments

It is a pleasure to salute the many people who have lent accuracy, astuteness, and style to my account of Cole Porter's life.

I'm often asked what led me to write a biography of Porter. The story of this book begins with Annie Dillard, a writer I admire and a dear friend. It seems that *Interview* magazine was in search of a likely writer to do a short piece on Cole Porter, and consulted Annie, who had liked *Stevie: A Biography of Stevie Smith*, which I'd recently coauthored with Jack V. Barbera. No doubt she recalled how, as fellows at the Ossabaw Island artists' colony, we several times sneaked into the vacant composer's studio, played and sang Cole Porter songs, and danced (at least the fleet-footed Annie did, even on the tables, the piano, and the window ledges). So she kindly recommended me to *Interview* and I wrote "Cole Porterland," which people seemed to enjoy. The little research I managed to do revealed to me that, with the exception of George Eells's biography, good as far as it goes, Robert Kimball's elegant *Cole* (a suavely scholarly collection of stunning photographs with linking commentary), and Brendan Gill's essays, too little serious attention had been paid to Porter in print.

I approached Robert Montgomery, trustee of the Porter estate, for permission to consult the Porter Archives, and he graciously granted my request. Throughout the years of my research and writing I have found him to be always urbane, generous, and supportive. He opened many doors for me, often persuading the reluctant to admit me to their corner of Porter's world. I owe Robert Montgomery special thanks.

The Cole family have been encouragingly warm and cooperative. The late James O. Cole escorted me around Peru, Indiana, and the places Cole frequented there. He answered all my questions and introduced me to directors of what were then the Porter Archives in Peru. His daughter

Margaret Cole, Porter's cousin, and her husband, Ralph, have been no less encouraging.

Carol Porr has kept the watch with me since I began writing this book. She has tolerated with the greatest grace my authorial vagaries and transformed my sorry script via the computer into beautifully legible print. I can never exaggerate the assistance she prodigally provided. My reliable major-domo at Hofstra University, Keith Dallas, has also offered me invaluable aid for which I am hugely grateful. My colleagues in the English department at Hofstra University have cheered me on, Robert Sargent and Dana Brand especially. And the administration kindly awarded me special leaves that facilitated my task. I thank them all.

The person whom I thank most is my sister, Suzanne Burnett. She has fed and housed me, looked after me when I was ill, discussed my text as it progressed, and offered invaluable editorial suggestions. In fact she has proved herself to be an editor of the first rank, dogged and discriminating in her perspicacious pursuit of my intentions and my realization of them in the manuscript. Her loving companionship has helped dispel the loneliness of which all working writers complain, and sweetened my tasks.

I thank, too, Robert Kimball, the dean of Porter studies, without whose writings on Porter, especially his book *The Complete Lyrics of Cole Porter*, I could not have completed this biography. He also read my manuscript and gave me informed and clever criticism about the shape of my work. I am touched that he found time in his busy life to offer articulate, abundant, and nourishing appraisals of this book.

Professor Jack V. Barbera, with whom I coauthored three books (one a biography) about Stevie Smith, is a dear friend who sacrificed weeks of precious summer holiday time to assessments of my work. I value his companionship even more than I do his critical brilliance.

Finally in this listing comes my editor at Knopf, Victoria Wilson, who more suitably might appear first. I shall always be grateful to her for smiling on my proposal for this book and deciding to acquire it. Since that time she has known when to slacken the reins and when to tighten them. (Ditto for Lee Buttala.) Both her taste and intelligence have resulted in a shapelier, more beautiful book. Both Victoria Wilson and my agent, Georges Borchardt, believed that the time had come to have a full biography of Cole Porter and that I might be the person to write it. Was it Hippolyte Taine who said success in writing came from a felicitous conjunction of *l'homme, moment, et milieu*? I believe, as do my publishers, that this book represents such a conjunction. I can only hope that it will give pleasure to the audience who already know and love Porter's work. If others happen upon it, my hope is that they will sample the sortilege that only a Cole song can supply.

Unfortunately I have not the space to describe in detail the assistance so many friends and professional associates of Porter offered me. I name them here with gratitude, well-aware as they must also be of the magnitude of their varying contributions:

David Acheson; Audrey Aurette; Lauren Bacall; Stephen Bach; Ben Bagley; Nelson Barclift; Jerry Barone; Ben Hur Baz; William E. Beaudreau; Earl Blackwell; Charles Bowden; Hazel Bowland; Dr. Leonard Brand; Charlotte Breese; Mrs. Francis Brennan; Bricktop; Mrs. John Otto Briney; Helen Brundage; Frank Campbell; Carmen Capalbo; Margaret Carson; Al Cendry; Cyd Charisse; Saul Chaplin; Mrs. Eleanor Childs; Walter Clemons; Jack Coble; Mrs. Gary Cooper; Anita Colby; Mr. and Mrs. James O. Cole; David Columbia; Betty Comden; Mrs. Howard Cullman; Tony Curtis; Jack Daney; Raymond Daum; Richard DeMenocal; Agnes de Mille; Honoria Murphy Donnelly; Peter Duchin; Louise Dushkin; John Eaton; Tanya Elg; Richard Falk; Joseph N. Farrell; Prince Jean-Louis Faucigny-Lucinge; J. Barry Ferguson; Cy Feuer; Geraldine Fitzgerald; Joan Fontaine; Colin Leslie Fox; Gant Gaither; Helen Gallagher; John Galliher; Nancy Gardiner; Betty Garrett; James Gavin; George [Jongeyans] Gaynes; Leonard Gershe; Elisabeth Giansiracusa; Brendan Gill; Robert Giroux; Carol and John Glanville; Frances Gershwin Godowsky; Leonard Goldstein; Richard Goldstone; Dr. Edward and Marion Goodman; Dolores Gray; Adolph Green; Dick Haas; Jean Haas; Marty Hall; Aurand Harris; Jones Harris; Kitty Carlisle Hart; June Havoc; Anthony Heilbut; Katharine Hepburn; Jane Hermann; Hildegarde; Fred Hill; Dorothy Hirshon; Hanya Holm; Mrs. Arthur Hornblow; Mark Horowitz; Horst P. Horst; Bart Howard; Jean Howard; Henry B. Hyde; Maria Cooper Janis; Polly Kahn; Richard Kamror; Garson Kanin; Frank Kellogg; Mr. and Mrs. Ray Kelly; Edwin Kennebeck; Michael Kidd; Eve Auchincloss Kingsland; James Kingsland; Joseph Kissane; Miles Kreuger; Gavin Lambert; Mark Landeryou; Ward Landrigan; Burton Lane; Paula Laurence; Nicholas Lawford; Florence Leeds; Richard Lehan; Richard Lewine; Lilo; Mrs. Donald J. MacDonald; Dominique Marteau; Ernest Martin; Ava Astaire McKenzie; Alleyn McClerin; George Melly; David Midland; Joyce Miller; Jules Modlin; Ethan Mordden; Patricia Morison; Sheridan Morley; Mr. and Mrs. Bearrs Muhlfeld; Senator George Murphy; Peter Murphy; Charles Nicholson; Jarmila Novotna; Kathleen O'Brien; Gretchen O'Reilly; Valerie Paley; Catherine Paura; Michael Pearman; David Peck; Charles Perrier; Mrs.

Alton Peters; Michelle Phillips; Harold Dutch Rader; Charles Reilly; Margaret Cole Richards; Ralph D. Richards; Comtesse de Rochambeau; Gloria Romanov; Steve Ross; Nedda Rubinstein; Keith Runyon; Mrs. John Barry Ryan; Stuart Scheftel; Fifi Laimbeer Schiff; Louise Cole Schmitt; Ann Kaufman Schneider; Marian Seldes; Artie Shaw; Bobby Short; Allen Silverstein; Babs Simpson; Donald Smith; Elise Smith; Sally Bedell Smith; Sam Stark; Stephen Stempler; Roberta Statts; Marti Stevens; Mrs. John Sturges; Arnold Saint Suber; Gisela Svetlik; Selma Tamber; James Tamulis; Samuel W. Thomas; Louise Thwing; Theodore Uppman; Amanda Vail; Jean Vanderbilt; Benay Venuta; Gwen Verdon; Gore Vidal; J. Watson Webb; Elisabeth Welch; Charles Whaley; Robert Wheaton; Janet Wightman; Billy Wilder; Julie Wilson; William Wright; and Gretchen Wyler.

I should like to thank the staffs of libraries, special collections, and archives who made available to me papers, pictures, and other items that often helped my research. These include: Academy of Motion Picture Arts and Sciences; The Margaret Herrick Library; University of Arizona at Tempe, Special Collections, in particular, Kathy Hrzys and Marilyn Wurzburger; Harry Ransom Humanities Research Center, University of Texas at Austin, especially Professor Thomas Staley, Sally Leach, Raymond Daum, and Kathy Henderson; Baylor University Libraries; Armstrong Browning Library at Waco, Texas, especially Betty A. Coley; Bernard Berenson Archives (Harvard University) at I Tatti, Florence Italy; Boston University (Mugar Memorial Library) Special Collections; British Theatre Library (London), especially Claire Hudson; Columbia University Libraries, especially Oral History Research Office and Special Collections. I am particularly grateful to Ronald Grele; The Condé Nast Library (New York), thanks to Andrea Payne; The Filson Club Historical Society (Louisville, Kentucky), especially James J. Holmberg; Isabella Gardiner Museum (Boston), special thanks to Susan Sinclair; Harvard University Libraries, including the Harvard Theater Collection, Annette Fern was especially helpful; Library of Congress, Music Division, I thank Mark Horowitz particularly; Lilly Library, Indiana University; Miami County Museum (Peru, Indiana), especially Mary L. James, Joyce Miller, and Mildred Kopis; The Museum of the City of New York and the curator Michael Jacobs; Museum of Modern Art Film Studies Center (New York), Anne Morra was especially helpful; Museum of Television and Radio (New York); New York Genealogical and Biographical Society (New York City); The New York Public Library of the Performing Arts at Lincoln Center; The Players Club (New York); The Hampden-Booth Theater Library, particularly Raymond Wemmlinger; Schola Cantorum (Paris), *merci beaucoup* to Mme. Treel; The Shubert

Archive (New York), thanks to Regan Fletcher; State Historical Society of Wisconsin (Madison), Elise Yee was helpful; Yale University Library, the Beinecke Rare Book Manuscript Library, especially Patricia C. Willis, curator. At the Music Library, I must mention Ken Crilly. Most important to my research at Yale was the expert and gracious assistance of Richard Warren Jr., curator of Historical Sound Recordings; University of Southern California, Special Collections; University of Wisconsin Library, special thanks to William E. Beaudreau and Harold L. Miller; The Worcester Academy Records, Worcester, Massachusetts.

COLE PORTER

Chapter 1

We Open in Peru

In 1905, when Cole Porter, a boy of fourteen, boarded the train for Worcester Academy in Massachusetts, he must have felt both triumphant and troubled. His struggle to free himself from his wealthy grandfather's demands that he remain at home in Peru, Indiana, and attend local schools had succeeded. In this he was abetted by his redoubtable mother, Katie Cole Porter, who in her youth had herself acquired an eastern education, at Colby Academy in New London, Connecticut and then at Brooks Seminary in New York. There is no evidence that J. O. Cole opposed this move by the daughter upon whom he doted. In fact, in August of 1882 J.O. and his wife "gave a reception and dance, honoring their daughter, Miss Kate Cole, just returned from college in the east." But when it came to his grandson, J.O.'s attitude was entirely otherwise. Interestingly, Cole's father took no part in this quarrel.

By now J.O. presided over a financial empire of vast proportions, all of it self-earned, and he had promised his grandson a large share of his fortune. So Cole was jeopardizing an enormous inheritance in countering J.O.'s will. Cole knew his grandfather's promise of a fortune was not ironclad, or at least that is the conclusion he must have drawn from the experience he once related to a biographer. When he was only eight years old, Cole recalled, J.O. used to drive him a couple of miles out into the rolling Indiana countryside and rein in his horse at the top of a rise. He would point with the end of his buggy whip at a large rather bleak gray building. That, Cole, he would say with satisfaction, is the place where you will end up. It was the county poorhouse.

When J.O. threatened to terminate Cole's allowance, Katie did not waver. She responded to her father's refusal to finance Cole's education by using her own money, and by opposing her father's tyranny she taught her son courage and perseverance. "Tyrant," by the way, is a word Cole himself used to describe his grandfather. Annually on J.O.'s birthday his wife gave what Cole called " 'too long dinners' which all were obliged to attend." Everyone hated it because his grandfather was so "dictatorial"— "the strong man."

J.O. seemed not to realize, when his daughter announced to him her plan for Cole to be educated at East Coast schools, that Katie was exercising the very determination she had inherited from J.O. himself. Cole left for Worcester amid this tempestuous family quarrel, which resulted in his mother and grandfather refusing to speak to each other for two years. Perhaps to finesse this standoff, Cole, very much his mother's boy, visited Peru only rarely in his adolescence, nor did any family members go east to visit him.

Why was J.O. determined that his grandson attend school locally? Why was Katie determined that her son go to Worcester Academy? And why was her husband silent on the matter of his son's education? To better understand the drama, one must know more about the cast. Certainly they and their forebears played a part in teaching Cole the strength of character that helped him in later life to cope with pain and to combat censorship and all restriction of freedom.

The name Cole first surfaces in local history in the person of A. A. Cole, great-grandfather of Cole Porter, who came with his family from Connecticut to Peru, Indiana, in 1834. His son, J. O. Cole, was six at the time. Albert Cole was a soldier under Andrew Jackson and an engineer on the Wabash-Erie Canal before he became a distinguished lawyer and judge and the co-owner of a dry-goods store, Cole and Bearss (pronounced "bars"). Ironically, in light of J.O.'s insistence that Cole attend school locally, A.A. wanted his son to return east for his education. A.A. had been born in Connecticut, and many of his ancestors had lived and died there.

J.O. resisted his father's wishes that he study in the east and enrolled instead in the Peru Collegiate Institute, which was founded by leading citizens "to furnish a thorough academic course" and was said "never to have been excelled by any [school] in the country." For a time he worked as a clerk in a local store. By 1850, however, at age twenty-two, J.O. decided to seek his fortune in the California Gold Rush. With six hundred dollars A.A.

had borrowed for him, and accompanied by a fellow Peruvian, J.O. went by canal to Defiance, Ohio, then by the Ohio Canal to Cincinnati, where the young men boarded a steamer to New Orleans via the Ohio and Mississippi Rivers. From there they sailed to the Isthmus of Panama and by another boat down the Chagres River as far as Cruces, and then traveled by foot to the Pacific, with trunks carried by donkey. From the Pacific coast of Panama another sailing vessel took three months to reach San Francisco.

Except for visits home in August 1855 and February 1860, J.O. spent more than a decade in California strenuously attempting to make his fortune. His first job was helping to build a mining dam on the Feather River; when he saved up six hundred dollars, he sent it home to repay his father. Deciding the work was too hard for the meager monies he earned, J.O. clerked in a store, then bought a building at Oak Valley, where he prospered almost from the start. He came to realize that, rather than panning for gold, he could make more money by setting up a general store, selling water, and constructing a flume and dam. "It has always been my aim to be what is called rich," wrote J.O. to his brother, Alphonso, in 1858, and so in time he was, although, along with others who had made their way to El Dorado, he battled illness, fierce weather, and loneliness.

As the 1850s passed, he seemed more and more to tire of California and to regret his bachelor existence. While J.O. was in California, Alphonso married Sara Bearss. "Married life is indeed the happiest way of living when a man is in luck enough to find one who *truly* loves him," J.O. wrote to his brother, "(but that is the catch.) I do not know whether it is luck or good judgment. It is a mixture, in my opinion, of both." J.O.'s letters have a richness of sentiment and give an impression of him as a person with deep feelings, although he was always intent, as he said, on "making a pile."

In 1860 J.O. returned to Indiana and married Alphonso's cousin-in-law Rachel Henton. The morning after their wedding, he and his bride began the journey back to California. Once there, they settled in Brandy City. Two years later, Rachel Cole gave birth to a daughter, Katie, who was destined to become the woman Cole Porter worshiped and celebrated throughout his life. In 1865 Rachel gave birth again, this time to a son, Louis. J.O. finally sold his properties in Brandy City in 1867 and returned with his wife and two children to Peru.

J.O. had amassed a considerable amount of money in California, which he cleverly invested not only in Indiana farmland but in acres of West Virginia forests as well. When the timber was exhausted, the land was found to have rich deposits of coal and oil. J.O.'s wealth was estimated at $17 million and in time he was judged to be the richest man in Miami County. At home

Cole's grandfather, J.O.

in Indiana, J.O. farmed the fertile acres he owned which were watered by the Wabash River.

J.O.'s son, Louis, was educated in Peru schools and at Notre Dame University in Indiana and "assisted in the management of his father's immense lumber interests at Cincinnati." Eventually he married a Cincinnati girl, and the couple had four children: Louis, Omar, Kate, and Samuel. Rumors reached Cole as a child that J.O. had sent his son to West Virginia to work in the family business, but he had gotten into some kind of trouble there and his father had had to pay off the authorities. Louis was an alcoholic, but his untimely death in November 1903 was attributed to the ill effects of a hernia operation. Only a few months earlier, he had given a dinner-dance just before "the gay season which the young people have been enjoying [shut down] owing to the advent [sic] of Lent." Cole believed that his uncle must have found himself in further troubles, because when Louis died, J.O. said, "It's the best thing that could have happened." Ironically, in light of his son's troubles with alcohol, one of J.O.'s successes was the establishment of a brewery: "As his family went regularly to Church on Sunday, being in the brewery business was okay with the majority of his fellow townsmen," said a jocular friend of Cole who remembered J.O.

Cole's mother, Katie

Cole's maternal grandmother seems to have had a more poetic and metaphysical temperament than her husband, at least as evidenced by the preface she wrote in a kind of autograph album she kept: "These pages and the hands which made their record here will pass away but the thoughts recorded shall remain; and as true as it is that 'the heart of man answereth to men' so true is it that the sympathies and affections of pure hearts are immortal as the human soul." In the summer of 1890, Katie's mother died in Peru, and in the winter of 1892 her father married Bessie LaBonte.

On April 9, 1884, years before her mother's death, Miss Kate Cole, then twenty-two years old, married Samuel Fenwick Porter, who was twenty-six, at her parents' house. The wedding took many by surprise, so unannounced and so quietly executed was it. Sam Porter had migrated as a young man from Vevay, an Indiana town on the Ohio River. Little is known of his mother, Catharine McCallum, whose father had emigrated from Scotland. Sam's father and paternal grandfather were both farmers, his father having the distinction of serving in the Indiana House of Representatives, and his grandfather, of serving as a captain in the War of 1812. Sam Porter gave the commencement oration at his graduation from Vevay High School in 1875. He moved to Peru, Indiana, and went on to become "a parvenu druggist,"

Father and sister of Cole Porter

Cole's father, Samuel, and sister, Rachel

or at least that was the impression Cole gave one of his Yale friends. Sam had found employment as a drug clerk, and later purchased a drugstore. "His business profited and he expanded and later became the city's leading druggist, owning and operating three stores." A brother of Sam's served as best man at his wedding. Today in Peru no trace remains of Porter's paternal family, nor of the Porter drugstores, one of which stood, until 1924, opposite the courthouse that dominates the town square. Sam's brother, Andrew, joined him in opening a combination drug-and-restaurant business, and they named the latter Cafe de la Paix, which suggests a flair not foreign to Cole.

Another business structure in town with family associations was the Cole Building, erected in 1886 by Sam's father-in-law, J.O. And on the same block as the Cole Building was the popular shop of one of Peru's colorful characters, the confectioner Robert Pelky. Long after his death, Peruvians remembered Pelky, who boasted a snow-white beard that reached to the floor. In cold weather, old-timers recalled, "he used his whiskers for a muffler and kept warm."

When J.O. was in his twenties, he reported in letters home the large profits he was realizing from his dry-goods business in California. Samuel Porter's profits were not in the same league. Nonetheless, as one critic observed, "unconsciously J.O. probably preferred an obscure druggist dependent on his bounty to an equal, and in consequence a rival to his daughter's affection." Katie worshiped her father. At the same time she valued her freedom. A plain girl, she returned from finishing school to Peru and decided to wed the handsome Porter, despite the opinion of most Peruvians that she was marrying down. Porter was said to have been "rather dreamy" in temperament, but he surprised the town by protesting the "monopoly" he felt his druggist competitors exercised. Katie, who was not particularly jolly, said she married Sam Porter "because I just love the way he plays the guitar."

The house Porter lived in as a child, still standing, is a largish frame one, Victorian in style. It is in a neighborhood of other Victorian houses, at the corner of Third and Huntington Streets, just a few blocks from the town center. When Cole was in elementary school, "he gave shows on the sun porch at 102 East Third and charged a penny or a bottle cap admission." Peru is characterized by tall trees, luxuriantly leafy in summer, which stand amid spacious lawns and colorful gardens. Oak, walnut, ash, and poplar trees and in sunshiny nooks sumac, dogwood, and wild briar abound. Cows graze in fields, and in summer the landscape resembles a scene by Constable. The Porters' life in town must have been quite trim and contained: the First Baptist Church is located a few blocks from their home, for example, and Sam's drugstore was not much farther in another direction.

Seventy-five miles north of Indianapolis, Peru has changed very little since the 1890s, when Cole was a boy. Located on the banks of the celebrated Wabash River and near the juncture of the Wabash and the Mississinewa, it had a population of only twelve hundred when Cole was growing up. As a boy, Cole sang in the choir of St. John's Lutheran Church, as did Emil Schramm, who grew up to be head of the New York Stock Exchange. Two pictures always hung in Schramm's Wall Street office: one of Abraham Lincoln and the other of J. O. Cole. Covering in Cole's boyhood fifteen hundred acres, Peru already had a handsome public library, to which Andrew Carnegie donated $25,000. The farming country surrounding Peru, an amount of it waving with corn and wheat by high summer, is said to be the best in Indiana.

The Coles who survive today cheerfully admit to their lack of musical gifts. In reply to a question about this subject, his cousin James O. Cole emphasizes that neither in his generation nor as far as memory takes him

Cole (left) age eleven, with his cousin Louis

can he recall any other Cole with a musical talent. "It must be true," he said, when informed that some people recall the gift Sam Porter had in music. Hazel Bowland, a nonagenarian when interviewed, remembered Sam Porter vividly. She and her large family lived in her childhood years on the Porter farm, and she knew Cole well. Cole "had one of the most wonderful fathers," she said without any prompting. "He gave me my first music lesson. Cole got that musical genius from his father, not from his mother's rich family. His father was a good pianist. He had a lovely tenor voice. That's the truth."

In Mrs. Bowland's estimation, Sam Porter was "a good man but not burdened by religion." "Passive" was a word she applied to Sam, "a gentleman of the old school who was quite cultured . . . a very thoughtful person who would take pains at Christmastime, for instance, to make certain that children each received some special gift they wanted." Mrs. Porter she thought "spoiled" and "not very friendly." "But Cole was close to his mother and not very intimate with his father, who was a compassionate man. Everybody's sorrows became his sorrows. Mrs. Porter called him 'Sammy.' He'd telephone her every day round noon. 'Katie, Katie,' he'd say, 'this is Sammy.' He was a warmer person than she. The loss of his two children was very sad for him. Mr. Porter could have done with more affection from his wife, and less money."

These repeated references to Sam Porter's love for children make all the more mysterious his failure to be closer to his surviving son. Cole was born on June 9, 1891, and he was a healthy baby, which must have been a great relief to Katie and Sam after the deaths of their infant son, Louis Omar, and, just the year before Cole's birth, their baby daughter, Rachel, who died of tubercular meningitis. Sam was a reader, and it may be that with his encouragement Cole read such childhood classics as *Alice in Wonderland,* *Treasure Island,* and *The Swiss Family Robinson.* As is true for many children, reading was an escape for Cole and at the same time an enchantment. But more than fiction, Sam Porter liked to read poetry: the English Romantics but also the Victorians, among whom he favored Browning. Cole remained devoted to that poet. Although Cole recalled in later life the impatience of his father at Cole's failure to comprehend lines that they looked at, he somewhat grudgingly said, "I suppose he started me writing lyrics."

One can only imagine that mother and son, perhaps unconsciously, conspired from Cole's earliest years to create an intimate union from which Sam Porter was excluded. When Cole was about six years old, a Gypsy persuaded Katie that a person whose initials spelled out a simple word would be fortunate. Once convinced, she added "Albert" as her son's middle name (after his maternal great-grandfather, A. A. Cole) without any discussion of the matter with her husband. Regrettable was the assignment of Mr. Porter to the role of disciplinarian. On one of the rare occasions when his mother punished him, Cole said to her, "I thought that Sammy was the whipper."

Cole's first recorded appearance in Peru was remembered by his friend Tommy Hendricks (named for his great-uncle Thomas Andrews Hendricks, who had been governor of Indiana and vice president of the United States under Grover Cleveland). It was in July 1894, on the day when the first horseless carriage reached Peru. As it progressed down Broadway, a crowd gathered, among whom could be seen Sam Porter, standing in front of his drugstore with the three-year-old Cole alongside him.

Parades were not unknown to Peruvians; quite the contrary. Peru had for many years been the headquarters for the Hagenbeck and Wallace Circus. "As a circus center, Peru naturally was a wonderful town in which to be a boy. Elephants were known to enter drugstores and disrupt the soda fountain trade." Perhaps Porter's pharmacy had indeed been the site of such a bizarre occurrence. There is the tale still told in Peru of a malicious keeper

who one day led an elephant to drink in the Wabash. The elephant knocked
him down, thrust him into the river, placed his foot on the keeper's head,
and held it there until the man drowned.

Playing the steam calliope was the contribution Sam Porter made to the
village parades and is further evidence of his musical talents. "Here Comes
the Bandwagon," published November 1929 and sung by Gertrude Lawrence
in a film called *The Battle of Paris,* demonstrates the impact the circus parades
continued to have on Cole:

> *If you look your childhood over,*
> *There was nothing half as grand,*
> *As the old-fashioned circus parade.*
> *And the greatest thing about it*
> *Was the*
> *Oom-pah, oom-pah band!*
> *And the heartbreakin' music it played.*

"The lure and lore of the circus filled our thoughts," wrote Tommy
Hendricks, who met Cole when both attended kindergarten. Tommy's
father was the owner of the Blue Pharmacy—a Peru rival of Samuel Porter's
drugstore. "Cole and I were buddies from the first day we met," he went on
to say. The two boys lived nearby and met at the corner carrying lunch pails.
Much of their talk was about the circus, and Cole disclosed that his own
ambition was to become a circus performer. (A clown suit was one of his
favorite possessions.)

> *I'll remember forever,*
> *When I was but three,*
> *Mama who was clever,*
> *Remarking to me:*
> . . . .
> *Be a clown, be a clown,*
> *All the world loves a clown . . .*

Years later Cole wrote this song for a film, titled *The Pirate,* at Gene
Kelly's request, and although it took him only overnight to compose, in
some sense it had been gestating since those childhood days in Peru. The
boys were obsessed with the circus. Hendricks reported that it filled their
thoughts, and he reproduced in his writings bits of the kinds of conversa-

Cole (third from right, front row) c. 1899, in grade school

tion he and Cole had: "How many elephants are they going to have?" "Have they started training the bareback riders yet?" The Wild Man of Borneo was a familiar sight as he spent the winter months shining shoes at the village barbershop. The Fat Lady was also a favorite of Cole's, and he liked very much to drive her about Peru and its environs in his donkey cart. Sometime in spring the Wild Man would tell Cole and Tommy that the circus was resuming its life and that outdoor practice in the riding ring was to begin. On Saturday the two boys would hightail it to the circus grounds early to secure the best places by the rail. Once " 'the Royal Repenskis' were work-ing on their riding routine . . . teaching one of the youngsters not much older than either of us, to ride bareback . . . It took perfect timing. Time after time, hour after hour, they went through the intricacies of the maneu-ver, until it looked so simple that almost anyone could do it." Writing decades later, Tommy Hendricks insisted that Cole "learned the value of practice at first-hand from the greatest aerial and equestrian artists of the day—performers who knew that lack of practice might mean a mistake, and a mistake might mean death."

The perils of the bicycle were fewer, perhaps. As in many towns at the turn of the century, bicycles were the mechanical means most people used for transportation. Hendricks remembers Cole as a fast, fearless rider who "would dash in and out between horse-drawn vehicles, make handsome cir-cles around me, and even ride without holding on to the handlebars." Once when he encountered Tommy on his bicycle, Cole leapt onto the handlebars, but the two of them were unable to stop the speedy vehicle, and they crashed through the swinging doors of the town saloon and slid to a stop at the brass rail.

One of the places to which the boys cycled was the home of the bed-ridden "Aunt May" (a relative of two childhood pals), who delighted Cole and the others with the stories she read them and the verses she composed. According to Tommy, Cole learned from Aunt May that "persons who are alive can write things that may be printed in books . . . a wonderful thought, new and surprising."

The day after one visit to Aunt May, Cole went home and wrote "The Bobolink Waltz" (1902). This was not his first composition. How much Cole was motivated by the muse or by the desire to please is difficult to say, but nothing distracted him from music for long. The first work he com-posed, in 1901, "The Song of the Birds," is dedicated to his mother: its parts are labeled "Mother's Cooing," "The Young Ones Learning to Sing," "One Bird Falls from the Nest," "The Bird Is Found," "They Fly Away." Katie understandably approved.

Soon Cole and Tommy were joined by Desdemona Bearss, daughter of a long and distinguished line of Peru gentry. The Bearsses and the Coles argued furiously over politics and enjoyed their disagreements hugely. Des

Cole, with classmates; Desdemona Bearss on right

and Cole Porter talked more about the circus, a favorite meeting place for them, than about politics. Not surprisingly, Desdemona's mother read Shakespeare, and she was also interested in opera. Sometimes she took her daughter to Indianapolis to see the productions of visiting companies. So a lively exposure to music was another bond between Des and Cole, who by the age of six was practicing the piano daily and learning to play the violin.

That instrument he later studied at the Marion Conservatory of Music, thirty miles off. The train ride was congenial, but the boy began to rue the hours he had to while away until the arrival of the return train to Peru. In time, however, he stopped complaining, having discovered a shop that sold risqué books. Later in life he confessed that "some of my lyrics owe a debt to these naughty books." Once each year Cole's mother imported the Marion Conservatory Orchestra to Peru to play a concert that would include the boy's performance of a violin solo. She papered the house with Peruvians, and her son performed not with pleasure, but dutifully. In 1902, for instance, "the elite of the city" attended such a concert. "Master Cole was seated at the front of the . . . stage with the orchestra and those fortunate in being present were given a rare musical treat. . . . [He] made his debut with a violin solo in the second part, in which he completely charmed his audience with sweet music and gracefulness of rendition."

What Cole preferred was the piano accompaniment he sometimes supplied when films were shown at the Wallace Theater. Once, when he was eight years old, he climbed uninvited onto the stage and played happy music on the piano during a sad sequence in the film. He was asked to leave.

Katie Porter approved of Cole's learning to ride ponies but forbade football and other sports, which she considered less than gentlemanly. Dancing was a social skill, so Cole was sent off to dancing lessons. And he was tutored in French by Madame Cattin, who made dresses for the ladies in Peru. Madame thought Cole made rapid progress and attributed this partly to his musical ear.

The childhood photos of him that have surfaced depict Cole dressed in the attire of a dandy, a style he brought to Yale and refined in later life. "Other children didn't mix much with Cole," said Mrs. Bowland. "His mother dressed him up like Lord Fauntleroy and other children made fun of him. Cole was very shy as a boy." Perhaps some children are naturally inclined to form triangular friendships as they develop their identities. Tommy, Des, and Cole seemed to have remained for some time an amiable trio, and this configuration was one Cole kept to throughout his life.

Des and Cole met at kindergarten, but the intermingling of their families in this small town would anyway have resulted in an early meeting of the two. A typical adventure for these children was dressing up as country folk and peddling apples from the Porter trees. And then there was the cabaret they inaugurated. With sets that depicted Paris and Venice they afforded the townspeople musical entertainment. Hendricks reported that at one children's party the three attended, Cole and Des held hands and sang. The next day Cole told Tommy, "Des is the most beautifullest person in the world, outside of my mother." George Eells, his friend and biographer, quotes Cole as saying later in life that he liked Des, "even loved her, but . . . had never been *in* love with her."

Before dinner Cole had to practice the piano. "That was one thing Cole had to do—practice. Otherwise, I think his mother let him do almost everything he wanted to." In later life Cole told the columnist Leonard Lyons that piano practice nearly ruined his childhood. But, on the other hand, when he grew up, his passport everywhere was as a singer-pianist who often performed his own songs.

Lost to history is a photograph of Tommy taken on his sixth birthday along with his guests. Most of the guests (even some of the girls) are dressed in military or naval styles pointing to the national obsession with the Spanish-American War. But not Cole. Tommy describes Cole rigid in a black jacket, a vest, wing collar, black tie—utterly correct. Des, "the queen of our hearts," also attended, "with gigantic hair ribbon, round face, hair parted in the middle, very lovely and very dignified and confident." Hooney Causey, a black boy who sometimes played with Cole and Tommy, was not invited to the party.

Summer was idyllic at Indiana's Lake Maxinkuckee. Thirty miles from Peru, it had been a resort since 1836, when the first white man built a house there. Before that it was frequented in summer by members of the Miami and Potawatomi Indian tribes. Later it became a summer playground for wealthier midwesterners, including the Porters and the Hendrickses. Around the turn of the century, Cole's parents built a late-Victorian "stone cottage" on the east shore of the lake. The room on the left as one entered gave access to a boat garage built for Cole's use. In it he housed a steam-powered paddleboat (far too large for one person to paddle). "They wanted Cole—around whom their life was centered—to have everything," said a cousin. The main room was furnished with an enormous gaming table and a piano; the dining room could seat thirty. Upstairs were five bedrooms and two baths, and outside was a charming guest house. Cole and Tommy spent long days on or in the lake, netting turtles and minnows, boating and awaiting the steamer *Peerless,* which arrived amid the sounds of bells ringing and whistles blowing. Usually the captain let the boys climb aboard and up to a spot near the flagpole. As the *Peerless* backed away, the boys could dive off. Cole, however, took a different tack: in his wet bathing suit he'd head for the piano. The noises of the steamer would drown the music, but a moment of silence came when the ship was ready to depart, and everyone suddenly heard the piano. The captain would erupt in fury at the realization that Cole was ruining the piano stool, seated on it in his wet trunks. Abandoning the wheel, Captain Crook (who sounds like a J.M. Barrie character) tore after Cole, but not in time to catch the elusive musician, who somersaulted into the lake.

Time passed, and Cole and his piano became an attraction aboard the *Peerless* and other boats. In these years, sports counted very little for Cole, so that other boys easily outshone him. "But when night came it was different . . . sooner or later Cole would get into the vicinity of a piano and it was all over for the rest of us. . . . Gone were all the girls—Cole had them all." His repertoire was vast: from current hits to Gilbert and Sullivan and English folk songs. Often the boys took the steamers to dances in distant landings on the lake.

> Going to the dances Cole played the piano just to pass the time but it was on the trip back after midnight that he really played. Everything was still except the piano and the pounding of the engine, and Cole's one-toned voice. . . . Cole's singing was terrible, nearly a toneless talking affair; but the entire energy of his slight frame, his keen eyes, his changing facial expressions and his sly, humorous asides made his act. After the first song the crowd and the rest of the evening were his.

Cole played steadily until the steamer brought him home, usually at around 2 a.m.

> By that time not only did the youngsters crowd around the piano . . . but the older folk had boarded the boat at the various landings just to hear Cole play . . . Many [good musicians] played the piano better than Cole, but Cole was a natural showman, and he should have been, for he had seen the best there was in showmanship from his earliest days in Peru. And although showmanship may take on a form for the New York stage different from that of the circus ring[,] basically . . . it's all one and the same—and Cole had never forgotten, never underestimated and never neglected that fine art.

Tommy Hendricks had an interesting theory of how Cole accommodated his piano playing to the rhythms and sounds of the Lake Maxinkuckee steamer as "night after night, summer after summer, Cole hammered out his rhythm by the tempo . . . [of] that *Peerless* engine. That is where Cole got the heavy accented phrasing and that powerful punch in his music," Hendricks wrote.

Katie had two Indian maids who looked after some of the more burdensome household tasks and left her freer to move about town socially. An old Indian man who worked for her habitually went to town on Saturday nights to get drunk. Finally Katie decided to fire him. When she announced this to him, he looked at her and said, "Katie Porter, you can't fire me. I walked on this land before you were born." Cole told George Eells she had no choice but to keep him.

As a boy, Cole was several times in the spotlight. One was at the concert of the Marion Conservatory Orchestra, in which "Master Cole" performed a violin solo ("Serenade" by Silvestri) and played in the orchestra as well. He appeared, too, in a school production of *Snow White*—cast, of course, as the Prince. He was also given billing in a newspaper account of the marriage of a relative held in the Porter house: "The Wedding March was played by Master Cole Porter." Three years later, when the Metropolitan Opera went to Chicago, the Porters traveled there to attend performances of *Cavalleria Rusticana* (starring the great soprano Emma Calvé), *Tannhäuser,* and *The Barber of Seville.*

The time was nearing for Cole to set off for boarding school. As we have seen, Katie had detected in her son at an early age his gifts as a composer and performer, and she did what she could to encourage and develop those gifts. Her ambition for him may well explain the otherwise mysterious fact that Worcester Academy records identify Cole as twelve years old at the time of his registration when he was actually fourteen. (Having misrepresented himself at boarding school, Cole continued in later life to be cavalier about his age, and at least three of the passports he acquired show different dates of birth: 1891, 1892, and 1893). Katie probably thought her son would appear more of a prodigy if he was thought to be younger and that his way would thus be eased, later, into the Ivy League. That may also explain her choice of boarding school. Compared to the posher New England prep schools, the Worcester Academy is simple, reserved, but cozy, just the sort of place where Cole would shine. Founded in 1834, it originally had an affiliation with the Baptist Church; but although Katie was herself a Baptist, her tenuous attachment to that religion was scarcely enough to explain her choice of school. Probably of more importance in her mind was the solid training in the classics that the academy offered, and its preparation of its students for Yale, among other universities. Its dean, in Cole's day, proclaimed that "at Worcester Academy boys are treated as boys. Promptness, regularity, work, obedience, personal influence are not obsolete. The Academy is small enough for every boy to be personally known and large enough to give the strength and inspiration of numbers."

J.O. found himself positioned at the polar opposite of Katie's stand. He argued that his grandson should be educated in Indiana at a military academy or a business school, where he could train to become in time director of the Cole family conglomerate. His only son had died two years earlier, but even before that J.O. must have worried that Louis's alcoholism made him unsuited to administer a financial empire. As for Katie's musical ambitions for her son, J.O. had scoffed at Cole's early composition "The Song of the Birds" and continued to consider such pursuits not really serious. What was serious to J.O. was making and maintaining a fortune. After all, while his son-in-law was musically inclined, wasn't it as a businessman that Sam Porter supported his family?

And what of Sam Porter's silence during this conflict between his strong-willed wife and father-in-law? According to Mrs. Bowland, who recalled Sam Porter so affectionately from her childhood, although "Cole's grandfather wanted him to go into industry," Cole's father "very much approved his taking up music." By this time, however, Cole was his mother's boy, and Sam Porter probably considered it wiser to let his wife resist her formidable father.

After Cole's departure for boarding school, Peru ceased to be his world. However, the town and certain of its inhabitants surfaced for the rest of his life in artistic transformations. Of course, there were a few people he clung to emotionally: his mother and Des Bearss were two. "It was always toward Des that Cole looked whenever he sang 'Come, Come I Love You Only' [from a song titled 'My Hero'] . . . Des knew Cole was a non-conformist but she had more control over him than anyone—even his own parents." In an attempt to refine their styles, Des read a book to Tommy Hendricks and Cole about clichés and verbal pomposity and organized word games, which helped Cole later to be wary of trite and vulgar diction and cheap rhymes. She seems to have had less influence over Cole's haberdashery. Once when Cole made a rare return to Peru from boarding school he was walking along Broadway with Tommy and Des in his first pair of long trousers when he stopped, "lifted one trouser leg and adjusted his bright multicolored garter.

It was a horrible breach of conventionalities," said Tommy later, "and I can remember how terrible the act seemed to me." Tommy attended Indiana schools and eventually went off to earn a degree at Princeton.

Des married Milton Edwards, who was a big-game hunter. Then her life turned tragic. Her husband caught sleeping sickness in Africa and soon died. Shortly after his death, their young son died of meningitis in Arizona, where she had traveled for treatment of tuberculosis. Soon she too passed away. Cole was shattered by the news of her illness. He sent a five-page telegram to Des in the hospital. "Read it to her and she'll come back." But it never was read to her, as she was already dying. Years later, when Cole's cousin Louise Thwing went to visit him with Katie, Cole began to weep and sputtered out, "Oh Mother, I can't stand it, she reminds me so much of Des." In saying goodbye to Peru and the people there he cared for, Cole must have had many regrets.

Chapter 2

I Want to Be a
Yale Boy

Cole arrived at Worcester, short, slender, hair parted in the middle, with the rarest of gear: paintings and an upright piano in addition to several trunks. These were placed in his room at Dexter Hall, a large brick edifice still partly in use as a dormitory. Set atop one of Worcester's many hills, the campus now has buildings in other styles mixing with the austerely dignified old red-brick halls that fronted on the quad (or circle, really) when Cole lived there. Having discovered early in life that he could win the friendship of people of any age, boys as well as girls, with his music, he arrived at Worcester Academy with social strategies. And they were successful. The school had 240 boys when Cole arrived, and 21 teachers. All of the students were required to take English, mathematics, Greek, Latin, French, science, and history.

In such a small community Cole's prowess as a pianist quickly became known. On October 7, 1905, he followed a talk by the dean, Dr. Daniel Webster Abercrombie, with a piano solo. That same autumn, the school paper reported that on Thanksgiving Day, "after a hearty dinner . . . all remaining at school, gathered in the Chapel . . . and listened to an enjoyable programme . . . a piano selection by Porter and in response [to calls for an encore] he rendered 'Julia' in a surprisingly imitative manner." His gift for mimicry, which matured at Yale, seems to have been in evidence in his first year at prep school. More surprising is it to read that in the spring of 1906 Porter tried out for the position of pitcher on the baseball team. He didn't succeed; but he was successful, not surprisingly, in becoming a star of the academy Glee Club.

Faculty, and especially their wives, invited Cole to their homes, and his social gifts completely captivated them. Those of his classmates who were alive and talked with earlier biographers all remember the small youth playing the piano in the school auditorium after supper and leading in song boys who gathered around him. First among his fans was the dean, Dr. Abercrombie, a Harvard-educated Scotsman who aimed "to convert middle-class American boys into young gentlemen." "Democracy is not a leveling down but a leveling up" was one of his favorite mots. Abercrombie favored Cole over the school athletes and trained the boy with special care in upper-class fine points: "A gentleman never eats. He breakfasts, he lunches, he dines, but he never eats," was typical of the dictates he propounded.

Abercrombie taught one class in Greek, and his power to evoke characters from the classics and make them live again was formidable. "If Cole's father first aroused his interest in poetry, it was Dr. Abercrombie whom Cole later credited with causing him to realize that he (Cole) alone could match the rhythm of *his* words to the beat of *his* music." Another lesson credited by Cole to the dean was his dictum that "there is always enough money in the world—never enough beauty."

Mrs. Abercrombie was also fond of Cole; he was asked to teas and played the piano for her. Cole's friendship with the Abercrombies was noticed by faculty and students alike and soon placed this midwestern freshman in the front ranks of the academy.

Curiously, the boy Cole, much attached to his mother, didn't discuss his family at all. It is difficult to understand how he seemed not to suffer from the separation from home ties that boarding school entails until one realizes that although Katie cosseted her son, she also filled him with a sense that he was a child of unusual gifts, one whose destiny it was to go into the great world and make his mark there. One friend thought that Porter didn't discuss his family because he was deeply upset by the family rift he provoked by choosing Worcester Academy. In later life some of his classmates recalled their belief that Cole was an orphan being looked after by rich relatives. Cole's credo, according to George Eells, was "neither to show weakness nor to beg indulgence"—a stoic standard which helped, no doubt, to defeat negative emotions but at the same time distanced him from others.

One person to whom Cole confided some of his feelings was Donald Baxter MacMillan, who coached the school's athletic teams. Seventeen years older than Cole, he had accompanied Admiral Peary on his first attempt to reach the North Pole. At Worcester Academy, MacMillan also taught

French and mathematics. In 1964 he told George Eells: "Cole was a lonesome kind of boy . . . Didn't seem to have a home. Never heard him speak of his father, grandfather or any brother or sister. Rarely of his mother. They never visited. And either they didn't want him to come home or he didn't want to go. He went around like he hadn't a care in the world, but I could see something was bothering him." In effect Cole seemed to MacMillan an orphan, which in some sense he was.

At the end of his first year, in which he received honors for the winter and spring terms, Cole acted on MacMillan's advice and went to Camp

Cole Porter, c. 1910

Wychmere, one of the oldest nautical camps for boys in America. MacMillan had founded it a few years earlier on Bustin Island, in Casco Bay off the coast of Portland, Maine. MacMillan thought it would "put some iron in his spine." For two summers, with Katie's permission, Cole went directly to Wychmere and back to Worcester without any visit to Indiana—except once inadvertently in his first summer. On July 20, 1906, the *Peru Republican* published what probably was information supplied to them by Katie:

> Instead of returning home to Peru for the vacation immediately upon the close of school, [Cole] started with his teacher of athletics and a party of fifteen school mates for a yachting cruise along the New England coast. The boys . . . had established a camp on Bibber's [sic] Island in Casco Bay when they decided . . . to sleep in a loft. The boys slipped with their weight and carried Cole down an opening to [the] barn floor below. A fracture of the leg a few inches above the ankle joint resulted.

On July 27 the *Republican* reported that "S. F. Porter who went to Portland, Maine, last week to bring home his son Cole, who was in a hospital in that city laid up with a broken leg, has arrived [in Peru] safely with his patient."

By the summer of 1907 J.O. and Katie had reconciled and J.O. was concerning himself with Cole's education. No doubt this came about largely because Cole was at this stage a good student, earning high grades in the strictly classical curriculum that Yale demanded of its applicants.

And socially he was on the rise. In his junior year the Mandolin Club elected him its president, he was appointed co-pianist of the Glee Club, elected editor of the school paper (*Vigornia*—Greek for "Worcester"), ushered at the senior prom, and was a member of the Inter-Society debate team. On October 5, 1907, at a reception for the YMCA, "Cole Porter began the more formal exercises by seating himself at the piano and playing one of his . . . selections in the splendid way that those familiar with his music have learned to expect."

Cole told Eells that for a time he intended to pursue a career as an actor; and on March 21, 1908, after successfully persuading the director of drama to abandon the traditional Shakespeare play and stage instead Sheridan's *The Rivals,* Cole appeared in the leading role of Bob Acres, a part "I was crazy to play." *Vigornia* wrote: "Cole, as Bob Acres, was excellent. He was the carefree young man at first, then the bold fighter . . . and last the terrified duelist . . . shaking with fear. He was full of life and vim throughout." According to Eells, another actor received even better reviews than Cole,

who, refusing always to settle for second place, dropped his interest in acting. That same year, though, he won the first prize (twenty-five dollars) in
the speaking contest, reciting Wordsworth's "Complaint of a Forsaken
Indian Woman." Those who thought that Cole Porter could only specialize
in humorous selections were especially surprised by his choice.

While Cole enjoyed entertaining audiences with his piano playing and
recitations, he tried to distance himself from the violin, despite his skillful
playing on it. He appeared to dislike the instrument, eager perhaps not to
evoke criticism by the athletes and other boys who might find him effeminate. So he cleverly found a strategy to deflect any such inference. When the
Glee Club director requested that he prepare a violin solo to play at their
last annual performance, Cole agreed and offered a selection from Flotow's
Martha. At its conclusion the boys clapped and whistled, much to the
delight of Dr. Abercrombie, who complimented them for their good taste
and then urged Cole to play an encore. Cole switched to the piano and
played and sang several pieces satirizing the foibles of the academy faculty.
Cole, of course, had put the boys up to this trick, and it worked. His violin
career seems to have terminated with this *jeu*. It's not surprising to learn
from sources who knew and talked with Porter's teachers that the academy
faculty on the whole did not approve of the boy and in some instances
actively disliked him. An old boy recalled in 1983 that "Porter was reprimanded for writing ribald songs that included a lot of off-color puns about
the faculty. Unfortunately none of them have survived. But he did write the
class song and songs for class musicals."

In June 1908 Porter was awarded the Dexter Prize for excellence in
declamation. Debate and public speaking were two other interests the
young Cole pursued at school. Whether he was personally keen on oratory
and argument or simply found that they offered him another chance to be
on stage and garner applause is difficult to determine. Whatever his
motives, Cole exercised his rhetorical skills with some frequency: on March
6, 1908, he "gave a reading at the first concert by the WA Glee and Mandolin Clubs at Piedmont Church." On March 13 he performed again at
nearby Shrewsbury, giving a reading and playing a piano solo.

In 1908 Cole took the entrance exam for Yale, which qualified him in all
subjects except Greek. Perhaps he had recollections of his struggles with the
Greek classics when he wrote these lyrics for *Kiss Me, Kate:*

> *The girls today in society*
> *Go for classical poetry,*

So to win their hearts one must quote with ease
Aeschylus and Euripides.
One must know Homer and, b'lieve me, Bo,
Sophocles, also Sappho—ho.

Cole wanted to work with a tutor in New Haven, but J.O. insisted that he return for the summer to Peru. J.O. was threatening to terminate Cole's attendance at Worcester Academy because of a "terrible new income tax which would take one percent of his income." He had previously paid only property tax. Cole agreed to remain in Peru for the summer and was at home again for only the second time since he left for Worcester. As often as he could he spent time at Lake Maxinkuckee playing piano on the steamers, and often in the company of Des Bearss, whom he invited to his senior prom the following year. Des accepted.

Cole's senior year (1908–09) is described in a history of the Worcester Academy as "a great year." The boys were "thrilled by the singing of Geraldine Farrar [and] later they listened to two concerts by the Boston Symphony Orchestra and a performance by Paderewski." Cole dated a few girls, one of whom he met at a church reception for the academy boys. This was Beulah Mae Singer. She found him "fascinating . . . He wasn't what you'd call handsome. He moved like a frisky monkey and looked like a solemn bullfrog. With slightly buggy eyes. Well he captivated me by sheer force of personality. I took a fancy to him that lasted all my life." Once Beulah Mae refused Cole's offer to see her home to her door. Cole followed her to the trolley stop and when her companion left, "stepped out of the shadows . . . gave me an accusing look and said in a masterful way, 'I'm taking you home.'"

Cole and Beulah Mae enacted the classic stages of flirtation. On Easter Sunday Cole and a classmate, Martin Van Buren III, attended the Piedmont Church and sat down alongside Beulah. "Cole talked all through the service. He was one of the most irreverent persons I've ever encountered—but *so* charming," she said. "While he talked he cracked his ankle bones in a kind of castanet-like accompaniment. I'm certain he did it to draw attention to his new brown silk socks and snappy footwear. He was quite a Beau Brummell—even then." Eventually he left her for a Worcester girl called Gracie Allen.

Cole wrote a lot of original material which he performed for the academy students and a few of the more liberal instructors. "Fi, Fi, Fifi," "The Tattooed Gentleman," and "The Bearded Lady" were some of his titles, demonstrating the persistent influence of the Peru circuses on his imagination. (He wrote as well the class song of 1909.) Dr. Abercrombie got wind of Cole's performances and insisted Cole render one of these songs for him. Outraged by a few lines from "The Bearded Lady," he threatened Cole with expulsion and forbade any future airing of this material, leading Porter to go underground. Cole seemed to refer to such experiences in a lyric he composed in 1929 for a song titled "I'm in Love":

> At boarding school I was always taught,
> Not to reveal what I really thought,
> Nor ever once let my eyes betray
> The dreadful things that I longed to say.

On March 13, 1909, Cole, with two classmates, "successfully argued the judges into believing Uncle Sam should not establish a Parcel Post System, [his] chief point being that Uncle Sam could not begin to compete with the Express Companies in handling big parcels." One can't imagine that Porter had his heart in this exercise.

Cole gave his last talk in chapel on April 23, 1909. It was inspired by a theme dear to Des Bearss: "Are You a Bromide?" On May 28 he took part in Class Day exercises as historian. His salutatory address was titled "The Individuality of a School." Porter closed his talk with some sentimental verses from a poem by Richard Hovey, appropriately titled "At the Crossroads":

> You to the left and I to the right
> For the ways of men must sever.
> And it well may be for a day and a night,
> And it well may be forever.
> But whether we meet or whether we part
> (For our ways are past our knowing)
> A pledge from the heart to its fellow heart
> On the ways we all are going!
>   Here's luck!
> For we know not where we are going.

Vintage Porter themes are sounded—comradeship and the mysteriousness of human fate—but the verses of Hovey not surprisingly lack the wit, dexterity, and passion that came to be part of Porter's signature. The festivities concluded with the senior class promenade and Des Bearss on Cole's arm. It was held in "the beautifully decorated Gym, beside a pool transformed by underwater lighting, a fountain and a few gold fish."

J.O. was pleased with Cole's attainments and offered him any gift he desired. Cole chose a two-month trip to Europe. First he took again on June 30 the entrance examination for Yale and then embarked in early July for Paris where he boarded with a middle-class French family, the Delarues, and greatly improved his conversational French. From Paris he made sorties into the French countryside and saw something of Switzerland and Germany.

In late summer of 1909 Cole returned from France to Peru in time to pack some most unsuitable clothes and hasten to 242 York Street, New Haven, then the location of Garland's Rooming House (and now the site of Davenport College), where "the people who mattered" resided. One of his housemates in Garland House, and a classmate as well, was W. Averell Harriman. Another was Howard Cullman, who reported that from the start Cole flouted the standards of dress set by conservative upperclassmen. Instead, Cole wore colorful clothes which "were the uniform for Main Street in Peru" (not, though, of the average Peruvian). An upperclassman, Gerald Murphy, who was to become an important figure in Cole's future, recalled that Porter "wore salmon-colored ties and had his nails done." Despite that, he came to be a social success at Yale, where class rosters read like America's *Who's Who:* Auchincloss, Vanderbilt, Noyes, Phelps, Dodge, Plimpton, Acheson, Fenimore Cooper, among the more notable. Cole told a few friends that he had lived on an enormous apple farm in Indiana and that he had a cousin named Desdemona and that they both used to ride to market on the apple trucks.

Owen Johnson's *Stover at Yale,* published in 1911, during Cole's residency at the university, is a fictionalized account of a typical Yale undergraduate. As the novel begins, entering freshmen meet on a train bound for New Haven. "I'll bet you get a lot of fruits," says one freshman to an upperclassman. "Oh, some of them aren't half bad." The Yale men emphasize the correctness of student attire expected at Yale and insist on another point: "No fooling around women; that isn't done here—that'll queer you absolutely," Stover is advised by an upperclassman. Porter had the dandy's desire to stand out and to seem one of the swells. Later in life he told Tex McCrary and Jinx Falkenburg, "You might describe me as a cross between Eddie Cantor and the Duke of Windsor."

The first academic move a Yale student made in 1909 was to choose one of the three main divisions in which to concentrate: language, literature, and the arts; mathematics and the physical and natural sciences; and philosophy, history and the social sciences. As one would expect, Cole chose to take courses from the division of language, literature and the arts.

Cole's first experiences at Yale were not all agreeable. Freshmen did not live on campus and were cut off from the rest of the college. They were not permitted to smoke pipes in the street or on campus, carry a cane, be out of doors without a hat, dance at the junior prom, talk to upperclassmen about Yale's secret societies, dine at Mory's, or enjoy certain other pleasures. But doubtless he was free to view Nazimova when she came to New Haven in Cole's freshman year to play in *A Doll's House*. The next year Porter saw, among other stars, E. H. Sothern and Julia Marlowe, Peggy Wood, and Fanny Brice.

Even as a college freshman Cole knew that he had an unfailingly seductive power to summon audiences of all kinds with his songs and his showmanship. By 1910, in the spring of his freshman year, Cole had written "Bridget McGuire" and "When the Summer Moon Comes 'Long." (Throughout his career Porter used contractions in his song titles and lyrics. In some cases they serve his syncopations, and where no musical advantage is gained they convey a nonchalance that was part of Porter's aristocratic pose.)

In 1910 a football song competition was announced, and Cole submitted "Bingo Eli Yale":

> *Bingo! Bingo!*
> *Harvard's [Princeton's, etc.] team cannot prevail.*
> *Fight! Fight!*
> *Fight with all your might*
> *For Bingo,*
> *Bingo, Eli Yale!*

The song caught on at once and was copyrighted and published in November 1910. Other football songs followed: "Hail to Yale," "Eli," "A Football King" (first titled "If I Were Only a Football Man"). "I'd like to shine in a physical way" is a telling line from "A Football King." But no song was more relished then and in succeeding years than "Bull Dog." It immediately became a campus hit when it was premiered in 1911 at a Yale dining hall dinner concert:

> *Bull dog! Bull dog! Bow, wow, wow,*
> *Eli Yale!*
> *Bull dog! Bull dog! Bow, wow, wow.*
> *Our team can never fail.*

As the spring term ended in 1910, J.O. complained about the amounts of money Cole had spent as a Yale freshman. His allowance was said to be the second largest of any fellow in his class, topped only by that of the Cleveland millionaire Leonard Hanna, who became one of Cole's closest and lifelong friends. Len Hanna, who lived in Mentor, Ohio, outside of Cleveland, brought the first weimaraner dogs out of Germany. Later in life he bought an English castle and had it disassembled and each part numbered so it could be accurately reassembled in Ohio. The castle had an enormous hall with a large fireplace, alongside of which eight or ten weimaraners lay, Cole told a friend.

J.O. ordered his grandson home for the summer of 1910 in order for him to become familiar with the family's farming business. Katie opposed the idea and so did Cole. Eventually a compromise was reached, with all parties agreeing that Cole would study law. There is no indication that Sam Porter took any part in the discussion. No doubt he was busy planning the move he and Katie were to make from their home in town to Westleigh Farms, a house that J.O. was building for the couple. Contrary to what several commentators have written, the Porters did not move to Westleigh Farms until 1912. The house was begun in 1910 and took two years to complete.

Back went Cole to New Haven in the fall of 1910 and a single room he'd rented at 112 Welch. His courses were English (B), French (A), geology (A), history (B), and Spanish (A). ("A" indicated first-year level of a subject; "B," second-year level, etc. Few advanced to D level. Students were judged by the

Cole (far right) starring in *The Rivals* at Worcester Academy, 1908

levels to which they advanced.) He received credit hours as well for choir, in
which he sang for the remainder of his college days. In 1910–11 he joined the
Yale Glee Club and was eventually elected to a top fraternity, Delta Kappa
Epsilon, suggesting that his social stock had risen. This was due in no small
way to his friendship with Gerald Murphy, the heir to the Mark Cross
shops. In his years at Yale, Murphy was voted the "most thorough gentleman," "greatest social light," and "best dressed." Despite this last designation, Murphy was able to look beyond Porter's dandyish dress to his solid
gift for musical composition, not to say his attractive personal qualities.
Murphy told his biographer:

> There was this barbaric custom of going around to the rooms of the
> sophomores, and talking with them to see which ones would be proper
> material for the fraternities. I remember going around with Gordon
> Hamilton, the handsomest and most sophisticated boy in our class, and
> seeing, two nights running, a sign on one sophomore's door saying
> "Back at 10 p.m. Gone to football song practice." Hamilton was enor-
> mously irritated that anyone would have the gall to be out of his room
> on visiting night, and he decided not to call again on this particular
> sophomore. But one night as I was passing his room I saw a light and
> went in. I can still see that room—there was a single electric light bulb
> in the ceiling, and a piano with a box of caramels on it, and wicker fur-
> niture, which was considered a bad sign at Yale in 1911. And sitting at
> the piano was a little boy from Peru, Indiana, in a checkered suit and a
> salmon tie, with his hair parted in the middle and slicked down, look-
> ing just like a Westerner dressed up for the East. We had a long talk,
> about music, and composers—we were both crazy about Gilbert and
> Sullivan.

Cole also told Gerald Murphy that his submission to the football song competition, "Bull Dog," had just been accepted. According to Murphy, "Porter
did not fit easily into the social mold of a Yale man." However, Murphy persuaded DKE to elect Porter as a member and even succeeded in convincing
the Glee Club, which Murphy managed, to induct Porter, though the Club
had never before accepted an underclassman. In Porter's Yale years the Glee
Club had usually twenty-three members, among whom were Charles
"Buddy" Marshall, Dean Acheson, J. V. Bouvier III (the famous "Black
Jack" Bouvier, father of Jacqueline Kennedy Onassis), and Averell Harriman. Porter often told friends that Averell Harriman, despite all his family's
fabled wealth, never had a penny to spend; so Len Hanna and Cole would

take him to New York when they went. One of Cole's classmates, Johnfritz
Achelis, told George Eells in 1964 that he and Cole often went to Manhattan and spent an evening at Sherry's, an elegant restaurant on Park Avenue.
"We'd come down on the 6 o'clock train, change [into white tie and tails]
on the back platform . . . go to the theater, on the town and then take the
milk train home and change our clothes on the back platform." That train
left at four o'clock in the morning and stopped at every station to deliver
milk; they got back just in time for chapel, which they were obliged to
attend.

Soon after his induction into DKE Cole appeared at the Glee Club
concerts in a solo spot. Just before the finish, Cole came on stage and,
against a backup "zoom, zoom, zoom" from the boys behind him, sang
"The Motor Car," a satire on the pleasures of the automobile, which he had
recently composed:

> *Oh, the lovely motor car,*
> *What a wreck it's made of Pa!*
> *Over twenty doctor chaps*
> *Worked on him in his collapse.*

Cole (far right) with friends at Yale

Cole (on left) with fellow cheerleaders, 1912 season

Mother wears a sickly grin.
Where her face is dented in.
What do we care as long as we are
Having a ride in the motor car?

Porter also became a member of the Whiffenpoofs, the small singing group for senior class members which had been founded in 1909 at Mory's Temple Bar. More and more insistently music was demanding his attention, although throughout his four years in New Haven he took only four courses in music: History of Music, Instrumentation, Harmony, and Practical Music. According to *Stover at Yale,* in 1911 the musical education of the Yale student was lamentable. Dink says to his classmates: " 'I won't ask you the tendencies and theories of the modern schools—you won't know that such a thing as a theory in music exists. You know the opera of *Carmen* and the good old Toreador song. Do you know the name of the composer? . . . Do you know the history of its reception? Do you know what Bach's influence was in the development of music? Did you ever hear of . . . Verdi or that there is such a thing as a Russian composer?' Absolute silence. 'You have a hazy knowledge of Wagner, and you know that Chopin wrote a funeral march. That is your foothold in music; there you balance, surrounded by howling waters of ignorance.' "

In fall of 1992 eleven of Porter's college notebooks were presented to the Music Library at Yale by the family of Henry Humphrey Parsons, with whom Porter roomed in his senior year and who tragically committed suicide a few years later. As seniors, after Cole's three years of living alone in New Haven, he and Humphrey Parsons shared a suite in 31 Vanderbilt, which was located over the archway. When a member of the Vanderbilt family was studying at Yale, it was reserved for him. That year, Porter's friend and classmate, Vanderbilt Webb had gone abroad to study and so it was available to Cole. It was described as "sumptuous." Parsons served as manager of the Yale Glee Club and Porter as its president. Cole had often visited the Maine coast cottage of the Parsonses at Kennebunk and evidently left behind these notebooks and other music exercises.

The notebooks disclose much about Porter's life as a student. English was his major and music his minor at Yale. In later life Porter loathed writing, including the scoring of music for performances. His left-handedness may explain some of this dislike: in his day the world was arranged more conveniently for *droit* than for *gauche*. Anyway, it is notable that in these college books he wrote legibly and even primly, one could say.

William Lyon Phelps, Yale 1887, was perhaps the most legendary of all the Yale faculty in Porter's day. Besides courses in drama he taught a course in Tennyson and Browning which Cole took. Cole joined as well the Pundits, whose ten members—devoutly literary, and admirers of Professor Billy Lyon Phelps—met weekly at Phelps's home, where they were given dinner and lectures by Phelps on artistic topics. Porter paid rapt attention to these lengthy monologues. In one of Phelps's drama courses, which covered "contemporary drama in Europe and in America," Cole read plays by Ibsen, Hauptmann, Maeterlinck, Wilde, Pinero, Shaw, and many others. "A large amount of difficult reading will be required . . . Only those who can read French and German may take this course."

"In the mid-30's . . . figures with national reputations began discussing literature on the air." Phelps, the Lampson Professor of English at Yale, with an upper-class accent, became in time the most successful of these. The columnist Lucius Beebe proclaimed in 1939 that Phelps did more than any other living person to develop in readers reverence for the word. On the lecture circuit, he regularly drew audiences of two thousand people. "Nobody has ever said it until Billy Phelps says it," wrote the editor of the *Ladies' Home Journal.* His views were elitist and he rejected both modernism and so-called proletarian literature. This was in some ways a shift from his position as a young instructor at Yale, when he introduced contemporary drama

William Lyon Phelps, 1905

and fiction to the curriculum, rather to the disapproval of his Yale colleagues. After retirement from the university in 1933 he joined with the composer Sigmund Romberg in a weekly radio program where morality was as much a topic as the arts. A year after its inception, the program drew 16 percent of the radio audience, and Phelps became more influential than ever as a tastemaker.

In his Tennyson notebook, in which he took down Phelps's lectures, Porter writes reminders to himself: "Be prepared on subject matter," "Bring books to class." All these notebooks show a well-intentioned student who is orderly, writes neatly, and is attentive to detail. Often Porter paraphrased poems and sometimes quoted works redolent of adolescent angst—for instance, Tennyson's "All Things Will Die." Poems about unrequited love also had their appeal. No doubt friendships and music were two outlets for the young students—as they were for faculty members. The *Yale Banner and Pot Pourri* (the annual yearbook of the students of Yale University) for 1913 bears a dedication written by William Lyon Phelps to Charlton Miner, a lawyer who gave up his practice and became a member of the Yale English department. "During the last eighteen years," writes Phelps, "we have lived together in the closest intimacy as colleagues in the same department of a great university. Members of the Faculty have . . . the same sincere and ardent friendships that are found among undergraduates."

"Kind hearts are more than coronets" is a line Cole liked and one by which he tried to steer his life, despite the powerful pull that coronets and those who wore them always exercised on him. It is difficult at times to distinguish Phelps's judgments from Porter's, but in any case what Cole chose to take down in his notebooks is significant. Can one discover the subtext when he writes of "Supposed Confessions": "Man without faith begs God to enlighten him. He recalls his mother with her faith etc."? Although in later life Cole briefly considered embracing religion, he was never a believer, and his several comments about his mother's attachments to Peru churches were dismissive. In this course of Phelps's, St. Simon Stylites came under discussion. "Why was it good to get on a pillar?" Cole asks, and replies, "Away from temptation which was the attitude of Christianity of the time." (Cole's predilection led him to pursue temptation in reaction to the Puritanism that surrounded him.) In a discussion of Tennyson's "Ulysses" mention is made of the gods. Several times in his songs Porter refers to "the gods," always in the plural and depicting them as vain and spiteful. He also says about several male characters in "Ulysses," "This man is not a gentleman," a judgment he no doubt applied to the gods. In his senior year Cole was one of 69 (in a class of 292) who went to no church.

Once during Cole's days at Yale the British Catholic poet Alfred Noyes visited the campus and lectured on "Poetry and Faith." A university publication cited "fire, fancy, and faith" as the great qualities of his work. Cole cut and preserved this account, which went on to quote Noyes as saying, "A poet is great, and is not a mere metrician, when he can discern and express emotive and spiritual ideas that lie hidden in the minds of men . . . His art becomes almost a religion." In some sense it did for Cole.

Cole's judgment of poems is often decisive. He criticizes some as "false," "laid on too thick," "too much sentimentality." Tennyson's "The Miller's Daughter" he labels "a bore." (All his life, friends maintain, Porter was in frantic flight from boredom.) He appears to have learned a lot about technique in Phelps's course, particularly scansion, the relation of words to their rhythms, and the music inherent in diction. "The Princess" he thinks would make "an excellent libretto for a comic opera."

More congenial to Cole than Tennyson perhaps was Fitzgerald's translation of the *Rubaiyat* with its frank hedonism. Porter noted that Omar Khyyam's "philosophy of life . . . is Pleasure, Drink, Epicurean sensuousness of life, transitoriness of life," mentioning, by the by, that the poet "was a vegetarianism [sic]." This Omar was quite unlike the many Omars in Cole's family tree.

Oddly enough, Phelps's course had very little to say about Browning, the poet Porter kept an eye on from childhood. Perhaps the voluble professor ran out of time.

The most unexpected marginalia in Porter's recently discovered notebooks are the many drawings he did. Especially arresting are the accomplished depictions of his fantasies of Belle Epoque beauties hatted and gloved. Others, chic and a touch *farouche,* are dark-eyed sirens equipped for combat with ostrich plumes and décolletage. A few of the drawings are labeled: "Amor vincit omnia" is one legend; "Constance Collier" (the celebrated actress, who later became one of Cole's close friends) identifies another. A languid lady says, "Bill, let's go to the Women's Exchange instead of the University Club." One scantily dressed young woman is captioned "The Passing Parade." Many of the subjects of these cartoons typify women Porter sought out socially later in life—such international glamour girls as Merle Oberon, Jean Howard, Natalie Paley, and even Linda Lee Thomas, who became his cherished wife.

The other main subject of these Porter drawings is his signature. He repeatedly experimented with variations on the two words "Cole Porter" that ranged stylistically from rococo to art deco. Watching as he invents yet another decorative design for his name in those notebooks, one senses that the youthful Cole foresaw a future when the phrase "words and music by Cole Porter" would be emblazoned on theater programs and marquees around the world. Porter also drew a few circus characters—a motif moving from his childhood to his adult life. Included were "The Clown," "The Fat Lady," "The Bare-back Rider."

Eells's remark that Cole "majored in outside work and minored in the prescribed curriculum" seems severe, but there is some truth to it. He belonged to the Mince Pie Club and the Grill Room Grizzlies, among others, and more importantly the Yale Dramatic Association. During this time he composed more than one hundred songs. Although Monty Woolley was closely connected to the Yale Dramat, it was elsewhere that he and Cole met, nor did the meeting at first seem promising. During his sophomore year Porter was the sole member of his class invited to the *Yale News* banquet, where, as the evening progressed, he was asked to sing. He obliged by playing and singing several songs then popular and finally launched into "Bingo Eli Yale," which all the Yale men in the audience took up. The applause was clamorous, and Woolley, habituated to the starring role, was not pleased; he curtly accused Cole of showing off. But Cole's rejoinder was adroit: "Look, Mr. Woolley, if I broke one little pinkie, no one would give me a second thought." These words won Monty over. Cole became his protégé, and a lifelong friendship began. Cole considered his meeting with Edgar Montillion Woolley one of the major attainments of his years at Yale. More than forty years later Cole told an interviewer that "one of my finest experiences at Yale was Monty Woolley—who taught me how to listen."

The other person he met through the Dramat was T. Lawrason Riggs. Riggs came from a privileged background. His Riggs grandfather was a Yale graduate who financed the first telegraph line in the United States and handled the purchase of Alaska for the government. Lawrason's father, a pious Roman Catholic, was a pioneer in the liturgical movement that began in the Catholic Church about the turn of the century. His special efforts were

Drawings from Porter's notebooks when he was at Yale

Monty Woolley, 1923

devoted to ridding church worship of the operatic-style music that had gained ascendancy in the past and returning to Gregorian chant.

Small in physical stature, T. Lawrason Riggs—named for St. Thomas Aquinas, although St. Thomas More seemed more his enthusiasm in later life—was drawn to drama and invariably cast as the female lead, which required him to appear in drag, often in elaborate costumes suited to the characters he played. This was true even in the elegant Westminster School, where he prepared for Yale. His final role in the dramatic society offerings that year required him to play a woman who rode about on an elephant, although, like Porter, he was not at all athletic. Riggs could also summon easily a falsetto which fit these female roles.

Probably his father's passion for church pageantry and for piety accounts to some degree for Lawrason's twin lifelong pursuits. As a senior at Yale he served as president of the Dramat and was invited to be one of the

T. Lawrason Riggs

chosen ten in Phelps's Pundit Society. Phelps encouraged a natural tendency in Riggs: "his refusal to pander to popular taste."

In his junior year at Yale (1911–12) Porter lived again in a single room. One of the courses he took that year was devoted to nineteenth-century English poets. Wordsworth, Coleridge, Byron, Shelley, and Keats were the poets discussed. He made careful notes on the Romantic movement and the liberation it offered, but sounds in his written comments sympathetic to forms inculcated by his mother and his tutors at the Worcester School. "In the early 18th century the Poet must be refined, just as we are today in conversation. Example *ill* and not *sick*." Colloquialisms must be avoided. In the notebooks Porter and/or his professors paraphrase extensively and focus often on plots. He pays considerable attention to rhyme schemes and scansion. And he sometimes copies lines that attract him: "The music stirs in him / Like wind through a tree." He deplores in Wordsworth the lack of humor (an element Porter rarely neglected in his lyrics) and notes that, though pre-Romantics like Crabbe and Burns wrote poems about the lives of the poor, Shakespeare did not. Porter's sympathies here are with Shakespeare. Cole's description of Wordsworth's fertile friendship with his sister, Dorothy, points to the parallel relationship Cole later enacted with his wife, Linda: "Dorothy helped [William] to discover the elementary principles of

life. During this . . . time Wordsworth became a poet." He noted that
Wordsworth's marriage "was extremely unromantic. Dorothy went along on
the honeymoon. This has given clearance to critics to say W. was incapable
of passion." Even more revealing is Cole's observation that "once . . . on
being asked why he [Wordsworth] never wrote love-poetry, he answered love
was too strong a passion to be dealt with artistically. He always hated to give
free rein to this passion." Not so Cole Porter. One thinks of Alan Jay Lerner's
comment: "Everybody else, perhaps, when fortunate can write a tender song
or a romantic song or a wistful song or nostalgic song, but Cole could write
passion." More congenial to Cole were these lines of poetry: "To be beloved
is all I need, / and whom I love, I love indeed."

And then the class turned to Lord Byron, who, Porter noted, "was
always being charged with immorality." No doubt the aristocratic background of the poet attracted Cole. He comments on Byron's being from a
"very old family" who for a long time were ranked as peers. Porter briefly
notes the inadequacies of Byron's mother and goes on to say that Byron led
a riotous life at Cambridge: for example, he traveled to Brighton with a girl
dressed as a page. Refinement and form were concerns as Cole read through
the Romantics. In view of his elitism in later life it is curious to observe
what seems to be his enthusiasms for "the growth of democracy" and the
"demise of the over-value placed upon refinement."

Just then, in the fall of 1911 during his junior year at Yale, Cole, whose
academic achievement as an undergraduate had slipped badly, was occupied
with his songs and the fate of the football team. The *New Haven Register*
published an article on November 12, 1911, entitled "Football Song Writing:
Cole Porter, Latest Yale Composer of Big Game Choruses, Looks to New
Hits 'Bull Dog' and 'Eli' to Cheer Team to Victory Next Week." It begins
with the sweeping statement that Porter is "one of the best entertainers who
has ever been at Yale . . . Mr. Porter had no musical education [!!] but had
natural ability . . ." Then one discovers that this profile of Porter is a spoof
of the kind he invented often in later life, and one wonders if he didn't write
this send-up of himself: "Some of the peculiar and distinctive features of his
work," it continues, "have been explained by the fact that he spent several
years in the mountains of Roumania, and heard many strange birds while
up there. But it was probably the sight of Bill Howe's dog, 'Beans,' which
used to be in a continual brawl at Yale field last spring, but which had qui-
eted down on the gridiron this fall, which inspired the following song which
has been chosen as one of the official songs for the fall[,] 'Bull Dog.' "

The Yale–Princeton football game that November was a bitter contest
for Yale men; an unusually fine team suffered defeat on a rain-soaked grid-

iron. Afterward, the Yalies heavily patronized the bar at New Haven's new Hotel Taft, and many went on to view the Saturday-night entertainment at the Hyperion Theatre. The star of that show was Gaby Deslys, whom Tommy Hendricks, one of the Princetonians in New Haven for the game, called "the hot-cha baby of her day," leading "the biggest musical review of Broadway." But Mademoiselle Deslys scarcely got a hearing. So drunk and disorderly were the students from both universities that they hurled any and every movable object at each other and at the performers. The audience was sprayed with water, as were many of the performers. The uproar wakened the star of the Yale team, who had been sleeping innocently. As he ventured out onto the street to investigate the brouhaha, he was clubbed by a policeman and hauled off to jail. Six other innocent students were arrested along with him. Word of this reached the Hyperion, and students of both colleges vacated the theatre and "ran hellbent for the bastille to release the great [footballer] from bondage . . . Cole was among those who led the march on the bastille. Each student was armed with a brick. The bastille had to come down." But somehow the insurgents were quelled and a riot averted.

Although as Tommy Hendricks avers, "Cole Porter was definitely not a football king," by his junior year he was known to every undergraduate and recognized as the leader of most of the musical and theatrical activities on the campus. As the *New Haven Register* insisted: "Mr. Porter's work, it should be stated, is not confined to writing football songs. He has just been engaged to write an opera for the summer colony at East Hampton, L.I. for which 'Spud' Murphy of the class of 1908 will write the words. Another light opera by him is shortly to be produced." That probably refers to *Cora,* the annual production of the DKE that academic year, for which Cole wrote the songs, staged the production, and played the leading role. It was Porter's first musical comedy and was performed at the Phi Theatre, York Street, on November 28, 1911. The cast included such cronies as Len Hanna, as the mother of the character played by Cole; Humphrey Parsons; and Arnold Whitridge, who in later life was able to re-create some of the lyrics and tunes. Whitridge also recalled to Robert Kimball, the noted music scholar and former curator of the Yale Musical Theatre Collection, a couplet gently mocking Rufus King ('14), who was known for his female impersonations in college musicals: "Little Rufe King couldn't teach me a thing, / I'm the Queen of the Yale Dramat." Also extant are Porter's lines:

Oh, it's awfully hard to concentrate at Yale.
. . . .

For the extra curriculum
Makes the gay life at Yale.

Cora was "the event of the midwinter social calendar." And "The star of this particular performance was Cole, 120 pounds of fire and fight, strutting and striding across the stage in a large white turtle-neck sweater adorned with an oversized Y."

Many debs hoped that Porter might ask them to be his date. Instead he had invited Des Bearrs, who came east for the event. Tommy squired Des to the performance, and so these two childhood pals, who not so very many years ago staged their theatricals in Peru, found themselves watching the third of their trio advance on his way to Broadway and the Big Time.

None of these college shows offered Porter the kind of réclame that he noted in Byron's life: "After [*Childe Harold's*] publication he awoke and found himself famous." He does note that Byron "was the lion of a very speedy set in London" and that he was stimulated by his life with London's "corrupt set." In fact, the more one looks at Porter's notes on Byron, the more one suspects that this Romantic poet was a model whom Porter, in a less public way, imitated. Porter too moved in a "speedy set," and like Byron he had "wandered by the Rhine." "In Venice," Cole wrote in his notebook, "[Byron] led a very corrupt life, enjoying a succession of mistresses . . . All this he did on his wife's money." And he admiringly mentioned that Byron "lived in a palace on the grand canal." Byron's literary style impressed Porter even more than his life did. Byron, he says, adapted his style from Francesco Berni, a poet and satirist of the early sixteenth century. "Byron found this style attractive for he was getting tired of being intense, poetical, spiritual . . . He was free [in the style of Berni] to change his mood . . . from flippancy to poetry, from beauty to obscenity . . . This style dominated 'Don Juan.'" And dominates the work of Cole Porter, one might add: to examine "Don Juan" is to discover many characteristics Porter's lyrics copy. Most notable are the unexpected and witty rhymes and the lists, many of them devoted to society figures of Byron's day or friends from the fraternity of poets.

Porter read other writers in this course on the Romantics: Godwin he notes as an apostle of free love, but he was not "a libertine—far from it"; and Shelley, he observes, "wrote a novel before he went to Oxford and published another while a Freshman."

In a course on Shakespeare, Porter takes notes on *Othello* and domesticates Desdemona by calling her "Des." There is little about *Taming of the*

Shrew beyond an enigmatic mention that "we saw Katherine in *The Tam-ing.*" Porter sometimes jotted down in his pages dialogue that pre-echoes his later work with a soupçon of W. S. Gilbert:

> 2ND LADY: *Would I know something worse than this*
> *No doubt you've heard of Bella Bliss.*
> *I'm told she's the inventor of the first soul kiss.*
> ALL: *Oh, Deplorable!*

In April 1912 the Yale Dramat gave two performances—one in New Haven, the other at the Yale Club in New York City—of *And the Villain Still Pursued Her,* a spoof on *Uncle Tom's Cabin.* It was co-staged by Porter, who wrote as well the music and lyrics for the show. Buddy Marshall, another of Cole's wealthy and later celebrated friends, was in the cast. Rufus King performed as "the lovely heroine" and Monty Woolley played the villain:

> *I take delight*
> *In looking for a fight*
> *And pressing little babies on the head*
> *Till they're dead.*
> *I have gotten*
> *A rep for being rotten,*
> *I put poison in my mother's cream of wheat.*

That same year, Porter played "Mistress Aelinde" and had the role of the Abbess of Kirklee in *Robin of Sherwood.* "Much might be written . . . about the startlingly 'professional' annual musicals [Cole] wrote for the Yale 'Dra-mat' Smokers," said John Garth. "[I] still sing and play his 'Rick-Chick-a-Chicken.' " "Those Porter undergraduate musicals always contained spots of colorful original humor (for men only) like the one [*Kaleidoscope*] about the football hero who walked in from the shower to find his room full of his room-mates' lady friends, and their mothers, just arrived for 'Dawn Tea.' " In *Kaleidoscope* Archibald MacLeish played Butler, a baby. This is also the entertainment in which Cole published these now naughty verses:

> *Death hangs o'er us like*
> *The threatening sword of Damocles,*
> *We're so poor*

We can't afford a
Box of Rameses.

The summer of 1912 Cole spent with his family. Back home in Peru, he gave thought to the Christmas tour he would organize for the Glee Club, of which he was now president. Then there was the 1912–13 DKE smoker to prepare. Cole sought out as librettist Almet Jenks, '14, who had been awarded as a freshman the prize offered by the Dramat for the best play submitted by a member of Yale. Jenks agreed to the collaboration. Cole expressed to Jenks a practice he retained all his life: "Tell me whom you select for different parts, and I can write fitting songs the more easily." And so *The Pot of Gold* came to be. Four letters from Cole to Jenks survive; written from "Westleigh on the Mis-sis-sin-a-wa," they show Cole's industriousness when it came to creative work. "Dash off a scenario," he tells his collaborator, "so I can work on opening choruses . . . Don't forget color. We must have lots of that. Be naif and I can join you." Elsewhere in the letter he tells Jenks to be "obvious and uninteresting. Otherwise we will suffer defeat, for my music was never the result of inspired imagination."

From the start Porter eschewed the "Poeta nascitur, non fit" notion and emphasized craft as the primary component of artistry. With the Porter notebooks recently recovered is an almost complete manuscript of the Jenks/Porter collaboration, *The Pot of Gold*—a title the librettist invented and with which Porter was delighted. He thought Jenks had cluttered the show with too many characters and like a practiced showman anticipated the difficulties which a large cast would invite. The two Russian nihilists (reappearing again in *Silk Stockings*) had already inspired Cole to write a motif combining "the splendor of Wagner and the decadence of Strauss." Jenks thought of a three-act play, but Porter was against more than two acts because of the changes in scenery and costumes a third act would entail. "I wish we could make this play a little masterpiece in its own foolish way. Take it horribly seriously, and I will join you. It really is important, for after all it can never happen again." As a commentator points out, American musical comedy in 1912 was not auspicious, producing banal lyrics and rhymes. "Out in Peru, Indiana that same summer, a nineteen-year-old Yale undergraduate was working on the lyrics and music of a show called *Pot of Gold* . . . These early Porter lyrics . . . show that even at nineteen [Porter was in fact twenty-one] the composer-lyricist was moving considerably ahead of his professional contemporaries. The beginning of the Porter style, at once suave and audacious . . . can be detected in his undergraduate work, and even when the youthful hand falters, a turn of phrase, a novel conceit or an unexpected rhyme reveal the seeds of his later distinction."

Both Porter and Jenks worked strenuously at completing *The Pot of Gold.* Cole used flattery to hurry his collaborator on. "Perhaps I sound altogether too serious about it, but I feel that it's up to you to show New Haven a little of that brain. You have no idea how much is expected. You have a reputation." No doubt he was thinking as much and more of himself and the high expectations people had for him. Apart from a sejour with the Parsonses that summer of 1912, Porter devoted himself to the score for the DKE smoker. In late September he wrote to Jenks, "We leave for New Haven tomorrow morning. Let me know the minute you arrive."

The Pot of Gold was performed at the DKE fraternity house on November 26, 1912, and at the Hotel Taft in New Haven the following week. Porter starred in the musical and introduced, among other songs, one that was a nod to his fraternity: "I Want to Be Married (to a Delta Kappa Epsilon Man)."

Porter was astonishingly busy in his final year at Yale. He served as a cheerleader, wrote songs for other college shows, conducted the rehearsals for two productions and coached the performers. He was also now a member of the prestigious senior society, Scroll and Key. It is not surprising to read in Donald Ogden Stewart's memoirs that when he went, in Cole's senior year, to interview Cole in Vanderbilt Hall, he found him fast asleep at eleven a.m. Stewart considered this to be "extraordinary comportment." Meanwhile Cole had the Glee Club to look after. Their Christmas trip of 1912–13 took them to Cleveland, Chicago, St. Louis, Kansas City, Denver, St. Paul, Detroit, Niagara, Buffalo, Syracuse. Many dances and teas were organized for the Yale boys. "The average student sees the tour as hat boxes and white waistcoats, dancing all night and sleeping all day, much fun, little work, and less achievement." This journalist, writing in an unidentified newspaper, cautions that "the real purpose of the tour is to keep the distant graduates in touch with the University, to show them that a real, vital undergraduate life still exists at New Haven, and to remind them of the old days of Brick Row, The Wooden Spoon, or even Alumni Hall." A Richmond paper (undated) wrote of the Christmas concert: "But the glittering star of the concert was Cole Porter '13. This young man has a singing pianologue act that would easily make good in 'big time' vaudeville. He is a born comedian . . . plays piano very well and writes most of his own 'stuff,' which is unusually clever . . . he was made to sing six encores, all of them except one, presumably his own . . . Indeed we rarely have a man in any of our vaudeville houses as good as this Yale junior."

The choristers had a splendid time traveling in a luxury train over forty-seven hundred miles. Apparently none suffered from homesickness, although they were unable to spend Christmas with their families. On the contrary, the young men were cited by one newspaper for the "snap and dash with which they carried their work." In this program Cole did his much-praised imitation of Marie Dressler's "Heaven Will Protect the Working Girl." Indeed, in all the reviews of the Glee Club's performances on this tour, he is singled out with praise. At a concert President Taft (a Yale alumnus) attended in Washington, D.C., "the singing of Cole Porter was one of the features," and the reviewer praised his "good voice and being a clever imitator [and] a comedian." A Boston critic wrote that "a pleasing feature of Porter's work is, that while it is worthy of professional notice, it is not performed in that manner." A concert held at Princeton "featured Mr. Cole Porter, President of [Yale's] combined organization. Mr. Porter gave several attractive solos accompanying them himself, and in 'Football King' which he composed, his unusual voice was shown off to great advantage."

In Cincinnati, "Mr. Cole Porter . . . appeared in the program but once, but when the audience had him there it wouldn't let him go until his stock of 10 or 12 encores was exhausted." Other anonymous newspaper cuttings call Porter "the star of the evening." One goes on to say, "He is one of those musical geniuses to whom music is second nature, and he has not only written the score but the words of many of the songs . . . He could make his fortune on the vaudeville stage, for his specialty consists of a running commentary on people and things while singing topical songs to his own accompaniment or giving imitations. Among the songs he sang were some of his own, including 'Mercy Percy' [lost], 'No Show This Evening' [lost] and 'Music with Meals' [lost]. Porter's tactic was to delay his entrance until just before the Glee Club's last number, when he would step from the ranks of the second tenors and "with a perfect command of the keyboard . . . and a voice full of melody" evoke tumultuous applause from the audience. "His versatility is remarkable and there seems to be no end to his store of amusing stunts. He will be the 'headliner' at the concert, but where the Yale men look forward most to the enjoyment of his special gifts is at the smoker of the Queen City Club after the concert, where they will take possession of him and keep him at the piano until the dawn breaks."

If the Yale men looked forward to the après concert, imagine what Cole's pleasure must have been. He had traveled far from his early days at Yale when he was mocked for his alien appearance and ways.

Porter's last show as an undergraduate was *The Kaleidoscope,* staged by the Yale Dramat at the Hotel Taft in New Haven in April 1913 and a week later at the Yale Club in New York. "As I Love You" was later retitled "Esmerelda" and published by Irving Berlin, Inc. In 1915 Sigmund Romberg and E. Ray Goetz used "Esmerelda" in a show called *Hands Up.* Robert Kimball notes that it was the first of Cole's songs to be sung in a Broadway show. It is a list song reminiscent of Leporello's boastful enumeration of his master's conquests in Mozart's *Don Giovanni:*

> *Esmerelda,*
> *Then Griselda,*
> *And the third was Rosalie.*
> *Lovely Lakme*
> *Tried to track me,*
> *But I fell for fair Marie.*
> *Eleanora*
> *Followed Dora,*
> *Then came Eve with eyes of blue.*
> *But I swear I ne'er loved any girl*
> *As I love you.*

Most of the musical score of *The Kaleidoscope* does not survive. Several of Cole's allusions in the songs are literary, and at least one "Oh, What a Pretty Pair of Lovers," (to *Paul et Virginie*) is recondite. After the performance Billy Lyon Phelps told the audience that "every serious man and organization often turns to things in a lighter vein. All dramatists have written burlesque and the Dramatic Club is very fortunate in having one who is a real genius and who writes both words and music of exceptionally high order." With commencement a few weeks off, these words of Phelps constituted an *envoi* that must have pleased Cole.

The pace of Porter's life quickened during his last month at Yale. He played a butler in a show sponsored by the Dramat. On June 14 he appeared as Mistress Melinda, a country maid, in George Farquhar's *The Recruiting Officer.* Archibald MacLeish wrote to Eells in 1964 to say, "I have the clearest memory of rehearsals conducted by Cole Porter, including drinks prepared by Cole Porter, including the first Tom Collins I ever drank."

The Yale Glee Club regularly closed its concerts with a work by H. S. Durand called "Bright College Years." How filled with feeling Porter must have been on his last appearance with these young men in spring 1913:

> *Bright college years with pleasure rife*
> *The shortest, gladdest years of life*

How swiftly are ye gliding by!
Oh why doth time so quickly fly?
The seasons come, the seasons go,
The earth is green or white with snow;
But time and change shall naught avail
To break the friendships formed at Yale.

Chapter 3

Seeing America
First

In the summer of 1913, Cole traveled abroad again, though mostly in the British Isles, touring the English countryside with three other Yalies: Peter Cooper Bryce, Buddy Marshall, and Gurney Smith. Then, in the fall, Cole settled into his law school studies at Harvard. "Porter expects to enter the Harvard Law School, after which he will go into either mining, lumbering or farming," noted the Yale *History of the Class of 1913,* suggesting a scenario that briefly Cole seemed to be enacting. But not for long. Paul McNath, in the same class as Cole at law school, told about a day when Professor Bull Warren called on Cole "to recite a particular case, and Porter wasn't prepared. He naturally fumbled and made Professor Warren very angry. Finally Warren leaned over his desk and very superciliously said, 'Mr. Porter, why don't you learn to play the fiddle?' And Cole Porter got up, walked out of the class and never went back to the Harvard Law School."

Considerable apocrypha have been generated around Porter's Harvard years, some of it seemingly by Porter himself. At 404 Craigie Hall, Cole resided with Dean Acheson, a fellow law student (and future secretary of state), and T. Lawrason Riggs, Yale 1910, who was in the graduate school. Later in life Acheson many times repeated "as fact" to his son David a story of how the three young men returned to Craigie Hall one evening, celebrating a theater opening by holding an impromptu champagne party. Probably Porter played the piano, and the others may have shouted out songs. Next morning neighbors called the law school to complain about the late-night noise, and Dean Ezra Ripley Thayer summoned the culprits and threatened to expel them. Acheson insisted to his son that Cole went subsequently to see Dean Thayer and offered to leave the law school if the others would be allowed to continue. All the parties agreed to this arrangement.

Talking to Louis Sobol twenty-five years later, Porter said, "One day I was at a party and I played a piece I had written and the dean of the Law School said 'Porter—don't waste your time—get busy and study music.'" This sounds nearer the truth and is corroborated by an unidentified newspaper cutting in which Porter is quoted: "I'm used to being sat on in Boston. If Dean Thayer of Harvard hadn't been so thorough in refusing to admit that I could ever become a lawyer I might never have become a song writer. If he hadn't been so sure I could never become a judge in law—I might never have become such a good judge of other things. As a matter of fact he suggested I try song writing. So I took up music with a swell recommendation from the Dean of Harvard's Law School! Anyway I only studied law to please my father [grandfather?]." Cole had entered Harvard Law School on September 22, 1913, and he left on June 14, 1914. Dean Thayer then arranged his transfer to the Harvard School of Music. He had received the equivalent of present-day D's in Contracts, Criminal Law, Torts, and Civil Procedure.

In time Cole made up a song about 404 Craigie and his life there:

> *In four-o-four*
> *On the second floor*
> *Lives a crazy Craigie crowd.*
> *They play all day,*
> *All night they play.*
> *No work is there allowed.*
> *Away with law.*
> *It's an awful bore*
> *Their war cry rings out clear.*

Some of the sounds emerging from 404 Craigie that year may have been the efforts to put together *Paranoia,* a show Cole had promised to do for his fraternity's smoker before he left New Haven in spring 1913. Professor "Billy" Phelps opened the smoker, calling the authors "the Gilbert and Sullivan combination of collegiate dramatics." Indeed, both Porter and Riggs (who wrote the book and some of the lyrics) were worshipers of Gilbert and Sullivan, whose impact on Porter was lasting.

Paranoia, or Chester of the Yale Dramatic Association opened in New Haven's Hotel Taft on April 24, 1914. Directed by Monty Woolley, it featured characters with such comic names as "the Marchioness of Petunya" and "Doremi Fasolarma, the sweet warbler of the Balkans." Archibald MacLeish played a Nubian slave and Henry J. Crocker Jr. (of the wealthy San Francisco banking family), acted the part of the "Crown Prince of Aphasia." It had many musical, as well as verbal, felicities. The opening chorus of Act II, for instance, was a parody of Debussy's *Afternoon of a Faun.* "We had such fun that we kept the 1913 cast together after graduation," wrote one of the group, "hoping to find some place for a reunion." Only weeks later, at an annual meeting of the Associated Western Yale Clubs held in Cincinnati, Ohio, Cole and some of the others presented a satiric musical about the Mexican Revolution, *We're All Dressed Up and We Don't Know Huerto Go.* The players insisted on certain rewards which were forthcoming: "first class accommodations, cards for all clubs, unlimited signing privileges, invitations to all parties, etc. . . . We had a car of our own," wrote Johnfritz Achelis, Cole's classmate and president of the Yale Dramat in their senior year. "Each one of us was presented with cards to five clubs, we attended the final polo matches, and many parties." Cole's sybaritic tastes awoke early and are reflected, no doubt, in this list of luxuries. For this show Cole wrote "Cincinnati," and he easily replaced the song with "Cleveland" when the show was later done there, with Len Hanna as stage manager in his home town. Its final performance was staged at the Marshall Field House on Park Avenue and Sixty-ninth Street and was followed by a swank party.

In April 1915 Cole was in New York staying with his Yale classmate Buddy Marshall. He was to interpolate some of his songs into a new show to be staged by the Junior League. "Tell grandad Lew Fields gave me 50 dollars for each song I sold him, and four cents on each copy," he wired his mother, still concerned to diminish J.O.'s disapproval of his career.

Elizabeth Marbury, very rich and famous as a theater producer and agent, visited New Haven in June 1915 for the first night of Lew Fields's new play. She was Oscar Wilde's friend and agent when he first visited New York in 1882 and afterwards toured the country. The *New Haven Evening Register* quoted Miss Marbury: "I am convinced that Mr. Porter is the one man of the many who can measure up to the standard set by the late Sir Arthur Sullivan."

When Porter journeyed to Chicago is not clear, but an unidentified newspaper cutting presumably published circa 1915 describes Chicago's departure of a diva called Madame Edvina who was traveling to New York to sing at the Metropolitan. A party tendered to her by friends featured Porter, who sang his own compositions and accompanied himself on the piano. "He has written an operetta—words and music—and Miss Bessie Marbury is going to bring it out with him in the chief role."

By December Cole was busy with *See America First,* which was to begin rehearsals early in 1916, produced by Miss Marbury. Much of the score was written during the summer of 1915 at a country house of the Riggses in New London, Connecticut. On Valentine's Day, 1916, Cole wired his mother: "Everything going beautifully rehearsing from ten in morning until twelve at night tired but contented." *Le tout* New Haven was said to have been present for the New Haven tryout on March 22, 1916, and witnessed what a member of the audience called "the second-act embarrassment" with the Arizona mountain burro "who refused to enter on cue and then when he did . . . ! Porter hadn't learned about the behavior of donkeys when suddenly confronted with a large audience . . . 'a side-splitting disaster.' "

Although he received little attention, the then unknown Clifton Webb was a plus, and "I've a Shooting-Box in Scotland," revised and resurrected from *Paranoia,* became the first enduring Porter patter song:

Elizabeth Marbury

I've a shooting-box in Scotland,
I've a chateau in Touraine,
I've a silly little chalet
In the Interlaken Valley,
I've a hacienda in Spain,
I've a private fjord in Norway,
I've a villa close to Rome,
And in travelling
It's really quite a comfort to know
That you're never far from home!

There are three verses followed by three refrains, all adding to a strict and witty rhyme scheme. "Miss Browning's hair" and "Alfred Noyes" show Porter including in his list people encountered in his classes or on the lecture platform. The structure, incidentally, is not unlike that of the Christmas-list poem annually published in *The New Yorker:* both depend on startling and delighting the audience by linking the unlikely.

The next day a critic in the *Evening World* wrote that Riggs and Cole Porter did everything in their power to follow the earlier and excellent example set by Gilbert & Sullivan, but labeled the show "an achievement that college boys might have done in the way of entertainment." He also applied the adjective "patriotic" to the work. Of course the year was 1916, and World War I was underway. But however much fun is made of foreigners, one can't help judging the tone of the eponymous song as satiric of America:

Of the sturdy Middle West I am the patriotic cream,
I'm the enemy of European Kings,
. . . .
Don't leave America,
Just stick around the U.S.A.
Cheer for America
And get that grand old strain of Yankee Doodle
In your noodle;
Yell for America,
Altho' your vocal cords may burst;
And if you ever take an outing,
Leave the station shouting:
"See America First!"

The work also took a satiric poke at J. O. Cole by enunciating the doctrine to which he subscribed. Indeed, the following lines sound quite the advice his grandfather might have given to Cole:

> *Of European lands effete,*
> *A most inveterate foe,*
> *My feelings when my camp I greet*
> *Are such as patriots know.*
> *Condemning trips across the blue*
> *As dollars badly dispersed,*
> *I hold that loyal men and true,*
> *Including in the category all of you,*
> *Should see America first,*
> *Should see America first.*

The Pirates of Penzance was cited as a model, as was *Iolanthe,* and mention made of debts to Nijinsky in the musical parody of *Faun.* The plot involves a wealthy American senator who loves his country and hates everything foreign, while his daughter dotes on England and a duke. (This was the period of "Dooks for Dollars," the practice of wealthy American women marrying titled Europeans.)

The play opened in New York on March 28, 1916. Dorothie Bigelow, a socialite, sang the female lead. A pupil of Jean de Reszke, she had been singing in the trenches and in hospitals in war-torn Europe. She described how she met Elizabeth Marbury and Cole Porter, calling it "inevitable that he and I should meet at a party for after leaving Yale, Cole had become the pet of New York Society. He had an utterly charming Leprechaun [a word many people used to describe Cole] personality, which coupled with his gift of song, endeared him to everyone." Unfortunately Bigelow fared ill with the critics, who felt, in the words of one, that she failed to "project her personality into the audience room" (in contrast to Ethel Merman in subsequent Porter shows). One notice didn't hesitate to state that *See America First* was the "worst musical comedy in town. Don't see *America First.*" Perhaps Porter was anticipating the critics' rejection when just before the show opened in New York he added "Lima" to the score. Writing this not very subtle serenade to his hometown, he must have longed just then for the support and enthusiasm of his mother and his Peru pals.

Lima's the place
And I'd give a lot, I guess,
Back there to race
. . . .
I simply quiver—to drive my flivver
Along that lazy hazy crazy Wabash River
And if I ever, ever get home again,
Why I never, never shall roam again.

See America First closed after fifteen performances. Years later Porter told Ed Sullivan: "I'll never forget that night . . . when my first show closed . . . As they dismantled the scenery and trucked it out of the stage alley, I honestly believed I was disgraced for the rest of my life. I literally sneaked back to the Yale Club, rushed through the lobby to the elevator and hid in my room." Porter was also amused to say once on the *Jukebox Jury* television show: "For years New York critics have said, 'Cole Porter's score is not up to his usual standard.' My wife, who keeps the scrapbooks, decided to go back . . . and establish that standard the critics referred to. She finally found it in a clipping dated 1916 which said 'Cole Porter is a young man who ought either to give up songwriting or get out of town.' That's when I joined the Foreign Legion." As one of the songs in *See America First* says, "I've got an awful lot to learn." So Cole resumed music studies, this time with Pietro Yon, for many years organist at St. Patrick's Cathedral in New York.

Riggs's personal reserve may account partly for the tendency of commentators on *See America First* to feature Porter somewhat to the exclusion of Riggs. As it did Porter, the failure of the show shook Riggs deeply, and he announced to friends: "I spent the fall of 1915 in Cambridge, working on the book and lyrics of a comic opera, *See America First,* with Cole Porter, who did the music. It was presented in New York during the winter, but failed dismally. Owing to the fact that the composer and I consented to complete transformation of the piece to meet the capabilities of its interpreters and the supposed tastes of the public, we suffered, in addition to our disappointment, the unsatisfactory feeling that nothing had been proved as to the worth of our efforts. But we are wiser, as well as sadder, and for myself I have done with attempts at dramatic composition, so far as I can foresee." Riggs had invested $35,000 in the show, but with his family fortune he could afford the loss.

Having completed his M.A. in English at Harvard graduate school Riggs began work on a Ph.D. He was an instructor in English at Yale when

the United States entered World War I, and enlisted in the Yale Mobile
Hospital Unit, surrendering the "bachelor grandeur" with which he lived in
a large house on Whitney Avenue in New Haven. It was while serving
abroad that Riggs decided to become a priest. After ordination he was
appointed Yale's first Catholic chaplain, in which capacity he served from
1922 until his sudden death from heart failure in 1943.

Eventually he built the St. Thomas More House and Chapel. He continued to live with splendid style: his large home stocked with servants and
the finest furniture. Students and colleagues were often entertained stylishly, and in some ways Riggs functioned as a religious Billy Phelps. Among
his admirable attainments were his pioneer efforts to launch the National
Conference of Christians and Jews and the liberal Catholic magazine *Com-
monweal,* in which he published fifty or so articles.

On April 6, 1917, the United States declared war on Germany, and a few
weeks later Congress passed legislation allowing President Woodrow Wilson
to draft men between the ages of eighteen and forty-five. In the summer of
1917 Cole Porter embarked on the *España* for France. Main Bocher, later to
become a famous couturier and a friend of both Linda's and Cole's, crossed
on the same ship. Cole carried abroad with him a curious but very useful
item a Philadelphia friend had presented to him: he described it as a zither
with a piano keyboard about two and a half feet wide. "In form it looked
like a Baby Grand piano with collapsible legs. It had a big strap on it so that
I could swing it over my back. He had it made especially for me."

Porter's intent was to forget the failure, disillusion, and self-doubt that
followed his first effort in the professional music theatre. But he felt as well
that the decent thing to do was to join in some way with the men, many of
whom had been his schoolmates or good friends, now fighting for the cause
of Americans and their allies in World War I. His friend Riggs had pointed
the way. But Porter rejected any attempt to impute pious or patriotic
motives to his enlistment. In 1953 he told *The New York Times:* "A great
many Americans did it . . . Was it out of a desire to help in the war against
Germany? No, it wasn't as noble as all that. It was exciting. And I met my
wife in France; she lived there then. We remained in Paris until 1937. Then
my wife had a premonition there was going to be a war, so we moved out
and brought everything back here."

Just before America entered World War I, thousands of young adven-
turers attempted to join ambulance services connected with the French military. A Paris partner of J. P. Morgan recruited taxis, buses, and private
automobiles to transport the wounded from battlefields to Paris. These vol-
unteers were "inducted into the Foreign Legion. Later this ambulance ser-

vice became part of the American military." Few episodes in Porter's life
have generated more confusion than what precisely he did in wartime
France. Porter seems himself to have created part of the confusion, casually
dropping the name of the French Foreign Legion in regard to his service.

All his life Porter enjoyed inventing ruses and sponsoring masquerades,
traceable partly, perhaps, to his early exposure to the circus. An acquaintance recalls the many costume parties that Porter arranged in the flat he
had on East Nineteenth Street in New York, right after the demise of *See
America First.* One biographer sensibly assumes that "as Cole had done in
his unhappy childhood, he escaped a miserable present by playing at being
someone he was not."

Porter revealed the pleasure that he took in deception in a parody he
wrote of Jerome Kern's song "They Didn't Believe Me":

> *And when they ask us how dangerous it was*
> *We never will tell them, we never will tell them.*
> *How we fought in some café*
> *With wild women night and day—*
> *'Twas the wonderfulest war you ever knew.*
> *And when they ask us, and they're certainly going to ask us,*
> *Why on our chests we do not wear the Croix de Guerre,*
> *We never will tell them,*
> *We never will tell them,*
> *There was a front, but damned if we knew where.*

One friend insists that Cole never mentioned the Foreign Legion to
him but said that he served in an ambulance unit: "not the Red Cross
exactly but a Franco-American ambulance corps. That's what Cole told
me." Initially he worked for the Duryea Relief organization (founded by an
American socialite), he told his mother in a letter dated October 5, 1917, and
published in the *Peru Republican* as a "letter from Cole Porter at the Front."
The newspaper identified Porter, no doubt at his mother's dictation, as "personal aide to the president of the Duryea Relief party now at the battle front
in France." The letter is addressed not to both parents but to his mother.
There is, however, one mention in the letter of his father, whom he refers to
as "Sammie": Cole, probably jokingly, says his father "will be glad to hear
that I really am developing into quite a [auto] mechanic." However keen his
mother was about his gift for music, he felt a failure in his father's eyes,
though on the evidence this feeling was unwarranted. Early on Cole had
chosen, however subtly, to league with his mother, and he wasn't far into his

career before he was using "Kate" as a subject for songs. An early example, provided from memory by a friend of Porter's, is entitled "Katie of the Y.M.C.A."

Elsewhere Porter gave this description of his link to the Foreign Legion: "I went to a little office in Paris for my physical examination after having asked to enlist. There was an officer of the Legion there and several soldiers. The officer looked up my name and then asked me to get on the scale. After I had been weighed he said to me, 'Now you're in the Foreign Legion.' That was all there was to it and afterwards I was sent immediately to Limoges to go through preliminary training before being sent to the front." This more or less matches what Porter told the playwright Abe Burrows: "Cole was with the French Foreign Legion. He told me the reason he was able to join was that the only requirement for entering the French Foreign Legion was you had to get weighed. So he joined the Legion and became an artillery expert which he now finds very useful at ASCAP meetings."

Despite Porter's matter-of-fact account of his military service, his record, as a commentator in *Town and Country* put it, "is a case for Scotland Yard, although he maintains he joined the Foreign Legion as a private, transferred to the Ecole d'Artillerie at Fontainebleau and eventually saw service at the front with the 32nd Regiment, French Army." Monty Woolley, in Paris with the U.S. Army, recalls Porter strutting up and down the boulevards in uniforms ranging all the way from a cadet's to a colonel's. "Porter," says Woolley, "had more changes than Maréchal Foch, and wore them with complete disregard of regulation. One night he might be a captain of the Zouaves, the next an aide-de-camp."

Eells has checked the pertinent sources scrupulously and gives a helpful account of Porter's passage from Duryea Relief, where he visited war-torn villages with provisions for the needy, to a division of the American Expeditionary Forces headquartered in Paris on the avenue Montaigne. Subsequently he enlisted in the First Foreign Regiment, moving from one regiment to the next until his discharge in April 1919, the year in which he wrote "When I Had a Uniform On": "I find that life's not what it used to be / When I had a uniform on."

Others beside Monty Woolley recall seeing him during his years in the military. One of them, Sir Rex Benson, reminisced in 1967 about Porter in a letter to a Yale official. "I met Cole for the first time in the very early days of the war . . . 1918 when I was Liaison Officer between Sir Douglas Hay and Marshal Pétain . . . we had a little coterie of friends consisting of Cole, Alan Graham [an English officer], the Kingsland brothers, Count Antoine Sala, Monty Woolley and Howard Sturges who used to meet frequently at

Dorothy "Dickie" Fellowes-Gordon on the Venice Lido, 1926

22 Place Vendôme . . . and listen to Cole playing the piano and writing his songs . . . He used often in later years to make me play some of these songs to him, saying he had forgotten them completely."

Archibald MacLeish, Yale class of 1914, was thought by some to be "quite arrogant," proud of the wealthy family whose scion he was. Like Porter, he went on to Harvard Law School, but unlike Cole, he took his degree. It was in Paris that he began to write poetry. In spring of 1918, on a Paris boulevard, he encountered Cole, who invited MacLeish to a party "at his house," lent to him by a French friend. MacLeish accepted and was dazzled by the style and sophistication of the partygoers, not to say the host. "Cole . . . seemed to me the most cosmopolitan figure," the future man of letters stated.

In the years immediately following World War I, Cole Porter continued to write and perform his songs for socially smart friends, and in this he was greatly aided by the legendary Elsa Maxwell. Porter first met Maxwell at a party in the Washington Square home of Mrs. Bridgit Guiness, wife of a British banker. Elsa was accompanied by a great beauty called Dorothy "Dickie" Fellowes-Gordon, an Englishwoman and, according to Maxwell, "one of Europe's *femmes fatales.*" The *on-dit* was that these two women who lived together for years never had a sexual relationship. This perhaps affirms Maxwell's claim in her autobiography (where she referred to Dickie as "my oldest friend") that "I never had a sexual experience, nor did I ever want one." The only male admirer she ever had ended their relationship with these words: "There is something in you that will always stop you from becoming a real woman."

Porter recalled decades later that Elsa and Dickie entered the Guiness house arguing about *See America First*. According to Elsa, Cole sidled over to them and asked, " 'Are you paging me?' He was wearing a white carnation and was meticulously groomed. 'A gigolo,' I thought. 'You're broke, no doubt,' I said aloud, 'so you *have* to dress well.' He shrugged. 'All on tick,' he said, 'Grandpa's tick.' Cole Porter was then called to the piano to play and sing his songs . . . 'secret songs' he'd been writing for years and stuffing into a trunk against a day when he could place them . . . a handsome leather [trunk], brass bound . . . The buzz of conversation in the room went on when Cole sat at the piano . . . but [soon] everyone was straining to catch the droll nuances of his lyrics. He held a critical audience enraptured for a full half hour while he ran through his repertory . . . which he had been writing for years and hoarding until public taste and sophistication [were] ready to appreciate them. At the end of that half hour, I was a world fan of the most paradoxical man ever to invade . . . show business."

As she came to know Porter in Paris and love his music, she included his songs in her performances and many people first came to hear his music through her entertainments. Short, swarthy, and obese—quite the opposite of the fashionable women she moved with—she was an "entrepreneuse," an "example of how far you can get with cheek", but from the start Porter liked her, perhaps, a friend opined, "because she was so outrageous." In his auto-biographical volume *Present Indicative,* Noël Coward describes meeting Elsa "before the days when she became the Queen of Paris." To write her true story, Coward insists, "would be worth doing, but unfortunately quite impossible, for the simple reason that . . . the real mysteries and struggles and adventures, are untraceable." Coward admired the unique way in which Elsa blended in her parties the social and the bohemian graces. No doubt this skill attracted Cole to her as well: he too learned, and perhaps partly from Elsa, the art of accommodating both worlds.

Chapter 4

I'm Tired of
Living Alone

When the Armistice was declared in 1918, Porter—unlike most of the American servicemen—lingered in Paris. According to his friend Marthe Hyde, he was one of the most attractive men in the city. Michael Arlen's caricature of Cole, written in 1919, has the ring of Wodehouse:

> Every morning at half-past seven Cole Porter leaps lightly out of bed and, having said his prayers, arranges himself in a riding habit. Then, having written a song or two, he will appear at the stroke of half-past twelve at the Ritz, where leaning in a manly way on the bar, he will say "Champagne cocktail, please. Had a marvelous ride this morning!" That statement gives him strength and confidence on which to suffer this, our life, until ten minutes past three in the afternoon when he will fall into a childlike sleep.

Although never taken up by the old French society, Porter was, among the internationals then in Paris, the toast of the town. A number of people who knew Porter in Paris after the war, and later, recalled that his French was fluent but that he had an unfortunate accent. This may have been one of the deterrents to his acceptance by *la vieille France*.

As much a social passport as his art was the friendship that flowered after his meeting Linda Lee Thomas at the wedding on January 30, 1918, of Ethel Harriman and Henry Russell at the Paris Ritz. Linda was a descendant of the

Linda, age forty-three, 1926

Pacos, one of whom signed the Declaration of Independence, and, like Jacqueline Onassis, was especially proud of her descent from the Virginia Lees. She was thought by people who knew her to have been "the most beautiful woman in the American South"—some said in the world. Tall and blond, with deeply blue eyes and a peaches-and-cream complexion, Linda had as well a beautiful speaking voice and great charm. When Mrs. James Borden Harriman came in a private railroad car to view the Kentucky Derby, she found her a beguiling beauty and benevolently introduced Linda, whose financial resources were few, to wealthy friends. So Linda came to meet Edward R. Thomas, a newspaper mogul, who owned, among other publications, the *New York Morning Telegraph.* She married Thomas in 1901; the wedding took place in Newport just prior to Linda's eighteenth birthday.

The marriage appeared to be a brilliant one. The young, beautiful couple resided in a variety of houses they possessed in Newport, in Palm Beach, and on Fifty-seventh Street in New York City. Linda enjoyed all the accoutrements of the rich-rich: servants, a yacht, racehorses, and lavish jewels— in which she especially delighted. Her favorite department store, a friend said, remained throughout her life Van Cleef and Arpels. She didn't buy pictures or even own any of consequence. Her best piece was a Fabergé egg, and as her life went along, she amassed a lot of Verdura jewelry. "You look very lindaporterish" became a phrase in the expatriate lexicon, describing a style that typically featured plain dresses and bright jewelry. Linda often wore white kid gloves—but only once: then she would send them to a cousin in Louisville.

The lives of the Thomases darkened owing to Edward's cruelty, aggressiveness, and sexual infidelities. An automobile enthusiast, he had the distinction of being the first American to kill someone in a car accident. Significantly or not, it was at just this time that Linda first suffered from asthma and was required to leave Thomas to travel to a drier climate. In 1908 (in what later must have seemed a macabre coincidence) Thomas was in danger of undergoing amputation of a leg. Linda kindly agreed to return and help him regain his health. But as he recovered, he resumed behavior that Linda found intolerable, and in 1912 they divorced. Linda quietly received a settlement of a million dollars and more from her wealthy husband.

In 1915 Linda spent part of the summer in Colorado Springs, where Frank Crowninshield, then editor of *Vanity Fair,* wrote to warn her jocularly about the perils of assembling scrapbooks, which she continued to do with a passion. Linda, who suffered all her life from allergies, asthma, and other respiratory weaknesses, had gone to Colorado Springs in the company of two friends, one of whom was Elsie de Wolfe, "leading decorator of the nation," as Porter deemed her in one of his lyrics written just before his marriage to Linda:

> Now since my sweetheart Sal met Miss Elsie de Wolfe,
> The leading decorator of the nation,
> It's left that gal with her mind simply full'f
> Ideas on interior decoration.

In fact, Elsie virtually invented the profession of interior decoration. Besides, she was "a social powerhouse whose scope reached from show business to royalty"—both passions of Cole's—"without drawing a line." Her reputation was made when Stanford White persuaded a committee of women to engage Elsie to do the interior of the Colony Club. Subsequently Henry Frick hired her to furnish (or "foinish," as she always pronounced it) the second floor of his mansion on Fifth Avenue. Elsie's watchword was "suitability"—a term one critic claims was first applied to decoration by Edith Wharton. She had also, Diana Vreeland pointed out, "something else that's particularly American—an appreciation of vulgarity. Vulgarity is a very important ingredient in life . . . A little bad taste is like a nice splash of paprika." (Elsa Maxwell had an appreciation of vulgarity, and in some regards it linked both her and Elsie to Cole Porter.) Elsie moved in an international set, many of whom she could count on as clients. Count Robert de Montesquieu, whom Proust depicted as the homosexual Baron Charlus, was a friend. Her intimate circle was largely lesbian and included Anne Vanderbilt; J. P. Morgan's daughter, Anne; and Elizabeth Marbury. When the very rich Bessie Marbury died in 1933, she bequeathed Elsie all her money and her furniture, which Elsie sold at once. This "Sapphic trio," as they were sometimes called, left many auspicious and abiding monuments to their taste and intelligence, among them the Colony Club in New York, the Villa Trianon near Paris, which they made into an exquisite home, and Sutton Place, which they first colonized.

Elsie de Wolfe was attractive to both Cole and Linda for several reasons. As one of the biographies puts it, "She stood on her head when she was seventy years old. She was dieting long before anybody knew what a calorie was. She conducted a thoroughly unconventional relationship with theatrical agent Elizabeth Marbury for forty years, and even more scandalously, married at sixty a British diplomat, Sir Charles Mendl—who volunteered subsequently, with great good cheer, 'For all I know, the old girl is still a virgin.' " Debutantes some years later all knew by heart these verses about Sir Charles and Lady Mendl:

> *Elsie de Wolfe, old and weary*
> *Might have lived and died a fairy,*
> *But Sir Charles Mendl she met and wed,*
> *And* on dit, *they went to bed.*
> *But whatever it is this Mendl's done*
> *There never can be a Mendl-son.*

Deeply conservative in some regards and prone at times to send himself up, Porter, as he grew older, was devoted more and more to the traditionalism of the elite. Of course, throughout his life and in his lyrics, he subverted, often subtly, Victorian values. Sometimes he did so in the jolly and affectionate mood of Gilbert and Sullivan; at other times, mockingly and derisively. No doubt Cole recognized in Elsie de Wolfe a comrade in the struggle to break free from Victorian restraints, but always tastefully. In an effort "to stamp out the stuffy Victorian standards of interior design," Elsie pioneered the use of chintz, mirrors, trellis, decoupage, and black-and-white color schemes as decorating devices. Cole celebrated her style in a song written for *Hitchy-Koo of 1919* titled "That Black and White Baby of Mine." "The gloom of interiors in the Victorian Era reflected the guilt of double-standard morality; fruits of materialism cluttered all. Velvets and damasks masked the sins of repression and hypocrisy," wrote biographers of Elsie.

It must have been in 1918 that Cole Porter met Bernard Berenson at Elsie de Wolfe's Villa Trianon. The villa was a venue that Linda knew well, not only because of her friendship with Elsie but because she did extensive relief work for soldiers' families in Versailles as well as in Paris. (Elsie had served courageously as a nurse for the French in World War I, and France bestowed both the Croix de Guerre and the Legion d'Honneur on her.) Among the guests who came was one whom Berenson described as an "enchanting, rather negroid youth named Cole Porter [who] improvised ragtime music and words really drole." Berenson's biographer writes that "the meeting with the composer launched a friendship that lasted for forty years." Among their mutual friends was Marthe Hyde, who was close to both Edith Wharton's and Bernard Berenson's worlds. She was a particularly good friend of the Duke of Alba, or Jimmy, as friends called him. This crowd all knew Berenson, who collected people and loved the fashionable world. At the Villa Trianon Elsie de Wolfe hosted many literary, military, and political figures. On Boxing Day of that year, forty guests "listened to Cole Porter sing some of his 'delicious songs.'"

No doubt Porter's connection to Elsie de Wolfe came via Linda, and it was Linda who had been Berenson's friend and remained so for her lifetime.

Duke of Alba with Linda, probably Paris, c. 1918

Berenson and she corresponded over the years. According to one biographer, Linda "had the most faultless intuitive esthetic sensibility in relation to the first-rate in painting, architecture and sculpture of anyone [Berenson] ever encountered." (This makes all the more surprising the fact that Linda never acquired pictures.) Like Berenson with art, Porter came to admire Linda's "infallible judgment" about his music, which she criticized frankly as he played it for her. "Until she is sold on the song, Porter keeps working at it."

Linda first saw Cole at a wedding reception at the Paris Ritz in January of 1918. "Linda Thomas called me," wrote her friend Schuyler Parsons, "and asked who the man and girl [Mimi Scott] were who had played so well at the wedding, begging me to bring them to dinner with them and have them perform . . . I asked them but they took offense and asked if Linda thought they were public entertainers. After a while I pacified them however and they accepted." On the evening of Linda's party, Parsons called for the two at Mimi's flat and was obliged to wait a long time for them. He was furious when they appeared dressed like music-hall entertainers in the Toulouse-

Elsie de Wolfe in Venice, 1923

Lautrec era. Cole was attired in "a dreadful tail coat with high collar and with his hair slicked down. 'Now' they said, 'this will put you and your swell friends in their place.' " When they reached Linda's, Parsons raced upstairs to tell her "what a ghastly trick they had played." But Linda thought it all hilarious, as did the other guests. Less than two years later, Linda was Mrs. Cole Porter. Decades after that, the producer Arnold Saint Subber, a close friend of Cole's, said, "Linda was the air that made his sails move."

So Porter was in step when he became engaged to the beautiful, wealthy, well-connected connoisseur Linda Lee Thomas. A song he wrote at this time describes his sentiments: "Tired of Living Alone" was the title. Early in 1919, Porter sailed home in hopes of persuading J. O. Cole to give him the sizable allowance that he would need if he were to marry Linda. On December 6, 1918, J.O. had created a trust for Cole which derived from "one-half interest in certain real estate in the States of West Virginia and Kentucky," but Cole hoped to magnify that amount. Fatefully, Raymond Hitchcock, the comedian and theatrical producer, who intended to open a new show shortly in New York, was a fellow passenger and "heard Porter moodily playing 'An Old-Fashioned Garden' on a piano in the ship's lounge . . ." Hitchcock asked him to play some of the other things he had written, and he obliged with "When I Had a Uniform On," subsequently subtitled by some "Demobilization Song." On the strength of the several songs Cole played, Hitchcock engaged him to write the score for his new show, *Hitchy-Koo of 1919*. As Alan Jay Lerner noted, "When the musical theatre started in this country about 1919 or '20, when Jerome Kern led the break from the European operetta . . . you could follow a progression from Jerome Kern to Dick Rodgers to Gershwin, but Cole seemed to spring like Jupiter from Minerva's head—all made. What he did was so special and so unaccountable and unexplainable that he is really of them all, in a strange way, the most irreplaceable." Hitchcock recognized Cole's gift and the timelessness of it early on.

After a tryout in Boston, *Hitchy-Koo* opened in New York on October 6, 1919, and played fifty-six performances. The songs, a number of which were dropped before the show opened, bear what was to become traditional in the mature songwriter: lists, in one instance, of German royals; lists of champagnes; flowers; names that go in twos (including Mark Cross, the business owned by the family of Cole's college friend Gerald Murphy). The chic of black performers, which was to dazzle Paris and New York in the twenties, was addressed in "When Black Sallie Sings Pagliacci," dropped regrettably before the New York opening. The lyrics of "Since Ma Got the Craze Espagnole" depict the hilarity that obtains when mothers become ultraprogressive, for example, and "fads [grow] excessive": "To show to what limits our nerves have been taxed / Why, she just had the bathroom done over by Bakst." (The couplet is proof that Porter was *au fait* with the world of Diaghilev.)

"Old Fashioned Garden" is the song that won the hearts of not only those who saw *Hitchy-Koo of 1919* but the many who heard it rendered by dance bands or over the airwaves. Its sentimentality probably accounts for the song's success. (In later life Porter repeatedly referred to it, perhaps wryly, as his greatest popular hit). "I suppose the biggest song hit of my life was something called 'An Old-Fashioned Garden' which was in *Hitchy-Koo*. Sold 2,000,000 copies." (Others put the sales figure more conservatively at 100,000.) For those recovering from World War I and longing for the cozy pleasures symbolized by flowers and an old-fashioned "missus" and "beau," its appeal is obvious. And conceivably even Cole yearned occasionally for "a spot that I loved as a child." But the view of the composer's pal Jack Coble is also credible: "Cole must have written this song with tongue-in-cheek." Certainly in "Another Sentimental Song" (dropped before the show opened in New York) Porter mocks the genre of song to which "Old Fashioned

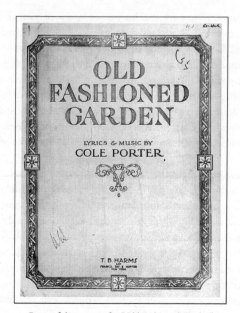

Cover of sheet music for "Old Fashioned Garden"

The house and gardens about which the song was written

Garden" belongs. Hitchcock and his backers acquired a set of dazzling floral costumes that had been created for the Ziegfeld Follies but never used. They queried Cole as to whether or not he could compose a song that would give the show girls a chance to wear them. This, then, was the etiology of "Old Fashioned Garden." Another amusing story that has attached itself to the song is the outrage of Brits whose familiarity with flowers could not tolerate Porter's apparent ignorance, which allowed him to depict spring and fall flowers blooming simultaneously in the garden. Perhaps this early faux pas accounts for the fastidious research Cole ever after conducted while composing lyrics.

J. O. Cole was unyielding when Porter journeyed from New York to Indiana to essay the major task he had set for himself on his trip to America: amplifying his income from family holdings so that his funds would approximate those of his future wife. His grandfather objected to Cole's persistence with the theatre and felt that all his grandson's education had been for naught. Upon hearing his request, "J.O. pounded the arm of his chair and shouted his refusal, adding that he had prophesied that no good would come of encouraging this musical nonsense."

Katie was of quite another mind, of course, and arranged secretly to increase Cole's income. The marriage to Linda suited his mother. Linda had already provided Cole a passport to social terrains he might never have entered on his own. Friends reported that before attaching himself to Linda, Cole was far from easy in mixing with the *gratin*. And, after all, in succeeding socially Cole was enacting his mother's own social ambitions and affording her a vicarious satisfaction. It was D. H. Lawrence who depicted in *Sons and Lovers* the theory that a woman marries, falls out of love with her husband after a time, and then if a male child arrives, shifts her passion from father to son. Something of this dynamic seems to have been enacted in the Porter family. Katie, rather than repulsing the competitor, welcomed her, aware of the social advantages Linda offered Cole. As George Melly wrote: "It was not for her money that Porter married Linda . . . What he needed was a mother figure to supplement, rather than replace, his own."

Back in Paris with additional funds from Katie, royalties from his songs (especially "Old Fashioned Garden") and a loan of ten thousand dollars from his Yale friend William Crocker, Cole and Linda were married on December 12, 1919, in the *mairie* of the Eighteenth Arrondissement and soon after were *en voyage de noce* for the south of France and Italy. "Les Colporteurs" was the breezy and affectionate designation used by French friends of Cole and Linda. Were people aware that *colporteur* designates in French one who traveled from place to place distributing Bibles, religious tracts, etc., or a peddler and newsmonger? The gospel Les Colporteurs circulated was one of refined hedonism and high style.

Linda was often called Linda Cole Porter. Bernard Berenson refers to her as such in a letter he wrote to Isabella Gardner in August 1921. He describes Linda as "the Beauty of the Peace Conference time in Paris—a lovely, lovely creature, whom both the Duke of Alba and Prince Beauvais were in love with but couldn't marry because she was divorced. She suddenly and to the surprise of everyone married a little musical man from the Middle West 15 years younger than herself and has nearly worn herself out going his rattling pace ever since. They came to us on their honeymoon, and I saw their future in the blackest terms."

"The 1920's was a period of license and iconoclasm, cynicism and sex emancipation, fads and rackets, uninhibited humor and freedom of behavior . . . Cole Porter is the spirit of the 1920's in song and lyrics . . . If his attitude toward love and romance reflected the spirit of the 1920's, so did his partiality for dilettantism and catchpenny philosophies . . . His lyrics sprawl across the worlds of esoterica, exotica and erotica." So wrote an early biographer of Porter in an assessment that is a half-truth. The 1920s for Porter were a decade of experiment and emotional maturation. Unlike the 1930s, which

Cole, Linda, Bernard Berenson, and Howard Sturges in Venice, 1923

he caught and conveyed with assurance in most of the scores he wrote, the twenties were for Cole a time of uncertainty, self-doubt, and confusion about his musical gifts, which he successfully disguised by assuming the role of a boulevardier. "Suppose I had to settle down on Broadway for three months just when I was planning to go to Antibes?" said Cole mischievously.

When the Porters returned from their honeymoon trip to the Côte d'Azur, the Italian Riviera, and Sicily, they went to live in Linda's elegant little house at 3 rue de La Baume. They visited America in October 1921. At that time Cole listed his temporary address as "The Plaza, Fifth Avenue and Fifty-ninth Street, New York City."

Early in 1920, Porter had enrolled at the Schola Cantorum at 269 rue St.-Jacques to study for two years harmony, counterpoint, and orchestration. This "*establissement libre d'enseignement superieur de musique, de danse et d'art dramatique*," founded by Vincent d'Indy and two others, had opened in 1896 in a quiet, tree-lined part of the street, not far from the Luxembourg Gardens. D'Indy still tutored students, though not Porter. Other instructors at the Schola Cantorum over the years included Edgard Varèse, Albert Roussel, Erik Satie, Isaac Albéniz, Darius Milhaud, and Olivier Messaien. Unfortunately the building was occupied by German soldiers in World War II, who used its archives to kindle fires. But the cream-colored stucco building is unchanged since Porter's days there. It has a faded elegance: winding wooden stairs with wrought-iron banister, a cobblestone courtyard bounded by a privet hedge.

According to Robert Kimball, "Between 1916 and 1928 . . . Porter struggled to find his own voice . . . It was his friend, Irving Berlin, who told him one of his problems was that he was trying to write like other people instead of his own style." In the early years of their marriage Linda had musical ambitions for Cole that miscalculated his talents and where they lay. Would he compose symphonies and piano music? Cole seemed equally bewildered. His popular songs had had very little success, so briefly he turned to classical composition. Years later Cole told the daughter of the composer John Alden Carpenter that "with all his success he would give anything if he had one tenth of [her] father's knowledge and genius for orchestration . . . I have little knowledge. John is a serious composer, and I would give my soul if I could believe that I was." Among his achievements at the Schola was an orchestration (dated May 7, 1920) of a movement from each of Schumann's First and Second Piano Sonatas. Linda, eager to do her part, wrote to English writers who were acquaintances of hers—John Galsworthy, George Bernard Shaw, and Arnold Bennett—and proposed to each that he write a libretto on which Cole might base an opera; but nothing came of the effort. Eventually, it is said, Porter left the Schola "when he found the influence of the French classical school was interfering with his own sense of rhythm."

Many commentators have spoken of the elegance and suavity of Porter's songs. It is in analyzing the structure of the music that one can appreciate the excellences of the songs. Two writers have been particularly insightful about Porter's elegance. Both understand it to be the result of "craftsmanlike problem-solving that goes with the concept of elegance." This is the opinion of Alan Rich, a trained musician and critic, who considers that "elegance in the mathematical sense . . . is the predominant quality in most of the great French music." He points to this "in the music of Couperin and Rameau, Fauré, Ravel and Poulenc. The emotional power of a Porter ballad likewise comes only after the song has insinuated itself into your consciousness by the utter, beguiling ingenuity and meticulousness of its over-all shape." He demonstrates his thesis by examining Porter's "Night and Day" and points to its harmonic richness (which, of course, works its spell whether or not we are conscious of it), resulting from "a constant fluctuation between major and minor (phrases that begin in one mode and end in another). Listen to the grabby modulation that starts the middle part of the song, and the way Porter gets out of that distant, new key and back to his tonic at the end. Those elements, the beautiful, clean, gradual rise-and-fall of the melodic line, the fascinating way the bass line descends over a repeated-note tune in the introduction—all those are the works of a master of his craft." So Porter's music studies at Yale, Harvard, and the Schola Cantorum were not missteps. At least unconsciously, he must have realized that these were readying him for his métier. "The stylistic overview that Porter got from his early training gave him a versatility that none of his colleagues could challenge," Rich says.

Leo Smit, distinguished as composer and conductor-pianist, is another person who has commented on the impressive technical dimension in Porter's songs. Once, listening to Schumann's song "The Lotus Flower," he was reminded of "Night and Day." "I had not previously associated American popular music with the romantic lieder tradition of the nineteenth century, but suspecting that my discovery could not have been a coincidence, I plunged into the deep, wide, and subtle world of Cole Porter." His inquiries were fruitful: Porter did know and love Schumann's music. Tchaikovsky taught Porter "an expressive declamatory style . . . appropriate for the verses that prepare the listener for the refrains." Smit's discoveries reveal "Porter as a composer who was consciously aware of the serious problems of musical craft and who, through an inspired gift, was able to conceal the many beautiful solutions from unsuspecting ears while easily charming them." Porter hinted at this when he replied to the host of a radio show, "My accompaniments are usually too complicated for publication and have to be simplified for general consumption." (The ability to make these simplified accompaniments was especially notable in Dr. Albert Sirmay, whom Cole met later in the United States and valued so greatly.) Smit's analyses of many Porter songs are convincing and illuminating and merit attention. The songs, he maintains, are "not the outpouring of a suave and urbane man-about-town"—though Porter was certainly that—"but of a passionate man who communicates his passions by governing them artistically."

The Porters found Linda's house too confining, so Linda sold it and purchased for approximately $250,000 a handsome, spacious *hôtel particulier* at 13 rue Monsieur in the elegant Invalides *quartier* (Seventh Arrondissement) near the Eiffel Tower. Cole and their friends mostly spoke of 13 rue Monsieur as "Linda's house," referring to the fact that she purchased it with her own funds. For most of the years from 1920 to 1937 this house was home to the peripatetic Porters. The street is just one block long, bounded by rue de Babylone and rue Oudinot. ("Monsieur" was a brother of Louis XVI.) Curiously, no plaque adorns 13 rue Monsieur, but on 15 rue Monsieur a plaque tells us that the Jesuit paleontologist and author Pierre Teilhard de Chardin lived there for some time. Odd neighbors—and the oddity is perhaps compounded when one hears that the Porters' garden backed up to Nancy Mitford's.

Thirteen rue Monsieur was described in a 1925 number of *Vogue* and elsewhere in the years to come. *Vogue* noted the predominance of Oriental art. The house had a circular entrance, in which, from a floor of black and white marble, marbleized columns rose. A staircase of white marble led to the apartments above. The grand salon, with white wainscoting and cream taffeta hangings, contained a collection of Chinese lacquered tables, statues,

Marthe Hyde, Linda, and Baron de Gunzburg

and bowls. Sofas and armchairs were upholstered in velvet of soft brown tones. Colorful rugs adorned the floors. The anonymous *Vogue* reporter noticed bowls of flowers everywhere. Other rooms became fabled because of their zebra-skin rugs and art deco furnishings. The full-sized ebony Steinway (donated to the Episcopal Cathedral in Paris, where it currently stands) was a striking contrast to red-lacquered armchairs. The library was covered in platinum paper. "Although it sounds garish today, the decor, replete with Chinese scrolls and Chippendale furniture, succeeded in creating the atmosphere [Linda] was after—one of restless simplicity." People recall the "ballroom" into which Linda transformed the basement. Hardwood floors were installed, the walls lined with mirrors and banquettes, and a bandstand was erected as well, and dances were held there. Diana Vreeland remembered parties at the rue Monsieur: "one of those rounded eighteenth-century streets which looked as if it had been designed by a swirl of *smoke,* and you'd ring the concierge's bell and the door would swing open and you'd find yourself looking through an orchard of apple trees at the kind of half-timbered house you'd find in Normandy. You'd go in and he'd play this little ditty: 'Here's Diana / Sittin' on the pi-ana.' " In the "pristine study" Linda created for Cole

she had imported and planted (an exotic) tree in the center of the courtyard, and Cole found it relaxing and drew inspiration while focusing on it. In order to provide sufficient light for him to work on his manuscripts, she had removed the rear wall of the room and replaced it with a huge sheet of frosted glass. But lest her husband be deprived of his inspirational totem, she had the center of the pane cut to the shape of the tree and filled with clear glass . . . The unadorned white walls, a white grand piano, a white working table, a hundred sharpened white pencils and a fireplace were all the minimalist room contained.

The Porters' friend Howard Sturges rented an apartment in the spacious house. Sturges, a native of Providence, Rhode Island, became Cole's closest friend. Son of a manufacturer of cotton and seven years older than Cole, Sturges attended Groton and Yale ('08), after which he went to Paris to study music. As a youth, Sturge—as friends called him—played the violin for a time in the New Haven Symphony. He always loved opera. So he had music in common with Cole. Another link was the circus and animals, which fascinated him. For a time in Paris he owned a black bear, and later he walked about with an enormous pig on a leash. Once he took the bear to the Ritz Hotel to meet his mother.

When World War I began, Sturges volunteered for full service, and was stationed in Paris. Inevitably, in the Parisian society he frequented there, he met Linda Porter. Both were friends of Elsie de Wolfe and probably met at one of her parties. As his friendship with the Porters deepened, he moved to the apartment in the house at 13 rue Monsieur. Horst photographed the Porters with Sturges in the mid-1930s at Carlsbad, the Czech spa where they went to take the waters. When World War II loomed and the Porters abandoned Paris, Sturges took a one-room apartment on East Sixty-fourth Street in New York City with a large bed: the room, a ballroom in a grand house, had been converted to an apartment with a small kitchen, bath, dressing room, and foyer. He had few if any detractors. Most found him a strong person. Latterly his income was small, but he remained cheery. He was addicted to gossip, and the Porters enjoyed the tales he brought to them.

One friend of Porter who did not admire Sturges was Colin Leslie Fox, an actor and model known principally as "the Man in the Hathaway Shirt," whom Cole entertained in New York. "Sturges sometimes made an ass of himself," said Fox. "In later years Sturge would just smile when Cole was carrying on about the delights of sex. But earlier, for example, he would spot a man at work on a garbage truck and try to make a husband or wife of him." Fox felt that Sturge, "at a certain age," should have conducted his sex life more discreetly, more privately. Linda and Sturge became friends years before Cole knew either of them. In these years Sturge appeared to have a penchant for trouble which was compounded by alcoholism. Once, in France, he befriended a circus that was impoverished. Sturge took the whole troupe on and became enamored of a young woman performer, whom he invited back to a beautiful home he had then outside of Paris. The woman had a "brother" in the town, who owned a garage and who appeared more frequently as time passed. Friends later thought the man and his "sister" were partners in crime. In a drunken state Sturge turned over all his property to this woman, who thereupon evicted him and took possession of it. Sturge went through three large fortunes. Years later he put it this way to Jean Howard: "Once I went through two fortunes, thank God I had another."

"Linda gave considerable time and energy to rescuing Sturge from the gutter," said Jean Howard. Early in their friendship, Sturges would sometimes disappear for a week and wind up in some drug den in Pigalle. They knew he was alive when a request for money or a check to be cashed came. According to Cole's friend Robert Wheaton, who was told the story by either Linda or Cole, Sturge's friends treasured him for his wit, warm nature, and elegance and worried over him a lot. Once Sturge disappeared for such a long time that they became extremely worried. They thought they knew where he was, but how to rescue him without involving the police? They hatched a plan. They invited a dozen or so very rich people living in Paris to attend the opera and to drive there in a convoy. However, they drove via Pigalle and went to Sturges's lair. All their bejeweled friends with fancy cars and in white tie and tails simply overwhelmed the people who kept the house. Porter's friends marched in, got Sturges, took him to the hospital, and proceeded to the opera. Linda grew firmer with Sturge. She recounted to Jean Howard her words to him: "If ever you go off again, I won't be there. It's up to you." Miraculously, Sturge stopped drinking and never again drank alcohol. Every year, on the anniversary of his renunciation of liquor, he gratefully sent Linda a beautiful gift. "Debonair" is an adjective repeatedly used by people to describe Sturges ("tall" and "elegantly slim" are other adjectives invoked.) His taste, said Jean Howard, "was always very, very smart, but just off the rack," perhaps because of Sturge's habit of traveling without luggage. When people would inquire how he managed, he replied, "I can always buy anything I want when I get there."

Gore Vidal described Sturges as "easier [for Cole] than Monty and right out of Edith Wharton." Indeed, he had connections with Wharton's world, although claims by Charles Schwartz and Jean Howard that Sturge was related to George Santayana seem to stem from the latter's mention in the opening pages of his novel, *The Last Puritan,* of a "Howard Sturgis." The Sturges family deny that Howard Sturgis had any link to Santayana. His pedigree, beautiful manners, old money, and humor ("terribly funny . . . he made me laugh all the time," recalls Jean Howard) were credentials that made him the perfect friend for both Porters. He loved travel and was the friend who most often accompanied the Porters on their journeys. So often did he travel to Peru, Indiana, with the Porters that one bedroom in Westleigh Farms is called the Sturges Room. Hollywood was his other American port of call, and occasionally Providence, where he owned a large home inherited from his family. His heirs now have in their possession a beautiful painting by Christian Bérard which he lent the Porters. For many years it hung on the walls of their drawing room at 13 rue Monsieur.

From childhood Cole was uncommonly curious, one of the personal qualities that led to his avidity for travel. Linda was keen on travel as well, and often in the 1920s and '30s the Porters were world travelers. When, at the conclusion of the twenties, Porter offered the public a song called "Why Don't We Try Staying Home?," he must have done so with tongue in cheek.

Since first we started out, we've simply run about,
And life's been one long rout unending.
We're always op'ning plays,
Or closing cabarets,
It seems to me our ways need mending.
. . . .

Why don't we try staying home?
Why don't we try not to roam?
What if we threw a party or two,
And asked only you and me?
I long to sit by the fireside
My girl, with me sitting by'er side,
Wouldn't that be nice?
We've tried ev'ry thing else twice,
So why don't we try staying home?

But they didn't. In February and March of 1921 the Porters were in Egypt, repeating more or less a trip that Linda and her first husband had made in 1909. The Porters chartered a ship called the *Chonsu* for the journey. With their friends Howard Sturges and Marthe Hyde in tow, they toured Luxor and Karnak, saw the Sphinx and the Aswan Dam, and rendezvoused with friends like Lady Ossey, Sir Ian Malcolm, and Jimmy, the Duke of Alba. For part of their expedition they had as a cicerone Linda's friend Lord Carnarvon, perhaps the most distinguished Egyptologist at that time.

> *The only thing they've got*
> *is ruins, ruins, ruins.*
> *They constitute our daily doin's.*

were lines Cole wrote (in a song called "Ruins" for *Nymph Errant*).

Besides Egypt, the Porters traveled during these first years of their marriage to Monte Carlo, Italy, London, Biarritz, Spain, Morocco, New York, and Indiana, among other places. Usually they were accompanied by a brigade of servants. And usually they invited a few friends.

In March 1922 C. B. Cochran, the English producer, presented *Mayfair and Montmartre,* and Cole wrote some songs for it, among them "The Blue Boy Blues," which Gilbert Seldes called "among the half-dozen best blues pieces." The song was inspired by the sale of Gainsborough's famous painting for $620,000. Porter ably invented a compelling American blues tune, and the song was strikingly staged. Nonetheless, the show soon shut down.

Another friend of Cole's in these years was Gerald Murphy, a Yalie he kept up with after their graduation, until the United States entered World War I. Gerald enlisted in the U.S. Signal Corps and trained as an aviator, but just as he completed his training, the war ended. Gerald, meanwhile, had married Sara Wiborg, a childhood friend. The Wiborgs had a large house in East Hampton. The young Murphys tarried for two years at Harvard, where Gerald studied landscape architecture, and in 1921, with their three children, they sailed first for London and then, in the fall, to Paris and an apartment near the Etoile.

In France, Murphy saw for the first time paintings by Pablo Picasso, Juan Gris, Georges Braque, and other modernists. He was thrilled by the work of these artists and began to study painting with Natalia Goncharova, who designed sets for Diaghilev. Goncharova persuaded the Murphys to help repair damaged scenery belonging to the Ballets Russes, and it was during this time that the Murphys met Picasso. Their charm and beauty attracted many artists and sophisticates. Picasso, like Hemingway and Fitzgerald (who modeled Nicole and Dick Diver in *Tender Is the Night* on the Murphys), would in time become infatuated with Sara.

The art critic Michael Kimmelman, writing of the Murphys, Cole, and Picasso—what William Rubin, a leading Picasso scholar, calls "the four-cornered triangle"—reports Rubin's use of the phrase "serious flirtation" to describe the relationship of Sara and Picasso. *The Pipes of Pan,* one of Picasso's best-known pictures, is addressed in Rubin's essay, which is subtitled "Picasso's Aborted Love Song to Sara Murphy." "Picasso decided to use *The Pipes of Pan* as a vehicle for his infatuation with her," writes Rubin. As Rubin points out, the music of the pipes of Pan has been, since ancient days, the music of love. For unknown reasons, Picasso eventually painted out the figures of Venus and Cupid and left only the two men on the canvas. The males appear to be versions of Gerald and Picasso—not Gerald and Porter, as some have contended. Rubin is of the opinion that hundreds of drawings and many paintings of what were thought to be idealized depictions of Picasso's wife Olga are in fact depictions of Sara Murphy. Calvin Tomkins, a biographer of Sara and Gerald, and John Richardson, Picasso's biographer, to some degree share this opinion.

Picasso was struck not only by Sara's beauty but with Murphy's gifts as a painter. In fact it was Picasso's pictures, which Murphy saw shortly after his arrival in Paris, that led Gerald to choose painting for a time as a métier. Gerald painted only from 1922 to 1929, and critics now write of his output as small (perhaps fourteen pictures) but brilliant. "Gerald Murphy was on his way," says Tomkins, "to becoming an American artist with an original and significant talent" when the death of his son Patrick seemed to shatter all of his plans to continue as a painter.

In 1921 Cole had taken the Château de la Garoupe in Antibes and invited friends to visit, among them the Murphys and Picasso. Cole wrote that "we rented the Château de la Garoupe for two summers—1921 and 1922—and enjoyed every moment. But in those days we were considered crazy, and it was before the days anyone went to the Riviera in the summer, as the weather was considered too hot." Pictures survive of the Porters and some of the friends they entertained in 1921 at La Garoupe. The house was very elegant, bright with many windows, and had a large garden, with a cypress tree and other beautiful shrubs. A chauffeur stood by with a Rolls-Royce. According to Gerald Murphy:

> Cole always had great originality about finding new places and at that time no one ever went near the Riviera in summer. The English and the Germans—there were no longer any Russians—who came down for the short spring season closed their villas as soon as it began to get

Gerald Murphy, Jinny Carpenter, Cole, and Sara Murphy in Venice warm. None of them ever went into the water, you see. When we went to visit Cole, it was hot, hot summer, but the air was dry, and it was cool in the evening, and the water was that wonderful jade-and-amethyst color. Right out on the end of the Cap there was a tiny beach—the Garoupe—only about forty yards long and covered with a bed of sea-weed that must have been four feet thick. We dug out a corner of the beach and bathed there and sat in the sun, and we decided this is where we wanted to be. Oddly, Cole never came back.

Eventually the Murphys decided to buy a place of their own in Antibes, and it became famous as the Villa America.

Porter returned to New York to spend the winter at 735 Fifth Avenue. On February 3, 1923, he received the news that at age ninety-four, his grand-father, J.O., had died, and Cole hurried to Peru to be with his mother. "Dis-

Porter on the Lido, 1923

Porter in Venice, 1923

tinguished Citizen of Peru and a 49er," the *Peru Republican* called him: "one of the wealthiest citizens of northern Indiana." The obituary goes on to say that "one cannot help but feel a distinct loss in his departure." Cole felt little sense of loss. Mostly he had encountered from J.O. withering disapproval of his musical ambitions. At J.O.'s death the Cole-Crane Trust had enormous financial worth from coal, gas, and timber. He left, as well, large parcels of land and, one account said, one million dollars in cash. Cole later told an interviewer:

> True to his word, I wasn't mentioned in Grandfather's will . . . But he left my mother over two million dollars, and she generously gave me half of it—with the remark that she wanted me to feel completely independent. A few years later, when she inherited two million more by the terms of the will, she again gave me half. So altogether I received over two million dollars . . . People always say that so much money spoils one's life. But it didn't spoil mine; it simply made it wonderful.

Chapter 5

Raising Hell in Europe

It was at a party in London that Elsa Maxwell and Dorothy Fellowes-Gordon invited Noël Coward to accompany them to Venice, expenses paid. None of them had ever visited Venice, and in his autobiography Coward recalled their intoxication when they descended the railway station steps and boarded a gondola.

> Elsa led, of course. Propped up against a cushion in the back seat she let forth a stream of enthusiasm into the gathering dusk . . . The air was clear and pure. A "Serenata" passed close by us on its way to the lagoon, already lit with coloured lanterns and crammed to the gunwales with stout little tenors wearing white shirts and coloured sashes . . . Our gondoliers gave sharp, atmospheric cries, and the sun set considerably as we arrived at the hotel, plunging the whole scene into a misty Turneresque beauty that robbed even Elsa of further adjectives.

This was the beginning of Elsa Maxwell's long love affair with Venice.

In 1923 she was engaged by the Italian government to turn the attention of her wealthy, cosmopolitan circle to the Venetian Lido. The Cole Porters were among her major assets. Some say a company whose acronym is CIGA was responsible for the revival of the Venetian Lido in the early twenties. Others give all the credit to Elsa Maxwell: "Her international reputation as an impresario of social functions is such that people do seriously discuss whether she, alone and single-handed, put the Lido on the map." Maxwell's success resulted from her reconciling the two grandes dames who captained contentious social factions in Venice. One was the Countess Morosini and the other, a great friend of the Porters, Princess di San Faustino of Rome, who had for many years visited the Lido in season. The regal countess loathed the Lido and considered it suitable only for the nouveau. Conscious of her pedigree (several Morosinis had been doges), she led a cluster of distinguished Venetians who haughtily dismissed the parvenus who came more and more to situate themselves on the Lido. However, the "Lido-ites" had a brilliant leader in Princess di San Faustino (the former Jane Campbell of New York City). She and her crowd were reputed to be bright, malicious, and flamboyant. They included "a large number of men who might have been safely described as effeminate." These friends of Princess Jane's were labeled by Italians as "Settembrini," meaning between the seasons. They set a twittering and bibulous tone for life on the Lido, managing meanwhile to ignore Venice proper. Anthony Heilbut notes in his biography of Thomas Mann that "Settembrini" was also the name given to those "September men" who visited Venice in early autumn to procure boys for smaller fees when summer ended. Mann gave it to a character in *The Magic Mountain.*

Maxwell assessed the situation and saw that for the Lido to succeed she must "collect all the Venetian socialites of every description." She invented a number of compelling entertainments which eventually the old Venetians and their entourage felt they could not miss. The Queen of Romania came to visit. Speedboat races were inaugurated; festive dinner parties were devised. Cole became part of Elsa's act one night at the princess's charity ball when Elsa donned an 1890s bathing costume and sang a Porter song about the Settembrini with the line "These Lido boys are mere decoys." Finally the princess and the countess confronted each other, and the result was amicable. From the early twenties until the end of the decade, Venice and its Lido was "the world capital of diversion."

For years Elsa organized treasure hunts as amusement, and she arranged some on the Venetian canals. Once, one of the clues was a key in the pocket of a young man's trousers. But the Italian word for key—*chiave*—is close to the slang word for penis. Venetian police, already on the alert, got wind of what they decided was scandalous behavior, arrested several guests, and ultimately halted a riot which ensued. Elsa was delighted. At last the Morosinis and the Settembrini were united.

In June 1923 the great excitement in Paris was the premiere of Stravinsky's ballet *Les Noces.* The pianist Marcelle Meyer, who played one of the four pianos scored by Stravinsky, was a friend of the Murphys, so they were tuned in to the mounting excitement and decided to invite everyone con-

Elsa Maxwell with Cole

nected with *Les Noces* to a gala opening-night party on a large canal boat on the Seine. Among the forty-some who attended were Diaghilev, Jean Cocteau, and Boris Kochno, who was soon to figure so importantly in Porter's life.

Darius Milhaud was at that time at work on his ballet *La Création du Monde* for the Ballets Suédois, with Fernand Léger and Blaise Cendrars providing the mise-en-scène. Swedish dancers and staff largely made up the company for the five years of its existence (1920–25). It was based in Paris, where it made its debut in October 1920. The audience celebrated the company's youthful beauty and its distinctiveness. The company became noted for the extraordinary attention its director, Rolf de Maré, gave to the visual arts. The repertoire was a rich mix of traditional ballets with more revolutionary works. *Jeux,* a ballet choreographed by Nijinsky for Diaghilev's Ballets Russes, had music by Debussy and backdrop by Pierre

Bonnard. This merging of music, painting, and dance, while to some degree a characteristic of the Ballet Russes, became the signature of the Ballets Suédois.

Gerald Murphy was invited to concoct a ballet that would be a curtain raiser. Murphy agreed and proposed that Cole Porter write the musical score. Gerald recalled that "Porter had not yet become a popular success on Broadway, and his wealthy and socially ambitious wife rather hoped that he would devote his talent to 'serious music.' The preceding summer, in fact, she had invited Stravinsky down to Antibes to teach her husband harmony and composition; . . . Stravinsky had declined."

In Paris, Cole and Linda became part of the world of Princesse Edmond de Polignac, daughter of Isaac Singer, the sewing-machine mogul. She was the center of a gifted society of writers, painters, and musicians, among whom were Stravinsky, Fauré, Satie, and Auric. The princess was an enormously generous patron. Grateful composers dedicated works to her: Ravel his *Pavanne,* Stravinsky his opera *Mavra.* It was in the home of Winnaretta Singer that Cole met Milhaud, who at the suggestion of the Murphys personally offered to Cole the opportunity to compose the ballet that would precede *La Création du Monde.*

In 1923 the Porters had engaged the fourteenth-century Palazzo Barbaro, which in the nineteenth century was beloved by Henry James, who set the climax of *The Wings of the Dove* there. They journeyed that summer to Venice, their customary style requiring them to reserve eight or nine compartments, depending on the number of guests in their entourage. Cole and Linda had each a private compartment, as did his valet and her maid. Another was used as a room where the servants pressed and generally attended to the Porters' sumptuous wardrobes. The sixth compartment functioned as a bar. The remaining compartments were assigned to guests of the Porters, whose travel expenses were absorbed by their hosts.

Cole accepted Milhaud's proposal and he invited the Murphys to join him and Linda in Venice for three weeks in order to facilitate his collaboration with Gerald on the ballet. In Venice, Gerald and Cole worked on *Within the Quota* (earlier titled *Landed*)—"a lively thirty-minute work satirizing the impressions of a young Swedish immigrant to the United States." *Within the Quota* has been described as "a pantomime ballet which wants to show what's forbidden in America," a theme congenial to Porter. The foreigner disembarks, and each time he desires something, he discovers it's forbidden: alcohol, dancing, love. "An immigrant wanders off a steamship pier and gets his first impressions of America as a huge yellow journal . . . as he tries to digest this a nouveau-riche lady saunters on stage,

Princesse de Polignac, 1923

as do a fundamentalist reformer, 'a colored gentleman,' a jazz baby, a tax agent, a cowboy and 'Everybody's Sweetheart,' a Mary Pickford look-alike." "Porter," one paper said, "used the musical scale to interpret the hurly-burly of superficial American life." The orchestration was done by the renowned French composer, Charles Koechlin. The plot was devised by Murphy, who painted a backdrop that satirized the Hearst newspaper of that time. "It included an ocean liner standing on end beside the Woolworth Building and a variety of lurid headlines, and across the top ran a banner reading, 'UNKNOWN BANKER BUYS ATLANTIC.'" Vladimir Golschmann conducted the world premiere at the Théâtre des Champs-Elysées in Paris on October 25, 1923.

Cole's music for this piece, labeled "the first jazz ballet," was called "futuristic . . . Instead of the ballet interpreting the music, the music appears to interpret the ballet. For instance, before the curtain goes up . . . [it] suggests a ship entering the [New York] harbor. You hear the whistle blowing in the distance. Gradually they come nearer. There is a roar of traffic, a hurdy-gurdy blowing a few strains—in fact the music is New York. It is not beauti-

ful harmony, but vivid musical description . . . the only word that describes
it perfectly is Truth . . . a truly marvelous blending of discord and harmony."
In the end the order of the ballets was switched because of the fear that
Within the Quota might overshadow the featured work, *La Création du
Monde*. Both ballets gained praise, but of course it is Milhaud's score that
attained lasting fame.

Le Figaro labeled *Quota* "triumphal" and mentioned that Rudolph
Valentino and his wife attended the opening. An unidentified review
praised Porter's music, which "comprised some very good jazz and some
polytonal dissonances that were evidently meant to be as funny as they
sounded." Not long after, the Ballets Suédois disbanded." In 1954, Porter
told a biographer, Richard Hubler, "The original music sheets are lost and I
have no copies. My one effort to be respectable must remain in limbo."
Thanks to a successful search on Robert Kimball's part, the score was recovered after Porter's death, and the conductor John McGlinn recorded it with
the London Sinfonietta in 1989.

Venice was a city that had first caught Cole's imagination when he sat
as a boy in the little Peru Emeric Theatre on West Fifth Street, where the
curtain was decorated by a picture of the Grand Canal with a gondola drifting towards the Rialto. Long before Porter visited Venice, the people of Peru
seemed especially conscious of that serene city. "Lieber & Co. have just
framed a magnificent embroidered picture worked by a lady of Peru . . . It
is a Venetian scene from a painting . . . The ladies should call to see it. Mrs.
Omar Cole is the fair workwoman." (Presumably the work would have no
appeal to men, or so Peruvians seemed to believe.)

One of their guests in Venice was Diana Vreeland, who described Cole
rising at six a.m. and setting off in a gondola on the Grand Canal, the
gondolier seated in Cole's place in the bow, and Cole standing in the back
of the gondola with the long oar "wearing a little navy pullover, and the little fluttering ribbons in his gondolier's hat, and he would feel the rhythm
of the gondola. The gondolier would correct him. Isn't that divine? Everything with him was rhythm. That's why he's so contagious, that's why he
never dies."

It was fortunate that a friendship developed between Cole and the
Princess di San Faustino. The *principessa* contributed to the gaiety of Venice
by producing amateur entertainment in the ballroom of the Excelsior
Hotel. "Scions of proud old Italian houses, members of the British nobility
and daughters of American magnates combined in a jazz revue . . . Bill
Reardon danced; the Duke of Verdura led off a trio of eccentric dances;
Prince Jit of Kapurthola did a lively ukelele number"; Count Volpi's daugh-

Princess Jane di San Faustino, 1923

ter did the black bottom. Lady Diana Cooper served champagne, as did Countess di Frasso, Linda Porter, Lady Abdy, and others. Prince Frederick Leopold of Belgium attended, as did Sir Charles and Lady Mendl. Some of the princess's friends were already pally with the Porters, and others they met in her coterie: Arthur Rubinstein, Lady Manners, later the John Barrymores, Sir Oswald and Lady Moseley. As an acquaintance of the Porters recently remarked, "Titles in those days were as common as measles." Diaghilev and Serge Lifar also mixed with this set, and in time Irving Berlin and George Gershwin visited.

Gilbert Seldes wrote in *The Dial* magazine that there were two possible successors to Berlin if he decided to retire: "I am sure of Gershwin and would be more sure of Cole Porter if his astonishing lyrics did not so dazzle me as to make me distrust my estimate of his music." Seldes was referring to songs from *Hitchy-Koo of 1922,* another of the revues starring Raymond Hitchcock (this one supervised and produced by the Shuberts), for which Porter wrote most of the score. It was not a success and closed after a dozen and more performances in Philadelphia. "The Sponge" may be one of

Porter's first ventures into the world of aquatic imagery and is a pale version of "The Scampi," which was written to amuse his friends in Venice, and demonstrates Cole's capacity to transform his social forays into art.

> *See him on his silver platter,*
> *Hearing the Queens of the Lido chatter,*
> *Getting the latest in regard*
> *To Elsa Maxwell and Lady Cunard.*
> *Thrilled little Scampi.*
> *See that ambitious Scampi we know*
> *Feeding the Princess San Faustino.*
> *Think of his joy as he gaily glides*
> *Down to the middle of her Roman insides.*
> *Proud little Scampi.*
>
> . . . .
>
> "*For I've had a taste of the world, you see,*
> *And a great princess has had a taste of me.*"

One of Cole's college chums never far from his side was Monty Woolley, who had returned to Yale, where friends tried to secure for him an appointment in the English department. The Yale Corporation refused to do so but named him director of dramatic production in the arts, with the rank of lecturer. Woolley came to see the Porters in Venice, and he and Cole wandered elsewhere together in Europe. Decades later Cole mentioned that "in 1923 Monty Woolley and I were drinking dark beer in Europe. We started wondering where the *lightest* beer was made: After about 145 miles, we traced it to Pilsen—did we celebrate! Later when we met my wife in Venice, she was disgusted with both of us . . . we were that fat."

In the summer of 1924 in the garden of the Palazzo Papadopoli, a Renaissance palace built in the sixteenth century, which the Porters occupied that year, they hosted an evening of ballet staged by Diaghilev and Kochno. They constructed a stage which backed on the Grand Canal. Three vine-covered arches were installed as frames, and three statues lent by museums formed the background. Two male duets from *Les Matelots* were danced, along with a tarantella and a selection from *Les Biches*. According to Kochno, he had to hum the music of *Les Matelots* to Cole so he could play it, as no scores were available. The Porters considered the evening a great success, despite a thunderstorm at its start. But this storm did not compare in violence to the storm that overtook Diaghilev when he learned that the Porters, in their enthusiasm, gave the dancers, besides their fees, special presents. "How dare they give presents to my artists—my artists have no need of such paltry sops!" He learned that after the performance the Porters had sauntered over to Piazza San Marco with some guests. Diaghilev rushed after them and at the piazza confronted Cole and Linda, denouncing them for this faux pas. Kochno claimed that "a first-class scandal . . . spread over the town."

Cole Porter could conceivably have first encountered the Ballets Russes in his student travels during the summer of 1909. That was the year that Serge Pavlovich de Diaghilev brought the company to Paris for the first time as part of what some called his "export campaign." Gifted with both exquisite taste and rare imaginative power, he had as well surprising skills as an organizer. In a letter Diaghilev once wrote to his mother he included a winsome self-portrait: "I am first a great charlatan, though with brio; secondly, a great *charmeur;* thirdly, I have any amount of cheek; fourthly, I am a man with a great quantity of logic, but with very few principles; fifthly, I think I have no real gifts. All the same, I think I have just found my true vocation— being a Maecenas. I have all that is necessary save the money—*mais, ça viendra.*" In 1898 he founded an important journal, *The World of Art,* and by 1909 staged highly successful exhibitions featuring the works of young Russian painters, all of this in an effort to educate the taste of Russian society. And he succeeded in so doing. As one student of the scene observed, people dressed differently, changed their furniture, and decorated their homes in a new manner as a consequence of Diaghilev's presentations. And he brought about a major revival of ballet in the world.

Diaghilev had met Kochno when the impresario was recovering from the heartbreak of parting with then the most famous male dancer in the world, Léonide Massine, whom he had recently banished from the ballet company when Massine announced his intention to marry a dancer in the company called Vera Savina. (This was, of course, a repetition of the fracas that followed the decision of Nijinsky to marry.) Kochno was described in 1920 as "a handsome seventeen-year-old Russian poet . . . bright, sensitive, eager . . . he set about creating a role for himself that brought an infusion of new life to the Ballets Russes. He wrote the libretto for Stravinsky's opera *Mavra* and was to provide the 'poetic argument' for many Diaghilev ballets, including the Rieti-Chirico *Le Bal,* the Nabokov-Tchelitchev *Ode,* and the Prokofiev-Rouault *Prodigal Son.*"

In time Kochno became régisseur of the company and Diaghilev's lover. Diaghilev had already mixed privately and professionally with some of the most gifted musicians. Rimsky-Korsakov, Glazunov, and Rachmaninov were among the important composers who came to Paris to conduct their works in concerts organized by Diaghilev. Eventually he added ballets to his offerings, and so began the Diaghilev Ballet, which counted among its artists such legends as Anna Pavlova, Michel Fokine, Vaslav Nijinsky, Tamara Karsavina, and Lydia Lopokova (who years after married John Maynard Keynes). Later, two dancers who would one day appear in a Cole Porter show—Anton Dolin and Alicia Markova—joined the company.

Within a month of their first meeting Kochno had become a member of Diaghilev's suite. Serge Grigoriev, who managed the Ballets Russes for all twenty years of its life, described Kochno as "a well-educated and intelligent young man, given to writing poetry and eager to contribute to the work of the Ballet." It may have been Linda Porter who brought Diaghilev and Cole together, believing, as she continued to do, that her husband's musical gifts included an untapped vein, classical in character, and that if commissioned to do so, he could produce an impressive ballet score for the Diaghilev company. Kochno gives the year as 1927 that Diaghilev sent word to him from Venice that "Cole is writing a ballet . . . Danger!" (More likely the year was 1923.) Diaghilev despised jazz and seemed mistakenly to place Porter's music—indeed all popular music—under that rubric. Kochno described Diaghilev as "a friend of Cole Porter . . . but Diaghilev never talked to him about his music and pretended not to know that this charming, high-living 'American in Paris' was a composer." Diaghilev, he said, was "outraged by the jazz invasion of Europe and by its influence on young composers." Porter once invited Diaghilev and Kochno to lunch along with George Gershwin, who played his *Rhapsody in Blue* in hopes that it would be performed by the Ballets Russes. Diaghilev listened to the work and commented that he would think of using it for a ballet but Gershwin never heard a word more about it. Throughout all of his career, Diaghilev never commissioned an American composer.

In 1924, while still in Venice, Cole set about scoring John Murray Anderson's *Greenwich Village Follies*. Anderson, who favored spectacle, couldn't appreciate Cole's sly lyrics or his sensual tunes. (Anderson found his stride later with the Ringling Brothers Circus.) The show opened in New York on September 16, 1924. Anderson sensed that the show wouldn't succeed and implored Porter to rework the score, but Cole—off on one of his jaunts—could not be reached in time. Nonchalance of this kind helped Cole to continue thinking of himself as a *flâneur* who dabbled in the music world, a pose not at all reflective of his deep yearnings to compete successfully with the pros. Such behavior led producers to be wary of engaging

him. Kitty Carlisle Hart put this pithily: "Cole Porter's passion was to be a
success as a songwriter but he so feared failure that he pretended in the
1920s to be a playboy who incidentally wrote songs."

Greenwich Village Follies had 127 performances, during which one after
another of Porter's songs was dropped. When it went on the road, none of
his songs remained. Among the numbers Cole had written for *Greenwich
Village Follies* were "Two Little Babes in the Wood" and "I'm in Love
Again," which the discerning Gilbert Seldes called "Mr. Porter's best song."
In 1927 Porter wrote a long letter to his mother about the fate of the song,
describing how to great applause he had played and sung it all around Paris
and "always with howling success, as the melody was very simple and the
sentiment appealed to everyone." Nonetheless it was soon dropped from
Follies, although Cole often heard it performed in cabarets in New York and
abroad. "I went to the band leader and asked him who wrote it, and he said,
'Oh, a Harlem nigger wrote it.' Now . . . comes a wire from Harms, offering me an excellent royalty to publish this song and do everything they can
to make a big hit out of it . . . I shall be surprised if I don't make a lot of
money out of it."

The song, both words and music, describes very well the intoxication of
falling in love:

> I'm in love again,
> And I love, love, love it:
> I'm in love again,
> And I'm darn glad of it,
> Good news!

Verse 2 has a striking line: it describes "someone sad" who meets "someone
bad / But the kind of bad that's sweet," and probably to some extent was
launched by Porter's infatuation at the time with Boris Kochno.

In the latter part of 1925, Porter wrote to Boris Kochno a series of
undated love letters that have recently surfaced. In the first of these Porter
refers to having not long ago spent "black weeks in the hospital in New
York." (In 1920 Porter had had problems with gonococcal urethritis and
tested positive for syphilis. The painful treatments for syphilis in pre-
penicillin days may have been what Porter was alluding to.) He implores
Kochno not to be "such a prima donna. Please write to me. I've been in
Paris three weeks—we're going to Spain for Easter—to Seville for Feria—
Paris month of May, & Switzerland June–October." Porter complains,
"You're so silent, & as for me, I'm so pleased to be back & so happy to

return to life . . . & I feel like seeing you. Is it possible that you've forgotten me? Even if so, tell me."

At two a.m. one Sunday morning—an hour at which Cole Porter seemed much of his life to write love letters and song lyrics (and these two were often interchangeable for Porter)—he sent ardent words to Kochno, who the day before had met Linda and found favor with her. "Boris," he writes,

> You made a great friend today—it was Linda. After everyone had left, she came to my room, to see me—And she spoke to me only of you—saying that you had been charming, that she found you *very* kind, and that you [both] had laughed a great deal together this afternoon.
>
> I place the third item at the end of this list: because I believe that it is the most important, considering that very few people amuse her, and that—I don't know how to tell you how grateful I am—you did it. And that makes everything so much easier.

Reading on in this letter Porter wrote to Kochno, one encounters the loving sentiment of which Cole was capable. Kochno was en route to Naples and his ardent lover already missed him:

> As for your departure, I'm trying to console myself by thinking of your return, but it's quite difficult. And the only thing that I really want to do, is to climb to the top of the belltower and announce to the *piazza* that I'm desperately in love [literally, in the original French, I'm in love to the point of dying] with someone who has taken this evening's train to Naples and that I'm going to follow him . . . Oh, there's nothing to say, Boris, I love you so much that I think only of you—I see only you and I dream only of the moment when we'll be reunited. Goodnight darling. C.

The passion here may startle those who know Porter only from the nonchalant persona he chose to present in society. But these words help those who are moved by Porter's songs to understand the origins of the ardor that is replicated in lyrics and in his throbbing rhythms and intoxicating melodies.

Diaghilev went often to Venice, and Kochno with him. Cole Porter, enchanted from childhood by his fantasies of Venice, spent summers from 1923 to 1927 there. It was probably in 1925 that he wrote to Kochno that their meeting before an evening at the Danieli "is the only thing in the world that matters." One is mildly amazed to encounter, in this same letter, Cole apologizing for being late. Linda had long been known as a woman who insisted on her household staff's comporting themselves with exactitude. She set the regimen and tone, insisting that lunch or dinner begin promptly, even if guests were late arriving. At the outset of their marriage, Cole was more cavalier in his habits, and Linda excused him as a genius for whom exception had to be made. Nonetheless, Cole came around to Linda's ways and, for example, imitated her habit of beginning his meal, whether in a restaurant or at home, exactly at the time announced on his invitation, regardless of his guests' whereabouts. To some friends this seemed almost pathologically compulsive.

All too soon Cole seems in the position of a supplicant that characterized him throughout his life when it came to romantic affairs.

> When will I find you again? There are not enough letters . . . I went this evening to the Grand Hotel—*Niente!* And since you left, six days ago, I've had only one letter. Don't bother telling me that you haven't had time, because I know perfectly well that if you wanted to, nothing would be easier. And I want to underline the fact that I'm becoming a bit furious about it. I miss you so much that I am falling apart & if this continues—this utter silence—I don't dare think what I could do. Oh, Boris, write me and tell me that you love me as much as I love you. You can't say it too often, because you are so far from me and it makes me so miserable.

In another letter Porter recognizes his need to have love reciprocated. He protests Boris's "calm":

> You write to me like an old philosopher . . . [as if] you thought of me as some crazy person who has to be humored. And that bothers me.
>
> Am I making myself understood? I mean, here I am bowled over since your arrival in Venice. I write you absurdities & that's all I feel like writing. And you answer me in a manner that is so tidy, so placid, that I wonder—"Does he really think I'm some sort of radio that broadcasts his thoughts to everybody?"
>
> It's that you are becoming too much the recipient. And I need to get something back from you, too. Maybe it bothers you to tell me such things, but that is what I ask of you. I'm so hungry for you to tell me that you love me & thousands of times, so I can look at your written

words in the night when I long to have you pressing against me, your lips on mine—your lips that I caress so often and so tenderly, my Boris . . . I'm leaving Florence Wednesday in order to avoid seeing you. It would be easy to arrange it but I realize that we must not.

On another trip to Florence Linda and Cole went to the Pitti Palace gallery, where he writes to tell Boris: "After lunch, I come back to the hotel to sleep a bit in my room #28. This will be from 3:00 to 4:00. Why not come see me there?"

Before and during the periods the Porters summered in Venice, they motored through Italy, stopping on one Italian tour at Ravenna and Rimini, Perugia, Florence, and Milan before returning to Paris. Travel attracted Porter throughout his life, and he was given to urging friends to voyage afar and to put up with whatever inconvenience they encountered in order to see as many of the sights as they possibly could.

Almost certainly on that same jaunt, Porter writes to tell Boris that they have arrived in Ravenna to see its treasures, although this was not Cole's first sight of them. "If you aren't familiar with them," he tells Boris, "perhaps we could come here next summer to see them together." He wonders "why instead of seeing this with all these people, [Boris] isn't here, alone with me? This is a city just made for offering unforgettable joys to the two of us. And moreover, you know, it must happen—our trip to Ravenna." Again Porter complains about his failing to find a letter from Kochno. "Undoubtedly, you didn't receive my plans in time," he writes, consoling himself with this supposition and the hope that they will meet a few days later in Florence, where "I will have the great pleasure of looking into those beautiful eyes of which I dream day and night, my Boris. Goodnight & don't forget for an instant that I love you."

That the nonchalant Porter felt uneasy at times with his passionate expression seems likely and perhaps accounts for a song he published in the twenties called "Love Letter Words":

> When somebody writes you a letter
> In the style that you've always admired,
> You say, "This could never be better,
> It's something that love has inspired."
> Then you read through the lines and discover
> Many words that you already know,
> For the phrases you find in the letter,
> Were first written ages ago.

No doubt a part of Porter observed with some irony the phenomenon of his falling so desperately in love. In 1929 he aired all this in a song that Jessie Matthews introduced in *Wake Up and Dream*.

> *I loved him,*
> *But he didn't love me.*
> *I wanted him,*
> *But he didn't want me.*
> *Then the gods had a spree,*
> *And indulged in another whim.*
> *Now he loves me,*
> *But I don't love him.*

The correspondence with Kochno does eventually cool: "Leaving this evening from Cherbourg my dear. Sorry not to have seen you before leaving for America. Affection—C." But this undated note is preceded by many more anguished and loving ones. "This is just a word to let you know that I first left you a quarter of an hour ago, & that I miss you—*tanto*. And to apologize if I turn out the light & take you in my arms & tell you that you are the only thing in the world that is dear to me."

Many of the songs that Porter wrote in the 1920s seem rooted in the feelings Kochno engendered in him, but none seems to say more exactly what he felt than "Dream-Dancing," one of his most beautiful songs, published in 1941 and danced in the film *You'll Never Get Rich* by Fred Astaire and Rita Hayworth.

> *When day is gone*
> *And night comes on,*
> *Until the dawn*
> *What do I do?*
> *I clasp your hand*
> *And wander through slumberland,*
> *Dream-dancing with you.*
> *. . . . .*
> *Oh, what a lucky windfall!*
> *Touching you, clutching you, all*
> *The night through,*
> *So say you love me, dear,*
> *And let me make my career . . .*
> *Dream-dancing with you.*

Boris Kochno and Serge Diaghilev in Monte Carlo in the early 1920s

One year the Porters discovered they'd "done something stupid—we've stayed too long in Venice." But they enjoyed very entertaining company, including Arthur Rubinstein, "who, as always—played pretty well before dinner, & marvelously afterwards." Nonetheless, "there was a sense that everyone was thinking about the end of their holidays & the atmosphere was predominantly melancholic." So the Porters and their friends moved on, among them Lady Abdy, a great friend of Diaghilev's, and Princess di San Faustino. The Porters had their car and first headed for Ravenna and then to Florence, where they hoped to meet up with Lord Berners, a colorful and aristocratic English composer, whose house at Farringdon remains a showplace. Berners and Diaghilev had met in Rome, where the Englishman had been a member of the diplomatic corps, and by 1919 Diaghilev was using pieces by Berners in the entr'actes during the London season of the Ballets Russes. Several years later, Kochno relates, when Diaghilev was pressing Berners to complete the score for *The Triumph of Neptune,* Berners replied in a note: "I don't feel too inspired at the moment. However, this morning I bought a very pretty Renoir, and hope that now things will go better." (That ballet, incidentally, has historical significance as the last ballet in which Balanchine danced with the Diaghilev company.)

Porter seems several times to have contributed to the support of Kochno and/or the Ballets Russes. In one letter Kochno is informed that checks sent to Morgan Bank for him by Cole and by Lady Mendl amount to 5,088 francs. And Guaranty Trust in New York wrote to tell Kochno that

the sum of 2,125 francs had been deposited for him by Porter, who helped as
well by mentioning Kochno's financial needs to wealthy friends.

In an early letter, before Cole began to *tutoyer* Boris, he wrote to
Kochno to say, "I have to see you before you [leave], because I want to take
care of the checks for the dancers. Also, we—Linda and I—would like all of
you to dine with us the evening before your departure." And he signs off
somewhat matter-of-factly: "Goodbye and see you soon." But as Porter confessed later to Kochno: "Even before daring to tell you the truth, before I'd
met you, I always wanted to chase away everybody there & must announce
to you that I adored you. So you can, perhaps, understand how hard it is for
me now. Because, I'm so chilled, Boris, & you aren't there. And I want you
in my arms—right now in my arms for always. Why are we so foolish that
you're not there? . . . Oh, Boris, how you have complicated my life!" he
writes, quickly adding, "How it makes me happy, darling."

Already in the 1920s ill health had begun to trouble Linda and led to
Cole traveling to America without her. "Linda's condition is very serious,"
Cole wrote to Boris. "I spoke with the doctor again this morning. He has
decided that it would be better if I were to leave for the States so that she can
get more rest here." This seems a curious prescription for a physician to dispense. One wonders if Linda was reacting painfully to Cole's profound passion for Boris. Linda seconded the doctor's suggestion. "She insists that
I leave," Cole tells his lover, and describes illness overtaking him. "You
remember the problem I was having with my head! Well I had to go to bed
for three whole days because of it. I went out for the first time today & I'm
starting to feel alive once more. But only gradually." Porter's decision to
leave seems at least in part motivated by his decision to break with Boris. "I
won't see you again before I leave, darling . . . Don't be furious—you should
understand & believe me when I tell you that I love you more than ever."

Horst recalled the passionate affair between Porter and Kochno, whom
he saw together at the Ca' Rezzonico. He remembered as well that Linda
suddenly discovered this affair one summer in Venice. "She took it very
hard," said Horst. "A very nice woman," he called Linda, and "very naive"
as well.

One commentator remarked, Linda "realized Porter was gay at first
meeting and, on condition that he maintain a minimal facade, was prepared
to accept it. It is likely that sex repelled her." Another explains the marriage
by insisting that "great beauties don't want sex—don't want to be pawed by
men." Indeed, this is a view that a number of Porter's acquaintances
advanced. "Linda became Cole's best friend," said the Comtesse de Rochambeau, Cole's godchild, "and they had a mother/son arrangement. Linda

brought sanity to Cole's life and was a wonderful foil for him." "It was always obvious to us," wrote a relative of Linda, "why she married Cole Porter. She was so abused by a heterosexual [Edward Thomas] she most probably would never have married again."

Speculations about Linda's sexuality abound: Rocky [Mrs. Gary] Cooper, for instance, is convinced that Linda was lesbian. The most recent biography of Irving Berlin asserts that she "tolerated [Cole's] homosexual affairs as he tolerated her lesbian encounters," but gives no evidence for this claim. Porter's friend Ben Baz thought Linda "not at all lesbian—she was sexless—but absolutely in love with Cole who adored her." What can be said is that Linda moved easily and comfortably with lesbian friends, though in other regards acquaintances found her "old-fashioned, not modern at all." One of the forms that this took was the kind of elegantly Victorian manners Linda maintained. "She didn't know how to open a door," said a friend, "she'd just stand and wait for someone else to do it for her." Cole, too, had beautiful manners, and Linda found his careful attention to her comforting. He always rose when she left or returned to a room, and generally his gallantry charmed her.

In all of his homosexual love affairs, Porter seemed deeply concerned to encourage friendship between his lovers and Linda. Usually one encounters the husband or wife who cannot detach an extramarital affair from feelings of guilt, but Porter was homosexual and not bisexual—which no doubt diminished the tensions that otherwise might have ruptured their relationship.

Porter's friend Michael Pearman remembers that before he met Porter, he heard of a "big sex scandal" involving Cole Porter in Venice. This most probably was the affair with Kochno.

By the late 1920s Porter and Kochno had grown apart, and their lives took very different directions. In 1928 Diaghilev left the production of the ballet *Ode* totally in Kochno's hands. By this time Boris was responsible for many of the scenarios of new ballets, and Diaghilev viewed Kochno as his successor. "The Young Oak," Diaghilev called him, and insisted that he preside over this effort with no assistance from him. During Diaghilev's last illness in 1929, Kochno was one of the very few admitted to the sick room, and it was he who sent to Grigoriev the terrible news: "Diaghilev est mort ce matin. Kochno."

The Porters' life in Venice continued into 1927. In their last years there, they rented for $4,000 per month the Ca' Rezzonico, one of the most majestic of the Venetian palazzi. Of special interest to Cole was its purchase in 1887 by the son of Robert Browning, Pen, who had married an American

heiress. According to Henry James, the restoration Pen had overseen in Ca'
Rezzonico "transcends description for beauty." In 1889 Robert Browning,
visiting Pen, caught cold and died there.

In 1926 Lorenz Hart and Richard Rodgers traveled together to Europe
and soon found themselves in Venice. Strolling on the Lido, Rodgers heard
someone calling his name and saw it was Noël Coward, with whom he was
slightly acquainted.

> Noël was in Venice, he told me, visiting an American friend he was sure
> would love to meet me. We strolled over to his friend's cabana, and I
> was introduced to a slight, delicately-featured man with soft saucer eyes
> and a wide, friendly grin. His name was Cole Porter, but at that time
> neither the name nor the face was in the least familiar to me . . . When
> I told the two of them that Larry Hart was staying with me at a hotel in
> Venice, Porter insisted that we both join him for dinner that evening at
> the place he had rented in the city.

Palazzo Ca' Rezzonico

Promptly at seven-thirty, Porter's private gondola pulled up outside our hotel. Larry and I got in, we wafted down the Grand Canal and were deposited in front of an imposing three-storey palace. This was the "place" Porter had rented, which we later found out was the celebrated Palazzo Rezzonico . . . We were assisted out of the gondola by a liveried footman wearing white gloves, and ushered up a massive stairway, at the top of which stood Noël, Cole and his wife, Linda. During the delicious and elegantly served dinner Cole kept peppering me with questions about the Broadway musical theatre, revealing a remarkably keen knowledge of both classical and popular music. Since he impressed me as someone who led a thoroughly indolent, though obviously affluent, life, the sharpness of his observations was unexpected. Unquestionably, he was more than a social butterfly.

After dinner they repaired to the music room, where at Porter's request Rodgers played some of his songs, followed by Coward at the keyboard. Then Cole sat down to play.

As soon as he touched the keyboard to play "a few of my little things" I became aware that he was not merely a talented dilettante, but a generally gifted theatre composer and lyricist . . . Why, I asked Cole, was he wasting his time? Why wasn't he writing for Broadway? To my embarrassment, he told me that he had already written four musical-comedy scores, three of which had even made it to Broadway. But little had come of them, and he simply preferred living in Europe and performing his songs for the entertainment of his friends. Later he did admit that he hoped someday to be able to have the best of both worlds: working on Broadway and living in Europe.

Most people found the hospitality of the Porters dazzling, although there were occasional exceptions. Lady Diana Cooper, famous as a beauty and for her triumphs on the stage, was frequently on the Porters' guest list, and one could say she was their true friend. Ditto for her husband, the elegant and handsome Duff Cooper; nonetheless, writing to his wife from Venice, he noted: "Dinner at the Coles' last night wasn't bad. No charm at all. I played chess with Monty Woolley afterwards, the others went on to the piazza where we joined them later." Many people are ready to rise and proclaim the charm of Cole Porter, but then a surprising number of Porter's good friends insist that Porter was at times "withdrawn and aloof . . . not exactly fun to be with." A lot of people considered Cole to be "cold, indifferent, rude," according to the singer Bricktop and others. But she found him "interested in me as a person. He wanted me to be beautifully dressed. When we went out together, he bought me gorgeous clothes. One time . . . a set of silver-fox furs." Bricktop attributed Cole's apparent indifference to his shyness. Somewhat cattily she wrote, "If you were going to be pushy with Cole, you had to do it with flair, like Elsa Maxwell did." Porter could stand neither snobs nor social climbers. Nor was he good at dealing with ill-mannered people. "He could have told off a lot of singers, but he preferred to leave by the back way."

The entertainments Porter conceived in Venice were "on an oriental scale of magnificence and the already picturesque nights of the city were enriched by such splendor as the huge illuminated float moored out in the Lagoon which was the scene of lavish entertainment and known to the Venetians as 'l'arca di Noe.' " This was the notorious *galleggiante,* or "dance boat," that Cole and "three titled Italian aristocrats" launched. (The ornately domed boat was originally designed for the Excelsior Hotel.) A newspaper cutting calls it "a large barge, which has been specially constructed, contain-ing facilities for serving supper, [and which] will float out into the lagoon and, on still nights, even into the open sea. A negro jazz orchestra is being brought from Paris to play and there will be dancing. Invitations have been sent to a number of members of the summer colony, and the subscription list is to be limited to 150 members, with the proceeds going to several Venetian charities." The "arca di Noe" made only one journey owing to the slipperiness of the dance floor, the absence of toilets, and the noisiness of the blaring band. But Porter kept the musicians in Venice for the summer, entertaining at parties he and Linda hosted.

Diaghilev wrote complainingly to Kochno about the Porter hijinks:

The whole of Venice is up in arms against Cole Porter because of his jazz and his Negroes. He has started an idiotic nightclub on a boat moored outside the Salute, and now the Grand Canal is swarming with the very same Negroes who have made us all flee from London and Paris. They are teaching the "Charleston" on the Lido Beach! It's dread-ful. The gondoliers are threatening to massacre all the elderly American women here. The very fact of their renting the Palazzo Rezzonico is considered characteristic of *nouveaux riches.*

Decades later Porter wrote to his lawyer, John Wharton, saying, "It is always strange for me how many fables are connected with the facts of any-one's life":

Many biographies speak about me and Linda running a night club in Venice. This must stem from the fact that I had a huge barge converted into a dance floor. I imported a negro band from London and once a week this barge was towed around the lagoons of Venice. [Porter mistakes the frequency of the barge's use.] The membership consisted of about one hundred of our friends, who paid a certain amount for the privilege of belonging to this club. All the proceeds were given to a local charity. So much for the night club.

The jazz boat was the source of a perhaps playful "feud" that developed in Venice in 1926 between Porter and the famous conductor Sir Thomas Beecham, whose father, Sir Joseph Beecham, was the originator of the pills known worldwide by his name. (The musicologist Ernest Newman once said of Sir Thomas that when he lifted his baton you could hear a pill drop.) Beecham privately printed a pamphlet called *The Tragical History of Young King Cole* under the pseudonym Didymus Belcampus. "At the conclusion Young King Cole was swept out to sea and drowned for having brought jazz and a cocktail barge to Venice." Porter wrote a song which alludes to Beecham:

> *Tho' perhaps you be a scorner*
> *Of our concerts on the corner,*
> *Yet we know that they would please Sir Thomas Beecham.*

In her customary way, Elsa Maxwell contrived to kick up her heels. Princess Giardini described a party she and her husband ("Andy") gave in Venice at that time:

We gave an Eighteenth century ball the same year Andy and I got married. In every palazzo costumes were dusted and cleaned for the occasion. We wore two beautiful costumes that were kept in the showcase in the Byron room near the desk where the poet, who had spent two years of his life in Palazzo Mocenigo, had written part of *Childe Harold.* The big hit that evening was provided by Elsa Maxwell, an American journalist. She arrived in shorts while everyone was seriously dancing to a minuet. Furthermore, she wore on her head the authentic ducal horn that belonged to the seven Mocenigo dukes that she had taken from the glass bell in which it was jealously guarded. The orchestra put down its violins and the dance stopped. The aristocratic women: the Morosini, the Albrizzi, the Dona, and the Foscari all became pale. Elsa Maxwell invented public relations.

Along with Elsa Maxwell, three black entertainers contributed to Porter's social success in the 1920's: Bricktop, Josephine Baker, and Leslie Hutchinson. "My greatest claim to Fame," said F. Scott Fitzgerald once, "is that I discovered Bricktop before Cole Porter [did]."

Cole Porter met Bricktop, a West Virginian, around 1925 in Paris. She was an entertainer who first opened a small club called Le Grand Duc, where she danced the Charleston. One morning "a slight, immaculately dressed man came in . . . by morning I mean between 3 a.m. and 6 a.m. . . . I got up to sing and could sense that the man was watching and listening with more than ordinary interest. He applauded when I finished." After he left, Bricktop discovered she'd been singing a Cole Porter song ("I'm in Love Again") to the composer. "Everyone in Paris knew that Cole was funny about people singing his songs. If a singer didn't do it just right Cole wouldn't embarrass him or her but he'd leave quickly—and that would be the most embarrassing situation imaginable for the singer." Cole reappeared the next night, but instead of showing interest in Bricktop's voice, he inquired about her dancing. Did she know the Charleston? Yes, she had learned it in New York, although it was still unknown in Paris. A few nights later Porter returned with Elsa Maxwell and several other friends. Bricktop danced the Charleston and "Elsa loved it. She clapped and shrieked." Said Cole, "I'm going to give Charleston cocktail parties at my house two or three times a week, and you're going to teach everyone to dance the Charleston."

So Bricktop found herself at 13 rue Monsieur, with all its opulent decor. The three hundred-pound Aga Khan was there, as were Elsa and about fifty other "students." "I was about to become the dance teacher to the most elegant members of the international set." Dolly and Jay O'Brien were smart-set clients of Bricktop, as were Arturo Lopez, a Chilean millionaire, who saw less of his wife than he did of his lover, Baron Rede. The Rothschilds, Lady Mendl, and Consuelo Vanderbilt, the Duchess of Marlborough, also came to Bricktop (or she to them) for lessons in the Charleston.

Bricktop recalled the acceptance of black entertainers socially in Paris, where they entered by the front door—not as in American society, where blacks were admitted only at the service entrance. She also was sought after by lesbian socialites: "I could have had romantic involvements with women, but I never liked women. Consequently I was never big on the orgies that some people had." Bricktop considered Cole and Linda "real friends."

In Venice, summer of 1926, the Porters were in residence at the Rezzonico, but something was missing. The Charleston, they decided. So they asked Bricktop to come and spend the summer with them. Luckily, she was free in the months that Parisians spend *en vacances,* and she had never been to Venice. The Porters had already engaged Leslie Hutchinson to play and lead the orchestra intended for the dance boat and retained for summer parties. Bricktop had worked with his band before, so that was another lure. Hutch was a tall, handsome man born in Grenada in the West Indies, who drifted to New York with a few dollars and a desire to make his mark. He played for private parties in New York and soon was the darling of the smart set, first in Paris, then in London, where eventually he settled. Aspiring as a youth to be a classical pianist, Hutch went to study in Paris and earned money by playing evenings at Joselli's Bar in the place Clichy. Porter probably met him there. "I am a gentleman," Hutch said, "and I am always polite, always know my manners." Years later, when Porter would enter the elegant Quaglino's, or the Café de Paris, Hutch would swiftly segue into "Beguine" to signify that Cole was in the room. Many royals attended the cabarets that featured Hutch; one of them, Lady Mountbatten, was reputedly his lover for a time as well as his fan. The assertion has been made that Hutch was bisexual and the question raised whether or not he and Cole had been lovers, but there is at present no evidence for either claim.

The languorous Venetian summer of 1926 was punctuated by the arrival of many guests: Dorothy Oelrichs, wife of Herman, his friend from Yale; Dorothy "Dickie" Fellowes-Gordon; Noël Coward and his lover, John C.

Leslie Hutchinson with his band, Venice, 1926

Countess Dorothy de Frasso, 1926

"Jack" Wilson; Lady Abdy; the Duke of Verdura; Monty Woolley; Lady Diana Cooper; Jean Bouvier; the Mendls; Countess de Frasso; and Countess di Zoppola (the former Edith Mortimer). Alistair Mackintosh was another of Cole's guests that year, and Cole introduced him to Lila Emery, an heiress from Cincinnati. The two subsequently married, and lived for a time at 8 rue Monsieur, just opposite the Porters, in a house that resembled a miniature Greek palace. When daughters were born to them, Cole became godfather to one; Linda, godmother to the other. One of these daughters described the Porter marriage as "an arrangement of great coziness and deep friendship." Linda made their lives immensely pleasant. "She was the epitome of femininity." Cole, in the opinion of his godchild—now the Comtesse de Rochambeau—was "not a funny man, rather a dour man filled with depression." The Mackintosh butler, King, later wrote an entertaining memoir called *The Green Baize Door,* in which he depicts his former employer and comments on his neighbors. "I remember [Porter's] cigarette case and lighter were of heavy gold. He lost so many cases that in the end he always had engraved inside the lid: *Stolen from Cole Porter.*" Once when King went to inspect the drawing room while all the guests were golfing—or so he

Countess Edith di Zoppola, 1926

thought—he found Porter "seated at the piano, running through a chord or two, then several notes, then jotting something down on a sheet before him. 'Don't move, King!' . . . After about two minutes he turned to me and said: 'Thank you very much, King, that's fine. I've got it!' Judging by the notes and the chords I heard him strumming I feel pretty sure that it was the birth of 'Begin the Beguine.' " Eventually the Mackintoshes divorced, and she married the Duc de Talleyrand.

By 1925 Monty Woolley was settled in his position with the Yale University Dramatic Association and approached Cole about writing songs for the annual Christmas show, entitled that year *Out o' Luck*, written by Tom Cushing, class of 1902. Some friends felt that it was Cole's link to the Dramat and the success of the songs he wrote for *Out o' Luck* that had lured him back to songwriting. In 1968 the distinguished stage and film director H. C. Potter, a member of the cast back in 1925, sent to Robert Kimball these recollections of the show. Potter had heard often from Monty Woolley that Porter had been "in the doldrums in the long and unproductive period [the 1920s]." Woolley told Potter, then an undergraduate, "of Cole's despondency, how he felt that his style was hopelessly outmoded and old-fashioned, his conviction that he would never be able to 'get with' the music that was then being written. I know that Monty had to use every bit of . . . exuberant enthusiasm and persuasion . . . to nudge Cole out of what

Jack Wilson, Noël Coward, and Cole, Venice, 1926

he himself considered virtual retirement." Potter recalled that Monty's great friend Herman Oelrichs was also instrumental in getting Cole started again.

"Looked at in the cold light of today," Potter recalled, "the show . . . would seem terribly naive, démodé, and . . . 'campy,' the youth of today would call it. However . . . the New Haven audience ate it up and the 1925 Christmas tour was a huge success . . . so much so that the Dramat took the show out the following Christmas for another series of highly successful 'one-nighters' throughout the East and Middle West." Credit for the success went to Woolley's direction and Porter's three songs presented in Act Two "during an impromptu 'show' being put on by some . . . soldiers, dressed in spangled, chorus-girl 'tutus' (but still wearing their GI boots)." The third song, "Opera Star," was written by Cole after a cast member performed for

The Duke of Verdura, 1926

him a falsetto number he had invented, a burlesque of divas then in fashion. The song, said Potter, "proved to be what used to be known as a 'wow' ":

> *I'm a great success making love on the stage,*
> *But a terrible failure at home.*
> *I can find a nice fellow once in an age*
> *But in no time he starts in to roam.*
> *'Round the fireplace I'll admit I'm much too tame*
> *But they call the fire department when I sing* Bohème.

Fanny Brice was a guest Cole especially enjoyed. She arrived at the Ca' Rezzonico in the summer of 1926. Both Cole and Linda felt a frisson when

they learned how at home Brice was with hoodlums. Her estranged husband, Nicky Arnstein, had been well-known as a gambler. "Royalty and
gangsters were all the same to her," said Porter with amusement (or was it
envy?). Brice asked Cole to write some songs for her, and in Venice he composed two: "Hot-House Rose" and "Weren't We Fools?"

> I'm hot-house rose from God knows where,
> The kind that grows without fresh air.
> The whistle blows and work is done
> But it's too late for me to get the sun.
> They say that when you dream a lot,
> You always dream of what you haven't got.
> That's why I dream of a garden, I s'pose,
> 'Cause I'm only a hot-house rose.

Porter told a friend that by 1926 he had abandoned the idea that he would
ever succeed on Broadway and had taken up painting. Then Fanny Brice,
"whom we grew to know very well," asked Cole for the songs.

That was the reason for "Hot-House Rose." When I finished it, I
invited her to the Rezzonico to hear it and afterwards she always told
friends how wonderfully incongruous it was, that I should have demonstrated to her this song about a poor little factory girl as she sat beside
me while I sang and played it to her on our grand piano that looked lost
in our ballroom, whose walls were entirely decorated by Tiepolo paintings and was so big that if we gave a ball for less than a thousand people they seemed to be entirely lost. She never sang the song.

"Weren't We Fools" was sung by Fanny Brice next year during a week's
run at the Palace Theatre in New York City. One evening at the Palace she
decided not to sing the song: Nicky Arnstein was in the audience. Theirs
had been a tormented marriage, and Brice, although said by some still to be
deeply in love with Arnstein, had finally agreed to a divorce. "I long to put
my arms around you now," the song says, "but it wouldn't be the same,
somehow." The lyrics of the refrain, set to a hauntingly sad tune, make this
one of Porter's most affecting torch songs, though a neglected one.

> Weren't we fools to lose each other?
> Weren't we fools to say goodbye?
> Tho' we know we loved each other,
> You chose another,

> So did I.
> *If we'd realized our love was worth defending*
> *Then the story's broken threads we might be mending*
> *With perhaps a diff'rent ending,*
> *A happy ending.*
> *Weren't we fools?*
> *Weren't we fools?*

The narrative does resemble the plots of several well-known plays by Noël Coward, most notably *Private Lives* (though the Porter song is more heartfelt), and one can easily imagine how the song suggested itself to Coward's parodic powers:

> *Weren't we fools to lose each other?*
> *Though we know we loved each other*
> *You chose your brother, so did I.*

In mid-August 1926 Linda organized in Venice an annual benefit for the Tubercular Children of Italy—a cause dear to her heart. Inaugurated by the Princess di San Faustino, it was held on August 14—Eve of the Assumption, a great feast day in Italy—and presented at the Excelsior Lido. There was "a jazz revue which for swing and pep would yield place to no amateur show." The program lists: "Direttice Miss Bricktop." On her copy, Bricktop parenthetically scribbled "ha ha," a chortle over how far she had come since the days when she started out in Chicago. The Porters had arranged at a certain moment for the lights to be extinguished and a spotlight to fix on Bricktop. A birthday cake was presented to her, at which she began to weep. "At least something has impressed Brick," said Cole.

The apotheosis of balls given by the Porters in Venice was the now legendary Red and White Ball. *Gondolieri* in red and white costumes guided the guests, who by the hundreds glided into the Ca' Rezzonico and onto the dance floor. At midnight, however, the music ceased and the guests moved from the ballroom to the grand salon, where they found every conceivable item of red and white papier-mâché clothing, in which they were requested to outfit themselves. Back they then went to the ballroom and danced with extraordinary visual effect in their red and white costumes. Prince Faucigny-Lucinge, a connoisseur of galas and spectacle, was present: "I recall a tight rope dancer such as there were then still on the piazza, keeping all eyes riveted on him crossing over from the top of the illuminated courtyard, dressed in white and red, and with table and chair, affecting to have a meal over the anguished guests."

In August of 1927 Linda was spending some time in a Swiss sanitarium and Cole was at the Rezzonico, when news reached him that his father, aged sixty-nine, had died. Elsa Maxwell was with Cole, and he arranged for her to remain at the Rezzonico until his return, with the proviso that she lead a socially quiet life during his absence. Porter traveled alone to Indiana because of Linda's health. He seemed not to be personally wounded by the loss of his father but worried very much about his mother. The *Peru Republican* praised the thrift that had allowed Sam Porter to broaden his prosperous business in Peru at the same time he oversaw much of the management of Westleigh Farms, which he loved and from which he was buried. The obituaries printed the misinformation that "death came as the result of complications following a nervous breakdown." All the biographies repeat this as fact. Katie Porter (and other family members as well) must have decided to print this misinformation. A glance at his death certificate, available at the courthouse in Peru, reveals that Porter died from meningitis, the same illness that had killed his infant daughter, Rachel. What the family's motive in falsifying this fact could have been remains speculation. Perhaps they feared social ostracism: the same fear that cancer victims often felt until recent years.

Cole reached Peru about a week after his father's funeral. Although the *Republican* saluted Sam by printing his obituary on its front page and praised him as someone who had earned "an enviable reputation as a business man and had a wide circle of friends," he failed to win the love of his son, who remained convinced that his father had not valued him, and this despite the many efforts—mostly of his cousin Lou (Louise) Bearss—to persuade him otherwise. Lou Bearss became, after Sammy's death, Katie's confidante and traveling companion.

On the day of the funeral, Linda and Cole later learned, Elsa Maxwell had hosted a party at the Rezzonico. Cole was not surprised by this news, but it infuriated Linda, who never liked Elsa. She left the Swiss spa at which she'd been battling respiratory illness and demanded that Elsa leave at once. From then, Elsa was never again *en famille* with the Porters, but she kept close ties with Cole, who in the late 1920s in Paris wrote a song laced with affectionate wit for her birthday:

> I'm dining with Elsa, with Elsa, supreme.
> I'm going to meet princesses
> Wearing Coco Chanel dresses
> Going wild over strawberries and cream.
> I've got Bromo Seltzer

> *To take when dinner ends,*
> *For I'm dining with Elsa*
> *And her ninety-nine most intimate friends!*

Late in 1927 Porter was in New York and lunched with Louis Shurr, a theatrical agent who acted on behalf of several of Porter's friends, Clifton Webb and the opera star Grace Moore among them. Shurr was another of the raffish characters it probably amused Porter to see. According to Cole's friend the pianist, Lew Kesler, Shurr was sex-obsessed and had a trick of offering a woman a white ermine coat at the start of an evening and then, after he'd been to bed with her, demanding its return. In *Seven Lively Arts* Dolores Gray sang these lyrics in Cole's song "Wow-Ooh Wolf!," a cautionary tale about Shurr:

> *You can't scare me, Mister Louie Shurr,*
> *Though you're Hollywood's best-known agent.*
> *Just why should I let you handle me, sir?*
> *You're a much too famous-in-the-hay gent.*
> *For all your gifts, Mister Louie Shurr,*
> *I'll forever be your debtor,*
> *But why did you send me that rabbit fur*
> *When I know you like bare skin better?*

Whatever the vagaries of his private life, Shurr was an able agent.

La Revue des Ambassadeurs, Paris, and *Fifty Million Frenchmen* (all three were presented in 1928 or 1929), are in some ways a summation of Porter's Paris period. Years later, Porter described himself to a friend as having suffered at the whim of critics who "kicked us around for so long simply because we were raising hell on the Continent." All that was now to change.

Chapter 6

Mesdames, Messieurs . . .

At a party given by Elsa Maxwell in Paris in 1928, Cole Porter heard and admired Frances Gershwin singing some of her brothers' songs. On the strength of that, he drove her the next day to an audition for a revue that was being mounted "at a chic night club," The Café des Ambassadeurs, and Cole and the producer wrote her into the show. Backed by a full chorus and Fred Waring and his Pennsylvanians, Frankie (as she is called) sang with great success a medley of Gershwin songs, introduced by these verses composed by Porter:

> *I happen to be the sister*
> *Of a rhythm twister.*
> *No doubt you know him as Mister*
> *George Gershwin.*
> *If you're prepared for an orgy*
> *Of music written by Georgie,*
> *I'll try to sing you some fav'rites of*
> *The man I love.*

On opening night George appeared at the piano accompanying his sister. Frankie recalls that she sat beside him on the stage in a very informal way, as if they were at home. In the spring of 1928 George Gershwin was staying in a hotel at 19 avenue Kléber, working on *An American in Paris*. His brother, Ira, was staying at the same address and remembered George playing late into the night with Cole Porter.

The year before *La Revue des Ambassadeurs* opened, Cole and Linda spent the winter in New York, where he was among the "few hand-picked men" to meet, at the home of Schuyler Parsons, the great hero of the day, Charles Lindbergh. Earlier in 1927 Lindbergh had made his famous transatlantic crossing to France, and Cole, with his irrepressible curiosity, drove out to Le Bourget to be part of the crowd who welcomed Lindbergh on his arrival. A year later, on May 10, 1928, *La Revue des Ambassadeurs* opened, and Paris was entertained by the double entendre of:

> *Pilot me,*
> *Pilot me,*
> *Be the pilot I need.*
> *Please give my ship*
> *A maiden trip,*
> *And we'll get the prize for speed.*
> *So cast away your fears,*
> *Strip my gears,*
> *Let me carry you through.*
> *And when afraid you are*
> *Of going too far,*
> *Then I'll*
> *Just pil-*
> *Ot you.*

The opening of *La Revue des Ambassadeurs* was brilliant and set the style for the many Porter opening nights to come. People sat at tables and there were many standees. One paper predicted that the Café des Ambassadeurs "will be the great rendezvous for those in search of late night evening amusement from now until the end of the season." Celebratory parties were given all over Paris, hosted by such notables as Elsa Maxwell, the Prince and Princesse de Polignac, Lady Cunard, and William Randolph Hearst (whose guests included Mr. and Mrs. Cornelius Vanderbilt). Linda came to Paris from Italy, where she'd gone to recover from a recurrence of respiratory illness.

Eventually Clifton Webb and Dorothy Dickson joined the cast, and they inspired Porter to write one of his loveliest songs:

Looking at you,
While troubles are fleeing.
I'm admiring the view,
'Cause it's you I'm seeing.
And the sweet honeydew
Of well-being settles upon me.
What is this light
That shines when you enter?
Like a star in the night,
And what's to prevent 'er
From destroying my sight,
If you center all of it on me?
Looking at you,
I'm filled with the essence of
The quintessence of
Joy.
Looking at you,
I hear poets tellin' of
Lovely Helen of
Troy, darling.
Life seemed so gray
I wanted to end it,
Till that wonderful day
You started to mend it.
And if you'll only stay,
Then I'll spend it looking at you.

The song became a hit, and Cole used it again in *Wake Up and Dream,* in which Jessie Matthews introduced it to London and New York.

Irving Berlin and Cole Porter first met in New York at the home of Elizabeth Marbury. Berlin was captivated by Porter's musical knowledge and gifts. In time the two became fast friends. In 1926, Berlin wed Ellin Mackay, daughter of the wealthy telegraph magnate Lawrence Mackay, who bitterly opposed the marriage and continued the opposition. Linda Porter had dated Mackay years earlier. But both the Porters warmly backed the Berlins who accepted their invitation to stay with them while in Paris. So the two couples grew close.

Berlin's first wife, Dorothy Goetz Berlin, had died soon after their marriage. Her brother was E. Ray Goetz, a songwriter as well as a composer and playwright. He was determined to stage a musical in which his wife, Irene

Bordoni, would star. He consulted with Berlin who advised him to go and find Porter on the Lido. In 1927, Louis Shurr, Cole's agent arranged a meeting in New York between Porter and E. Ray Goetz. Negotiations began and Goetz agreed to engage Porter as composer and lyricist. So *Paris* was launched.

The tryout earned high praise from hometown critics. After the tryout, in Washington, D.C. (which was attended by the then mayor of New York, Jimmy Walker), the show opened in New York on October 8, 1928, and ran for 195 performances. *The New Yorker* declared itself "ecstatic" about Porter's songs, with the rare insistence that the songs were "up to Mr. Porter's best and there is no better. No one else now writing words and music knows so exactly the delicate balance between sense, rhyme and tune." Most of the New York notices were enthusiastic. Richard Watts in the *New York Herald Tribune* praised "the absent Mr. Cole Porter" as "the flaming star of the premiere of *Paris*." He was one of the earliest commentators to invent a legendary Porter: "This Mr. Porter is a wealthy American who occasionally finds the time to sit down in his Riviera chateau and write a song. It is the misfortune of musical comedy that he writes them too seldom and it is the triumph of *Paris* that five of his works have been gathered together for it."

"Let's Do It" remains one of Porter's most admired songs. When the show was on tour in Chicago a year later, a critic wrote of "Let's Do It" as "this joyously tuned and worded anthem with which Bordoni rang twelve bells."

Porter's use of the pronoun "it" is masterful. He follows Mallarmé's advice to suggest rather than to name. Everyone knows what "it" means (when a man asked his young daughter to join him singing "Let's Do It," she said, "Daddy, if you don't want me to do 'it,' why do you want me to sing about 'it'?"). Porter plays tricks with the audience: we first think that the antecedent of "it" is sex, but the *faux naïf* speaker is more loftily proposing not sex but love:

> *And that's why Chinks do it, Japs do it,*
> *Up in Lapland, little Lapps do it,*
> *Let's do it, let's fall in love.*

(Seeking not to offend, Porter changed the opening lines of the first refrain to "Birds do it, bees do it, / Even educated fleas do it," etc.) Some years later, in *Esquire*, Gilbert Seldes wrote that "Porter discovered the facts of life and zoology at the same time—he became the great leader of the habits of rabbits school of popular song . . . He worked this vein, if not to death, certainly to corruption. 'Let's Do It' is the best of the kind."

"You've Got That Thing," written for *Fifty Million Frenchmen* (1929), is another instance of suggestion. We're never told what "that thing" is:

> Your fetching physique is hardly unique,
> You're mentally not so hot;
> You'll never win laurels because of your morals,
> But I'll tell you what you've got
> You've got that thing, you've got that thing,
> That thing that makes birds forget to sing.
> Yes, you've got that thing, that certain thing.

That the undefined "thing" has some sexual import Porter makes clear in the four-line alternate finish he composed:

> You've ideas inside your head
> That make me order an extra bed
> With an extra spring.
> You've got that thing.

Another and less well-known song that Porter wrote for this show is "Don't Look at Me That Way."

> When you tell me sweetly you're mine completely,
> I always give a long cheer;
> But those sudden flashes behind your lashes
> Are nobody's business, dear.
> Since you began to play your role,
> I've lost my heart and I've lost my soul
> But as for losing my self-control,
> Don't look at me that way!

A cautionary tale, but at the same time the typical "sweets of sin" theme which delivers a delicious shiver to the listener. Another song from 1927 introduced at the Café des Ambassadeurs, "Let's Misbehave" was used in the original score of *Paris* but was replaced by "Let's Do It" before it opened in New York. The verse impudently asks: "If you want a future, darling / Why don't you get a past?" and then seductively suggests how:

> *It's getting late*
> *And while I wait,*
> *My poor heart aches on,*
> *Why keep the brakes on?*
> *Let's misbehave.*
> *I feel quite sure,*
> *Un peu d'amour*
> *Would be attractive,*
> *While we're still active,*
> *Let's misbehave.*
> *You know my heart is true,*
> *And you say, you for me care;*
> *Somebody's sure to tell,*
> *But what the hell do we care?*

Then comes the zoological bit:

> *They say that bears*
> *Have love affairs,*
> *And even camels;*
> *We're merely mammals,*
> *Let's misbehave.*

With the success of several such "bright and snappy tunes" Porter's star was in its ascendancy. His next venture was to write the score for a revue produced by Charles B. Cochran with a mere thread of a plot. Cochran described the origins of *Wake Up and Dream* in the *Star*. John Hastings Turner, author of the book, Porter, and Cochran conferred many times. All made suggestions about songs, scenes, dances, etc. and Cochran acted as a kind of editor-in-chief discarding and appraising. The show starred Jessie Matthews and her husband, Sonnie Hale, Tillie Losch, a stunning dancer who co-choreographed the show, and George Metaxa. The show opened at the London Pavilion on March 27, 1929, and ran for 263 performances.

Later *Wake Up and Dream* moved to New York, where it opened on December 30, 1929, and ran, in that ill-starred year of the stock market crash, for 136 performances. The debonair Jack Buchanan joined the cast in New York. One of the scenes in the play mentioned by many critics was "San Francisco—the Gold Rush, 1849," about which Cole Porter had knowledge and sentiments conveyed to him by his grandfather. "The Banjo That Man Joe Plays" may have derived from an anecdote J.O. told to Cole.

> *When that man Joe*
> *Makes that banjo*
> *Play that old tune I adore,*
> *San Francisco,*
> *Dear old Frisco,*
> *Calls me 'cross the prairies once more.*
> . . . .
> *Whenever Joe starts that old song of mine,*
> *Somehow my mem'ry strays*
> *Back to the Gold Coast in forty-nine.*

The Gold Rush figures as well in a song called "Entrance of Emigrants," whose lyric links to the theme of *Within the Quota,* but its mood is scoffing, poking fun at those who upon hearing of the discovery of gold in California "hopped aboard a clipper / And simply told the skipper / To take us to the Golden Gate." Counted among the emigrants are "the Astors, the Vanderbilts, the Morgans, and the Fricks, the Mackays [Irving Berlin's in-laws] and the Guggenheims."

The title song is replete with Porter's philosophy and shaped probably by his Worcester Academy skirmish with Plato and his lifelong belief in seizing the day. "Every moment you're bored is a sword / Of hari-kari in you." (These verses show Porter's skill with internal rhymes.)

> *If you wake up, you'll find you've the mind*
> *Of Master Barrie in you.*
> *Listen, young man,*
> *You were once Peter Pan*
> *And you've simply forgotten your theme,*
> *Wake up and dream.*

The haunting "I Loved Him, but He Didn't Love Me" was sung in the English production by Jessie Matthews (The *Sunday Pictorial* urged that this song be dropped as "too cruel," and it was dropped from the New York Production.) "Looking at You" was lifted from *La Revue des Ambassadeurs* and brightened the score of both the London and New York productions. Leslie Hutchinson performed in the show and was praised on all sides. The London *Sunday Express* printed the vociferous demand by his fans that he not remain in the pit but appear on stage. Hutch was described as being at his best when he was playing "Looking at You" and the orchestra accompanied him "with a delightful counter-melody."

"What Is This Thing Called Love?" is perhaps the loveliest song in *Wake Up and Dream,* and both words and music are echt Porter.

> *Love flew in through my window,*
> *I was so happy then.*
> *But after love had stayed a little while,*
> *Love flew out again.*
>
> *What is this thing called love?*
> *This funny thing called love?*
> *Just who can solve its mystery?*
> *Why should it make a fool of me?*
> *I saw you there one wonderful day.*
> *You took my heart and threw it away.*
> *That's why I ask the Lord in heaven above,*
> *What is this thing called love?*

When Walter Winchell heard the score, he singled out "What Is This Thing Called Love?" for praise and predicted that it would be remembered. Winchell was right: in 1945 it was listed one of the top forty all-time song favorites in the United States. Nearly every review complimented the composer for this song: one spoke of its "wailing, moaning, anxiety-making quality." The insistent rhythm parallels the poignant melody. Cole Porter later told an interviewer that the title gave him a haunting melodic phrase and the song practically wrote itself: the words and music formulated themselves almost simultaneously in his mind. The whole song was the work of a few hours.

"Operatic Pills" brought Porter back to Sir Thomas Beecham and their Venetian exchange. This song from *Wake Up and Dream* (alternatively titled "If You Take One Pill") bemoans the English preference for revues over operas.

> *'Twould be infinitely prop'rer*
> *If they went to hear the op'ra*
> *'Stead of going to these barbarous revues.*
> *So, convinced that the British nation*
> *Cares for nothing but syncopation,*

> *I have sworn that their education*
> *Somehow I will form.*
> *I'm determined that I shall teach 'em,*
> *And decided the way to reach 'em,*
> *As a dutiful son of Beecham*
> *Is in pill form.*

Emerald Cunard gave a party in honor of Cole Porter and insisted oddly that each of her guests make a speech on politics and music. "This cast a slight gloom over the party," wrote one reporter, "as everyone was in trepidation that they would be called upon next to deal with this difficult subject, and most people's fears were justified, as very few escaped Lady Cunard's single eye. In fact Lady Stanley was forced to take cover under the table in order to avoid oratory. The display of jewels was remarkable: every female arm was adorned from elbow to wrist . . . Lady Mendl had a cluster of cabochon emeralds . . . on one of her bracelets, and Mrs. Reggie Fellowes wore the most lovely necklace of the same stones."

"I'm a Gigolo" is droll but tragic too in its depiction of the man whose nature has in it a dash "of lavender" and who is fated to find himself beside "some dowager who's wealthy rather than passionate." "Ev'ry twenty-fifth of December" he gets "stocks and bonds from faded blondes" rather than love. "The Extra Man" is another number intended for *Wake Up and Dream,* but not used, where the man feels "quite the most pathetic of all the clan." Of course Porter had averted this fate by marrying an understanding woman who loved him. But he seems throughout his life to have had an especially deep sympathy for lonely males.

Wake Up and Dream had a bumpier time in America, where many reviewers compared it unfavorably to *Charlot's Revue* and Noël Coward's *This Year of Grace.* Cole was referred to as "the expatriate," and John Mason Brown called the revue "flat."

Despite the American rejection of *Wake Up and Dream,* by 1929 Cole had shed his losing streak and gained the respect of the critics: "Porter is a young American," wrote one, "who spends his time between Paris and Venice. Last year he wrote more New York hits, than any American composer. Perhaps the greatest tribute to his ability as a song writer is that Irving Berlin has signed him up to do the music of a revue which will be presented at Irving Berlin's Music Box Theatre in New York in the autumn." This was *Fifty Million Frenchmen.* Berlin originally thought that he might write the score, but when he read the story, with its Parisian setting and decadent or bohemian characters, he correctly concluded that this was not

material that suited him. Porter was clearly the man for the job. It was produced by E. Ray Goetz and staged at the Lyric Theatre.

In these late-1920s shows Porter had many hits, but he complained to a
critic at the start of 1930: "No sooner am I engaged to write the lyrics and
music of a revue than the producer comes to me and asks me to be sure and
write him a few hit numbers. Of course he realizes that nobody can predict
which tune will catch on with the public, and which will not . . . No one
can tell beforehand a song that will gain wide popularity. All a composer can
do is write the melodies as he feels them and then hope for the best."

Fifty Million Frenchmen opened on November 27, 1929, after a tryout in
Boston. It had a book by Herbert Fields and was directed by Monty Woolley. *The New York Times* made an effort to profile Porter and his art as the
twenties segued into the thirties:

The words and music leap light-footed from Cole Porter—the Mr.
Porter who never wrote a mammy song, who never even whirled away
an idle hour in wheedling thoughts of Dixie out of his boxed piano . . .
The local loop may fight back starvation for however long they can
bandy 'blue' and 'you.' Mr. Porter does not. He looks about with an eye
for subtle things, and so his song stories are apt to be satirical treatments
of little but unblushing girls and the piquant matters that lead up to her
jewels and motors . . . Then too you learn about life from Mr. Porter's
biological ballads . . . It has been plain to the point of irritation that
Mr. Porter has worked when, and no oftener than he chose to. Though
it detracts from the ethics of a struggle-and-success story, his ballads are
shot through with a quality of cynical ho-hum that breathes of the Ritz
and the Lido.

"Cole Porter," said Moss Hart once to Agnes de Mille, "was the greatest
amateur [I] ever met." "By this he meant," said de Mille, "that Porter wasn't
a man of the theatre." Others have a different view. The producer Carmen
Capalbo calls Porter "a great man of the theatre."

"The best musical comedy I have seen in years" was one puff offered by
Berlin; and another: "It's worth the price of admission to hear Cole Porter's
lyrics." Otherwise the critics were tepid, and some feel that Berlin's public
endorsement of the show was what kept it alive, especially at that econom-
ically depressed time. There is, of course, the view (probably true too) that
Fifty Million Frenchmen and other musicals in the 1930s afforded a few
hours of escape from financial, not to say political, worries, and so ironically

people spent prodigally for admission to theatre and films, in fact diminishing their already shrunken funds.

Fifty Million Frenchmen is the tale of a rich young American male in Paris who bets a friend that without his line of credit for a month he can nonetheless win the love of a young woman dear to him. He makes money by working as a magician, a gigolo, and a tour guide, which facilitates the depiction of many Parisian venues familiar to Porter: Longchamps, the Ritz bar, the American Express, the Café de la Paix among others. Porter the lyricist, like all storytellers, reveals himself in amusing ways. The show originally opened at the Ritz bar with the male ensemble singing "A Toast to Volstead"—the congressman who introduced the Eighteenth Amendment, prohibiting the sale of liquor in the United States. For whatever reason, the number was dropped five weeks into the New York run, perhaps because Volstead was still alive. The male chorus wish

> . . . *a long life to Volstead,*
> *Our senator from heaven sent.*
> *Let us give our endorsement*
> *To his act of enforcement,*
> *What a noble experiment!*
> *Let's sing a swan song to liquor*
> *That blight with which we once were cursed.*
> *Here's a long life to Volstead,*
> *And I hope he dies of thirst.*

The naughty nine lines in French attached to this seem not quite to follow:

> *Bonsoir, ma cherie,*
> *Comment allez-vous?*
> *Bonsoir, ma cherie,*
> *Je vous aime beaucoup.*
> *Avez-vous un fiancé?*
> *Ça ne fait rien.*
> *Voulez coucher avec moi*
> *Ce soir?*
> *Oui, oui, combien?*

Volstead was a natural target for Porter, who opposed the Puritan tendency of some Americans to try to legislate against personal freedom, especially sexual freedom.

Porter has been accused of racial prejudice by some, who cite, for example, a song from *Fifty Million Frenchmen* titled "The Happy Heaven of Harlem":

> *There's a happy heaven of Harlem*
> *In a country over the sea*
> *Where there ain't no rule*
> *Against white mule*
> *And all lovin' is free.*
> *There's a happy heaven of Harlem,*
> *Twice as nice as heaven above,*
> *Where you're never blue*
> *'Cause all you do*
> *Is eat, sleep and make love . . .*

A number of people have commented on the insensitivity of these verses. Of course they depict the typical naiveté and insensitivity of some white Americans in the early decades of the twentieth century. Cecil Beaton, replying to the question "Why do you think T. S. Eliot was anti-Semitic?," said, "Dear boy, why ask me that? Why did Cole Porter detest colored people?" Of course, Beaton's words in interviews and in his *Self-Portrait with Friends* and *The Selected Diaries of Cecil Beaton* have reportedly been unreliable. Monty Woolley apparently told David Grafton, one of Porter's biographers, that he and Cole often went to Harlem for sex. "Harlem was regarded as the next-best thing to an anything-goes madcap heaven in Depression-bound America. Woolley, with that intensity he gave to the first reading of a play he was about to direct, extolled the physical virtues of the young black studs who inhabited the many houses of male prostitution that dotted the Harlem landscape during this period. A favorite 'house' for Cole and Monty was an establishment operated by Clint Moore . . . Whenever Monty and Cole visited this house they first would spend a prolonged period in Moore's ornate offices, sipping the finest French champagne from Baccarat crystal flutes. Then Moore's newest male acquisitions were paraded around the office for their approval." According to the historian Eric Garber, "Moore had a fondness for celebrities, and his parties allegedly attracted luminaries like Cole Porter, Cary Grant, and society page editor Maury Paul." Porter always paid for sex, according to his friend Arnold Saint Subber. But there is no evidence that he treated these men cruelly or felt in any fashion superior to them.

Porter worked on another and probably earlier version of "The Happy Heaven of Harlem," titled "The Heaven of Harlem." His advice here is: Go sing in Paris,/You'll be an heiress/Soon,/Coon. "My Harlem Wench" plays with the same theme:

> *When for red-hot kisses I'm thirsty*
> *Then my thirst I just gotta quench*
> *But the more I take,*
> *The more I ache*
> *For my Harlem wench.*

None of these songs would be published today, at least not with approval. But the attitude of the late 1920s was different and perhaps even found such lyrics friendly. Porter could be patronizing with blacks, but he also associated them with spontaneity and vigor—qualities he greatly admired. And one must not forget his great admiration of the art and charm of Lena Horne, Ella Fitzgerald, Mabel Mercer, Hutch, Bricktop (who was his houseguest in Venice), and many other black performers.

Dropped before the New York opening of *Frenchmen* was "The Queen of Terre Haute," which displays Cole sending himself up:

> *For instead of being famous*
> *I'm an unknown ignoramus*
> . . . .
> *Why did the gods decree*
> *That I should only be*
> *The Queen of Terre Haute?*

Robert Kimball labels "You Do Something to Me" as "*Frenchman*'s most famous song," and this seems true. By now it has attained the stature of a standard, because both the ecstatic lyric and the amorous tune are convincing and recognizable. It is one of the many times Porter's art stirs recognition in the listener and offers a vocabulary for feelings that would otherwise be inarticulate.

> *You do something to me,*
> *Something that simply mystifies me.*
> *Tell me, why should it be*
> *You have the pow'r to hypnotize me?*
> *Let me live 'neath your spell,*

> *Do do that voodoo that you do so well,*
> *For you do something to me*
> *That nobody else could do.*

"Find Me a Primitive Man" announces:

> *I could be the personal slave*
> *Of someone just out of a cave.*
> *The only man who'll ever win me*
> *Has gotta wake up the gypsy in me.*
> *Find me a primitive man.*

There's also the racy "I'm Unlucky at Gambling":

> *I went to Monte Carlo the other day,*
> *I went to Monte Carlo to have some play;*
> *I went to Monte Carlo and, straightaway*
> *I went and fell in love with a croupier.*

"It's bad enough to lose your purse," sings the overwrought mademoiselle, "but when you lose your heart, it's even worse." The narrative continues:

> *I took the croupier to a picture show,*
> *I took the croupier to a picture show,*
> *And though I snuggled close when the lights were low,*
> *The croupier impressed me as rather slow.*
> *I said I like John Gilbert a lot, don't you?*
> *I said I like John Gilbert a lot, don't you?*
> *He didn't answer but when the show was through*
> *I realized that he liked John Gilbert too.*

This is the first of Porter's lyrics that allude to homosexuality.

"The Tale of the Oyster," previously titled "The Scampi," had earlier amused Venetian society. Porter reworked the lyric and inserted it in the score of *Fifty Million Frenchmen*. The words as well as the music appear to be a parody of a Schubert song, perhaps "The Trout."

> *Down by the sea lived a lonesome oyster,*
> *Ev'ry day getting sadder and moister.*
> *He found his home life awf'lly wet,*

> *And longed to travel with the upper set.*
> *Poor little oyster.*

Not very different from the frog prince or many of the melancholic myths poets provided for the Romantic composers. A kind fate brings the oyster to the Park Casino (a favorite boîte when Porter was in New York), where the chef places him on the menu.

> *See him on his silver platter,*
> *Watching the queens of fashion chatter.*
> *Hearing the wives of millionaires*
> *Discuss their marriages and their love affairs.*

The oyster is consumed by the rich Mrs. Hoggenheimer, gliding "to the middle of her gilded insides." After lunch Mrs. H. feels unwell and decides to return on her yacht to Oyster Bay. Then the song grows *agitato*:

> *Off they go thru the troubled tide,*
> *The yacht rolling madly from side to side.*
> *They're tossed about till that poor young oyster*
> *Finds that it's time he should quit his cloister.*
> *Up comes the oyster.*

Writing in the *Evening Graphic*, Gilbert Seldes found *Frenchmen* "as near to a perfect musical as you are likely to see" but objected to "The Tale of the Oyster": "It should be cut out instantly as it has no virtue whatever." And shortly after that it was cut. Seldes was only one of several critics who objected to all the animal imagery. Earlier on, the critic of the *New York Telegram* wrote that "among the Elegansia they're asking if Cole Porter . . . frightened in his cradle by a box of animal crackers—is an officer of the Humane Society, while the intelligentsia are murmuring, with lifted eyebrows, polysyllabic uncertainties about zoo fixations." In reply Cole said, "I love animals . . . I was born next door to a circus. Frequently we used to go hunting tigers down the main street and find elephants swimming around in our back yards. It's literally true about the elephants. I was born in Peru, Indiana, which, as everybody knows, is the home of circuses. And once there was a flood and two of the elephants were drowned and washed up in our back yard. I began feeling sorry for animals right then and there . . . Of course there's something to be said for flowers," alluding no doubt to his best-selling "Old Fashioned Garden."

Everyone admired the speed with which Porter worked. He had arrived in New York on August 20, 1929, having sailed from Paris aboard the *Vulcania* and on November 27 *Frenchmen* opened on Broadway. In an interview published in the *New York Herald Tribune*, Cole—commenting on the interviewer's statement that "for every tune that enlivens *Fifty Million Frenchmen*, six were written"—observed, "The sad part is that when I work on a song for a long time I usually have to throw it away . . . I wrote about thirty-five songs for this show and the ones that are in it now are the ones I did during rehearsals." This confirms the recollections of Fifi Laimbeer, whose socialite family were friends of the Porters'. When Fifi's parents died and left her and her siblings orphans, Cole found a part for the sixteen-year-old in *Frenchmen*. As Sylvia (a tourist), the young girl had ten lines to sing. She especially remembers rehearsals when a blustery Monty Woolley, Muriel cigar in his mouth, would shout out to Porter, "We need two minutes of music to let people get off!" Cole sat down and dashed off the music. Said Leonard Bernstein decades later, "Writing for musical comedy was harder than writing for a symphony . . . [when] you are your own boss. If you are writing for a musical comedy you are subject to dozens of strictures. You finish a piece and the choreographer calls up and says, 'I will have to have six more measures of this. I can't get the ballerina off the stage.'"

Fifi's first dinner party was one that Cole gave at the Ritz (then at Madison Avenue and Forty-seventh Street). Fred and Adele Astaire were there, as was Douglas Cosden, "a great friend of Cole's who owned oil wells." Fifi remembers Cosden's purple Rolls-Royce with gold fittings, in which he drove her home. She married and left the theatre but often sent opening-night telegrams to Cole. His typical reply was: "Thank you for your opening-night telegram. Cole." Once, soon after a son was born to her, Porter sweetly inquired, "Do you know of a young man, twenty-four hours old, that I can star in my new show?" Porter, she recalls, could be snobbish. "He disliked boring people and tremendously valued people who enlivened dinner parties."

One element in *Frenchmen* that did not survive the Boston tryout was the brief ballet "The Snake in the Grass," staged by Léonide Massine, depicting a boy and girl dancing in the Bois de Boulogne. When the ballet was cut, one of the loveliest songs in the show replaced it, "You Don't Know Paree":

> *Though you've been around a lot,*
> *And danced a lot, and laughed a lot,*
> *You don't know Paree.*

. . . .
Paree will still be laughing after
Ev'ry one of us disappears,
But never once forget her laughter
Is the laughter that hides the tears.
And until you've lived a lot,
And loved a lot, and lost a lot,
You don't know Paree,
You don't know Paree.

In some ways this song seems a parting salute from Porter to the city he loved beyond all others. He seemed to sense that the zeitgeist had shifted from Paris to New York and that the moment when he was to reach his apotheosis had arrived with the 1930s. For much of the 1920s,

> Broadway pleased [Porter] so little and the imagined joys of travel tempted him so much that he washed his hands of the theatrical business. But . . . even after he had decided to quit and do nothing but travel and laugh at the worries of song writing, he was fashioning tunes and juggling words into lyrics. The virus was in his system and neither the Riviera nor Munich beer gardens could get it out. Porter came back as his friends on Broadway knew he would. For ten years he stayed away, trying to tell everyone he was not working but filling a trunk with manuscripts and scores just the same. He has learned now that he can't quit, but he stays away always as long as he can.

On April 22, 1930, the *Indianapolis Star* mentioned that Cole Porter of Peru, on a trip around the world, had written his latest song in the Malay Straits. He had sailed on January 1, 1930, with Linda and their friend Mrs. Herman (Dumpy) Oelrichs, for Venice via Hollywood, Hawaii, China, and Japan. Before his departure he had agreed that E. Ray Goetz, Herbert Fields, and he would write a new show in Venice, where *Paris* and *Frenchmen* were composed. Cole seemed to be enacting the advice he gave to the readers of a Syracuse paper in December 1929: "[Life] would get pretty dull if you didn't find something to work at. Just sitting back . . . and living off money is no fun. It would drive you crazy. You've got to have something to do." Once, when people were astonished at the Porter style of life, Cole said, "What they don't understand is that everyone lived that way then."

Chapter 7

Take Me Back to Manhattan

The list of Porter's 1930s musicals is glittering: *The New Yorkers* (1930); *Gay Divorce* (1932); *Nymph Errant* (1933); *Anything Goes* (1934); *Jubilee* (1935); *Born to Dance,* a film, and *Red, Hot and Blue!* (both 1936); *Rosalie,* a film (1937); *Leave It to Me* (1938); *DuBarry Was a Lady* (1939). In this decade Porter also wrote the scores for the unproduced *Once Upon a Time (Ever Yours)* (1933–34); the unproduced movie *Adios Argentina;* the unproduced *Greek to You* and *You Never Know.* Before 1930 Porter wrote successful songs and shows, and certainly he had many hit shows after 1940 (*Kiss Me, Kate,* arguably his finest single achievement, premiered in 1948); but such songs as "Night and Day," "Begin the Beguine," "Just One of Those Things," and "Easy to Love" remain Porter's signature tunes, telling us who Cole Porter was and illuminating both his and our ecstasies and desolations.

"All these [songs offer] sophisticated views of love; they express erotic feeling rather than tenderness or exhilaration; in them ardor is firmly controlled, even subordinated, to elegance of style," wrote Dale Harris about Porter's thirties songs. He continued: "In his music he showed himself to be wise to the ways of life, cagey, self-protective, something of an aristocrat in preferring restraint to the open display of passion." Display, no; but sublimination often seems to make his music throb with powerful passions just below the blasé veneer. True, too, is the observation of many that wit serves as a conduit of passion in Porter and also speaks in a special way to the habitués not so much of high society as of café society.

As the 1930s dawned, the Porters left New York for the West Coast and their first stop on what was to be a six-month trip around the world: to Japan, China, Indochina, and the Malay Peninsula. *The New York Times* reported that "Cole Porter started around the world . . . with a piano"—a "trifely-bored-piano," it is called later in the article—"and some notes on where a song might be expected to fit into a plot." The Porters were due to arrive in Italy by April, when E. Ray Goetz was to meet Cole and make further plans for the opening of *The New Yorkers,* which tried out first in Philadelphia where "Mr. Porter . . . killed some time by writing 'Take Me Back to Manhattan,' " and then Newark, New Jersey, before opening at the Broadway Theatre on December 8, 1930. Herbert Fields's book was based on a story by Peter Arno and Goetz. Elizabeth Marbury had first called Goetz's attention to the possibilities in the Arno book for a musical. She suggested it be called "Manhattan Parade." Monty Woolley directed a cast that included Hope Williams, Jimmy Durante, and his sidekicks Eddie Jackson and Lou Clayton and Fred Waring and his orchestra.

Girl Crazy, Three's a Crowd, and *Fine and Dandy,* were installed in Broadway theatres when *The New Yorkers* arrived. It opened in B. S. Moss's Broadway Theatre, then the largest theater in New York. For a time it was a big hit, earning a larger gross, but since it had to do a huge business—owing to the size of the house—it closed after 168 performances. Mrs. Joshua Cosden, "well known in turfdom," was the principal backer of *The New Yorkers.*

The plot of *The New Yorkers* featured the customary fluff that Porter found hospitable to his tunes. It tells the story of Alice, a young socialite (played by Hope Williams, who was herself in the Social Register but was dropped when her show-business career and divorce became known) and her romance with a bootlegger, Al Spanish, which leads her to many louche venues before Alice and Al are wed. Gangsters and their sordid situations scarcely seem the subject for the elegant Cole Porter, who was nonetheless an ardent fan of Dick Tracy in the funny papers. But because they are cardboard characters, these gangsters, and others who appear in later Porter musicals, have considerable comic effect. Or did have. If one thinks of how heavily cops and robbers were featured in entertainments of the 1930s, especially films, one can only conclude that tales of gangsters afforded audiences then, as to a great extent they do again in the 1990s, an opportunity to flee from harsh social and political realities. Porter escaped the Depression unscathed: although his mother invested in the stock market part of the fortune left her by J.O., Cole wisely did not. One of the songs he wrote for *The*

New Yorkers concerns "The Poor Rich," but it was dropped discreetly before the show came into New York:

> *I receive ev'ry morning*
> *A request or a warning*
> *That I help out some fund for the poor.*

Porter jocularly catalogs the woes of the rich:

> *I admit that big cities*
> *Have to have such committees,*
> *And they're all very worthy, I'm sure.*
> *But why don't they start saying prayers*
> *For poor millionaires?*
>
> *Have you heard that Missus Burr*
> *Has had to fire her pet masseur?*
> *And you can b'lieve me, baby, that was some rub.*
>
> *Have you heard that Missus Pennall*
> *Has auctioned off her kennel*
> *And all that she has left is one bitch?*

In an effort to make this play, which seemed to take lightly the underworld, more acceptable to audiences (not to say censors), it was depicted as happening in the dream of an exhausted socialite. Despite this accommodation, several critics anticipated the trouble it ran into with censorship. In a scene that one critic called "filthy," a white prostitute sang "Love for Sale." To suit the critics and other censorious people, the scene was shifted from Reuben's to the Cotton Club in Harlem, and the white Kathryn Crawford, backed by three girls, was replaced by a "colored girl." This was Elizabeth Welch, who had been brought a copy of the song by Peggy Hopkins Joyce and advised to incorporate it into her cabaret act. She did, and one night Irving Berlin, Monty Woolley, and Ray Goetz came to hear her and recommended her to Porter. She went on in January and remained with the show until it closed. For many years the lyrics of "Love for Sale" could not be broadcast on American radio. Probably because it was so maltreated, Porter referred to it as his favorite among all the songs he wrote. "I like it best because it's kind of a step-child . . . I can't understand it. You can write a novel about a harlot, paint a picture of a harlot, but you can't write a song about a harlot."

When the only sound in the empty street
Is the heavy tread of the heavy feet
That belong to a lonesome cop,
I open shop.

When the moon so long has been gazing down
On the wayward ways of this wayward town
That her smile becomes a smirk,
I go to work.

Love for sale,
Appetizing young love for sale.
Love that's fresh and still unspoiled,
Love that's only slightly soiled,
Love for sale.
. . . .
If you want the thrill of love,
I've been through the mill of love,
Old love, new love,
Ev'ry love but true love.

The uproar that greeted the song arose from people who refused to accept Porter's poignant depiction of a prostitute who is not blamed for her lot.

Other songs for *The New Yorkers* included "Venice" (a recurrent subject), "Say It with Gin" (intended no doubt to ridicule the prohibitionists), and "Sing Sing for Sing Sing." When Fred Waring played these songs on his radio show, prisoners wrote from Sing Sing asking for copies of the song to sing at Sunday football games as their official anthem—not quite the Yale equivalent, but the request amused Cole. More memorable are such contrasting, uptempo numbers as "Take Me Back to Manhattan" and "I Happen to Like New York" (with its triple rhymes):

I like the city air, I like to drink of it,
The more I know New York, the more I think of it.
I like the sight and the sound and even the stink of it.

The history of this song suggests the shifting character of the score. After the opening, Porter soon sailed off to Europe and while en route composed this song. He sent it to Ray Goetz, who found a spot for it in the show three weeks after the opening. Throughout the run Goetz made changes in the plot to lend it an attractive trendiness. Porter husbanded his ambivalence and wrote "Let's Fly Away":

> HE: *I've such a hate on Manhattan lately,*
> *That I'd gladly die.*
> SHE: *Your conversation excites me greatly,*
> *For so have I.*

They list the places and people who fatigue them, including "the Paramount's gaudy gilding"; the Chrysler Building; Texas Guinan, and Walter Winchell, who resented being mentioned and labeled Porter's reference to him as "mean" and "a travesty."

> *There's only one solution, dear.*
> *Let's calmly disappear.*
>
> *Let's fly away.*
> *And find a land that's warm and tropic:*
> *Where Prohibition's not the topic*
> *All the livelong day.*

Leaders of New York society mixed with Porter's pals at an *après*-theatre party hosted by Elsa Maxwell at the Ritz-Carlton for more than three hundred costumed guests. On arrival they found the walls covered with large posters advertising the newest books to be published by "Maxwell Publishers," including: *If You Would Have the Form Divine, Try the Elsa Maxwell Method; Galloping Through Society,* by Mrs. Vincent Astor; *Life's Hard Luck Stories,* by millionaire James B. Duke; and *My Early Training for Monastic Life,* by Laddie Sanford, a polo star and playboy. Guests were asked to wear costumes depicting the opposite of themselves. Elsa came as President Hoover. "Mr. Porter," a journalist reported, "the guest of honor, wore the uniform of a football player in the 'gay nineties' "! Linda came as a housemaid.

Reviews for *The New Yorkers* were mixed. Virtually all the critics quote the line "Park Avenue—the street where bad women walk good dogs." Broadway was agog, and a Tuesday matinee was held in Christmas week to allow actors in other shows to attend, including Fred and Adele Astaire, Ethel Merman, Fanny Brice, Clifton Webb, Al Jolson, Marilyn Miller, Fred Allen, and Ruby Keeler.

One of the more perspicacious reviewers was George Rosette writing in the *Jewish Examiner:*

"Take me back to Manhattan / That dear old dirty town." The satire
inherent in these lines has been concealed by a genius with a diabolic
flair for the concealment of satire. Their quaint, dry wit will not at once
be apparent . . . But then, this is not a review for stupid people. Such
would not understand the weltschmerz that must have led the writer of
those lines to only seem to scoff at Manhattan by calling it a dirty town,
while he really was choking back a wave of deep emotion that insisted
on finding expression in the use of "dear" and "old."

Interesting that the Brooklyn *Jewish Examiner* should have been the only
paper to comment on the plangent character of Porter's melodies. In 1926
Cole told Richard Rodgers that in order to have hit songs, "I'll write Jewish
tunes." In his autobiography Rodgers wrote, "I laughed at what I took to be
a joke, but not only was Cole dead serious, he eventually did exactly that.
Just hum the melody that goes with 'Only you beneath the moon and under
the sun' . . . or any of 'Begin the Beguine,' or 'Love for Sale,' or 'My Heart
Belongs to Daddy,' or 'I Love Paris.' It is surely one of the ironies of the
musical theatre that despite the abundance of Jewish composers, the one
who has written the most enduring 'Jewish' music should be an Episco-
palian millionaire who was born on a farm in Peru, Indiana." Cole himself
often referred to "Easy To Love" as a "Jewish song."

A recent commentator, Stephen Citron, disputes the accuracy of this
contention: "My ears tell me that some of this shifting from the major to
minor more closely resembles the ambivalent French chansons popular
around Pigalle than true Yiddish music. (None of Cole's tunes has the interval of a step-and-a-half, the augmented second, so much a trademark of
Hebraic or Jewish song.)"

On January 18, 1931, a performance of *The New Yorkers* was given for
Mayor Walker's Unemployment Fund, but Cole had already started on his
yacht trip around the world. And on January 31, Ray Goetz went to London
to arrange the opening of *The New Yorkers* there. Meanwhile, the fashionable press had discovered Cole. In February 1931 *Vanity Fair* published "A
Close-Up of Cole Porter," which profiled him in these words:

He is wholly unable to shave himself, which operation must be performed at an average of twice a day. He never carries a walking stick or
gloves and wears a hat as little as possible. Most of his suits are gray and
he has a passion for soft shirts with collars attached. He writes entirely
with his left hand, at an angle almost upside down. He loves a good

dirty limerick . . . His dislikes are many and varied, among the more pronounced being golf, steam-heated rooms, pressed duck, English railway hotels, Belgium, and poetry. He delights, however, in all kinds of scandal and crime news. He is five feet, seven and a half inches tall and weighs a hundred and forty pounds. In America he likes town; in Europe he prefers the country. He needs only five hours' sleep and, save for an occasional headache, keeps in pretty fair trim. During the writing of a musical show or revue score he lives with his music, day and night. He is able to concentrate on work in the centre of the liveliest doings, just as he is a fellow of many moods. He has often played for the King and Queen of Spain and the Prince of Wales. His Paris house in the rue Monsieur has a room done entirely in platinum. He is prone to seasickness and takes Mothersill's by the bottleful. He has studied at the Schola Cantorum in Paris, under the eminent master, Vincent d'Indy. In playing the piano he uses his left hand little—though with great effect. He whistles a fifth higher than he plays. He averages at least two baths a day and owns sixteen dressing gowns and nine cigarette cases. His favourite *hors d'oeuvre* is a *trenche* of melon eaten simultaneously with a slice of *jambon de Parme*. He is an ardent movie fan but doesn't give a whoop for baseball.

The author of this piece perpetuates a number of errors: for example, in Europe he seemed to prefer the cities, and Vincent d'Indy was never one of his teachers. But as a collage of Cole it succeeds.

In 1931 the Porters still spent a good segment of each year in Europe—Paris principally—and parties were still a preoccupation. That year Cole had written a string of wonderful songs for *Star Dust*. The book was the work of Herbert Fields, and E. Ray Goetz was again to produce. But owing to newly imposed tobacco taxes, the principal backer withdrew, and plans for the show were dropped. Believing in recycling as much as did Bach, Handel, and many other composers, Cole placed the songs for a brief period in the trunk. They included some of his best: "I Get a Kick Out of You," "The Physician" (first titled "But He Never Says He Loves Me"), "I've Got You on My Mind," "I Worship You," and "Mister and Missus Fitch."

Perhaps the most celebrated of Cole's hoaxes was one he concocted with Elsa Maxwell and a few close friends, involving a fictitious family he called Mr. and Mrs. S. Beech Fitch. As he customarily did, Cole cannibalized the Fitch saga for a song (it was finally sung in *Gay Divorce*). The Fitches hail from Tulsa, Oklahoma, and are parvenues who started out

On a farm far from pleasant,
No pair was more peasant
Than Mister and Missus Fitch.
Their days, each one duller
Were so lacking in color
They didn't know which was which.
When suddenly tilling the soil
Mister Fitch struck oil.

Again Porter satirized nouveau-riche Americans in a wickedly witty way. (In some ways the scenario seems a mock version of Henry James's stories about Americans in Europe.)

"Mister and Missus Fitch one day / Hit town, determined to play," and Cole announced their arrival in letters sent to newspaper columns, describing their progress in international society. Sonia, the Fitches' daughter, although she doesn't appear in the song, is featured in the letters; and from Nice a nephew of the Fitches wrote:

It is well for all to know that the U.S.A. is able to take the lead in art-work, music and writing as well as in business, politics and warfare.

I know what I am writing about for I have lived in Europe for nearly eight years but that is on account of taxes, prohibition, expenses, and my one desire here [is] that they should know all about the glory of Uncle Sam.

Mr. Fitch chimes in with similar chauvinistic sentiments: "The U.S.A. to all good Americans, always has been and always will be the greatest country on earth." As was true in his song lyrics, introducing the names of real friends of his into these letters gave Porter particular pleasure. Marthe Hyde, for instance, was said in one letter to have given a dinner attended by the Porters and the Fitches, who were going onto the Szechenjis in Hungary and eventually stopping with the Marquis de Talleyrand, "who has arranged for them an audience with the Pope." Another contributor suggested that Mr. Fitch forsake Carlsbad in favor of "one of the various homeland spas out in the desolate stretches of Indiana where everybody is 100 per cent American."

By now the imaginary couple had become sought-after celebrities:

And soon the crowd they call "elite"
Were fighting madly to meet
The young, attractive, and rich,
Mister and Missus Fitch.

Then Porter decided to halt the hoax by killing the couple off in an auto-mobile accident. He and Lady Mendl sent an obituary note to the papers, and soon after both Walter Winchell and "Cholly Knickerbocker" exposed the deception. The unfortunate Fitches fared badly in the song too—but came off no worse than the idle rich:

> *When they called for champagne,*
> *Champagne arrived.*
> *An aeroplane,*
> *The plane arrived.*
> . . . .
> *But when they called for cash*
> *The Crash arrived.*
> *Now men who once knew Missus Fitch*
> *Refer to her as a bitch.*
> *While the girls who once loved Mister Fitch*
> *Say he always was a son of a bitch.*
> *So, love and kisses,*
> *Mister and Missus Fitch.*

In the published version, "witch" and "son of the rich" are substituted for the offending words. Luella Gear, who presented the song in *Gay Divorce*, told Robert Kimball that "she had an arrangement with the show's drummer to drown out the allegedly offensive words so they could be sung but not heard."

Porter seems never to have lost his delight in hoaxes. A writer sailing from Le Havre on the same ship as Cole once stumbled into a trap when he picked up the phone at the Fraschotti Hotel in Marseilles on the eve of sailing and asked for a porter. The operator mistakenly rang Cole's room, and when the writer asked for ice water, Cole in a faked French accent asked countless questions about the size of the ice the man wanted. "He had me screaming with annoyance. I must have told him about 25 times just any size ice would do—just to bring a pitcher of ice water and not to mind the discussion. It was several days before I knew of the hoax."

Against a drab Depression background, the smart set continued to create a brilliant social life in New York and Paris. Ethel Harriman Russell (at whose wedding Cole met Linda) gave after-theatre parties in New York, and it was at one of these evenings in 1931 that Jean Howard, appearing then in the *Ziegfeld Follies* and who was to become the closest of friends with Linda and Cole, met the Porters for the first time.

In June of that same year, Baron Nicholas de Gunzburg, the wealthy young son of a banker, joined with Elsa Maxwell to host a "country ball" at an exquisite house which had been a small pavilion he rented from the city of Paris. It was in the Bois de Boulogne between the Seine and the Longchamps racetrack. The guests were required to arrive either in a horse-drawn carriage or by bicycle. Christian Bérard and Boris Kochno decorated the house and garden, draping the façade of the pavilion in blue, white, and red satin. They used giant paper flowers, artificial fruit, and domestic animals fashioned of papier-mâché. The lighting was indirect and made the place seem like a stage set.

The Porters attended in a Sicilian donkey cart loaded with orchids and gardenias. (This entrance was topped by Serge Lifar, who arrived on a white horse, his body painted entirely in gold.) Pictures of this sumptuous party show many of Porter's closest friends, including one of Lady Abdy, Dolly O'Brien, and Baron Robert de Rothschild milking a papier-mâché cow. Another is of Elsa Maxwell dressed as a peasant. "Cole and Linda were great friends of ours," writes Prince Faucigny-Lucinge, "and I remember with nostalgia those lovely evenings in their Paris home . . . when [with] Cole at the piano, Elsa Maxwell and Noël Coward improvised tunes and lyrics. Linda was very beautiful, and her world had been very different, but Cole gave her a bright and bohemian life which she loved, and I think that in spite of her husband's escapades theirs was a happy marriage." Among the partygoers with whom Cole and Linda mixed in those years were Coco Chanel, Georges Auric, Serge Lifar, and Arthur Rubinstein, who loved to sit at the piano and play Cole Porter songs. At Nicky de Gunzburg's *fête champêtre* Lauritz Melchior and Frida Leider sang the *Liebestod* from *Tristan und Isolde*.

In November 1931, Bricktop opened a club at 66 rue Pigalle. The photographer Horst, among others, accompanied Cole on some of his visits there, just as in New York, they would go to Harlem nightclubs together. Horst had met Porter in Paris in the 1920s, and their friendship endured, despite the fact that Porter could sometimes be cruel in his remarks: once when Horst was dressed in brown Porter remarked that "no gentleman wears a brown suit." Horst's lover of many years, fellow photographer George Hoyningen-Huene, had done the lighting of the large room, which seated about a hundred people. The walls were lined with banquettes, and Hoyningen-Huene "lit them from behind and created a cozy kind of mysterious atmosphere," according to Bricktop. "There were heavy patent-leather curtains across the door, and as you approached you could see only shadows—the silhouettes of people's heads." The carpet was red, the banquettes red and black. The general effect was stunning and caused a great sensation when the club opened.

So into the 1930s Cole continued his playboy life. "Because I had plenty of money, they began calling me 'Playboy' . . . you should have heard all the Broadway producers—Take a chance on a songwriter who's *prosperous?* Absurd! If I had climbed up out of the gutter . . . or if I'd once been evicted for non-payment of rent . . . if I'd ever been hungry, then recognition might have come a good deal sooner." A favorite refrain of Cole's as the years passed. But by 1932 and the opening of *Gay Divorce* Porter had attained international fame.

It was in 1932, Ray Kelly remembered, that he met Cole Porter. Linda and Cole were crossing from Marseilles to New York on a small passenger ship whose owners employed Kelly to work as a sailor. He met Linda first, when the captain assigned him to show her around the ship. A few days out to sea, he met Cole. (In conversations he repeatedly stressed his friendship with Linda.) When they disembarked in New Jersey, the Porters invited Kelly to visit them in New York. Having completed *Gay Divorce,* Porter was setting to work on a new musical, and Kelly took this invitation to be "a shipboard pleasantry" courteously extended by a man who was deluged with work. But on a subsequent visit to New York, he rang up the Porters and was asked to dinner. Over the next few years he "called in on the couple and met with Linda and Cole."

There is no doubt that, like Howard Sturges, a number of Cole's other friends were first acquaintances of Linda's, and that if they were not, and Cole felt they were destined to have any future with him, as we've seen, he would urge them to befriend Linda. In time, through Linda no doubt, Ray Kelly came to be a friend of various members of the Porter circle, among them Jean Howard, for whom he later named a daughter. He always found Cole "generous," "unable to save money." When Cole acquired a Capehart phonograph which people admired, he sent maybe forty of these to the admirers. (In the case of Porter's friend Michael Pearman, he sent two, which irritated Pearman, who felt burdened by Cole's excess.)

Meanwhile the Porters were crossing the Atlantic in a life that shuttled principally between Paris and New York. Marthe Hyde and her son, Henry, went to lunch on rue Monsieur some time around 1932 in what the boy considered a not terribly attractive house: dark drawing room at the head of the stairs and a dining room off it, in the corner of which stood a grand piano. After lunch Cole moved to the piano and played songs from *Gay Divorce,* which they had not heard as the show was yet to open. Among the songs was "Night and Day," which delighted them. Linda was present. Henry

Ray Kelly, c. 1945

Hyde remembers her as shy rather than cold, which some people judged her to be. At this time Sturges lived around the corner from the Porters on rue Madame and was often with them. Cole struck the young Henry Hyde as "comfortable in his own skin," "self-satisfied," "no hangups." "When Cole was young the tensions of his marriage didn't show," said Hyde.

Gay Divorce "came to be known as the 'Night and Day' show," said Fred Astaire, for whom the song was written. He didn't recognize it first as a potential hit, but it has been steadily such over the decades and is one of ASCAP's top ten money makers of all time. Tailoring a song to a performer's vocal range and style became more and more a practice of Porter's. Astaire was first skeptical about its being a song for him and undecided about accepting a role in the show, partly because he wasn't sure that he was ready to go it as a single after the retirement of his sister, Adele (his only dancing partner until then), following her marriage to Lord Charles Cavendish. According to one account, Cole sat down at the piano and played "After You, Who?" and Astaire was won over. The song, one of Porter's loveliest, was a particular favorite of Mabel Mercer's.

> *Though with joy I should be reeling*
> *That at last you came my way,*
> *There's no further use concealing*
> *That I'm feeling far from gay.*

For the rare allure about you
Makes me all the plainer see
How inane, how vain, how empty life without you would be.

After you, who
Could supply my sky of blue?
After you, who
Could I love?
After you, why
Should I take the time to try,
For who else could qualify
After you, who?
Hold my hand and swear
You'll never cease to care,
For without you there what could I do?
I could search years
But who else could change my tears
Into laughter, after you?

The melody to which this simple yet touching lyric is set aptly approximates the emotional state of one who is joyfully in love and simultaneously saddened by the threat of losing the beloved. "How inane, how vain, how empty life without you would be." Porter allows us to experience (or perhaps experience again) the melancholy that even the putative loss of a lover entails. What if I never met and fell in love with her (or him, as it was in Porter's life)? How inane life would be. But a more frightening feeling emerges from words and music, which suggest that love might yet disappear. So the lover emphasizes a list of losses he would suffer if he were to lose the beloved. He implores her to "Hold my hand and swear / You'll never cease to care / For without you there what could I do?" The fragility of love; the rarity of finding it; its capacity to light up the landscape; but the deeper darkness its disappearance occasions. The variation of short with long lines conveys the alternating moods of the lover, as do the rhymes and repetitions.

" 'Night and Day' has a long range," Astaire said—"very low and very high and it was long . . . and I was trying to figure out what dance could be done to it." Commenting on the song, Cole said, "I wrote 'Night and Day' in forty-eight bars, against the sixteen bars traditional in popular songs up to 1932, and I widened the voice range to four notes over an octave. Both innovations handicapped the song at the beginning." Cole was living at the Ritz-Carlton when he wrote "Night and Day." "I put the tune together, I remember, on a Saturday and wrote the lyric the next day while lying on a beach in Newport." In composing the tune before the lyrics Porter practiced a rare reversal of his customary crafting of the words first. Porter's locating the birthplace of the song in Newport lends credibility to the story of him lunching at Mrs. Vincent Astor's in Newport that weekend and listening to the steady downpour. Mrs. Astor is said to have remarked: "I must have that eave mended at once. That drip, drip, drip is driving me mad." Cole leapt up with a shout of elation on finding the perfect start for his lyric: "Like the drip, drip, drip of the raindrops." Porter appeared to have recovered from the discouragement that overtook him the night before when Monty dropped by and after hearing Cole play the music for "Night and Day," said, "I don't know what this is you are trying to do but whatever it is throw it away; it's terrible!" However, Cole said, he tried it on some of Mrs. Astor's guests and they liked it. Perhaps it was experiences like this that led Porter to say to a journalist about the theatre: "A crazy business, but lots of fun, mind you." (The etiology of the song was located half a world away from New York and Newport when Cole later told a reporter that he had got the music when, in Morocco, he heard a Mohammedan priest summoning the religious to prayers. One must not forget that this is the same man who invented the Fitch hoax.)

Gay Divorce opened at the Ethel Barrymore Theatre on November 29, 1932, after tryouts in Boston and New Haven. It starred Astaire and Claire Luce (a former Ziegfeld girl), and the supporting cast included Luella Gear (who sang "Mister and Missus Fitch"), Betty Starbuck, and Eric Rhodes and Eric Blore, both of whom appeared, as did Astaire, in the 1934 film version, *The Gay Divorcee* (the title changed to suit the censors, who could not concede that a "divorce" could be something joyous). Considerable critical attention was given to Astaire's first appearance on the stage without his sister. As it turned out, this was Astaire's last stage performance, as he left New York soon after for Hollywood.

Pandro S. Berman, the producer of the film version, recalled that when he approached the producer, Lou Brock, about RKO purchasing *Gay Divorce,* the arrogant Brock said, "I could blow a better script out of my nose than *Gay Divorce.*" But Berman had his way, and *The Gay Divorcee* became one of the two delightfully escapist films RKO produced each year. They didn't try to make it a backstage musical, but opened it up, emphasizing bright sets. Regrettably, the film features only one song by Porter— "Night and Day."

One critic called the New York opening night of the stage production "the most brilliant gathering of the season," and Cole Porter "one of the social and musical favorites of our international set." Perhaps it was the social credentials of the audience and of some of the players that led one critic to refer to Cole as "the international society pet." However, both actors and critics complained of the "brandied roarings of . . . Mr. Astaire's fashionable friends." Astaire later recalled these friends caustically: "We had a rather rocky first night . . . It was rather elegant . . . the Swells were really out that night! White ties, beautiful chinchillas and minks and jewels . . . they were rather obnoxious. They ran up and down the aisles and sort of talked to one another and that upset . . . us, on the stage . . . But when we came to the numbers . . . there were standing ovations and sitting ovations and lying down . . . ovations."

Nearly all the critics panned the book, now more or less familiar to everyone who has seen the Astaire/Rogers film, one labeling it a failed imitation of P. G. Wodehouse. Few, though, were the complaints about Porter's score. Burns Mantle wrote: "Cole Porter has done a fine job with *Gay Divorce,* with the music which sets him apart as a modest Gershwin and especially with the lyrics, which have wit and form and a provocative lilt. He can be audacious without being offensive, bold without being cheap, amusing without being low." Ring Lardner was even more rhapsodic:

Mr. Cole Porter . . . shares the mantle of W. S. Gilbert with Ira Gershwin, Lorenz Hart [et al.] . . . In ["Night and Day"] Mr. Porter not only makes a monkey of his contemporaries but shows up Gilbert as a seventh-rate Gertrude Stein, and he does it all with one couplet, held back till late in the refrain and then delivered as a final, convincing sock in the ear, an ear already flopping from the sheer magnificence of the lines that have preceded. I reprint the couplet:
     Night and day under the hide of me
     There's an Oh, such a hungry yearning burning inside of me.

But only a short time later Lardner was said to have complained about "suggestiveness and dirt in songs on the radio." These songs, said Lardner, "crop up in every review, largely under the influence of Mr. Cole Porter."

Two of the many congratulatory letters especially pleased Cole. One was from Irving Berlin, who, all in all, was the colleague Porter valued most. "Dear Cole," wrote Berlin in January 1933 to Porter in Paris: "I am mad about 'Night and Day' and I think it is your high spot. You probably know it is being played all over, and all the orchestra leaders think it is the best tune of the year—and I agree with them. Really, Cole, it is great and I could not resist the temptation of writing you about it. Love from us to you and Linda. As ever. Irving."

The other letter was from Dr. Albert Sirmay, dated February 2, 1933. Filling many roles—friend and music editor—Sirmay was Budapest-born and had himself written many songs, not to say a string of musicals which were staged in several European capitals. His best friend was Ferenc Molnár, on whose play *Liliom, Carousel* was based. When Sirmay emigrated to America in 1921 he worked primarily arranging and editing music. He was employed by Max Dreyfus, the head of the music publishing house T. B. Harms, which published Porter's work during the 1920s, and he became a faithful and discriminating amanuensis to Cole. Sirmay's salary was paid by Dreyfus, who himself was a man immensely important to Cole. Dreyfus and his brother, Louis, were music publishers all their lives. Harms was later acquired by Warner Bros., and in 1935 they left Harms and began a new music publishing house called Chappell, which became very successful. Max ran Chappell Inc. in America, and Louis ran the London office, Chappell Ltd. Porter told Robert Montgomery, his lawyer, that in early 1935 he was in financial trouble (or thought he was). He telephoned Max and asked if he could borrow some money. How much did Cole need? "Twenty-five thousand dollars." In the same hour Max arrived with a check for fifty thousand. Cole never forgot Max's generosity and resisted all temptations to leave Chappell for another publisher. Max lived in the Astor Hotel on Forty-third Street. Both brothers lasted into their mid-nineties.

In the old days the composers would assign the music to the publishing company except for the Grand Rights, and the company collected all the royalties. "An outrageous arrangement," Montgomery called it. Change came in the 1950s, when a composer would create his own publishing company, assign all the rights to that company, which would then work out an arrangement with Chappell to administer the copyrights, pay a royalty to the composer, and pay back about 50 percent of the profits to the composer's company. That is the reason Cole's lawyers founded the company called Buxton Hill. Cole owned 50 percent of Buxton Hill and 50 percent went to Chappell. After Porter died, the trust dissolved Buxton Hill and made a deal with Chappell that paid Porter's estate a larger percentage—75 percent in some instances.

Cole was reluctant to found Buxton Hill, fearing Max Dreyfus would be offended. But Dreyfus said Cole was the only composer who hadn't yet founded his own company and of course he should do so. Only then did Porter agree. He was very loyal to Dreyfus, with whom he had long telephone conversations. Cole was a person who valued loyalty in others and demonstrated it in his own life. "His loyalty was great," said Ray Kelly, recalling a night when Linda and Cole were discussing the soprano Grace Moore. Linda said: "Her voice is gone. She never did have a voice to begin with." "Cole immediately got up in arms and stomped around the place, had a big scene for himself, and stamped out without his canes. He was a terribly loyal person. If you once sat well with him you could do no wrong." Kelly, and Cole's bequest to him, was another example of Cole's loyalty.

Sirmay served George Gershwin, too, as music editor, and collaborated with Oscar Levant on an unsuccessful musical called *Ripples*. Some considered him a father figure to Jerome Kern, George Gershwin, and Richard Rodgers. In time he became the chief editor at Harms and later at Chappell. Sirmay faithfully took down the melodies as Cole dictated them. "You know," said Sirmay, "Cole was a highly educated musician. So he helped himself by dictating. He was a left-handed writer and it was not easy for him to write down music. But he gave me everything worked out to perfection. Occasionally I corrected a bar or two that I disliked, but I was an intimate advisor." Nonetheless, Sirmay was a better musician than Cole, and though the melodies came from Porter, it was Dr. Sirmay, some say, who supplied the harmonics. His chordal ideas were often superior to Porter's. Sirmay did the voicing of the chords, not changing a note of the composer. Perhaps Sirmay's greatest contribution was arranging the piano copies. He excelled at preserving the composer's intention and having, at the same time, a sense of what the average piano player could and could not do. He was a superb editor with a superior sense of how to syllabify the lyrics so that the right syllables coincided with the right notes. Porter's lyrics, insist many commentators, have the same musical quality as the notes. Therefore, Porter objected years later when Frank Sinatra sang "I've got, got, got you under my skin." "Don't sing it," he told Sinatra, "if you can't keep to the line I composed." Gershwin, unlike Cole, wrote out detailed piano parts to all his songs with harmonies and accompaniments exactly as he wanted them. Perhaps it was left-handedness that contributed to Cole's "novel way of working" with scores. He developed the habit of writing music with the lines and spaces of the paper facing him vertically instead of horizontally.

Porter was always squeamish about criticizing colleagues, not to say dismissing them. So he found Sirmay a convenient cover. "The Doc doesn't like it," he'd call out at rehearsals. Ray Kelly remembered that when a show was in preparation, Sirmay and Cole worked together for many hours a day. "At the Waldorf," said Kelly, "Cole had two grands back to back and he and Sirmay would play like crazy—Cole Porter tunes." Kelly recalled Sirmay as an elderly man in the 1930s. He remembered Sirmay's very thick accent and the practice, which Sirmay encouraged, of addressing him as "Doctor," despite the fact that he was, according to his nephew, merely a failed doctoral candidate in music at the Hungarian Academy. But his musical ear was indeed sensitive and discriminating, as Cole came to realize, and as a consequence he relied heavily on an imprimatur from Sirmay and was buoyed up by his praise.

However, Porter with his penchant for practical jokes sometimes found Dr. Sirmay a likely victim. (Sirmay was often the butt of people's jokes: perhaps it was the Hungarian accent. But he took it very well.) The composer Irving Caesar told of one such joke that took place in the Boston Ritz—Cole's favorite place in that city. The two composers were dining together in Cole's suite, discussing the two different shows they were trying out in Boston. After a few drinks, Cole said, "Let's call Sirmay," who was staying on a lower floor of the hotel. Cole got on the phone. "Dr. Sirmay," Cole said in a disguised voice, "get up here right away. There's a fellow here who's broken his leg." Sirmay said, "You don't understand, I am not a medical doctor. I am a musicologist." Cole shouted into the phone, "I don't give a goddamn what your specialty is. Get up here right away. Didn't you take the Hippocratic oath?"

In February 1933 Dr. Sirmay wrote the rue Monsieur to tell Cole, "It gives me great satisfaction that the victory which I predicted for your music didn't fail to cover [sic]. That goes especially for 'Night and Day' which can be heard all over New York, on the air and otherwise. I think this is the finest and most artistic song which has been written for many years. In the meantime I saw *Gay Divorce*. It was a delightful evening. That's about all I wanted to tell you. I envy you your Rue Monsieur. But come back soon." By February 1933 more than thirty artists had recorded "Night and Day," including Astaire, Hutch, and Morton Downey. And it was not only all over town that the song was to be heard. In 1935 Porter experienced what he called "the greatest surprise I ever had" when, arriving in Zanzibar, he went to a little hotel with a patio, and "all these ivory dealers from East Africa were sitting around in their burnouses and listening to 'Night and Day' being played on an ancient phonograph." The "surprise" must have been a pleasant one for Cole, although he added: "People like to think that composers get great pleasure out of hearing their songs played. I suppose some do. I don't, particularly."

Gay Divorce played 248 performances in New York before touring America. In November 1933 the musical opened in London. An English critic called it "an utterly sophisticated farce. It is beautifully dressed and daringly undressed. The main-spring of the humor is infidelity, and the sub-

Dr. Albert Sirmay with Cole

ject is garnished with . . . innuendo and . . . spiciness." Astaire, Claire Luce, Eric Blore, and Eric Rhodes traveled to London to do the show. W. A. Darlington, a critic of considerable stature, wrote, "Fred Astaire and Claire Luce 'stopped the show' last night at the Palace more completely than I have ever seen that feat performed." "Everybody loves dear Coalie," sighed the *Bystander,* using a name by which Cole's mother addressed him (and later, to his pleasure, Saint Subber). In later life Cole dismissed *Gay Divorce,* although not the songs. A friend who saw the 1960 revival told Cole that "it was no good." Cole replied, "It never was." Fred Astaire felt the same. His wife, Phyllis, came backstage after the opening and said, "What a dwedful [sic] audience!" He replied, "So is the show!"

Michael Pearman met Cole in a not unusual way—via Linda. When the Porters were in New York, both Michael and Linda often attended lunch parties hosted by Lily Havermeyer in her house on Sutton Square.

Eventually Linda invited Michael to lunch at her apartment, where he was introduced to Cole. Then Michael contracted pneumonia and, in those pre-antibiotic days, was ordered by his doctor to go to Arizona to recover. Linda, suffering as she did from emphysema, accompanied him. They went for six weeks to a dude ranch called Triangle Field. It was supposed to be *grand luxe,* but they both loathed it. The only excitement came when they went to Tucson and lunched in the El Conquistador Hotel.

Linda had sent her car and chauffeur out to Arizona as well as Weston, her Scottish maid, "who had been with her forever"; and afternoons Michael and Linda would drive in the country. Linda talked very little because she kept a handkerchief to her mouth to block the dust. Once she rapped on the glass and said, "Weston, where did you get that dreadful hat?" "It's one you gave me, Madam, it was one of yours." (When, many years later, Weston died, she left a large amount of cash in trunks in the Waldorf basement.) Maury Paul, in his column, "Cholly Knickerbocker Says," announced in April 1934 that in the winter of 1933–34 Linda for several months had been sunning herself in Arizona; she hadn't felt able to endure the rigors of winter in Manhattan. "She will return to us completely restored to health," Paul promised. Linda's plan was to pause for a month in New York before sailing for London. It was mentioned that she was to be seen often in the company of Lily Havermeyer. From the El Conquistador Hotel in Tucson she wrote to Bernard Berenson ("Dearest B.B.") to say how happy his letters had made her and how ill with grippe she had been. "When Cole sailed for London . . . I came, more dead than alive, to Tucson." She describes her medical progress and writes also about her bewilderment over business matters, investments, and the like. Along the way she denounces President Roosevelt for ineptitude. These two topics would not have interested Cole, and one wonders if they engaged Berenson's interest. "After New York—London to join Cole for his opening—No Paris this year. I cannot afford to open the house, which leaves me planless." Linda goes on to tell B.B.: "What I should really like . . . is to own a ranch in Arizona, spend at least six months of the year here & *feel well.*"

"The great love of Cole Porter's life was Eddy Tauch," said Michael Pearman. During the early 1930s Porter's intimates were Sturges, Jack Coble, and Ed Tauch, according to Coble, who was, like Tauch, an architect. Tauch surfaces first in Cole's life in the summer of 1933 when he and Cole were, as Tauch called them, "Wasserwanderers." That year he and Tauch took a three hundred-mile trip down the Danube in a small boat called *Steffi.* The two visited Augsburg, Regensburg, Passau, Melk, Vienna.

On this Danube trip Porter spent time with his friend Michael Strange, the writer (born Blanche Oelrichs of Newport), who was thrice married, once to John Barrymore, by whom she had a daughter, Diana. In pictures taken at Gmunden Strandsee other men are present—some very scantily clad, a few nearly bare-bottomed. Austria as well as Germany, in the early 1930s (as the writings of Isherwood and Spender demonstrate) were favored by homosexuals, and partly for the nude sun-bathing they offered. Perhaps all that inspired Porter to compose a song for *Nymph Errant* which was discarded during rehearsals. It is called "Sweet Nudity":

> GIRLS: *No hats to choose, no frocks to tear,*
> BOYS: *No studs to lose and no stiff shirts to wear,*
> GIRLS: *No ladders running up and down our hose,*
> BOYS: *No drawers to open and no drawers to close.*

Eventually Porter and Tauch visited Salzburg and then returned to France, a country Cole associated with an appealing hedonism in one of the songs he wrote for *Gay Divorce* called "I've Got You On My Mind":

> SHE: *You don't sing enough, you don't dance enough*
> HE: *You don't drink the great wines of France enough!*
> SHE: *You're not wild enough,*
> HE: *You're not gay enough,*
> SHE: *You don't let me lead you astray enough.*

Tauch was in some ways ill suited to Porter. "He was a crazy boy," according to Pearman, "but a good architect." Luckily he clicked with Linda and they became good friends. He came from a simple family. When Cole, who had never met them, invited Tauch's family to visit, he was shocked to discover they were German peasants. Horst, who knew Tauch in Paris and whose home in Oyster Bay was designed by Tauch, spoke of Tauch as "Porter's great friend, for whom he wrote 'Easy to Love.'" But another of Porter's pals disputes that and insists that Tauch was the lover for whom Cole wrote "Night and Day." The dates favor the latter opinion.

In June of 1933 *Variety* announced that Porter was back in Paris from Carlsbad with the script of a musical play to be called *Nymph Errant*. The book was adapted by Romney Brent from the novel of the same name by James Laver, an assistant curator of the Victoria and Albert Museum and art

critic of the *Daily Post*. Laver as an undergraduate at Oxford had won the
Newdigate Prize for poetry. His father, a part-time Methodist preacher,
never attended the theatre out of principle. Brent, a Mexican-American
actor and writer, had been appearing in Noël Coward's *Words and Music* in
the West End when the producer Charles B. Cochran requested that he
write an outline for a musical version of Laver's story. Porter liked it, and on
June 29, 1933, he and Brent met in Paris and decided that Brent would
accompany the Porters and their friend Mary Cass Canfield to Carlsbad,
where the two collaborators would work while Cole took the cure. The
scene Brent depicted at the Gare de l'Est confirms the style with which the
Porters customarily moved around: maid and valet, ample and elegant luggage. Brent was especially won by Linda's warmth and charm: "Nothing of
the bitch about her," he said, contradicting the impression some had. In the
sumptuous railway car, with separate bedrooms for Cole and Linda, bedrooms for the others, a drawing room, and workrooms for the servants,
Cole summoned Romney Brent to his room to discuss *Nymph Errant,* all
the while applying creams to his body, swallowing pills, and indulging in
other health routines. Brent thought it was freedom from puritanical shame
for his body that allowed Porter to be so at ease in these circumstances, as
well as on their walks, when Cole would swallow large draughts of mineral
water and from time to time wander off to use the toilets that bordered the
paths. In Brent's view, "Cole was a first-rate hypochondriac. He really had
nothing wrong with him. He was a man of forty-three or so, full of piss and
vinegar, but he thought he was sick and that this was doing him a world of
good."

Mornings after these walks, Cole would retire to work, usually from ten
until one. His habit was to require that a scene be completed before he
began to invent the lyrics. "In order not to make the songs seem intrusions,"
said Brent, "the music began long before the song came into the scene. The
music was there a long time before Gertie Lawrence began singing. That
was Cole's idea and he was one of the first to use it."

The part that Romney Brent played in the evolution of this show can
scarcely be exaggerated, for bad and for good. Many London critics praised
his adaptation of the Laver novel, although other critics faulted him for
bringing the heroine, Evangeline, through all sorts of threats to her virginity without her losing it—a dénouement quite the opposite of Laver's in his
notorious novel. Brent has her return to England still inexperienced and
unhappy; but having failed to be seduced at Neauville, the Café du Dôme
in Paris, a Venetian palazzo, and in a Turkish harem, she is finally (with a

nod to D. H. Lawrence) propositioned by the family gardener. The *Observer* critic called *Nymph Errant* not a play but "a pantomime for high-brows." Perhaps this helped dissuade Cochran from taking the show to New York. The costumes in the Paris scene were called "the most daring ever seen on the English stage" by another critic: a further deterrence, perhaps.

It was Romney Brent and Arthur Schwartz who convinced Agnes de Mille to act as choreographer for *Nymph Errant.* Despite the poor pay ($40 a week) she considered a Porter-Cochran show "the big time, and she did not hesitate to accept the offer." A choreographer's observations of a person's appearance are often revealing. De Mille remembers Cole Porter as "quiet and deferential . . . finely boned and fastidious." She thought his head to be shaped like a doll's and noted his dark, staring eyes. "He walks mincingly," said the dancer, "and very gingerly [this was 1933] with tiny steps . . . but . . . he is the most powerful person in this theater."

Just before the Manchester opening Cochran sent Porter a note saying, "I want to express to you my eternal gratitude. You have been a tower of strength not only in your own department but with valuable suggestions to the good of every department." It was about this time that Porter met Douglas Fairbanks Jr., a lover of Gertrude Lawrence's. Fairbanks recalls that *Nymph Errant* "had a big, ballyhooed preview at the Opera House in Manchester . . . It seemed to my starry eyes that much of the trans Atlantic theatre world came up for it . . . My old childhood friend, Agnes de Mille, who had been living and struggling in England for some time, had done the lovely choreography. I was as professionally pleased by her success as I was by Gee's [Gertrude Lawrence's] and Cole's triumph." (One of the dances de Mille created was what she called a "Greek dance." She asked Cole to write an appropriate piece in 5/4 time. "That should be interesting," said Cole, and quickly wrote a captivating bit of dance music.) Then came the great supper afterwards—Cocky (as Cochran was familiarly called) had taken over the whole of the large ballroom at the Midland Hotel. The *monde* was certainly there: Noël Coward, the Fairbankses Junior and Senior, Dorothy Gish, Lady Mendl, Elsa Schiaparelli, and, of course, Linda Porter had all traveled up to Manchester for the opening. In London, at a pre-opening performance on October 1, such royals as the Prince of Wales, the exiled King Alfonso XIII of Spain, the deposed King George II of Greece, and Princess Helen of Rumania attended. The performance purported to be a typical rehearsal and was broadcast from London to America. Some time earlier, Porter had dined with the Prince of Wales, who said to him, "Tell me about your score," referring to *Nymph Errant.* Cole said it would be easier to play it—whereupon the Prince clapped twice and three men entered the room pushing a Steinway grand and brought the keyboard right to Porter at the table. "Now that's what I call service," said Porter, describing the evening later to a friend.

On October 6, 1933, *Nymph Errant* opened in London and began "the Little Season." As in Manchester, police had to be called to cope with the crowds. Douglas Fairbanks Jr. called the audience "the most elegant-looking . . . I had ever seen . . . Cole was justifiably ecstatic, as was Cocky." Cochran always did things lavishly. Traveling to and from Manchester, he hired a private car on the railroad reserved for the cast and others connected with the production. A keg of sherry and proper glasses would be brought aboard and offered to all. After the show there were champagne parties. Elizabeth Welch, a featured singer, and her two roommates—Queenie Leonard and Anita Leslie (daughter of the Irish poet Shane Leslie)—would bide their time and then creep down the hall collecting discarded bottles. The drops that remained were used by these girls to shampoo their hair. Lady Cunard hosted an after-the-opening party which "the Duke of Verdura . . . helped make . . . most amusing . . . The Duke, better known as 'Fulco,' is a Sicilian, very gay and a perfectly wonderful dancer."

Fulco Santostefano della Cerda, Duke of Verdura in Sicily, (called a latter-day Benvenuto Cellini by some), went to work for Chanel in the 1930s and made a big contribution to her success, creating work, said Diana Vreeland, like someone from the Renaissance. (His cousin the Prince of Lampedusa was the author of the beautiful novel *The Leopard*.) Verdura had met Cole and Linda Porter earlier in Paris, and they remained fast friends for life; great admirers of his art, Cole and Linda often commissioned Verdura to create jewelry and decorative items, including the cigarette cases Linda gave Cole to commemorate the openings of new shows.

An unidentified reviewer called Porter's lyrics in *Nymph Errant* "the best the stage has known since Gilbert, because while achieving wit they do not leave out silliness and *are effective in the theatre* . . . Mr. Porter's music is the brainiest I have ever known in this type of entertainment." The writer quotes this couplet as "proof": "Though aware the place is nothing but a washout, / We get the jolly little mackintosh out." Among the verses invented by Porter for *Nymph Errant* are many other instances of clever rhymes. Gertrude Lawrence considered the show to have four big tunes, among them "The Physician," one of her numbers. Dropped from *The New Yorkers* and then intended for the unproduced *Star Dust,* it scored a success in *Nymph Errant.*

> *Once I loved such a shattering physician*
> *Quite the best-looking doctor in the state.*
> *He looked after my physical condition,*
> *And his bedside manner was great.*

But the patient's consuming question is "Do you love me, / Or do you merely love your work?"

> *He said my vertebrae were "sehr schöne,"*
> *And called my coccyx "plus que gentil,"*
> *He murmured "molto bella,"*
> *When I sat on his patella,*
> *But he never said he loved me.*

Porter's finding the rhymes for anatomical parts is virtuosic and very funny—as is the double-entendre.

Another illustration of Porter's sauciness appears in "Si Vous Aimez les Poitrines," a song from the score of *Nymph Errant* (1933). The refrain features the macaronic verses Porter enjoyed:

> *Si vous aimez les poi-trines*
> *Come to Gay Paree.*
> *Si leur beauté vous a-nime*
> *Come and call on me.*
> *I will show you how di-veene*
> *Parisiennes' poi-trines really are,*
> *If you promise me, you naughty boy,*
> *Not to go too far.*

"Experiment" is charming, and its message is the leitmotif of the show, and in many ways the motif, too, of Porter's life. The novices are advised by the worldly commencement speaker:

> *Before you leave these portals*
> *To meet less fortunate mortals,*
> *There's just one final message*
> *I would give to you.*
> *You all have learned reliance*
> *On the sacred teachings of science,*
> *So I hope, through life, you never will decline*

> *In spite of philistine*
> *Defiance*
> *To do what all good scientists do.*
> *Experiment.*
> *Make it your motto day and night.*
> *Experiment*
> *And it will lead you to the light.*
>
> . . . .
>
> *Be curious,*
> *Though interfering friends may frown.*
> *Get furious*
> *At each attempt to hold you down.*
> *If this advice you'll only employ*
> *The future can offer you infinite joy*
> *And merriment.*
> *Experiment*
> *And you'll see.*

"Neauville-sur-Mer" was originally titled "Deauville-sur-Mer," and its lamentation of the visitor trapped indoors by the rain there can be attested to by everyone who's visited that resort:

> *For here when the rain comes and drives you indoors,*
> *It pours and it pours and it pours and it pours*
> *With persistence so wearing, you find yourself tearing your hair.*

"The Cocotte" pairs with "I'm a Gigolo" as laments of social oddities who might be said to be the comic counterparts of the pathetic prostitute in "Love for Sale." "They're Always Entertaining," the complaint European servants voice about American employers, could easily have been whisperings Cole and Linda caught from the back stairs in their own dwellings:

> *Ev'ry day they ask a bunch*
> *Of celebrities for lunch.*
> *If you think that that is all,*
> *Ev'ry night they give a ball.*

This was sung by a sextet that included a young woman named Sheila Marlyn, who later was known as Sheilah Graham, F. Scott Fitzgerald's lover.

The score of *Nymph Errant* is a blend of wit and romantic passion that traditionally characterizes the Porter idiom. "How Could We Be Wrong" is a lovely ballad that Gertrude Lawrence introduced and which continues to be programmed by artists today:

> *How could we be wrong*
> *When we both are so set on it,*
> *How could we be wrong?*
> . . . .
> *Why should it ever die?*
> *Darling you and I*
> *Are too wonderfully happy today*
> *To throw it away.*
> *Now life is a song*
> *If we build a duet on it,*
> *How could we be wrong?*

According to Elizabeth Welch, two songs in *Nymph Errant* stopped the show—"The Physician" and "Solomon"—and she never could comprehend why they were placed back to back in the production. Before being cast for the part in *Nymph Errant,* early in 1933, Welch was performing at a night-club in Paris when Porter sent word to her, inviting her to 13 rue Monsieur for what amounted to an audition for a part in *Nymph Errant.* She recalls that he first sang for her "Solomon," which subsequently she made famous in the show. "He had a terrible voice," she remembered, "slightly high-pitched"; nor did she greatly admire his piano playing: "not much left hand," she said. But his face—dark, sad eyes, like a rabbit's, and gentle features—made her overlook his voice. When she arrived in Porter's home, Linda was just leaving and rudely ignored her. "Linda Porter didn't like me and I didn't like her," she said years later. "She was beautiful but pompous." When she learned that Linda grew up in the South, Elizabeth Welch said, "Oh, that explains it. She probably thought I should be in the cotton fields." Cole, though, Welch venerated all her life for the poignance, wit, and elegance of his work. "Irving Berlin," she said, "wrote for the general public but Cole for a much more sophisticated audience." She found him quiet, very dignified. "That he was homosexual everyone in the theatre knew, but it was not discussed."

At her audition, Cole told Welch that he had "dreamed up" a song called "Solomon." The song stemmed from an experience he had traveling in Turkey, where the sultan invited him to coffee. In the distance Cole could hear the concubines in the sultan's harem wailing in a melismatic manner.

When he left the premises, he immediately took down the melody, which had now re-emerged as "Solomon":

> So———olomon had a thousand wives
> And being mighty good, he wanted all o'them
> To lead contented lives;
> So he bought each mama a plat'num piano,
> A gold-lined kimono and a diamond-studded Hispano.
> So———olomon had a thousand wives.

Nymph Errant has never received a proper production in the United States. Despite Gertrude Lawrence and other strong performers in the cast, it enjoyed only 154 performances in London, and the film of it that Twentieth Century–Fox was to make never materialized. In 1957, terms were discussed for the acquisition of off-Broadway stage rights for *Nymph Errant* by Lawrence Kasha, who had been stage manager for *Silk Stockings*. But this effort was soon abandoned. Porter wrote to his lawyers to say, "I have no objection to an off-Broadway production of *Nymph Errant* . . . I feel that this is a very good score of mine but the actual book would have to be entirely re-written to be suitable for today." Perhaps Porter regarded this show as another badly treated offspring and so valued it all the more. No doubt he knew the worth of the score and sensed, quite rightly, that the songs would survive.

In late October Elsa Maxwell gave a party in New York and pared Mrs. Astor's "400" to 160, "eliminating the bores." It was held in honor of George Gershwin, Grace Moore, and Cole Porter. The newspaper account read "Exclusive Gathering Includes Notables of Music and Theatre." Four grand pianos were placed in the Astor Gallery of the Waldorf-Astoria, and both Gershwin and Porter played. Porter, aided by a pianist from the Paul Whiteman orchestra, also played songs from *Nymph Errant*. Events such as this gala amplified Cole's celebrity so that in 1934 a journalist wrote, "Cole Porter seems to have edged Noël Coward completely out of the spot as the reigning sophisticate. While he has none of the conversational acerbities of the Englishman, he has become almost a cult—the Indiana lad with the Buddha gaze."

Chapter 8

Anything Went

In 1933 Hildegarde, the chanteuse from Milwaukee, opened at the elegant Café de Paris, and Cole Porter attended with H. G. Wells (a friend of Linda's) and Charles B. Cochran. Later in life Hildegarde realized she hadn't sufficiently prepared for a stage debut. The audience was restive and inattentive. Sensing an incipient disaster, Porter and his party shouted out, "Sing 'Listen to the German Band,'" which was then a hit in Paris. The audience loved the song, and this saved the evening for Hildegarde. Other evenings in her engagement Porter returned to the Café de Paris with such friends as Lady Mendl. And in New York she and Porter met at parties hosted by William Rhinelander Stewart at River House—the same Stewart that Porter enjoyed teasing in the lyric of "Buddie, Beware," a delightful song dropped early in the run of *Anything Goes*:

> Now and then I like to see
> Willie Stewart and Company
> 'Cause I hear divine voices
> When their Rolls-Royces
> Come and honk for me.

Hildegarde found Cole "kind, gentle, very elegant," and undeserving of the soubriquet Gilbert Seldes gave to him in those years, "the leader of the habits-of-rabbits school."

In 1934 Arthur Arthur published a profile of Cole Porter subtitled "The Town's Topnotch Tunester Today," a description confirmed by the superb score Porter provided for *Anything Goes*. By New Year's Day 1935 *Variety* wrote, "This is the Cole Porter year. Almost every platter, chatter and radio gives out something by Porter." And indeed, critics today divide on their choice of Porter's best score: *Anything Goes* or *Kiss Me, Kate*.

It was Vinton Freedley's idea to create the show that became *Anything Goes*. That was in the summer of 1934, and Porter was boating on the Rhine with Ed Tauch. Freedley sailed to London that summer and arranged that Guy Bolton, living in the English countryside, and P. G. Wodehouse, living in France (and whom Porter several times over the years named as his favorite librettist), meet with him and Porter. In fact, when it was time to get together, Bolton, still at his country residence, had a ruptured appendix and resultant peritonitis, so Wodehouse took over. Eventually Wodehouse and Bolton devised an outline about the wrecking of a gambling ship, called it *Hard to Get,* and Freedley sent it to Cole. After a short while, Porter arrived in London with a collection of songs which captivated Freedley. Some of these had been in Porter's trunk; others he presumably turned out in a few weeks. Among the most enduring was "I Get a Kick out of You," which before its recycling had been a a song intended for *Star Dust;* Freedley paid Charles Cochran $5,000 for these measures of music. What did not please Freedley was the Bolton/Wodehouse libretto. Then the book, revolving around a shipwreck, was rendered useless by the terrible fire aboard the U.S.S. *Morro Castle,* a pleasure ship in the waters just off the New Jersey coast. Many lives were lost. Now this topic was suddenly devoid of any mirth: Freedley could hardly hope to fashion a comedy hit out of a plot that centered on shipwreck. Moreover, Bolton and Wodehouse by this time had other commitments and were unable to resume their efforts. Howard Lindsay, already engaged to direct the show, agreed to take the book on, provided he would have a collaborator. Cole was in Hollywood for the nonce, at work on the score before returning to Paris and a few weeks with Linda. Then he went back to New York and the rehearsals for *Anything Goes*. In a story Ethel Merman told, neither Freedley nor Porter—who arrived in the United States on August 16, 1934, aboard the *Ile de France*—was able to find someone for the task of co-author till Porter's friend Neysa McMein, a highly successful magazine illustrator, contacted Cole and told him that in a dream the name of Russel Crouse had surfaced. Apocryphal or not, the dream came true, and Lindsay and Crouse famously co-authored the book for *Anything Goes*.

They did the book in great haste, composing the final scene on the train speeding to Boston on November 5 for the opening night of the tryout. The first act had been written in ten days, and the second while the actors were rehearsing the first. When Donald Oenslager, the scenic designer, asked how he could do the sets for the second act, Crouse replied: "Oh, but you can do that at the rehearsal in Boston." "Having given us the backbone of the score, [Porter] had to wait for scenes to arrive in order to know the situations for the remaining songs," said Crouse.

> Mr. Porter was equal to all the emergencies we created and I think we hold the record. The show did not even have a name for days and days . . . Billy Gaxton finally baptized it accidentally. In answer to a question as to whether he would mind making an entrance a minute after the curtain went up, Mr. Gaxton replied "In this kind of a spot, anything goes!" We all leaped on the last words and an electrician started spelling them out in electric lights. Mr. Porter dashed off to write a title song. He came in with it the next day . . . Mr. Lindsay and I struggled for several days to get a second act started and found opening night sneaking up on us . . . Finally, one night, we telephoned Mr. Porter and told him there wasn't going to be any second act unless he could find a way to get it started musically. He came in the next morning with "Hymn to the Public Enemy," one of the finest bits of satire both musically and lyrically, I've ever heard . . . With the score Cole Porter wrote for [*Anything Goes*] nothing could have stopped it.

One critic, in an understandable but mistaken conclusion, wrote "Such works of art as Mr. Porter dashes off should . . . come out of anguish, of which Mr. Porter hasn't any . . . He is one of the gayest men I have ever met."

Ethel Merman, née Zimmerman (not Jewish, as many thought), had already been cast as the leading lady when Porter returned for the rehearsals. "Cole and I liked each other immediately. He said a lot of nice things about me, such as 'She sounds like a band going by.' People tell me he referred to me as La Merman and The Great Ethel." Others cared less for her, among them Ray Kelly, who called her "a stage bully." She did win the friendship of Kelly's wife, Virginia. The Kellys remembered an evening at dinner with Cole and Merman where the topic of both women's talk was domestic and especially concerned with how to raise children.

Odd indeed that Porter and Merman took to one another. It says something for the breadth of Porter's predilections that this singer from a simple Queens background appealed to him. All reports describe her speech as obscene much of the time; in the words of Garson Kanin, she had "the vocabulary of a longshoreman." Nonetheless, Porter submitted the book of *Anything Goes* for her parents' approval and rewrote "Blow, Gabriel, Blow" to suit her. This last is amazing, because Porter was famous for refusing to rewrite songs, preferring instead to begin anew. He said he'd rather write songs for Merman than for anyone else in the world. She, no doubt correctly, ascribed Porter's admiration to her fidelity to the text: "I never change a word. I also try, when possible, to include the verse as well as the choruses. I don't tamper with the melodies or rhythms." Merman starred in thirteen Broadway musicals in her career, and five were by Cole Porter.

Anything Goes opened in New York at the Alvin Theatre on November 21, 1934, starring Merman, William Gaxton, and Victor Moore; Vivian Vance was among the other cast members. Michael Pearman, a very handsome young man at the time, appeared in the show as Buddy Birmingham (near which city in Warwickshire he was born). Gaxton's character was called Billy Crocker—a nod to Cole's Yale classmate William Crocker, who helped finance some of his early theatre ventures.

In the show, Billy Crocker falls in love with Hope Harcourt and stows away on a ship she is taking to London. His efforts to win Hope are helped by Reno Sweeney, an evangelist who has given up the choir for nightclub singing, and by Public Enemy No. 13 (a.k.a. Moonface Martin), who has come aboard disguised as a clergyman. The show was an immense hit and was said by many to be the brightest moment in the theatre since the start of the Great Depression.

The songs cheered up many who could not attend the show but who heard the tunes on radios or in clubs. Reactions to the songs were raves. Porter, in an interview at the Boston Ritz, said, "My favorite tune in *Anything Goes* is a song Ethel Merman sings, called 'I Get a Kick out of You.'" The song is among the best of Porter's paeans to romantic love: it has dash, as well as the desperation the loss of love brings.

> *My story is much too sad to be told,*
> *But practically ev'rything leaves me totally cold.*
> *The only exception I know is the case*
> *When I'm out on a quiet spree*
> *Fighting vainly the old ennui*

And I suddenly turn and see
Your fabulous face.

I get no kick from champagne
Mere alcohol doesn't thrill me at all,
So tell me why should it be true
That I get a kick out of you?
Some get a kick from cocaine.
I'm sure that if I took even one sniff
That would bore me terrific'ly too
Yet I get a kick out of you . . .

The 1920s and early 1930s were times when cocaine was in considerable use internationally by members of café society, particularly in Paris. Not unexpectedly, Porter had problems with censors about this reference; but Robert Kimball assures us that "any substitutes for . . . 'Some get a kick from cocaine' are incorrect . . . 'Some like the perfumes of Spain . . . whiff' and 'Some like a bop-type refrain . . . riff' are particularly prevalent and equally objectionable." Presumably this includes the substitution of "Guerlain," which a Hollywood columnist attributed to Cole. On another matter Kimball is illuminating: he reminds us that the Lindbergh kidnapping occurred after this song was written, "so Porter removed the reference to Mrs. Lindbergh and revised the lyric." According to Merman, when Cole first delivered the song to her, the famous rhyme sequence "Flying too high with some guy in the sky / Is my *i*—dea of nothing to do, / Yet I get a kick out of you" was not in it. "Cole substituted that for some lines about the fair Mrs. Lindbergh spending nights in the air, for reasons of taste." His curiosity about Lindbergh's achievement was not rare. A somewhat related pursuit points to Porter's avid curiosity. In 1934 the Dionne quintuplets were born, and Cole, driving cross-country, suddenly changed his itinerary and sped to Canada in hopes of seeing the babies. "I got a letter," he said, "from Jean Hersholt, who played the part of Dr. Dafoe in the [movie version of the Dionnes' story]. When I got there I found that the doctor had never heard of me, and even the letter from Hersholt didn't get me in to see the quintuplets privately—only a letter from the King of England could have done that."

Merman recalled that Porter often rewrote the choruses of his songs, but not in "I Get a Kick out of You." "Of course, the line 'It would bore me terrifically too' I sang 'ter—riffff,' and he fell down. He loved that." From the start of his work on *Anything Goes* he knew who the leads would be: "Naturally I knew what type of song they sang and it made matters a lot more simple composing numbers for them."

Ed Sullivan in his widely read column described the swank of the New York opening of *Anything Goes:* "Many gorgeous girls and so many orchids . . . limousines clogging traffic, long lines of curious, special details of police at the Alvin, flare of photographers' bulbs." In *The New York Times* Brooks Atkinson said, "Cole Porter has written a dashing score with impish lyrics." And Robert Garland in the *New York World Telegram:* "Mr. Porter is the bold, bad, let's-call-it sophisticated, words-and-music man of America." The *Herald Tribune* reviewer wrote: "No less a minstrel than Cole Porter . . . is the composer of the songs, sentimental and ribald, in a hymnal fully up to his standard."

"All Through the Night" was written by Porter as a replacement for another of the most touchingly tender of his love songs, "Easy to Love," whose high notes Billy Gaxton claimed he couldn't reach.

> *All through the night I delight in your love.*
> *All through the night you're so close to me.*
> *All through the night from a height far above,*
> *You and your love bring me ecstasy.*

The melody that Porter invented to suit these lyrics is richly sensual: the song is another depiction of the Porter persona who can only find his beloved in a world to which the passport is nocturnal.

"Anything Goes," the title song, was a signature tune for both Merman and Porter and seems his broadest, most mirthful celebration of what the freer spirits in America have achieved in their tussle with puritanism. One critic, writing in 1935, saw *Anything Goes* as one of the American musicals that outclass serious drama even with regard to satirizing faults in society. "Kaufman and Gershwin led off with *Of Thee I Sing;* Hart and Berlin followed with *As Thousands Cheer. Anything Goes* follows in this vein. All in the tradition of Gilbert and Sullivan." Porter no doubt would have protested this as pompous, but there is truth to it.

> *Times have changed*
> *And we've often rewound the clock*
> *Since the Puritans got a shock*
> *When they landed on Plymouth Rock.*

. . . .

> *Good authors too who once knew better words*
> *Now only use four-letter words*
> *Writing prose,*
> *Anything goes.*
> *If driving fast cars you like,*
> *If low bars you like,*
> *If old hymns you like,*
> *If bare limbs you like,*
> *If Mae West you like,*
> *Or me undressed you like,*
> *Why, nobody will oppose.*
> *When ev'ry night, the set that's smart is in-*
> *Truding in nudist parties in*
> *Studios,*
> *Anything goes.*

In the second refrain Porter introduces names from the *beau monde,* many of whom were his chums. Rockefellers, Vanderbilts, and Whitneys are invoked, and in the third refrain, the Roosevelts:

> *So Missus R., with all her trimmin's*
> *Can broadcast a bed from Simmons*
> *'Cause Franklin knows*
> *Anything goes.*

(Simmons Mattress Company was a sponsor of Mrs. Roosevelt's radio show.) According to George (later Senator) Murphy, who in these years danced often with his first wife as stars of the show at the Central Park Casino, where Porter and his friends came to see them perform, the government brought some pressure on Cole to suppress these lines, but nothing came of it. (Murphy later also starred in a West Coast production of *Anything Goes.*) Whatever the White House's sentiments, it requested that songs from *Anything Goes* be included in its New Year's Eve party ushering in 1935.

"You're the Top" was composed in Paris, according to a *New Yorker* writer, Margaret Case Harriman, "during a supper at Boeuf sur le Toit when Cole and Mrs. Alistair Mackintosh entertained themselves by making up a list of superlatives that rhymed." According to one columnist, Porter considered the song "just a trick" and thought people would soon be bored by it.

You're the top!
You're the Colosseum.
You're the top!
You're the Louvre Museum,
You're a melody from a symphony by Strauss,
You're a Bendel bonnet,
A Shakespeare sonnet,
You're Mickey Mouse.

To make the lyrics of *Anything Goes* more suitable for the English audience, "an Ascot bonnet" replaced "a Bendel bonnet"; "Saks" became "Patou"; "Irene Bordoni" became "Tallulah Bankhead." No names of royal persons were used.

Eventually composing parodies of these lyrics became a popular pastime. In November 1934, Daniel Klein was among the many who sent Porter additional lyrics for "You're the Top," describing himself in a letter to Cole as "a struggling composer and lyricist." Porter replied, saying that the lyrics "are so good that if your music approaches them it is difficult to understand why you should be a . . . struggling composer and lyricist." The lyricist Mr. Al Stillman was paid two hundred dollars for some choruses he composed and was promised royalties if the choruses were used. Garson Kanin recalled that some of the parodies were "dirty." Porter himself wrote a parody which a radio station refused to let him broadcast. A Rhode Island churchgoer who had just seen *Anything Goes* wrote Porter: "Why was it necessary to bring so much ridicule on the church and to mention mockingly Bishop Manning, the Episcopal bishop of New York?" ("You're a Nathan panning / You're Bishop Manning / You're broccoli.") This New England puritan asked that the book be rewritten, omitting all references to religion.

Newspapers continued to report that the game around town in the winter of 1934–35 was writing new verses to "You're the Top," sometimes lewd ones. (What Porter's lawyer Robert Montgomery labeled "a fine ribald version" was written by Irving Berlin. It turns out that the mention of Mussolini was the contribution of P. G. Wodehouse for the London production and not Porter's work.) Harms, the music publishers, were prosecuting when they could. Some Porter songs do invite parodies, and in fact Cole was provoking parody when some years earlier he contacted his cousin Ted Fetter and encouraged him to compose parodies on "Let's Do It" and others of his songs. According to Fetter, "Cole would get stuck sometimes, he would call me up and say, 'Maybe you could suggest something,' and that's what I did. I did it on several shows and he used some of them." In 1935, when preparations were underway for the film of *Anything Goes,* Porter said, "I have engaged Ted Fetter to help me write lyrics for the picture version of *Anything Goes,* especially 'You're the Top.'"

In writing the song, said Merman, "What Cole had done was to analyze my voice and turn out songs which showed off its variety. 'You're the Top' brought audiences to their feet because it was a new kind of love song. There had never been a song like it before. A complete original. So I wasn't surprised that at the peak of its popularity Cole received three hundred parodies a month." Porter's favorite lines in the song were said to be in the fifth refrain:

> *You're romance.*
> *You're the steppes of Russia,*
> *You're the pants on a Roxy usher.*

Legend has it that Porter sometimes wrote, besides his frequently "naughty" lyrics, lyrics that could be called "dirty" versions. Not much evidence exists for this notion. In *The Collected Lyrics of Cole Porter* Kimball does print "the famous parody" of "You're the Top" often attributed to Porter, but written, in fact, by Irving Berlin. Garson Kanin was once present when Cole played and sang it:

> *You're the top!*
> *You're Miss Pinkham's tonic.*
> *You're the top!*
> *You're a high colonic.*
> *You're the burning heat of a bridal suite in use,*
> *You're the breasts of Venus,*
> *You're King Kong's penis,*
> *You're self-abuse.*
> *You're an arch*
> *In the Rome collection.*
> *You're the starch*
> *In a groom's erection.*
> *I'm a eunuch who*
> *Has just been through an op,*
> *But if, baby, I'm the bottom*
> *You're the top.*

Walter Clemons wrote, "The complexity of Porter's best work sets him somewhat apart from the other great songwriters of the first half of this century—Kern, Berlin, Gershwin and Rodgers. A Porter song is a luxury item, expensively made ('Begin the Beguine' is 108 bars long) and extravagantly rhymed. In a way no other songs of the period quite did, Porter created a world. It was a between-the-wars realm of drop dead chic and careless name-dropping insouciance. And it was a sexy place to be invited."

"Cole had a worldwide reputation as a sophisticate and hedonist," wrote Merman. "I suspect he capitalized on those traits. No other Broadway tunesmith enjoyed a similar image." In what appears to be a non sequitur Merman adds, "Cole and Linda . . . always responded most enthusiastically to people who had the courage to be themselves." Cole had this courage to some extent: he was not afraid to demonstrate, though never vulgarly, his pursuit of pleasure. When plans were announced for a film of *Anything Goes,* a young singer called Benay Venuta tried out for the Merman role on Broadway. Vincent Freedley told Venuta, "We'd like you to take over for Ethel Merman. Can you learn the part in three weeks?" She was directed to Cole's apartment, where he was to teach her the songs, but he was unable to sight-transpose the songs to her key. (She sang one tone lower than Merman.) "He couldn't play his own songs in my key," said Benay Venuta decades later with some incredulity. So Lew Kesler replaced Cole at the piano. Monty Woolley came each day and played the Billy Gaxton part, which he loved to do. These rehearsals took place in the afternoon, and sometimes, according to Venuta, "Cole would be a little bombed." (Benay Venuta thought of Cole as an alcoholic even in the 1930s and said that "so did most others of [their] mutual acquaintances.") There was, however, little discussion, she said, of Cole's homosexuality: "In those days people didn't talk about it."

Some years later Porter invited Benay Venuta to his Brentwood home and played her the score of *Out of This World:* "You'd be perfect for Juno." She declined, and after the show failed, Cole leaned over to her at a party and said jokingly, "How right you were to turn down the Juno role."

By 1935 Cole was "composing and writing his glossy tunes and lyrics in a niche of one of the Waldorf's highest peaks." After he moved in, Porter was presented with a Steinway grand piano as a gift from the management—a floral-print piano currently on view in the hotel's Peacock Alley. Porter decorated the suite with two grand pianos placed curve to curve, the players facing. For one room he imported antique parquet floors from a French chateau, and for two others, exquisitely beautiful oriental rugs. The Porters occupied apartments on the forty-first floor of the Towers, just below the top floor, which later became the residence of the United States ambassador to the United Nations. Former President Herbert Hoover had the floor below. Many other luminaries dwelt in the Towers. Cole set to work "after midnight in a lengthy, cathedral-like room surrounded by pianos and dressed in slacks and a polo shirt with wide belt. His getup is as comical as some of his jingles." No party seemed able to get along without Cole. Another writer found Porter to be without affectation—an unexpected virtue, he thought, in someone who had spent years of his life in Europe. However, he seems to have disapproved of Cole's traveling with his own bedsheets; "and his dress and manners still faintly suggest his native Peru, Indiana." In this respect the mature Cole continued an eccentricity that made him stand out as a Yalie. It is a mild kind of exhibitionism, related to his dandyism, but surprising nonetheless in someone who "clings to the background and is rarely seen in the lobby buzz at theatre intermissions."

Linda Porter had moved into the Waldorf Towers when Cole did, but eventually had her own suite—really a separate apartment—on the same floor. She had it "daily redecorated" with fresh flowers—all white: roses, gardenias, virgin orchids.

One of the reasons Cole and Linda lived in separate quarters was his work habit. With his inclination to settle into work after midnight, he had acoustical "mud" installed to deaden the sound of his piano so as not to disturb his neighbors. In August 1935 Cole told a reporter that he worked about four hours a day, but "I never stop thinking of songs. I wrote 'Night and Day' in a taxi." Perhaps the rigor of Porter's art accounts for a columnist's mentioning that "Porter looks partly fatigued and sleep weary." This profile captures Cole then forty-three years old:

Wears black tie with blue shirts, likes Harlem, can [mix] cocktails as dexterously as the best . . . Won't touch a piano while composing because you feel your fingers in the tune . . . Writes close to 25 numbers for each show—then discards 10 or so during rehearsals. Used to throw away as many as 30. Now discards fewer because he's a better judge . . . Cole Porter says his greatest trouble has been unintentionally offending audiences by writing cynically. When he first heard "I'm a Gigolo" from your side of the footlights he felt that "it definitely left an unpleasant taste."

In this interview Porter says some things about his art that are notable. He thinks that the great danger for inexperienced songwriters is "not realizing the importance of 2/4 and 6/8 tempos every so often in the score. Americans are too inclined to write everything in 4/4 fox trot time. That's our national tempo." He now says that it was "What Is This Thing Called Love?" that "grew out of a series of notes heard on a Moroccan visit." He says he knew "Night and Day" was a success when Mrs. Vincent Astor got up to dance. He thinks its best line is "under the hide of me," although "some friends object to it as 'unpleasant.'"

At that time the Porters had a dachshund and a cat. Much later Cole had two cats: one called Anything, the other called Goes. According to Michael Pearman, the cats never left the luxurious confines of the Waldorf Towers.

The opening of *Anything Goes* in London on June 14, 1935, was deemed the most fashionable first night of the season. C. B. Cochran had obtained an injunction prohibiting performances of the songs before *Anything Goes* opened, so its vintage score seemed all the more bewitching to the first-nighters. Wodehouse, years later, wrote of his amazement that *Anything Goes* ran some thirty weeks in London: "In those days there was no more horrible spectacle than English performers portraying American characters." Cochran, who claimed the show satirized America's hero worship of the gangster, was congratulated by the press for having "done it again." The reviews were laudatory, praising the show for its style and animation. Cole lingered for a time in London. One reporter noted that he saw Porter at a recital Vladimir Horowitz gave at the Queen's Hall. Unfortunately lost is the name of the soprano who amused him so much at another recital: he described to Gerald Murphy how she stood with hands folded on her abdomen and sang off-key the lyric "A deer ran into the forest *ma-a-d* with his own perfume." He told Murphy that he "fell off his seat on to the floor rocked with laughing."

One of the most charming incidents concerning *Anything Goes* is told by Mercedes de Acosta, beautiful, legendary, a friend of Garbo—both of them friends of Cole Porter. "One afternoon a Metro story editor sent a script via messenger to Garbo at her home in Santa Monica. At the end of the day the messenger returned to the studio—script still in hand. He'd not been able to make the delivery: He could hear laughter and music coming from inside the house . . . It was Cole Porter's 'You're the Top.' The kid rang the front bell . . . If Garbo heard him, she wasn't letting him in. When he went to knock on a window, he peeked inside, and saw Garbo dancing with a woman friend of hers—they were playing a certain verse of the song over and over, laughing about the lyrics. [The messenger] decided not to intrude." Of course, de Acosta was notorious for inventing stories.

Another big bash Elsa Maxwell arranged took place at the Starlight Roof of the Waldorf-Astoria before the Porters and friends sailed on a round-the-world voyage. The party began at eleven p.m., preceded by a number of small dinner parties. Condé Nast gave one; Mrs. William Randolph Hearst another; Princess Mdivani a third. Seated at the entrance to the roof garden were two attendants: one announced the guests; the other ensured against gate crashing (not rare for Elsa's parties). Johnny Green (composer of "Body and Soul," "I Cover the Waterfront," and "Out of Nowhere," among many wonderful songs) led the orchestra from his piano. After some dancing the show, with Miss Maxwell as mistress of ceremonies, began. She announced Cole Porter and then unveiled a huge cake reaching almost to the ceiling. As the guests applauded, two folding doors parted at the base of the cake and out walked Cole Porter. He was placed in the seat of honor, and Elsa opened the entertainment by imitating Ina Claire's version of "I've a Shooting Box."

The guests included the Vincent Astors, the Averell Harrimans, Noël Coward, Prince Serge Obolensky, Yvonne Printemps, and Fritz Kreisler. At Elsa Maxwell's parties Park Avenue mixed with Broadway—two worlds to which, since his childhood days in Indiana, Cole Porter aspired ardently to belong. But the appeal of Porter's music was not restricted to the wealthy or the glamorous. Brian Friel's play *Dancing at Lughnasa* (1990) depicts five "brave" (his word) Irish women living in what was once the domain of the pagan Celtic god Lugh and repressed by forces that render their lives drab and deprived. Nonetheless their spirits soar when one of them turns on the wireless and Porter's "Anything Goes" fills the air; they erupt into rapturous dance. When Friel searched back over the decades for a song that would timelessly proclaim the pluckiness of the human spirit, both in the 1930s and today as well, he chose a Cole Porter song.

Chapter 9

World-Famous Tunesmith

On January 12, 1935, Cole Porter, along with Linda, Howard Sturges, Monty Woolley, Billy Powell, Moss Hart, two maids, and a valet, boarded the Cunard liner *Franconia* in New York for a journey that was to take them around the world by way of California and the South Sea islands.

It was at the Ritz bar, in Paris, in the early thirties, that Moss Hart, with a letter of introduction from Irving Berlin in his pocket, first met Cole. The bar at the Ritz, rendered memorably in Fitzgerald's "Babylon Revisited," had been a haunt of Cole's and a rendezvous for Linda and him early on. The Right Bar, that is; the Left Bar was called the Men's Bar, and its clientele were often homosexuals. Beverly Nichols meanly wrote that "Cole Porter, looking like a startled leprechaun [in the Left Bar], could sip a Pernod and cast his dark, little syrupy eyes to the white and gold ceiling, and think out his devastating little rhymes." In 1919 Cole wrote a song about the Ritz:

> I simply adorn a secluded corner,
> A cozy corner in the Ritz Hotel.
> When I wander each afternoon for tea,
> 'Cause I like to see the kings
> And let the queens see me
> In my corner, my dear little corner
> Where I gather up the spicy bits.

Billy Powell, Sturges, Linda, Monty, Cole, and Moss Hart onboard the *Franconia*, 1935

The code is simple to decipher. A friend of the Murphys wrote of a meeting he had with Cole in the Ritz bar. "He introduced me to the Duke of Alba who was costumed as a chorus man and trailing a dog named Snookums on a silver chain. An odd object. Hurried from this exalted society around the corner and saw remains of Scott Fitzgerald propped on a chair. Fled before recognition could ensue."

Hart also brought a gift to Cole from the dancer Georgia Hale—a pair of garters with gold clasps, which led Cole in a now legendary gesture to remove the garters he was wearing, also fitted with gold clasps, and casually make a present of them to the bartender. The next evening Hart dined in Paris with the Porters and discussed a possible collaboration, but nothing eventuated until five years later. Nonetheless, by the late twenties, as Moss Hart wrote, he and others "were aware that a new musical voice of immense vigor and freshness was making itself heard—a forcible talent . . . that had great elegance . . . no one could write a Cole Porter song but Cole Porter. Each song had a matchless design and a special felicity of its own that stamped it as immediately and uniquely his." "Gaiety," "impishness," "audacity," and "insouciance" are qualities Hart noted in Porter and in his songs.

"Little Bill Powell," as people called him, was a Yalie and a great friend of Len Hanna's. Not well-off when he graduated, he was a travel writer but went to work as a publicist for the Johnson Wax Company and proved ardent and relentless in his tasks. Before the opening of *Kiss Me, Kate,* he pestered Porter to use the name of the wax in one of the composer's list songs. Finally the irritated but amused Cole wrote to tell Powell: "We've decided to call the show *Kiss Me, Johnson's Wax.*" Powell's first coup had been to persuade Helen Morgan, whom the elder Mr. Johnson worshiped, to slide a bit when she slithered onto the piano (her characteristic bit) and say, "Oh, that Johnson's Wax!" She did so and thrilled Johnson, who always had a ringside table when Morgan appeared in a New York club. Years later, Powell persuaded Jacqueline Kennedy to be photographed in the White House near a table on which a can of Johnson's Wax stood. Powell, who eventually married the actress Irene Purcell, was just the kind of quirky and amusing character who appealed to Porter's sense of fun, and so Cole invited him into this intimate company.

"When Messrs. Porter and Hart return to New York," said the *New York Herald Tribune,* "they expect to have on paper a complete score and book for a new show." This was the musical titled *Jubilee.* Porter and Hart were by this time stars. The *Tribune* called Cole "heir apparent to the throne of Jerome Kern as the nation's top balladeer," and Hart had for half a decade been much admired, especially for his collaboration with George S. Kaufman on *Once in a Lifetime* and *Merrily We Roll Along* as well as for the Irving Berlin shows *Face the Music* and *As Thousands Cheer.* Hart had hoped to spend the winter months in Morocco. Couldn't they work there? he asked. But Porter suggested instead the South Seas and ultimately a voyage around the world. Hart agreed, and the others acquiesced as quickly, including Woolley, to whom Cole proposed the trip only a few days before the scheduled departure. Several commentators have itemized part of the impedimenta Cole brought: a metronome, a small piano-organ, pencils and paper, a phonograph and recordings, a typewriter, and cases of champagne. The jesting Lindsay and Crouse, meanwhile, sneaked into Cole's cabin "an ugly carved statue with a bulging figure" which delighted Cole. Instead of tossing it overboard, he dressed it up in the native costumes of the countries they visited and gave parties in her honor.

Hart, who was something of a dandy, had brought aboard an enormous wardrobe and wore jackets and ties when others were mostly informally attired in shorts and polo shirts. According to one account, Linda was irritated by Hart's lack of *comme il faut* and one morning went to his stateroom, gathered up all his clothing, and tossed it overboard. Hart was understandably perturbed and could not be mollified by Linda's promises to replace his wardrobe. She did do so, and eventually Hart forgave her.

Moss Hart, 1935

(Although this voyage preceded by many years Kitty Carlisle's marriage to Hart, she had never been told this tale by him, nor did it sound to her or to other friends of the Porters at all like something Linda would do.) In *My Trip Around the World,* Hart's unpublished account of this journey, he notes that he is a good traveler and has, above all, one quality that he thinks all good travelers must possess: an infinite capacity for being astonished and amused. "Every new sight excites in me complete wonderment." This was a capacity he shared with Cole, who even in his later years, loved travel and went far out of his way to see the sights.

In the log Hart kept of this voyage, he begins at Kingston, Jamaica: "I knew instinctively . . . that Kingston would offer no more than the regulation Botanical Gardens, banana trees, a stream of dissatisfied looking British Army officers." So after they saw their shipmates depart on a tour of the island, Cole's party headed off to a luxurious pool set in the midst of a tropical garden overlooking the sea and felt "New York sliding off." From the pool Porter and his party moved to a café, where they drank "potent Planters Punches."

Oddly enough, Hart does not mention in his journal what Kimball calls "one of the most acclaimed songs in the score [and] the first song composed for *Jubilee* soon after the visit to Jamaica." The song is called "The

Kling-Kling Bird on the Divi-Divi Tree," after exotic specimens Cole saw in Jamaica. It is sung by the character called Eric Dare in the show, a thinly veiled version of Noël Coward (who indeed had a brother called Eric):

> *Then we sailed and sailed for miles and miles*
> *Till we came one day to the Cannibal Isles,*
> *Where I soon enjoyed a great success*
> *With a very broad-minded cannibaless.*
> *We had dallied for a week or more,*
> *When she said one ev'ning, in front of her door,*
> *"Won't you come inside and make poi?"*
> *Then I heard that bird say, "Listen, little boy!"*

The kling-kling bird sings his customary caution: "Oh, beware, beware of the ladies fair / In the countries across the sea."

From Jamaica the *Franconia* traveled through the Panama Canal on its nine-day run to California. Hart remembered that Balboa had walked across the isthmus; Cole perhaps recalled that J.O., his grandfather, had done the same. Cole was bequeathed a hearty heritage—a resource he was soon to need badly. The *Franconia* pleased the Porter party. It was small, accommodating 250 passengers, among whom were eccentrics such as an elderly French lady, Madame Piaget, who met the blistering heat of Panama by donning black velvet, a fur neckpiece, and a steamer rug; and Porter and his party amused themselves by inventing legends about these passengers. The *Franconia* was built for cruising rather than being a converted transoceanic liner. (It pleased patrons that they saw the seas from anyplace they sat or stood.) The ship boasted swimming pools indoors and out, a sun deck, air conditioning, and good food. With their days left entirely free, Cole and Hart found themselves working steadily without stress. "Cole Porter 'worker' and Cole Porter 'playboy' were two different beings." The secret of *Jubilee*'s marvelously gay and seemingly effortless songs was a prodigious and unending industry. "He worked around the clock," said Moss. "He used work as a weapon to shield himself from a boredom whose threshold was extremely low; he could withdraw and disappear before one's eyes with an almost sinister facility."

When the ship reached Los Angeles, however, the tempo quickened. In Hollywood there was a series of lunches, cocktail parties, and dinners in what Hart called "thoroughly exhausting days." Irving Berlin, George Kaufman, Max Gordon (who coproduced *Jubilee*), Jerome Kern, Oscar Hammerstein II were among the friends they encountered. From California the ship proceeded to Honolulu and then to Tahiti, which was in the grip of a typhoon, so the passengers were unable to land. In the end the stormy weather prohibited a landing on any of the Tahitian islands, so they proceeded on an eight-day voyage to Samoa and the Fiji Islands. The ship made an unscheduled stop at Pago Pago, where Hart was so thrilled to be in Somerset Maugham country that he fired off a telegram to Tallulah Bankhead, who had just opened in Maugham's *Rain.*

Cole adopted a routine early on in the voyage. Breakfast on the deck and a visit to the barber. From eight to twelve Porter, clad in his bathing suit, worked on the deck, occasionally halting for a dip in the pool. Lunch at one and then a nap. From four to six Cole worked again and then had a session in the gymnasium, after which he dressed for dinner. Cocktails, dinner, backgammon (or some other light entertainment), and then to bed at ten p.m. Of course, when the ship docked and the passengers went ashore, Cole, the irrepressible tourist, went off to see the sights.

On their nearly five-month cruise Porter and Hart heard the choir of a boys' school. Moss Hart referred to them as "magnificent specimens of young Samoan manhood . . . We were all . . . more moved than we cared to admit. So much so that Cole Porter arranged to go back and have them sing again in the afternoon . . . When the revolution comes, we shall all make a bee-line for the island and meet at the Boys' School."

After unremarkable tours of New Zealand and Australia the *Franconia* continued to Port Moresby, Kalabahi, Bali, Mombosa, Zanzibar, Madagascar, India, Africa, and South America. As they sailed away from New Guinea Cole wrote on the untitled score the words "End of Act I"; Act II was begun on the day the ship landed in Kalabahi. As Hart remarked, "two pretty strange places to see the birth of a Broadway musical comedy." In Bali the beauty of the natives made it seem as if the Americans were "constantly coming upon bronze gods and goddesses." And the music of the gamelan pleased them immensely.

Eventually the cruise reached Africa, where the travelers took an airplane flight over that continent. In Zanzibar Cole and Moss and their party were entertained by the sultan. The British authorities there arranged the audience. Porter, who'd always had a fondness for *The Arabian Nights,* was very excited by the prospect. They were required to dress in white suits, white headdresses, and black tie. Outfits were borrowed from the captain and the crew. When the launch bearing the sultan's equerry came alongside the *Franconia,* Porter was informed that he could expect something extraordinary. The sunshine in Zanzibar was dazzling. They drove to the palace— a two-storey, rambling, pure white structure, in the Moorish doorway of which stood a sentry in red fez, a sight that delighted Moss: one red dot against the whiteness of the palace and the cloudless, azure sky. They approached the throne room on the second floor by an ebony staircase. Somewhat rickety gilt chairs were all around, and portraits of Queen Victoria and King Edward VII hung behind the sultan's throne. The sultan arrived with a single escort who spoke perfect English. The Americans were disappointed that neither a eunuch or a Nubian slave was to be glimpsed: "The scene wasn't story bookish at all." Pink sherbet with almonds was served and warm, sweet champagne. When the sultan clapped his hands, Hart thought dancing girls would appear and said to Cole, "The weird strains of Oriental music presently will assault your ears and the dancing girls of Samarkand will make you swoon." "Samarkand is in India," Porter replied. "Hello. What's that?" Instead an attendant removed a screen revealing an old-fashioned phonograph with a big tin horn. He turned a lever and the sultan's eyes lit up as a scratchy recording of "Let's Do It" commenced. "Your song, Mr. Porter," said the sultan. "I have it played often when I am feeling . . . liverish." And the audience ended.

While crossing the South Atlantic the English ship received news of the twenty-fifth anniversary celebration of the coronation of King George V. Suddenly the Hart/Porter creation had its title: *Jubilee*. Hart had completed the book at Cape Town, a week before schedule. At Rio de Janeiro Cole finished the score. According to one of his accounts, he also had a musical dividend while approaching the harbor of Rio. "It was dawn . . . As we stood on the bow of the boat my exclamation was 'It's delightful!' My wife followed with 'It's delicious!' And Monty, in his happy [squiffy] state cried, 'It's dee-lovely!' " Cole's other version of the etiology of his song (which Merman and Bob Hope introduced in his 1936 show *Red, Hot and Blue!*) is as follows: "I took a world tour a couple of years ago, and I was in Java with Monty Woolley and Moss Hart. We'd just been served that famous Eastern fruit—the mangosteen . . . Moss Hart said 'It's delightful!' I chimed in with 'It's delicious!' and Monty Woolley said, 'It's dee-lovely!' "

When the *Franconia* arrived in New York on May 31, 1935, Cole and Moss found their mothers awaiting them. Evidently the women had arrived early and made themselves known to each other. Moss's mother later commented, "You know, that Mrs. Porter—she's very nice, very, very, very nice for a country woman."

Porter and Moss Hart had only a month and a bit to attend to their affairs before flying in July to the West Coast, where they stayed at the Beverly-Wilshire Hotel for nine days conducting auditions as they cast the musical, engaging, among others, Porter's cousin Ted Fetter as an usher and a teenage Montgomery Clift as a prince.

In mid-August 1935, the *Cleveland Press* reported that a bright red airplane flew over the swimming pool at Len Hanna's farm in Ohio and dropped a cardboard box scrawled with messages announcing that Len and Cole Porter would arrive shortly. Hart, Woolley, and Derek Williams (who was to play Eric Dare in *Jubilee*) were with them. It was there at the farm that Cole wrote "Just One of Those Things," a song that did not really take hold for nearly a decade. The story is that Moss Hart told Cole they needed a song for Act II. Although Porter disliked being advised about the score, he accepted Moss's advice and next morning when Moss came downstairs there on the piano was the score for "Just One of Those Things." (Only one word resisted Cole's imagination, and when he mentioned this later to Ed Tauch, Ed immediately suggested "gossamer," giving Cole the line "A trip to the moon on gossamer wings.")

> *So goodbye, dear, and amen.*
> *Here's hoping we meet now and then,*
> *It was great fun,*
> *But it was just one of those things.*

The plot of *Jubilee* is slight: as one critic put it, "very much the sort of idea clever college boys get and develop for their varsity shows." Rumor of revolution offers the royal family of a fictional country a chance to roam about incognito and pursue the pleasures previously unavailable to them. The king becomes chummy with a famous hostess, Eva Standing (a caricature of Elsa Maxwell); the queen pursues an actor-swimmer, Charles Rausmiller, or Mowgli, who, like Johnny Weismuller's Tarzan, often appears in no more than a loincloth. The royal daughter earns the love of Eric Dare, an actor, playwright, and composer. Eventually the threat of revolution is discovered to be a hoax and the royals resume their duties, sweetened now by the company of their new pals. Sets for the show were by Jo Mielziner and costumes by Irene Sharaff. Monty Woolley began as the director. At a rehearsal during the tryouts in Boston he became infuriated when Michael Pearman flubbed some tricky lines. "Get off the stage!" Monty roared. Pearman went backstage only to discover a fire beginning to blaze. He walked back onstage. "I thought I told you to stay backstage!" growled Monty. "I tried to, but the theatre is on fire," said Pearman as he sauntered up the aisle and out of the theatre. Hassard Short was soon engaged to replace Woolley as director.

Theatre people are inclined to superstitiousness, or so we are meant to believe. The singer and dancer June Knight thought that *Jubilee* was jinxed. Troubles began when members of the cast rehearsing in New York received letters threatening their lives if they went to Boston. Arriving at their Boston hotel, the actors received further death threats. Leading lady Mary Boland slowly succumbed to drink and as a result missed some performances, although by opening night in New York she was in good form and played brilliantly. In the Boston tryout, besides the fire which broke out backstage, the mothers of Mary Boland, Max Gordon, and the chorus girl Jeanette Bradley all died. And during one performance a musician in the pit keeled over dead. Later, in New York, a second fire broke out backstage in the theatre, damaging some props and costumes, so that a performance had to be canceled. And in January 1936 George V, died which some felt doomed the show to a shorter run than otherwise it might have had. In fact, before the show opened rumors flew about that the British Foreign Office was concerned that it might be irreverent about the royal family. In an effort to please the Brits, Hart and Porter made revisions. "There'll be no war if I can help it," said Moss Hart. The beard was removed from the King George character, and Mary Boland changed her makeup in order to look less like Queen Mary.

John Simon's comment that "*Jubilee* is definitely one of Porter's lesser efforts" can be questioned. One should recall that the songs—at least four or five of them—have become standards. "Why Shouldn't I?" describes the reaching for love of someone too long deprived of it:

> All my life I've been so secluded
> Love has eluded me,
> But from knowing second-hand what I do of it,
> I feel certain I could stand a closer view of it.
> . . . .
> Why shouldn't I
> Take a chance when romance passes by?
> Why shouldn't I know of love?
> Why wait around
> When each age has a sage who has found
> That upon this earth
> Love is all that is really worth
> Thinking of.

The sentiment is sad but hopeful and admirably served by the shortened lines and both end and internal rhymes. The clever rhymes in "We're Off to Feathermore"—"*dix-huitième*"/"B.T.M." and "buttons on"/"Edward F. Huttons on"—are central to Porter's style and idiom. "When Love Comes Your Way," with its plangent melody and bittersweet lyric, is a song Gertrude Lawrence sang in *Nymph Errant* tryouts. It was dropped from the London production and successfully recycled for *Jubilee.* The song is replete with Porter's *carpe diem* convictions.

> *When love comes your way*
> *Take ev'ry bit of joy you can borrow.*
> *Be carefree, be gay,*
> *Forget the world and say*
> *Goodbye to sorrow.*
> *Simply live for today,*
> *And never think at all of tomorrow,*
> *For just when you are sure that love has*
> *Come to stay—*
> *Then love flies away.*

"When Me, Mowgli, Love" mentions Walter Winchell, Elsa Maxwell, and, more daringly, Will Hays, the well-known censor, one of Porter's puritan targets. In the most famous number from *Jubilee,* "Begin the Beguine," Porter, possibly feeling the oppression of censorship, decided to change the penultimate line, "And we suddenly know the sweetness of sin," to: "And we suddenly know what heaven we're in."

Lists are to the fore in a few of the songs written for *Jubilee.* In the anthem "Gather Ye Autographs While Ye May," which derives from Herrick's famous poem, the lyrics cite Toscanini, Dizzy Dean, Josephine, Clarence Darrow, and Haile Selassie. These juxtapositions always work in Porter's lyrics to comic effect and, perhaps more importantly, show, as metaphysical poets like Donne did, some planetary unity in apparent discord.

"Good Morning, Miss Standing" pokes friendly fun at Elsa Maxwell and gave Cole the chance to mention his illustrator pal Neysa McMein and also the journalist Herbert Swope, the Dionne quintuplets, and the Sultan of Zanzibar. "My Most Intimate Friend" also caricatures Elsa Maxwell. One of its lines jests about George Gershwin, who was famous for seizing the piano at parties and playing ceaselessly. "T'will be new in ev'ry way / Gershwin's promised not to play." Lines that follow were later on scotched:

Has Mussolini been invited?
What, Benito? Why he's delighted,
He's my most intimate friend.

Another song from *Jubilee* that becomes more popular as time passes is "A Picture of Me Without You," again in large part a list. "Picture Av'rell Harriman without a train . . . Picture Clifton Webb minus Mother Maybelle"; in every case these deprivations translate into "just a picture of me without you!"

Jubilee opened in Boston on September 21, 1935, and on October 12 moved into the Imperial Theatre in New York. "Not since *Show Boat* has Broadway seen a musical comedy which holds such promise of making theatrical history," wrote one reviewer. Another located *Jubilee* between musical comedy and opera, retaining the best features of each—a cross between Gilbert and Sullivan and opera bouffe.

In Boston, the *Herald* called *Jubilee* "a brilliant musical play," and *Variety,* monitoring the Boston tryout, called *Jubilee* "unquestionably a hit." Soon after the opening in Boston, Ned Saltonstall, a great friend of Cole's, threw what some of Porter's friends called a "boy party." Porter came, somewhat to the surprise of Michael Pearman, who was also there. Generally, according to Pearman, Cole was very careful about his sexual affairs; "always correct." This must be the same "wild party" at the Boston Ritz that the writer Schuyler Parsons alluded to in his book *Untold Friendships.*

The New York opening was opulent. Mary Margaret McBride, then the grande dame of radio commentators, wrote that "not since 1929 had there been such a convocation of ermine, mink, Russian sable, diamond dog collars and star sapphires as was brought forth by the opening night of *Jubilee.*" Linda wore a new diamond-and-aquamarine necklace which Cole had designed; and she, as had become the custom, commemorated the opening of the show by presenting Cole with a beautiful cigarette case. The audience boasted a prince (Obolensky) and a duke (of Verdura) as well as many of the theatre's greats: Laurette Taylor, Katharine Hepburn, Mady Christians, Ina Claire, Tallulah Bankhead, George S. Kaufman, Franchot Tone, Joan Crawford, Libby Holman, Edna Ferber, Jerome Kern, Norman Bel Geddes, Howard Dietz, Lee Shubert. And from Cole's other world, that of high society, came Mrs. Belmont Tiffany, William Rhinelander Stewart, Mrs. Irving Berlin, Ethel Harriman Russell, Elizabeth Arden, Bernard Baruch, and Len Hanna. People were offering two hundred dollars for a pair of tickets, but there were no takers. Hundreds of celebrity seekers lined the sidewalks.

Brooks Atkinson led off the reviewers: "*Jubilee* is a tapestry of delights," he wrote in *The New York Times*. The *Daily News* enjoyed the show's "gay, noisy, truthful . . . caricature of the Premiere Playgirl of her day . . . The buxom Miss Maxwell is an excellent target . . . for such darts. Her rabbity career has consisted in thinking up childish games for adults to play." Burns Mantle in the *Sunday News* proclaimed *Jubilee* to be "much more than just another musical comedy . . . it is poured from a new mold . . . *Jubilee* is . . . the most notable contribution to the American theatre this generation has had a chance to welcome."

Albertina Rasch, one of two *Jubilee* choreographers, insisted to a reporter that the beguine is not South American or Spanish but "distinctly a South Sea melody." The jungle drums, temple gongs, and "clinker" symbols in the orchestra "all confirm its origin: It came to [Porter] . . . on his cruise around the world." "The beguine will probably become a popular ballroom dance," she correctly predicted.

Cole with Amelia Earhart, c. 1935

Years later a journalist wrote to ask Cole the origin of the word, for which he could only find the name of an order of French lay sisters. Porter replied that somewhere around 1925 he was living in Paris and went to see "the Black Martiniquois . . . do their native dance called The Beguine . . . I was very much taken by the rhythm of the dance, the rhythm was practically that of the already popular rumba but much faster. The moment I saw it I thought of BEGIN THE BEGUINE as a good title for a song and put it away in a notebook, adding a memorandum as to its rhythm and tempo."

"About ten years later," Porter continues, "while going around the world we stopped at an island in the Lesser Sunda Islands, to the west of New Guinea, at a place called 'Kalabahi,' my spelling of Kalabahi is entirely phonetic. A native dance was stated [sic] for us, the first bars of which was to become my song. I looked through my notebook, and found again, after ten years, my old title BEGIN THE BEGUINE. For some reason the melody that I heard and the phrase that I had written down seemed to marry. I developed the whole song from that." The Préfet of Martinique entered the fray with an authoritative statement:

The beguine is the popular dance in the French West Indies. It is derived from the "bel-air" . . . the dance of liberation of the slaves . . . Like it, the beguine was a quadrille dance, similar to the lancers on the "Haut-taille." According to an old man, the leader of the ball, who always stressed the rhythm of the dances with a drum, got the bel-air dancers started with the signal of "beguine" . . . this word is the imperative of the English verb "to begin" which means "begin" . . . the beguine has become standardized under the influence of the fox-trot, being executed more by movements of the waist and legs [rather than rhythmic poses and facial expressions]. Nowadays, it is . . . following the rhumba rhythm which causes great dismay to the ones over thirty.

In 1938 Artie Shaw recorded the famous swing version of "Begin the Beguine," which moved, in Shaw's words, "a latin beat to a swing time." Porter was pleased with Shaw's version and invited him to a party, where Cole greeted him: "Happy to meet my collaborator." "Does that involve royalties?" asked Shaw. "I'm afraid not," countered Cole. Shaw remembers that Porter "behaved like a very rich man" and that he moved gracefully. Shaw always called him "Mr. Porter," nor did Porter invite him to call him "Cole." Shaw thinks that his recording of "Begin the Beguine," which sold 6.5 million copies, may be the single most popular recording ever made.

And it continues to sell. (In 1954 Shaw made a second recording of the song.) Shaw was particularly interested in Porter's habit of mixing major and minor in a single song, not to say his departure from the traditional ABA length in "Begin the Beguine." Recently, Sam Kusumoto, president of Minolta, said: "The culture shock that followed Japan's surrender to the Allies changed the Japanese completely . . . The first music we heard was 'Begin the Beguine' by Artie Shaw's band. If you talk to Japanese of my generation and mention 'Begin the Beguine,' everybody will rise and smile because that song represented a new era for the Japanese."

Writing in *Life*, George Jean Nathan called Cole "the lyricist of the boulevard" and said that he "has worked himself up into the unhappy position where, unless every song he now writes is Gilbert and Sullivan plus, his customers begin to shake their heads and allow that he is slipping. That his light songs are generally as good as anyone has a right to expect of him doesn't seem to count. They apparently should be even better . . . Thus there has been some growling over his score for *Jubilee* simply because it doesn't make his score for *Anything Goes* look third-rate. Such is the attitude of Broadway."

On the fifteenth of November, the Porters and their guests, Moss Hart and Mrs. Herman Oelrichs, boarded a cruise ship bound for Bermuda, where they occupied the Vincent Astor house for three weeks before Cole was due to make a Hollywood film.

Chapter 10

Like Living on
the Moon

Late in 1934 and early in 1935 Porter composed a score (six songs) for a Fox film to be titled *Adios, Argentina*. The picture was never produced, nor were the songs published, except for "Don't Fence Me In," which the public didn't hear until it was sung in the 1944 film *Hollywood Canteen*. None of these song lyrics is memorable. This is inexplicable, as Porter in these years was writing at the top of his form. His mother told a reporter that Cole "likes to do shows much better in New York, but I guess everybody has to go to Hollywood on account of the prices."

Nineteen thirty-five brought Cole a contract from MGM, and he and Linda went in December of that year to Hollywood, a place he liked from the start. "Hollywood," Cole said to Garson Kanin, "It's like living on the moon, isn't it?" For the rest of his life he lived in Hollywood for four to six months of the year. On this first visit the Porters rented a very large, elegant house on Sunset Boulevard. In subsequent visits they decided a smaller house with only one guest room and a pool was what suited them. In Hollywood, Cole saw friends like the Astaires but seldom went to the studio. Fred Astaire was Porter's ideal: how he wished to see himself. If the Astaires came to Cole's home for dinner, Phyllis Astaire would send cream from her cow, Alexandre, and Porter would serve a tart with "creme Alexandre." But Linda liked Hollywood far less than Cole; as one of their acquaintances succinctly explains, "Porter's homosexuality, fed by opportunity, had become more blatant."

Dorothy Kilgallen reported from California that this habitué of Paris, Manhattan, and the Riviera had "gone Hollywood." In a lengthy interview, Porter described the more discreet of his West Coast pleasures, among them horse riding. "He would rather compose on a horse than on a piano . . . 'When I write a song at the piano it is always lousy' he said." Reading non-fiction is another pleasure he names, along with jigsaw puzzles (he kept a couple scattered on white tables in the living room all the time). He never played tennis, but told Kilgallen (perhaps jocularly) he ran around the block every morning for exercise. He wore mostly blue, but liked bright red best of all colors. To Kilgallen's ear he talked swiftly and somewhat indistinctly. "The important thing about a song today," Porter said, "is not so much the way it's sung as the way orchestras take to it. If orchestras pick up a song, it sweeps the country." In the mid-thirties Porter felt that swing was possibly on the wane and he wasn't sure what manner of song would take its place. "Casually sentimental songs," he guessed, "love with a laugh." He felt that better times would produce brighter songs.

In California Cole exhibited a persona that seems outré and recalls the dandy he was in prep school and college. In the matter of dress, for instance, "Cole liked rather boisterous colors at times," said Ray Kelly, who describes Cole's visit to a tailor in Hollywood. "He wanted sports coats made to mea-sure and requested the man show him swatches of material. The tailor brought one piece of cloth to which were attached many patches, each a dif-ferent color. He invited Cole to make a choice. Cole said, 'I'd like the whole thing; make it out of that.' It caused quite a riot. He wore it constantly. It was great large patches of orange, blue, and reds—he called it his David's coat." (He must have meant Joseph's coat.)

Porter's two principal tasks in 1936 were the scores for the film *Born to Dance* and the Broadway musical *Red, Hot and Blue!* Before the Porters trav-eled to Hollywood, Cole was busy with *Red, Hot and Blue!*, with a libretto written by Howard Lindsay and Russel Crouse. The show—which starred Ethel Merman, Jimmy Durante, and Bob Hope, and was produced by Vin-ton Freedley and directed by Howard Lindsay—tells the tale of a rich widow, once a lowly manicurist, who, with assistance from her aide, an ex-convict, tries to benefit a lawyer who lost a great love at age six when he forced her against a waffle iron and branded her on the behind. The Mer-man character, "Nails" Duquesne, inaugurates a lottery to find the lawyer's lost love; the plot thickens, but not compellingly.

Cole's mother saw the show and told an interviewer, "I think a lot of the time Cole's words aren't as good as his tunes . . . But of course he has to write the words for the show like they want him to. I don't like his

Sheet music for *Born to Dance*, 1936

new show, *Red, Hot and Blue!* It's too rowdy. It's not my style, but it is funny." On this same occasion she wished Cole would change the lyrics of "Love for Sale" "so people could hear the pretty tune on the radio." All of this seems to prove that Katie was conversant with her son's songs and aware of the sass and sex they sometimes featured. Katie was described in 1936 as a "sweet little grey-haired woman" and characterized herself as "just a plain, dirt farmer." Cole, she said, did some of his composing at West-leigh Farms "because it's so quiet" (although, as we know, Cole seemed able to compose with ease in crowded rooms, on beaches, trains, wherever life led him). Cole had tried to persuade her, after his father's death, to live in Paris, Katie said, but she preferred the farm. "It's a real farm with livestock and everything." Interestingly, Katie told an interviewer, "We had other plans for Cole. We wanted him to become a lawyer. He said to me, no Mom, I guess I disappointed you. I'm just a song writer."

On June 1, 1936, Linda sailed for Europe, where she made an unsuccessful attempt to sell her home in the rue Monsieur but did succeed in sending many of its valuable furnishings to the United States. The *New York Evening Journal* erroneously attributed her move to the Porters' passion for California. Linda was still in America when the state of Indiana proclaimed May 23, 1936, "Cole Porter Day." Booth Tarkington said about Cole: "Of course it's something to be a Hoosier who became a Hollywood and Broadway celebrity; but when a New York and Broadway celebrity becomes so celebrated that he's known in Indiana too, he touches the mantle of fame itself."

On June 2, 1936, Sam Katz the executive producer, had phoned Cole Porter and asked him to come to the studio and play and sing his songs for *Born to Dance* for Louis B. Mayer and Irving Thalberg. He agreed to do so, but "with dread." Next day he arrived to find Katz, Mayer, screenwriter Sid Silvers, and leading ladies Eleanor Powell and Virginia Bruce; Thalberg, according to Cole, was

Red, Hot and Blue, 1936

looking more dead than alive, and obviously angry at being disturbed to hear this score . . . By the time 'Rolling Home' was over, I realized that the atmosphere was friendly. When I finished "Hey, Babe, Hey," there was wild applause and L. B. Mayer began jumping around the room, whispering to people. I attacked "Entrance of Lucy James" next and it was during this that Thalberg suddenly became a different person and began smiling . . . The moment I finished the finale, Thalberg leaped out of his seat, rushed over to me, grabbed my hand and said "I want to congratulate you for a magnificent job, I think it's one of the finest scores I have ever heard." He was followed by L. B. who came up and put his arms around me and said, "Cole, how about coming into the next room and signing your contract for next year," to which I replied, "No, L.B., I don't understand money matters."

Cole describes how whiskey-and-sodas were served and then everyone gathered around the piano and sang.

Mayer told Katz: "Now, Sam, this material is so fine that I don't want you to take any chances with it. I want every lyric heard, and in order to insure that, I want you to make 'rushes' of these numbers and then show them in theatres as shorts to find out whether audiences can understand every word. And . . . this finale is so brilliant, that I want you to go to town and spend $250,000 on that number alone." A few days later, Cole signed a three-year contract with Metro "to turn out 'ditties' which are paying him a king's ransom."

July of that year Cole spent at the Waldorf. According to his close friend Jack Coble, "[Eddy] Tauch soon became the 'center' of Cole Porter's life." Porter may have spent time with Tauch at the Waldorf or on weekends twenty miles north of Manhattan at Sneden's Landing, where another of these intimates, Oliver Jennings, had a house. (At the time, Coble says, Tauch was *his* "best friend.") It was Tauch who first introduced Coble to Cole, and they remained close friends until Porter's death. Coble described Tauch in those days as very attractive, five-foot-eleven. He was a graduate of the Cornell School of Architecture, which was also Coble's alma mater. He had gone to Paris intending to stay and lived there from 1930 to 1936, during which years he became an intimate of Horst and of the Duke of Verdura. His travels with Cole included both Rhine and Danube excursions. According to Coble, Tauch was "lots of fun, in no way artificial"—a quality Cole appeared to appreciate, even if it couldn't be predicated of all his friends.

According to Coble, Ollie Jennings was an exceptionally sweet person, "a good man, enormously rich, but very plain and unaffected." When he built the house in Snedens Landing everyone was scrambling for invitations. An heir to the Standard Oil fortune, he married, but he and his wife led entirely separate lives, she well aware of his sexual preference, and he not dismayed by her affair with another man. "Cole was fascinated by Ollie," said Coble, and on weekends often traveled up to Snedens Landing to party until dawn with male friends. Cole loved late hours. Often he drove up after a Saturday-night performance. Linda was not included, but "she was friendly about it." Cole Porter loved those weekends with "choice chums" and seemed to have more fun there than elsewhere. Sometimes he'd fill his car with chorus boys. Once he hired a bus to transport a crowd of weekend guests. According to Coble, Linda certainly realized what Cole's interest was in these weekends and the nature of her husband's relations with Tauch, and others.

"It is hard, at this distance in time, to recreate the exact contours of the image that America, and in particular American music of the 30s, projected for many Europeans who had never seen the country." By the mid-thirties Cole's music was well-known and much admired by Europeans as well as by people around the world.

In November, according to a diary he kept, Cole went to MGM to discuss a film. This was *Born to Dance,* in which Jimmy Stewart sang one of Porter's most celebrated love songs, "Easy to Love." Stewart later said he rehearsed the song and found some notes very high. "I asked Cole Porter could you knock some of the notes down a bit but he didn't go for that." In fact the song was first written for William Gaxton to sing in *Anything Goes* and rewritten for *Born to Dance.* Because of the censorship exercised by the Hays Office in the thirties, the original lyric "So sweet to awaken with, / So nice to sit down to eggs and bacon with" had to be changed to "So worth the yearning for, / So swell to keep ev'ry home fire burning for."

"I've Got You Under My Skin" is another of Porter's songs from the film that has now the stature of a standard.

> I've got you under the heart of me,
> So deep in my heart, you're really a part of me,
> I've got you under my skin.

Some lines in the song displeased one man who wrote to ask: "How can you 'stop before you begin'?" Given the letter to read Fulco di Verdura scribbled in a margin a message to Cole: "Don't you hate logical people?" The success of this song was indicated more impressively when the Columbia College yearbook, edited that year by Thomas Merton (later to achieve fame as a Trappist monk and best-selling writer), announced that a poll it conducted cited "I've Got You Under My Skin" as the best popular song of 1936. Earlier, *Variety* listed three Porter songs among those "most played on the air": "I've Got You Under My Skin," "Easy to Love," and "It's De-Lovely." A number of Porter's acquaintances, commenting on "I've Got You Under My Skin," claim that Porter was alluding not only to sex but to drugs, which were popular with some of his café society friends.

One of the songs Porter wrote for Frances Langford in the film, "Goodbye, Little Dream, Goodbye," was dropped. Merman sang it in the Boston tryout of *Red, Hot and Blue!* Judged "too somber," perhaps because of its being in a minor key, it was retired a second time. But in recent years it's enjoyed something of a revival:

> It's done, little dream, it's done,
> So bid me a fond farewell, we both had our fun.
> Was it Romeo or Juliet who said when about to die,
> "Love is not all peaches and cream,"
> Little dream, goodbye.

The Economist years later wrote: "There is a story that when he introduced his song 'Goodbye, Little Dream, Goodbye' for the film *Born to Dance,* the MGM executive Sam Katz told him 'That song is beautiful. Why it's . . . it's Jewish.'"

"Swingin' the Jinx Away," which Langford sang and Eleanor Powell danced, is another anthem to swing. "Rap-Tap on Wood" has also climbed in popularity. "Upbeat," "positive," it caught the mood of better times in the United States:

> When you sit down, one day,
> Look over yourself and say,
> "You're very good,"
> Ra-ap tap on wood.

Said *The New York Times* on December 5, 1936, " 'Rap-Tap on Wood' and 'Swingin' the Jinx Away' should be items of importance for the swing set."

As Porter cheerily told Dorothy Kilgallen, "There aren't so many torches being carried this season." Although Kilgallen insisted that "[Porter] writes music for . . . New York audiences," Cole was more and more fascinated by

Hollywood. Said Cole, "It is such a struggle to do a show, and it is so simple in Hollywood, 'I'd like to do a show every year to keep from softening up,' he said . . . In Hollywood, they give you everything you want on a silver platter." "Oh, yes," said Kilgallen, "Cole Porter, the smooth continental music master, is sold on Hollywood, from the sunshine to the sound sets."

As they were in Paris, clubs in New York and Hollywood were creative venues for Cole. In fact one commentator wrote, "Cole Porter gets his inspiration from night clubs," and he quotes the composer saying, "Recently I visited a night club six times to get a feeling of swing in the new tunes played there." Of course he had other sources of inspiration: "I go to the theatre constantly to keep in touch with popular musical taste. My interest in composition is modern, but I like going back to the classics. I am especially interested in providing dance forms that haven't been used recently. In *Born to Dance,* for instance, I use an old-fashioned horn-pipe, and in *Red, Hot and Blue!* the czardas. In every show I always try to use my favorite tempo, one seldom used in America—the paso doble—or three/two time, a lively tempo." Porter always insisted that he carefully researched the backgrounds of his shows, which "forced me to learn a great deal about geography." He was concerned, too, that however timeless the songs turned out to be, they needed to be timely as well, and this led him to search "for that elusive topical idiom." He wanted to know "the newest wisecracks and cliches" so that his song lyrics appealed to different audiences.

At that time Porter claimed he worked from eleven a.m. until four p.m. "officially" but kept at his work wherever life took him. Many people heard from Porter a version of what he told Anita Colby when she sympathized with his being afflicted by a boring dinner partner: "I just close my eyes and write the most beautiful music." And even in the after hours, Porter persisted with his work. In 1936 Winsor French, Len Hanna's companion, was living with the pianist Roger Stearns in a house near Porter in Hollywood. "Porter 'retired' at 10 in the evening to his piano inevitably to leave it at some ungodly hour . . . it was his unfortunate habit to drift toward [our house] so that [Roger and Cole] could sit down at the piano together and spin his latest brain child into an endless duet." Once he listened to "Rap-Tap on Wood" for six hours. In the summer of 1936 Porter visited Cleveland twice, filled with the latest news about the film, and played sample recordings of the tunes for French, Stearns, Len Hanna, and their Cleveland chums.

He started writing a song by selecting a title. "From this title I work out the psychology of the tune. Next I write a lyric backwards, and in this way build it up to a climax . . . if I can't find a good climactic line I throw out the tune." He was quick, as always, to acknowledge his debt to rhyme dictionaries. "For long easy rhymes I use Andrew Loring's *Lexicon*. Other books I have in constant use are Roget's *Thesaurus,* an atlas, Fowler's *Modern English Usage,* and a dictionary." Porter's industry paid off. Very often, remarked a critic, Cole strove strenuously to avoid the triteness of lyrics, harmony, and thirty-two-measure choruses. His lifelong flight from triteness was a legacy from Desdemona Bearss, his childhood playmate who cautioned him about clichés. Nor did he relax his vigil with films, which brought additional challenges. "Motion pictures are more difficult to write for than the stage. I must deliver my tunes in a shorter time. I have only seven numbers in pictures, but twenty-one in an ordinary show." Nonetheless, Porter said, "It's fascinating work, entirely different from musical comedy for the theatre, and I hope to do more pictures."

Commentators called the plot of *Born to Dance* "gob-meets-girl" and the film "a mammoth musical." The combined stages were two hundred feet long, eighty feet deep, and one hundred feet high. More than three thousand people figured in the production: one thousand carpenters, painters, and steel workers constructed the set; fifty men cleaned and repolished it; one hundred wardrobe workers assisted the costume designer, Adrian, and another fifty kept the costumes in good condition. One hundred makeup artists and beauticians were employed, as were one hundred and twenty-five electricians, twenty-five prop men, seventy-five camera men. Not to speak of such specialists as glass blowers, who were part of the production staff, and the three hundred dancers. The film's grand proportions are partly explained by the studio's wish to make the film a worthy follow-up to *Broadway Melody of 1936* and *The Great Ziegfeld.*

Cole was leery of getting the sea slang wrong, so he solicited the help of the U.S. Navy in the person of Commander Harvey Shadle Haislip to look over the technical terms in the lyrics. "Nearing the starboard beam," he discovered, was less precise than "approaching the starboard beam."

"Research is absolutely essential in the writing of lyrics," Porter said referring to his errors in "An Old-Fashioned Garden." "Since that time I have been extremely careful. I took a course in anatomy before I wrote the lyrics for 'The Doctor's Song' ["The Physician"] and I studied all manner of insect and animal life before I started on the words of 'Let's Do It.'"

No doubt Porter is having us on a bit; but certainly he was meticulous in checking the accuracy of his lyrics.

Cole in Hollywood with Fred Astaire and Eleanor Powell, 1936

Meanwhile, Cole enjoyed his life in Hollywood. The retired opera diva Mary Garden joined him for a party at George Cukor's, where Cole sat at the piano playing and singing his songs. When occasionally Porter flubbed a lyric, Greta Garbo would sing out the correct words. The elusive Garbo even visited the set of *Born to Dance* to watch Eleanor Powell tap. As Christmas neared, Adrian gave a dinner for Mary Garden to which Linda and Cole came. Beneath the gardenia floating in each finger bowl was an oyster, which when pried open, revealed a pearl.

Born to Dance was released in November 1936. After the preview a studio official telegraphed Cole: "Your score applauded from beginning to end and when your name appeared on screen the ovation accorded you topped everything." Many critics called *Born to Dance* the greatest musical Hollywood had yet made. This notice in *Hollywood* is typical: "The Cole Porter music and lyrics will delight the common run of tune devotees as well as the more cultivated; two or three will certainly reach the popular hit level, especially the swing waltz 'Hey, Babe,' and 'Easy to Love.' Songs have color and novelty, and in the extravagant production numbers, especially the resound-

ing finale, they have the surge and vigor to go with pictorial spectacle."
Porter was particularly put out by the number of reviews that used the
words "suave" and "sophisticated." He said in an interview he'd rather be
called a "Rotarian" or a "Babbitt." "I've worked like a dog to keep all
["sophisticated"] implies out of my music . . . At best it means only worldly
wise and artificial but it now covers all sorts of bad taste and vulgarity . . .
[it] means nothing more than the bawdy ballads heard in the bluer New
York night clubs . . . Smart alec is more like it." The interviewer notes that
what Porter really wants to do is write genuine American folk songs. "Those
great popular songs are hard to write," said Cole. "They're so hard in fact
that few have ever been written. They just happen. Irving Berlin comes closest to writing real American music . . . without being banal. It's something
I admire."

But Porter continued to be unhappy about commentators connecting
him with a coterie. "Sophisticated allusions are good for about six weeks . . .
Sophisticated lyrics are more fun but only for myself and about eighteen
other people, all of whom are first-nighters anyway. Polished, urbane, and
adult playwrighting in the musical field is strictly a creative luxury." The raffish characters and their tough talk may have been Porter's nod in the direction of a less elite audience. Certainly "The Ozarks Are Calling Me Home,"
from Porter's new Broadway show, was an appeal to the proletariat, though
the ultimate effect is tongue-in-cheek:

> I've a feelin' the Ozarks are callin',
> And I've also a feelin' I'm fallin',
> So I'll soon be leavin' town,
> 'Cause the city has let me down,
> And the Ozarks are callin' me home.

Even in this song Cole couldn't keep entirely with the folk. For example
there's "Aunt Eliza in the rocker / Readin' Andy Gump and Cholly Knickerbocker."

Porter's adroitness in 1936 at scoring two major works being constructed three thousand miles apart is remarkable. *Red, Hot and Blue!* tried
out in Boston beginning on October 7, then traveled to New Haven for
a while, and came into New York on October 29. Len Hanna gave an
opening-night postplay supper for the celebrities who had traveled to
Boston for the show, among them Horst, who was so beguiled by the actress
Kay Picture when she arrived at Hanna's supper party that he wanted to fly
her to New York and photograph her. The first plan had called for the show

to open in New York a year earlier than it did, and Porter, then on his trip around the world, began work on the score during the return journey to New York, after he'd completed the songs for *Jubilee*. Initially it was to star Eddie Cantor along with Merman, but Cantor was otherwise engaged, so Freedley, late in 1935, hired Jimmy Durante. Ray Kelly thought Cole "was doing the show under great stress."

"I've never worked on a play in which everything has gone so smoothly," Cole told a reporter in Boston, despite the awkward length of the first act, which lasted for two hours and ten minutes. (One critic suggested they imitate Eugene O'Neill and do half the play one night and half the next.) Reviews in Boston were mixed, but a number of critics hailed the adagio danced by Grace and Paul Hartman, and everyone had praise for Merman, Durante, and Bob Hope. "Wait till you see Jimmy Durante," Cole said. "I think he's the biggest thing in the theatre today and he's terrific in this." The *Christian Science Monitor* reported some days after the Boston opening that Vinton Freedley and Porter were rewriting their new show; it was too sentimental and went "overboard on plot, on conversation, and on rowdy jokes." The reviewer said Porter drew "variously on Bizet, Sullivan, Ravel and others for his inspiration" but predicted "It's De-Lovely" would be a hit. It was at this time too, Porter recalled, that "we all decided another song should be added. It had to be done in a hurry, of course, but I didn't have any difficulty as I knew the situation in the show perfectly. I got my song in mind Tuesday, worked on it that night and Wednesday, and it was in the show orchestrated and sung by Ethel Merman on Thursday night." The song was one of his torchiest: "Down in the Depths." A familiar scenario: "The one I've most adored / Is bored / With me." The next lines were inspired by a rather touching remark of Merman's: "Nice people dine with me / And even twice." This song about unrequited love sung by a person perched in a New York penthouse has autobiographical echoes that persuade one that the song was gestating in Porter long before he wrote it down.

> While the crowds at El Morocco punish the parquet
> And at "21" the couples clamor for more,
> I'm deserted and depressed
> In my regal eagle nest
> Down in the depths on the ninetieth floor.
> When the only one you wanted wants another
> What's the use of swank and cash in the bank galore?
> Why, even the janitor's wife

Has a perfectly good love life
And here am I
Facing tomorrow
Alone with my sorrow
Down in the depths on the ninetieth floor.

Radio once found the reference to "the janitor's wife" class-conscious, and Porter for that one performance changed the phrase to "the analyst's wife." Another phrase bothered Porter and led to a brief misunderstanding. Several times Porter passed Russel Crouse without speaking. Crouse presumed he had displeased Cole in some way and was searching his memory to no avail when Porter suddenly smiled and said to him, " 'In my pet pailletted gown,' " ending Cole's search for the *mots justes*. (Ray Kelly also commented on Cole's concentration: "I'd think I was talking to him and he'd have every appearance of listening carefully to what I was saying and then suddenly it would dawn on me that he hadn't heard a word. I'd come up with 'There's a big black gorilla coming through that window.' His head would go up and down, 'yes, that's right.' And he hadn't heard a word. He just sort of carried around a little soundproof room of his own that no one could seem to penetrate. His work was constant.") Speaking of the beauty of Merman's performance of this song, Cole later reflected, "One thinks of these things on the morning after an opening, with affection and gratitude. For, after all is said and done, a song writer is very much at the mercy of his interpreters."

According to Ray Kelly, Merman, Durante, and Hope were all mischievous performers: "Every night the performance was something else because those three people would come on stage. Hope would carelessly toss a line up in the air and Merman or Durante would grasp it and many strange things would happen, but always funny. Some lesser person would come out and, bang, they would throw them a line having nothing to do with the book. They would sit there dumbfounded and the other three would carry on . . . kick it around. I don't think that show repeated itself three times in the whole run."

With Merman, of course, Cole felt entirely at home as she did with him. Merman and Durante had both been promised top billing, and the agents of both were unrelenting. It was Linda Porter who seemed to save the day, suggesting to Cole that both names should intersect. But the artists' representatives still fretted about which name the audience would read first. Finally it was decided that every two weeks the names be alternated. Cole, who was in Hollywood then, probably avoided this clash. But he could not avoid the disagreements with Vinton Freedley over "Goodbye, Little Dream, Goodbye" (too melancholic for the show) and the orchestration of "Ridin' High." Merman also feuded with Bob Hope about his mugging and moving on her laugh lines. Durante, though, Merman found "a dream." His number "A Little Skipper from Heaven Above" nightly convulsed the audience as Durante confessed in song he was not really a man but a woman: "I'm about to become a mother, / I'm only a girl, not a boy."

To commemorate the New York opening of *Red, Hot and Blue!* Linda presented Cole with what Michael Pearman considers the most beautiful of the cigarette cases the Duke of Verdura designed and executed. The platinum case featured diamonds, suns, moons, and zodiac signs; the top was entirely encrusted with rubies, diamonds, and sapphires (red, white, and blue) circling an enormous sunburst of diamonds. But Linda and Cole were by now beginning to be disaffected, and she did not attend the opening because, said Winsor French, she "was too ill to be at hand." Instead Len Hanna and Mary Pickford joined Cole with Merle Oberon on his arm. Oberon was a favorite of Porter's, although years later, chatting with Anita Colby about bequests people had sought from him, he said, "Merle wants everything!" On opening night, from the Alvin Theatre, Cole went to El Morocco with Winsor French and others and wound up at Len Hanna's bar at four a.m., waiting for reviews. The opening had attracted many celebrities, and police in large numbers had to protect stars from their fans. In New York J. Edgar Hoover and his companion, Clyde Tolson, attended. They'd become very matey with Merman because the Stork Club was their mutual oasis when in New York and they often met her there.

"The morning after an opening of one of my own shows," Porter a week later told *The New York Times,* "is more or less the same as any other morning—except that I sleep much later."

In the case of *Red, Hot and Blue!* I broke my record by exactly ten minutes. The reason for my behavior isn't that I'm confident of the play's success or that I'm totally without nerves. I'll put up my nerves against the best of them. But for some reason, the moment the curtain rises on opening night, I say to myself: "There she goes," and I've bid good-bye to my baby. During the months of preparation the piece itself has a way of becoming something of a person to me—not always a nice person, perhaps, but at least someone that I've grown fond of. The minute that it is exposed to its premiere audience, however, I feel that it's no longer mine.

In writing the score for *Red, Hot and Blue!* Cole produced a number of beautiful songs that seem enduring in their sentiment and musical appeal. Although a reviewer for *Time* called the show "of the second magnitude," its best songs belie that charge. One of these is "Ours," romantic, deeply felt, but *con brio* too. Again Porter's disapproval of:

> *The high gods above*
> *Look down and laugh at our love,*
> *And say to themselves, "How tawdry it's grown."*
> *They've seen our cars*
> *In front of so many bars,*
> *When we should be under the stars,*
> *Together, but alone.*
> *Ours is the chance to make romance our own.*
>
> *Ours, the white Riviera under the moon,*
> *Ours, a gondola gliding on a lagoon,*
> *Ours, a temple serene by the green Arabian Sea,*
> *Or maybe you'd rather be going ga-ga in Gay Paree,*
> *. . . . .*
> *Mine, the inclination,*
> *Yours, the inspiration,*
> *Why don't we take a vacation*
> *And make it all ours.*

The patter that follows and the second refrain poke fun at these romantic yearnings with self-directed irony, ending: "Why don't we stay in Manhattan / And play it's all ours."

"It's De-Lovely" finally was heard in the show, sung by Merman and Hope. The tale is told in two verses and five refrains, spirited and glamorous chat but attractively sentimental too. "The night is young, / The skies are clear," and the breezy lovers decide to walk. "Let yourself go" is the dictum.

> *So please be sweet, my chickadee,*
> *And when I kiss you, just say to me,*
> *"It's delightful, it's delicious,*
> *It's delectable, it's delirious,*
> *It's dilemma, it's de-limit, it's deluxe,*
> *It's de-lovely."*

In the verses of "Five Hundred Million" Porter appears to have vented some of his misgivings about the taxes the 1930s had brought:

> *The President*
> *Won't be content*
> *Till the government*
> *Has spent it all.*

And he laments "those days forever lost" when "any hospitable civilian / Could afford to give a big cotillion."

One of Merman's big numbers in *Red, Hot and Blue!* was "Ridin' High," the anthem that had troubled Freedley at the outset but which finally triumphed and remains among the finest of Porter's hits.

> *Life's great, life's grand,*
> *Future all planned,*
> *No more clouds in the sky.*
> *How'm I ridin'? I'm ridin' high.*

Why? Because of:

> *Someone I love,*
> *Mad for my love,*
> *So long, Jonah, goodbye.*
> *How'm I ridin'? I'm ridin' high.*

The patter allows Cole to drop the names of famous women of the time, whose beauty and wealth and wit matter not at all to the joyous lady who is loved. Those alluded to include Barbara Hutton, Wallis Simpson, Hepburn, Dietrich, Dorothy Parker, Eleanor Holm, and even Mrs. Roosevelt, who "gets pay to write her day" (her newspaper column was titled "My Day"): "If I could write my nights, hey, hey!" Tallulah appears, and Simone Simon.

> *So ring bells, sing songs,*
> *Blow horns, beat gongs,*
> *Our love never will die,*
> *How'm I ridin'? I'm ridin' high.*

Did Porter's rather muted marital troubles in 1936–37 shape at all "Hymn to Hymen"?

> Hymen, thou phony
> God of matrimony,
> Humbly we pray, keep away from our door.
> Those thou hast mated
> Say thou art overrated
> And call thee a dated, unmitigated bore.
> Why wouldst thou tie us
> In wedlock, holy and pious,
> Knowing as thou doest
> Love is truest when it's free.

The title song, sung by Merman, wittily voices her preference for music that is red, hot, and blue. Stravinsky sends her hurrying to Minsky's; she prefers Berlin and Vincent Youmans.

> If you want to thrill me and drill me for your crew,
> Sing me a melody that's red, hot and blue.
> . . . .
> I can't take Sibelius,
> Or Delius,
> But I swear I'd throw my best pal away
> For Calloway,
> So when we're all set and I get married to you,
> Don't let that violin
> Start playing Lohengrin,
> It may be as sweet as sin
> But it's not red, hot and blue.

This score of *Red, Hot and Blue!* was all bounce and style—as was Cole when he boarded a plane to California with Sturges in December of 1936. In Los Angeles they met Linda, who had gone ahead to rent a house.

Much of the first half of 1937 Porter spent in Hollywood at work on the score for the MGM film *Rosalie*, starring Nelson Eddy and Eleanor Powell. *Rosalie* was to be a film version of a 1928 Ziegfeld Broadway musical for which George Gershwin and Sigmund Romberg wrote the score. Everyone agreed that this Graustarkian tale of a West Point cadet and a princess from Romanza required an especially appealing title song. As Porter wrote nearly a decade later to Paul Whiteman, he composed six versions before he played the score for L. B. Mayer, who "liked everything in the score except that song, 'Rosalie.' It's too highbrow. Forget you are writing for Nelson Eddy

Cole, Sturges, and Ed Tauch on European walking tour, summer, 1937

and simply give us a good popular song." Porter told Whiteman, "I took 'Rosalie' No. 6 home and in haste wrote 'Rosalie' No. 7. Louis B. Mayer was delighted with it, but I still resented my No. 6 having been thrown out, which to me seemed so much better." This was a judgment with which even Dr. Sirmay disagreed. Cole insisted throughout his life that "Rosalie" was the dreariest song he ever wrote, despite Irving Berlin's advice to him: "Never hate a song that has sold a half million copies." The most beautiful of all the songs Cole wrote for *Rosalie* is "In the Still of the Night," which was in some danger of being dropped from the score because Nelson Eddy told Porter it was impossible to sing. Porter went to Mayer, who is said to have burst into tears when he heard the song. He quickly ordered Eddy to sing the song, and Eddy found the notes. Some months after the song was written, Cole told reporters that it was his best to date and that he preferred it to "Night and Day." The lyrics are eloquent, voicing the doubts of a person deeply in love but unsure that he is loved in return.

> In the still of the night,
> As I gaze from my window
> At the moon in its flight,
> My thoughts all stray to you.
> . . . .
> "Do you love me as I love you?
> Are you my life-to-be, my dream come true?"
> Or will this dream of mine
> Fade out of sight
> Like the moon
> Growing dim
> On the rim

Billy Powell, Monty, Cole, Linda, and Sturges, 1935

> *Of the hill*
> *In the chill,*
> *Still*
> *Of the night?*

The evanescence of this silver moon is beautifully suggested by the ono-matopoeia of the slender rhymes: "dim"/"rim" and "hill"/"chill"/"still."

"In the Still of the Night" was written with Cole's lover Ed Tauch in mind. Meanwhile, coolness characterized Linda's relationship to Cole in 1937. She had never liked California, claiming it didn't suit her frail physical constitution. But even more offensive to her was the increasing boldness of Cole's homosexual caperings. Her pleas that Cole give up Hollywood were unavailing, and she was deeply affronted by his decision to make another film in the next year. As Cole augmented his own crowd in Hollywood, many of them homosexual, Linda feared the loss of his companionship, which mattered enormously to her. She left for Paris, and this estrangement lasted over the summer and into the autumn. Cole eventually followed Linda to Paris, but neither of them would yield in the disagreement. Linda appears in some photos taken at this time looking cold and no longer beautiful.

Cole then commenced a walking tour with his pals Sturges and Tauch. The night of August 18 was apparently passed in what Cole called in a lyric "the dear, dear, clear Mussolini Hütte [hut]." Copenhagen and Elsinore Castle were next. Much of the trip is caught in photos, which feature handsome guides, attractive bellboys, statues of male nudes, putti. From Denmark the three traveled to Oslo, Stockholm, Helsinki, Danzig (where the snapshots include one of Hitler Jüngend), Warsaw, Cracow, Prague. Munich seems the nearest Porter got to the Nazi forces that were gathering strength in Europe in those years. One photo features many swastikas draped across a street, and others are marked "Il Duce with Der Führer" and "Modern Nazi Architecture," which would particularly have attracted the eye of the architect Tauch.

Back in Paris, Cole found Linda still angry. Neither seemed likely to capitulate. Cole had a score to do for the musical *You Never Know*. On October 4, 1937, he boarded the *Estonia* bound for New York.

Chapter 11
_____

Back in Stride

In October 1937, soon after Cole arrived from Europe, he accepted an invitation from his old friend, Countess di Zoppola (familiarly known as Tookie), to spend the weekend in her country house in Mill Neck, near Oyster Bay—a stretch of what people continue to call Long Island's Gold Coast. Among the other guests were the Duke of Verdura and Diana Vreeland. In those years the Piping Rock Club in Locust Valley, Long Island, rented horses to members. On that October 24 Cole seemed restless, and he arranged for a riding party. When he and his friends arrived at the Piping Rock stables he spotted a horse that appealed to him, and insisted on mounting this horse, despite advice that it was skittish. "If Cole were warned against a horse he chose to ride," said Michael Pearman, "it would be typical of him to spurn the advice and insist on riding the horse." In the woods his horse shied at something and fell, rolling over on Cole's legs. Porter suffered compound fractures of his legs, and eventually osteomyelitis (infection of the bone marrow) set in.

A member of the riding party rang the Locust Valley Fire Department, which sent its ambulance. (Once in World War II, Bart Howard, now known to many as the composer of "Fly Me to the Moon," was on duty in an army recreation room. One of his tasks was dispensing stamps. A young soldier dropped a letter on the desk addressed to Cole Porter. "Do you know Cole Porter?" Bart asked. Yes, he did. "How did you meet him?" "Well, when he had that accident I came by in a truck and picked him up." From then on, when a Cole Porter show opened, tickets for him and his wife would arrive without fail.)

Porter told friends that his mother had always stressed to him the notion that a gentleman never depresses his friends by relating his woes to them. Jean Howard said that Cole maintained a reserve, particularly where pain was concerned, that he never lowered. Cole liked to tell the story, which became a legend, that as he lay with his crushed legs, waiting for help to arrive, he took out a notebook and worked on his song "At Long Last Love," which though copyrighted earlier that month still lacked a verse. The song was introduced by Clifton Webb in Porter's 1938 show *You Never Know* and continues to be a favorite of saloon singers and their audiences.

> *Is it in marble or is it in clay?*
> *Is what I thought a new Rolls, a used Chevrolet?*
> *Is it a sapphire or simply a charm?*
> *Is it ———* or just a shot in the arm?*
> *Is it today's thrill or really romance?*
> *Is it a kiss on the lips or just a kick in the pants?*
> *Is it the gay gods cavorting above,*
> *Or is it at long last love?*

This tale, difficult to believe, suggests how eager Cole was to fend off the pity and depression news of his accident brought to his friends. Cole continued to be, as George Eells wrote, "a symbol of the invincible youth who rode unscathed from one triumph to another. Now . . . his colleagues seemed to realize that the golden period had come to an end." This recognition was repugnant to Porter.

Cole had the initial surgery on his legs at a hospital in Glen Cove and then, having been moved to Doctors Hospital in Manhattan, he underwent in late November the second of what were to be many, many operations over the years.

Linda (in Paris) and Katie (in Peru) were apprised of Cole's misfortune almost at once. From Paris, Linda wrote to Bernard Berenson a letter describing first, and at some length, her own illnesses that fall: a broken rib and bronchitis, "which was almost the worst thing that could happen, as, with constant coughing, the ribs refused to heal." But after weeks in bed she was better—able to take short walks when the weather permitted. She then

*Here the singer hums suggestively.

tells Berenson ("one of the few people in the world who matters") the news of Cole's accident: "To add to my distraction, Cole has broken *both* legs—his horse fell on him—& he is in the hospital on Long Island. Poor Soul! he must be suffering terribly. I am changing the date of my sailing from the 17th Nov to the 3rd so as to be with him . . . I really am worried to death & long to be near him."

Both Linda and Katie opposed the judgment of Dr. Joseph B. Connolly that Cole's two legs be amputated immediately. Linda secured a promise from the physician that he would not take any such action until she arrived. Friends criticized this decision, but Linda's assessment of the situation seems to have been correct: most probably the loss of his legs would have crushed Cole's spirit. Decades later, when one of his legs *was* amputated, he virtually shut up shop. Both women rushed to Cole's bedside. To Cole's friend Winsor French, Linda spoke about her decision to stand by her husband: "It's too heartbreaking. You don't desert a sinking ship." (For some time before the accident, according to Ray Kelly, Linda, in France after her flight from Hollywood, was making plans to divorce Cole.) For days after the accident he was in shock, at times delirious, at times unconscious.

Friends flocked to comfort Cole in the hospital. Among the earliest was Elsa Maxwell, to whom the heavily sedated Cole managed to mutter: "It just goes to show fifty million Frenchmen can't be wrong. They eat horses instead of ride them."

For some time the possibility of amputation was touch-and-go. An eminent specialist, Dr. John J. Moorhead, was brought into the case and first agreed with Dr. Connolly that amputation was the likely course to take, but he promised to delay. When Linda emphasized to him the psychological desolation the loss of his legs would bring to Cole, Dr. Moorhead said he would wait to see if fever developed. If it did not, he would attempt to rebuild the legs, but he advised Cole that he could give him no assurance that an alternate treatment would succeed and warned him that he would suffer agonizing and perhaps lifelong pain.

It was shortly after the accident, according to Ray Kelly, that Linda alerted him to Cole's condition. She knew that when Cole was discharged from the hospital he would need help and she turned to Kelly as the most trusted and suitable person. No doubt Cole concurred in the choice. Kelly, a tall, broad-shouldered young man probably fit Porter's sexual fantasies but he was also a loyal and affable companion who could assist with Cole's care needs. Kelly was employed by the Porters and paid the then princely sum of one hundred dollars a week and provided with a small apartment in the Waldorf.

Some years later, the composer Bart Howard remembered meeting
Kelly at Fort Benning, Georgia, and thinking how patently gay Kelly was. A
handsome man, Kelly swept Bart Howard up in his arms and kissed him. It
was while stationed in Georgia that Kelly met an attractive young woman
whom he eventually married and by whom he had four children. After the
war, the Kellys often dined privately with the Porters or were invited to dinner parties with guests as grand as the Duke and Duchess of Windsor.

At Doctors Hospital Cole underwent two operations to repair damaged
nerves. The pain was excruciating, but Cole, for the most part, maintained
his stoic behavior. Even the hospital staff was said to be impressed by his
control. Cole claimed it helped to make a game of his predicament. With
Elsa Maxwell the game took the form of assigning a personality to each leg:
the left he called Josephine, the right, Geraldine. Josephine was sweet and
obliging; Geraldine, "a hellion, a bitch, a psychopath," in line with the different degrees of pain the leg caused. Difficult as Geraldine was, Cole
insisted that he loved her as much as the docile Josephine and wanted to
hold on to her. To the physician's inquiry about how Cole found himself
one particular day, Porter replied, "There are about a thousand little men in
these legs with sharp knives and they're jabbing all over. I'm having awful
pain." Ray Kelly reported that at one point in the hospital Cole was taking
"14 different kinds of narcotics and hypnotics and sedatives daily. And there
was great fear that when he did get out of the hospital he'd have to go on a
cure. When he'd tell the nurse 'I need something, the pain is too great,' the
nurse would give Cole half a belladonna tablet and dispense placebos to
him." Kelly describes Cole in his hospital bed "with his eyes rolled back in
his head . . . and beads of sweat pouring off him. He suffered the tortures of
the damned."

Friends gathered in mid-January to welcome Cole, now discharged
from the hospital, and to celebrate his return to social life, restricted though
that life had become. Elsa Maxwell, as so often in the past, was mistress of
the revels. Like the guests at her gala, the Porters had sumptuous automobiles, but they had no reason that evening to summon them. (Each year
Cole ordered up a new black Cadillac, from which he had all the ornaments
removed; and he had made a present to Linda of a Rolls-Royce, which she
rarely used—when he inquired why, she replied, "Because it bruises my
sables.") On that January night in 1938 the Porters simply descended from
their suite of the Waldorf Towers. This evening he had to be carried by his
valet, Paul Sylvain, and by Ray Kelly. Porter had recently hired Sylvain, and
from the time of the accident he was the person most important to him:
"practically an extension of himself," said Jack Coble.

Paul Sylvain, Cole's valet for twenty-two years

Ladies dressed by Balenciaga and Main Bocher and spiffy gents in white tie and tails made their way through the elegant lobby to the Perroquet Suite, in the Waldorf-Astoria, where couples were already fox-trotting to music played by two society orchestras. The *gratin* had gathered that evening to cheer Cole up after his months of hospitalization and all the pain and depression consequent on it. Porter must have been especially pleased by the presence of his lover, Edward Tauch. The evening was a gala one, and Cole said afterwards he enjoyed being back in the spotlight, but he confessed he'd been still so heavily dosed with morphine that he had only vague memories of it all. Kelly found Cole "a tough little cookie who could adjust to all people and circumstances."

At home again, Cole arranged to have one of the twin pianos raised so that he could get near enough to the keyboard in his wheelchair. One of his legs reposed on a hassock, the other on a piano stool. He played for hours, mostly the classics. Meanwhile, reviews of *Rosalie,* which opened in December, were discouraging. The film was judged "lumbering" and "dull" despite Eleanor Powell's tapping her way down sixteen drums measuring from ten inches to sixteen feet in height. The score was judged "tuneful but not exceptional." The London *Times* called *Rosalie* "a simple little Ruritanian story . . . a dreary waste of magnificence."

On February 3 Cole again checked into Doctors Hospital, where further surgery was performed. Dr. Moorhead urged him to return to songwriting, hoping that this would head off the emotional collapse threatening Cole. Porter had promised Clifton Webb that he would ready the score of *You Never Know* for rehearsal in February, so he set to work on it and dropped plans to do a show called *Greek to You.*

You Never Know is an adaptation of a version by P. G. Wodehouse of a Viennese comedy called *By Candle Light.* Produced by the Shuberts, it opened in New York on September 21, 1938, and ran for 78 performances, after the extended tryout, which began March 3, 1938. Linda journeyed up to New Haven along with a number of celebrities for the opening night. Cole was unable to attend, so before departing for New Haven, the Shuberts brought eighteen musicians, along with several of the principals, to the Waldorf Towers, where they gave him a private peek at the show. The *New Haven Evening Register* panned the work: "Little song and not much beauty," it complained. Apparently Lupe Velez stole the show with her impersonations of Katharine Hepburn, Gloria Swanson, Shirley Temple, and others. The tryout continued in Boston in a swirling snowstorm ("uneven," "in need of surgery," "more good tunes than good singers," "the story . . . skirts the edge of naughtiness"). The Boston premiere nonetheless was called "the biggest night in the Boston theatrical season" and was graced by Mrs. Calvin Coolidge (who "came out of retirement" to do so), Marshall Field, Eleanore Sears, and the governor and his wife. Despite the attendant glamour, *Variety* wrote, "The premiere of Cole Porter's new musical was a distinct disappointment," singling out long-winded, dull passages in the book and the need for livelier singing and dancing, faulting the show for lack of singing voices and the paucity of laugh lines. And there was rancor among some members of the cast. No explanation was given as to why Lupe Velez had punched Libby Holman, but one newspaper proceeded to call Velez, who was married to Johnny Weissmuller, "Mme. Tarzan."

The rocky start of this new show doesn't seem to have been on Linda's mind when she complained to her friend Bernard Berenson that "this has been a dreadful winter." Linda had fled to the Triangle T Ranch in Arizona, her customary refuge from her respiratory illnesses for a three-month rest. She told Berenson something of Cole's ordeal and said optimistically, "With constant care he will make a complete recovery . . . The left leg (double fracture) is healed—he is free from cast and brace on the leg, so he can hobble about in his rooms at the Waldorf on crutches. He is as gay as a lark—has written a new score for *By Candlelight* which incidentally is a great success, & is now writing a second score." (Presumably this was the score for

Paul Sylvain and Cole's chauffeur, Bentley, assist Cole after surgery

Leave It to Me.) Of Cole, Linda adds, "He says his work saves his life, as it makes him forget his pain." Her displeasure with her husband in 1937 seems not at all present in her letter. "He is really a gallant soul," she writes. "There are no words to describe his patience and fortitude." Of her own life at the ranch: "I read all day long—with an occasional walk but am always out of doors & feel completely relaxed." She planned to return to New York and the Waldorf on April 2. In her farewell to "dearest B.B." Linda laments "the mess the world is in . . . Hitler means to 'inherit the earth'—will he?"

Like Linda, New York had great expectations for *You Never Know.* Lucius Beebe, who got a mention in one of the songs ("And the jelly? / What a very fitting present / For Lucius Beebe's belly"), wrote in the *Herald Tribune:* "Nothing in the Broadway year creates quite the excitement among the town's glamour folk as the evolution of a new Cole Porter musical. Its first inception [is] usually accomplished on a canoe trip down the Rhine or from his elaborate Hollywood chateau . . . About that time it has been named for the third time . . . heralds appear in the person of Linda Porter or [the producer] Dwight Wiman or Roger Stearns, whistling some of the more memorable tunes and quoting the catchier lyrics . . . [including] the rhyming of Elsa and seltzer and Colony and felony."

You Never Know was performed in Indianapolis on May 23, 24, and 25, and on opening night there was to be a reception and ball at the Columbia Club, which Cole, Katie, and other close friends were to attend. At the ball only Porter tunes were played by the dance band. Katie accepted the gold medallion for Cole. His stepgrandmother, Mrs. J. O. Cole, and his childhood chum Tommy Hendricks were among the audience.

In Chicago *You Never Know* was tried at the Grand Opera House. The *Chicago Tribune* said, "This was a premiere that recalled pre-Depression conditions in attendance and audience response." George Abbott spent five days in Chicago doctoring the play. As usual, puritans in the critical ranks warned readers of "tawdry vulgarities" and "obscenities" to be encountered in the show. When finally *You Never Know* reached New York, the critics were mostly negative. "Lacking in electricity" was one response. Walter Winchell knocked the show, as did Brooks Atkinson, although Winchell praised three of the songs. Richard Watts assessed the songs as "out of Porter's middle drawer." "At Long Last Love" did place first in one newspaper chart, but otherwise no memorable songs were sung. At the time Cole considered the new show his best to date, but some took this to be a judgment emanating from his drug-befuddled brain. He wrote twenty years later to tell George Eells, apropos a revival of this show: "Why anyone ever dug up *You Never Know,* I shall never know. It was the worst show with which *I* was ever connected."

Certainly the "glittering pals" turned up, as customarily they had done, in the front rows of the opening night in New York. And afterwards, there was a party given by Clifton Webb at his Park Avenue apartment, hosted by his mother, Maybelle; and another by Prince Serge Obolensky at the St. Regis. But Cole was still too ill to attend the parties, and Linda did not attend either.

Ray Kelly recalled that Cole could not always maintain his sangfroid when the pain became very acute. Once he asked Kelly to fetch his sleeping pills, but Kelly, aware that Cole had been drinking heavily, refused. Kelly was himself rather drunk and simply left the apartment when Cole kept up his demands. The next day Kelly failed to turn up for his customary drive with Cole. Later in the day Kelly received a package from the Waldorf florist. Inside was one dead lily and a note asking him to dine with Cole that evening.

Early in the summer of 1938—on his birthday, in fact—Cole tripped on a stair and broke his left leg. That put an end to the social sorties he had

begun to make. What to do? Cole was in no condition to travel and had to
be near to his doctors.

In 1938 Cole's friend Ollie Jennings built a house in Lido Beach, Long
Island, for himself and his lover, Ben Baz. Although Margaret Case Harriman's *New Yorker* profile of Porter asserts that "one summer he and his wife
experimented with a house near the Lido Country Club at Long Beach,"
most of the men who visited Cole there never recall seeing Linda, although
Jack Coble remembers that "Linda occasionally came out to see Cole."

In her delightful profile, Harriman notes that "the Long Beach Lido
bears no resemblance to the Italian Lido, and the house was small."
(Nonetheless the Lido Hotel on Long Island had been quite fashionable in
the 1920s and remained so well into the 1930s.) In fact this house still stands
at Lido Beach on Matlock Street, a cul-de-sac, facing sand dunes, the beach,
and the Atlantic Ocean only yards away. (A recent owner from Iran had
never heard of Cole Porter but was eager to tell about what must have been
a tenant subsequent to Cole, whose wife was discovered murdered in the
bathtub—still in use.)

Coble went to Lido Beach to visit Cole at "a house," said Coble, "which
I believe [he] used for little trysts." According to him, Porter also used Ollie
Jennings's house for trysts. Coble went there in a chauffeured limousine
with Cole and a male model, "a very attractive man who was the rage." The
three sat in the back of the car covered by a lap robe. Cole said he was working on a new score and had to do some research on a form of music with
which he was totally unfamiliar. Porter put questions to Coble, who had no
information to offer. "This was the only time Cole ever discussed a professional problem with me," he said.

Jack Coble remembers that "Ray Kelly, the great love of Cole Porter after
Tauch," was living in the house with Cole that summer, and a few young
men often stayed there, Tauch among them. Coble made "countless visits" to
Cole that summer at Lido Beach. "By now Porter and Tauch had separated
and Ray Kelly was Porter's lover," said Coble. "Kelly was husky but gentle
until he drank. Then he would fight and break porcelain." Coble thought
that Linda was aware of all this but "remained aristocratically aloof." Porter
had servants on Matlock Street, and food often, if not daily, was brought all
the way to Lido Beach from the "21" Club in Manhattan. As Porter's Lido
Beach house was only one short block from Jennings's house, their guests
often mingled. Servicemen stationed nearby sometimes turned up at Porter's
or Jennings's cottages. One army veteran stationed at Governors Island esti-
mates that many of the soldiers and marines billeted there were actively
homosexual. One of them, a handsome soldier named Frank Walsh, was

"very well-schooled in 'Who Was Who.' " At a Saturday-night party at Lido Beach in 1941, probably held at Jennings's house, Walsh and the other soldiers learned that the party was hosted by Cole Porter: "It was a drinking-and-sex party, nearly orgiastic—fifty or more soldiers kissing, drinking, and lots of very graphic sex." Cole was using a cane but mixed in with everyone. "Porter was definitely the boss of the crowd." A piano was prominent among the furnishings and several people played it, though not Porter.

Harriman reports that neighbors noticed twice each week a shiny delivery car with "Waldorf-Astoria" lettered in gold on the side, which called at Porter's house and paused only briefly before driving off. It did not deliver gourmet foods or rare and delicious wines, but rather on Mondays picked up soiled laundry, and on Thursdays returned the laundry clean.

Coble and Baz are two of the guests at the Lido Beach house who remember the word and card games that were frequently played. Jennings and Ben Baz, Elsa Maxwell, Neysa McMein, and Ray Kelly were among the players. Kelly was such a superior word-game player that Ollie Jennings in particular wondered if Kelly didn't assist Porter with lyrics. And indeed, as Kelly himself told it, he did, and in substantial ways. Stuck for a word or a rhyme, Porter would also ask the help of his secretary or a servant.

For the remainder of his life Cole had fond feelings for *Leave It to Me*, much of which he wrote flat on his back on the sun porch that overlooked the ocean at Lido Beach. Porter found it like a ship and claimed that the motion of the Atlantic stimulated him, indicating how many songs he wrote on ships. This show gave him the most satisfaction of any, representing as it did a victory over his crippling disability and proof to himself and others that he need not accept the role of a useless invalid.

It all began with a proposal to Cole and Vinton Freedley by the writers Sam and Bella Spewack, who by 1938 had several successful Broadway shows to their credit and now had revived the book for a musical comedy about Americans in the diplomatic service. Their book was originally called *Clear All Wires*. At the time Cole seemed to them "a sparkling and enormously talented writer of songs and song-shows," but not yet "a full fledged composer [nor] the incorrigible perfectionist" he ultimately became. Bella Spewack remembered Cole at about forty-five years old:

> small, dapper, with black velvet eyes and a ready, winsome smile. He was already crippled, but with the aid of crutches rose to meet us. He was an urbane host, and his facade at that time was that of a man who found musicals amusing. He was not enormously preoccupied with the book—that would be our department. I don't want to give the impres-

sion that he just tossed off such songs as "My Heart Belongs to Daddy" . . . for we knew better, but he certainly gave us that impression. And the tossing off, he would have you believe, came between and during bouts of pain. The unfortunate title [of *Leave It to Me* was] the producer's contribution.

Freedley sent the Spewacks a copy of *Anything Goes,* presumably as something of a model: "I would suggest that you give special attention to the musical layout as the numbers were well spaced, the tempos varied, and they at no time held up the continuity of the story." This was to be the first musical the Spewacks wrote, and a success, although Walter Winchell announced that "the show belongs to Mr. Porter."

Leave It to Me opened in New York on November 9, 1938, after a tryout garnering good reviews in New Haven and Boston. On Broadway it received excellent notices. In the opinion of most "he did a magnificent job of it." The cast included Gene Kelly and Mary Martin, both making their Broadway debuts. Reminiscing decades later, Kelly told of "the pride I felt at being in a Cole Porter show . . . I really didn't have a part . . . I came in with a telegram. 'My Heart Belongs to Daddy' made [Mary Martin] a star. I never got over this, and I thought, 'wouldn't it be great to have somebody like Cole Porter write a song for you?' And then, of course, it happened to me several times. I was very lucky."

Perhaps it was the play's subject that induced so many politicians and government officials to turn out for the opening, among them Governor Herbert Lehman (cousin of Cole's classmate Bobby Lehman) and his rival Thomas Dewey, former New York State governor Alfred E. Smith, and Postmaster General James Farley; Rockefellers and Warburgs turned out too. *The New York Times* found Porter "at the top of his form," and Richard Watts rejoiced that *Leave It to Me* had no social significance "despite a moment when Victor Moore kicked the German Ambassador in the belly and all applauded." "Cole Porter has provided . . . some lyrics in his most ingenious and unblushing manner and much music that finds him at his topnotch best," wrote John Mason Brown. When one looks at the song lyrics, it's easy to see what earned Porter the "unblushing" designation. "I've still got my virginity," sings one chorus girl, "but I'm hoping to lose it soon." Sappho is updated:

> As Madam Sappho in some sonnet said,
> "A slap and a tickle

> *Is all that the fickle*
> *Male*
> *Ever has in his head,"*
> *For most gentlemen don't like love*
> *. . . . .*
> *They just like to kick it around.*

(One critic erroneously predicted, "You'll never hear it on the radio.") Then these lines: "How often we meant to sup together / And ended by waking up together."

Of course the sexiest song in the show was "My Heart Belongs to Daddy," sung by Mary Martin. She had grown up in Weatherford, Texas, the daughter of the town's leading lawyer. As a young woman she started several dance schools locally and then went to Hollywood, where the studios all turned her down. She appeared at Hollywood's Trocadero, then went on to New York City, where Vinton Freedley heard her and hired her for *Leave It to Me.*

Cole Porter said years later, "Mary Martin, you know, is probably the most basically naive person I've ever met. I'm convinced she never had any idea about the many meanings of 'My Heart Belongs to Daddy.' But then, neither did the radio networks at first. They played it for quite a while before they discovered that some of the lines to 'Daddy' weren't quite proper."

> *If I invite*
> *A boy, some night,*
> *To dine on my fine finnan haddie,*
> *I just adore*
> *His asking for more,*
> *But my heart belongs to Daddy.*

The rumor was that finally Freedley and Porter had to ask Sophie Tucker, also in *Leave It to Me,* to have a long talk with Miss Martin about the double entendre in the lyrics. In the concluding lines Martin's character explains her peril: "I can't be mean to Daddy / 'Cause my Da-da-da-daddy might spank."

Victor Moore, playing Alonzo P. Goodhue, America's ambassador to Russia, sang "I Want to Go Home"—a song that shows nostalgic feelings Porter seems sometimes to exhibit:

Cole with Bella Spewack, 1948

> *Ev'ry afternoon when the sun goes down,*
> *I dream of Kansas and my home town,*
> *And I get so homesick I swear*
> *I just go silly.*
> *How I long at the drugstore again to sit*
> *And order a double banana split,*
> *And then wash it down with some rare old sars'parilly.*
> *The trouble is with this job*
> *You can't get corn on the cob.*

Of course Porter is in part (large part probably) satirizing American insularity, but one feels his affection too for his father's drugstore in Peru, where he spent many childhood hours.

According to Bella Spewack, she and her husband found Cole a modest, quiet man with whom they had affinities, though not socially or intellectually. "We got along with him," but "he had a lot of ideas [political ones] with which we couldn't agree." He was not, for example, a fan of Franklin Roosevelt; Mrs. Spewack, on the other hand, was. All of Porter's friends remembered that he was almost totally uninterested in politics.

Porter's distance from the didactic is remarked by several critics, as is his avoidance of boringly topical questions. One unidentified writer cited a line spoken by Sophie Tucker to her stage children—"You must never even hint to the English that Americans are civilized"—as "equal to several solemn tomes on the comparative sociology of England and America." This same writer attributes the success of Porter's shows to their avoidance of the grimness that characterized plays by Maxwell Anderson, Sidney Kingsley, and others. Except that their books were better. "My great professional tragedy," Cole said, "is that I have to be a book hunter . . . Such scoundrels as Rodgers and Hart . . . know how to write their own books." It's the Porter songs that are proving to be immortal, although *Kiss Me, Kate* is an exception.

In April 1939, Lucius Beebe ranked Cole the leading "creator of smart and glittering theatre lyrics of his time." Beebe brings up Cole's complaint about shows that have an *embarras du richesse*. Said Cole, "One really big hit song is all any show should have. I wish I could find some way to spread out successful lyrics to cover a number of productions. Four or five songs which catch the public fancy and become widely known tend to dissipate and defuse their own successful effect."

If we scan *Leave It to Me* for winners, there are "Get Out of Town," "Most Gentlemen Don't Like Love," "My Heart Belongs to Daddy," "Tomorrow," and "There's a Fan," which, although unused in the show, cabaret singers have recently taken up—another naughty number, about all the fans to be seen but

> *The nicest fan I've got*
> *Is that little fan*
> *That a trav'ling man,*
> *Who knew Mother, bequeathed to me.*

About songs, Cole's theory was that if several are released to bands and radios, audiences feel they're familiar with the entire score "and are bored or disappointed accordingly; whereas, if only one song stands out even if they have heard it repeatedly before, they look forward to it with pleasure and anticipation."

Most curious of all, thought Cole, was that neither the songwriter, the producer, nor the musical director can ever predict what will catch the ear of the public and become a hit. "I certainly can't," said Cole, "and for that reason some of my shows have been awash with hit songs and lyrics I should far have preferred to distribute over two or three productions."

Porter particularized his point to Lucius Beebe: "['Begin the Beguine'] wasn't at first famous because we didn't release *Jubilee*'s music to the radio at the time." Then Artie Shaw and his band made a hit recording of it, "with the result," said Cole, "that during the run of *Jubilee* 'Begin the Beguine' wasn't a tenth the hit it is at this very moment. There was a four-year delay before it became really big-time stuff. 'Daddy' was written in as a spot song with no particular relation to the book of the show . . . Along came Mary Martin and overnight the dingus became better known than the name of the show in which it is sung." In his experience, said Cole, "it takes up to two months to discover whether a song is a real wow or just a flash in the pan . . . It took all of three months to find out that [with] 'Night and Day' I had anything profitable."

In February of 1939 Cole, who in Ray Kelly's words "always had to be on the go somewhere," traveled to Cuba with Kelly and Paul Sylvain, who carried him to the beach, where he sunbathed and allowed the warm salt water to wash against his limbs, a treatment Dr. Moorhead advised. Daiquiris were among his favorite drinks, and they'd first been served at Havana's Florida Bar. Cole later said he was encouraged in Cuba by the sight of enormous yachts and private planes. "As long as there is that much money," he told Lucius Beebe, "there must be opulent audiences for [my] brittle and sparkling songs and lyrics, most of which [he rather snobbishly concluded] concern themselves with people who do smart and expensive things."

Leave It to Me gave 307 performances in New York before it shut down on July 15, 1939. It then went on tour. A toney opening in Chicago brought out the notables. Plans to do a Scandinavian production had to be scrapped because of war in Europe. Nonetheless Cole must have been greatly buoyed up that *Variety*, in its assessment of *Leave It to Me*, found him to be "back in stride."

Chapter 12

DuBarry

Linda's departure from 13 rue Monsieur in 1939 must have been wrenching. To please Cole, she sent all the furniture to California, where she planned to arrange it in the two houses (one by the beach) Cole was renting. Leaving it severed Cole and Linda from two decades of elegance and pleasure not again to be matched anywhere. "The wise lived yesterday," as the title of the *New Yorker* profile of Cole put it, must have been a thought in the minds of both Linda and Cole as the 1930s tottered toward World War II. Although the house survived the war unscathed, and was even improved by the addition of a first-rate heating system installed by the German official who occupied it, the Porters never again lived there.

In early 1939, while Linda was in Paris, Cole, leafing through a *National Geographic* magazine, became fascinated by a description of the ruins of Machu Picchu in Peru. With his customary curiosity he decided to travel there. Ray Kelly claimed that Cole put himself to the task of learning Spanish and did so in two or three weeks—sufficient at least to carry on simple conversations. He chose Kelly to be his companion on this South American journey and Paul Sylvain to attend to his personal needs. Howard Sturges also went along. Porter had just got to a point where he could manage to propel himself with two canes, wearing braces that reached up to his hips. The elevation was staggering, Kelly said—one seemed to look straight up at the mountain, which appeared to vanish from sight, so high was its reach—and while Cole used the crutches and a wheelchair, he relied heavily on

Kelly and Sylvain to lift him over difficult terrain. "It was completely primitive," Kelly recalled. "No comfort, not even a place to sit down except for a
rock." In order to ascend to the ruins, Cole had to mount a horse—which
without hesitation he agreed to do. He calmly sat on it as the party proceeded up "mountain trails with sheer drops on either side: one misstep and
that was it." Kelly described himself as "scared to death," but Cole had no
qualms. When they reached the top, a "hotel" with three rooms and no
bathroom was the only facility. "One washed outdoors with a bowl. If you
wanted to go to the bathroom you . . . found yourself a tree—and [Cole]
was delighted with the whole thing." Their guide had to catch and then
cook a chicken, which when they ate it was still partly unplucked. The fastidious Cole seemed to enjoy it all. Nor would he retreat when they came to
a frail wooden bridge and the others advised that they turn back. Ray Kelly
considered Cole a person of great physical courage, sometimes verging on
foolhardiness.

By the summer of 1939 he was in Hollywood. MGM had approached
him, proposing that he provide the score for *Broadway Melody of 1939*. By
early autumn Cole had completed his work, but others hadn't, and so the
film had to be retitled *Broadway Melody of 1940*. It was released on February
9, 1940, and starred Fred Astaire and Eleanor Powell, along with Frank
Morgan and George Murphy. Murphy, a dancer of very different style and
gifts from Astaire's, grew weary of Astaire's perfectionism and the practice it
required. He campaigned for more spontaneity and less rehearsal, but to no
avail.

Porter wrote some stunning numbers for the film, including "Please
Don't Monkey with Broadway," which Astaire and Murphy introduced:

> *Glorify Sixth Avenue,*
> *And put bathrooms in the zoo,*
> *But please don't monkey with Broadway.*
> *Put big floodlights in the park,*
> *And put Harlem in the dark,*
> *But please don't monkey with Broadway.*
> *Though it's tawdry and plain,*
> *It's a lovely old lane,*
> *Full of landmarks galore and memories gay,*
> *So move Grant's Tomb to Union Square*
> *And put Brooklyn anywhere,*
> *But please, please,*

> *I beg on my knees,*
> *Don't monkey with old Broadway.*

"Between You and Me" has been unfairly neglected:

> *Between you and me,*
> *To use the vernacular,*
> *You've got what they call "oomph" in your eyes.*

"I Concentrate on You," a sizzling torch song danced memorably by Astaire and Eleanor Powell, has become a Porter standard:

> *Whenever skies look gray to me*
> *And trouble begins to brew,*
> *Whenever the winter winds become too strong,*
> *I concentrate on you.*
> *. . . . .*
> *On your smile so sweet, so tender,*
> *When at first my kiss you decline,*
> *On the light in your eyes when you surrender*
> *And once again our arms intertwine.*

And a fourth song from the film, "I've Got My Eyes on You," is another standard. It was introduced by Astaire and danced by Eleanor Powell and him. In a very attractive way it laces the games of love with mordant wit—especially in the verse:

> *I don't want you to feel*
> *When you go out for a meal*
> *With my rivals in town*
> *That I mean to track you down,*
> *Or that when out you sail*
> *For a date down in the dale*
> *There's a Dictaphone*
> *Under ev'ry stone*
> *And a bloodhound on your trail.*
> *However—*

As June began, Cole was "ensconced in [the] cottage at Malibu Beach and taking daily dips in the surf. He reports that said dips have done much to help him recover the use of his legs." In Hollywood Cole had a coterie of twenty or so boys—"swimming pool boys," Jack Coble called them. "It was a way Cole had of amusing himself," he added.

Besides the film work, Cole had had several prospects, among them a musical to star Mae West and a show to be written in collaboration with Moss Hart and George S. Kaufman. But his choice was *DuBarry Was a Lady*. This seemed to come about because of a discussion the agent Louis Shurr had with Buddy De Sylva. De Sylva had written many successful songs himself, including "California, Here I Come," "If You Knew Susie," "Look for the Silver Lining," and "Avalon." Bert Lahr was completing *The Wizard of Oz* and was searching about for a vehicle. De Sylva immediately suggested Herbert Fields's script *DuBarry Was a Lady*, which he thought would suit Lahr, with Ethel Merman as the perfect leading lady. Shurr promised he could persuade Cole Porter to write the songs, and in time Cole did, although he held up the arrangement by pressing for a considerable advance. (Ray Kelly found Cole to be a spendthrift who immediately spent his royalties; nonetheless, Cole was unexpectedly cagey about advances and other financial dealings.) Cole was particularly enthusiastic about the selection of a nearly unknown Betty Grable as *DuBarry*'s ingenue, and he seemed to produce the score without any difficulty. Ray Kelly recalled the trunk that Porter carried with him from one residence to another and into which he would dip when a score was needed. Generally, Cole found that if fourteen songs were called for, six or seven songs already completed would, with a bit of tinkering, be suitable. Whenever he took on a task of some enormity, the trunk gave him the feeling that he had already half completed it. Though a hard worker who made severe demands on himself, he would joke with Kelly that "I have lots of time to fool around."

"When Lahr first heard the *DuBarry* score, he was not convinced of its excellence," writes his son, John Lahr. What distressed him, it turned out, was not the songs, but Cole's rendering of them on the piano. "Cole was a good piano player, but not a great one," said Ray Kelly, but Bert Lahr had a different opinion: "Cole was a horrible piano player. Oompah, oompah. He played with a slow, wooden tempo. If you didn't know who it was, you'd think it was a learner." This criticism is curious, because recordings available of Porter's piano playing all suggest a light and rather animated style—songs played and sung more quickly than one usually hears them. The misgivings Lahr had about the score were dispelled when he first heard the orchestrated versions.

Meanwhile, Cole continued to enjoy the summer weather in California. Ray Kelly spent much of the time at the beach house with him. Kelly loved the water and devoted himself to sunning on the beach, which must have pleased Cole. As the beach house was small, Kelly, who in the Waldorf had a small apartment of his own, saw more of Cole than usual. He was astounded by Cole's capacity for work and became more aware than ever of the anodyne it was for him. Once, when the cook was fixing lunch in the cottage, Kelly grabbed a knife and began to help her peel potatoes. When

Ethel Merman and Bert Lahr in *DuBarry Was a Lady*, 1939

Cole discovered what he had done, he became angry and told him, "You'll break down all discipline here. I won't have it." Linda was more equable. Kelly remembered sitting down for dinner on a chair of hers that once had belonged to Napoleon. He sat carefully, knowing that it was fragile, but during the meal he began to talk animatedly and moved too quickly, whereupon the chair fell apart. "Linda, I'm so sorry," he said. "Forget it, Kelly," she replied. "It was *old*." Linda was more acerbic when a visitor knocked an irreplaceable crystal off the mantel and it shattered. "I'll replace it," he said, and Linda replied, "Oh, no you won't." "She could freeze people with ten words," Kelly said.

In the fall of 1939 *The Man Who Came to Dinner* opened in New York with Monty Woolley as Sheridan Whiteside. The playwright and director George S. Kaufman, along with Moss Hart, asked Cole "to write a Noël Coward-type song for their play." The song is titled "What Am I to Do" and he signed the manuscript Noël Porter. Some time after the play began its run, Monty decided to give a grand party at the Ritz-Carlton. Linda didn't attend, but Cole did, and on his arm was a veiled lady who, when she removed her veil, was revealed to be bearded. This was Lady Olga, whom the writer, Joseph Mitchell described so deliciously in *Up in the Old Hotel*. It seems that Porter discovered the whereabouts of Lady Olga and went to her dressing room with an invitation to Woolley's party. He depicted Monty as a student of beards, "known as The Beard by his friends, and that he had always wanted to meet a bearded lady." He offered to pay her, but she demurred: "I and you and Mr. Woolley are all in show business, and if this party is for members of the profession, I won't charge a cent." As nonprofessionals were attending, she named a fee of eight dollars.

Late in the afternoon of the party Porter picked her up at her house. She wore a rhinestone-spangled gown, and her beard was hidden by a scarf, which she removed in the elevator of the Ritz-Carlton, "astonishing the other passengers." "There were more than a hundred stage and society people at the party, and Porter introduced her to most of them. Woolley . . . asked her to have a drink. She hesitated and then accepted a glass of sherry, remarking that it was her first drink in nine years. 'I like to see people enjoying theirselves . . . There's too much confounded misery in the world,' Lady Olga told Woolley." After an hour and a half she had to return home to cook dinner for her husband. Next day she told friends she'd never had a nicer time. "Some of the better class of the Four Hundred were there and when I was introduced around I recognized their names. I guess I was a curiosity to them. Some of them sure were a curiosity to me. I been around

peculiar people all my life, but I never saw no women like them before."
According to another account, Cole squired her about the room at the
party, introducing her to everyone as Monty's sister. Woolley niftily finessed
Cole by saying how pleased he was to have his sister attend the festivities.
Woolley told someone that she looked like Elsa Maxwell in a property
beard. When Lady Olga heard his remark, "she snorted with indignation.
'Mr. Woolley must not have good eye sight,' she said." Cole was no doubt
happy to be with someone who evoked recollections of his childhood and
the circus.

DuBarry Was a Lady had the first of its tryouts in New Haven on
November 9, 1939, and there were subsequent runs in Boston and Philadelphia. One of the cast, Geraldine Spreckles, the heiress to a sugar fortune,
was interviewed in the *Boston Advertiser:* "This girl has a sugar grand-
daddy—literally—named Adolph who left her $3,000,000." Miss Spreckles
complained about having "a name that gets you publicity every time you
sneeze [and] . . . which kept one from getting a fair evaluation of [her]
work."

Early reviews called *DuBarry* "on the crude, even the lewd side." The
play is set in a 1930s nightclub, the Club Petite, where Louie Blore (the Lahr
character) serves as a washroom attendant; he's in love with May Daley, a
chanteuse (played by Merman). Louie attempts to slip May's boyfriend,
Alex, a Mickey Finn but accidentally drinks it himself and dreams he is
King Louis XV and May, Comtesse Du Barry, living in *dix-huitième* Versailles. (A dancing couple were played by Betty Grable and Charles Walters.
Tito Reynaldo, who also danced in the show, was said by Porter's friend Ben
Baz to have been a lover of Cole's.) Eventually Louie awakes and realizes
that May is unattainable by him and he must settle for friendship with her.

The sets for the show were elaborate, and the costumes by Raoul Pène
Du Bois were excellent reworkings of the dress of French court paintings of
a period about which, surprisingly, Bert Lahr knew quite a lot. Lahr's son
tells us that his father had read Dr. Johnson and Boswell and discovered
much about the person and court of Louis XV.

Bert Lahr said that when Cole Porter got dirty, "it was dirt, without
subtlety. Nothing I sang in burlesque was as risque as his lyrics. It would
never have been allowed on the burlesque stage." The song to which Lahr
principally alluded was "But in the Morning, No," "a sophisticated song of
seduction set to a minuet. Lahr in high-buckled shoes, a lorgnette, and peri-
wig ridiculed the fustian eighteenth century." For many years "But in the
Morning, No" could not be sung on the air.

In Boston, where the show opened on November 13, 1939, everyone connected with *DuBarry* was fearful of John Spencer, the city censor; but after the performance he said he "saw little to blue pencil." "Musical of the Year," announced the *Boston Post,* although a few critics in Boston (as in New Haven) complained of the show's excessive length. Porter wrote uncounted refrains for "But In the Morning, No" (and many that he performed privately never reached print). The double entendres are patent. Typical are these verses:

> *Can you fill an inside straight?*
> *Kindly tell me, if so.*
> *I've filled plenty inside straight,*
> *But in the morning, no, no—no, no,*
> *No, no, no, no, no!*

There are also allusions to public figures: Nelson Eddy and the much-married Tommy Manville, who was said to have sadistic impulses. One of his many dates was with a showgirl from *DuBarry.* He tempted the girl with a diamond bracelet, implying that if she slept with him, she'd be rewarded with the bracelet. Cole Porter warned this girl to expect a flash of pain. When she sat down she felt a sudden sharp pain from a hat pin which had been strategically placed by Manville.

"Diamond clips and emerald rings" and other bijoux are part of the decor in "Give Him the Ooh-La-La," a song Porter wrote for Betty Grable, who did it for two performances before Ethel Merman took it from her. "What can I do?" said Merman. "They insist I do it." Grable detested Merman from then on.

> *If poor Napoleon at Waterloo-la-la*
> *Had had an army of debutantes,*
> *To give the British the well-known Oo-la-la,*
> *He'd have changed the hist'ry of France.*

Porter tailored tunes to suit Lahr's comic genius—"It Ain't Etiquette," for example:

> *If you meet J. P. Morgan while playing golf*
> *With the Long Island banking set,*
> *Don't greet him by tearing your girdle off,*
> *It ain't etiquette.*

. . . .

> *It ain't smart*
> *It ain't chic,*
> *It ain't etiquette.*

The concluding line of the song, "Now, for instance, Snooks," was sung by Lahr, "Now, for ninstance, Snooks." "Porter feels that syllables like those were obviously created so that Lahr could spray them at an audience," wrote Margaret Case Harriman. She added that Porter told her that the origin of this line is in a story about Peggy Hopkins Joyce (whom Porter seemed to take gentle pleasure in satirizing). Told by a friend that many attractive people were at the French Riviera one season, Joyce asked, "For ninstance, whom?"

Porter enjoyed writing macaronic verse, especially mixing English and French. Harriman gives a lively picture of Cole rehearsing the chorus girls in "Mesdames et Messieurs":

> Mesdames et Messieurs, écoutez-vous,
> *Pardon us if into French we fall,*
> *But King Louie's fav'rite beauty* nous
> Invite *to a* très *French ball.*

"Porter's trick of tossing a French phrase into a lyric now and then necessitates his carefully drilling the singers until they get the accent right," wrote Harriman, citing the line "*C'est pour l'amour de la France.*" Cole would stop the girls midway through the song to say, "You're getting in the habit of saying '*Pour l'amour dee la France.*' It's 'deuh,' 'deuh.'" "Later he would collect the girls around him in the back of the auditorium while another number was being run through on the stage and rehearse them for twenty minutes on that one line alone."

This upbeat song is one of Porter's standards, mixing romantic feelings with a fear of the loss of the beloved:

> *Do I love you, do I?*
> *Doesn't one and one make two?*
> *Do I love you, do I?*
> *Does July need a sky of blue?*
> *Would I miss you, would I,*
> *If you ever should go away?*
> *If the sun should desert the day,*
> *What would life be?*

In the show it was sung expressively by Merman and Ronald Graham. The *Boston American* wrote that an hour after the first curtain, dance bands at the Cocoanut Grove and the Mayfair were improvising on "Do I Love You?" Betty Grable and Charles Walters sang "Well, Did You Evah!" According to Porter's pal Jack Coble, "Well, did you evah!" was an expression of their friend Ollie Jennings which Cole appropriated. "Katie Went to Haiti," one of Merman's numbers, is another song in Cole's canon that has the element of a family joke.

> Katie stayed in Haiti
> Spending all her pay.
> Katie met a natie
> Ev'ry other day.
> . . . .
> After a year in Haiti
> She decided she should really go
> But Katie had lived at such a ratie
> That Katie had no dough.
> So Katie stuck to Haiti
> Delighted with her fate,
> 'Cause Katie still had Haiti
> And practically all Haiti had Katie.

"Friendship" was another great song success from *DuBarry* and something of a signature tune for Lahr and Merman. The song was such a hit in New Haven that Cole finally ran onstage with new lyrics he'd composed sitting in the second row. Whenever Lahr and Merman performed the song, the audience refused to let them go. In Boston, Lahr came down to the footlights and told the audience to turn up in Philadelphia for the final tryout. "There may be some new ones there," he added.

Rumors abound about the *froideur* that developed between Lahr and Merman as the show progressed. Tales are told of the lethal way in which Merman moved on Lahr's laugh lines and generally tried to get the spotlight. According to John Lahr, his father got on famously with Betty Grable (who, incidentally, was beloved too by the card-playing stagehands, whom she joined in moments offstage) but was less comfortable with Merman, "whose talent he admired, but whose strength made him nervous. . . . 'She's an individual with a special way of working. There was nothing vicious in what she did, she is a great performer. But she's tough. *She never looks at you on stage.*' . . . Lahr had his tricks too, and an inevitable, if friendly, friction developed. It fed their stage roles." Nonetheless, their huge success with "Friendship" had ironic overtones. Merman tried to be nice. "Bert Lahr knows all there is about the theatre and I can learn so much from him." She described herself as nice, not difficult, the "girl next door."

DuBarry was a hit, and not only for the reasons mentioned by a paper in Indianapolis, where it "helped audiences to forget there are so many overshadowing clouds." Lahr remained in the cast after the show closed in New York and went on tour, and he played to brilliant reviews. "Lahr is equally at home with the low jests of today or the gutsy carnality of . . . Rabelais." Bert Lahr did not travel with the show to England, where Arthur Riscoe replaced him. English reviewers were cooler, calling *DuBarry* not the best of Cole Porter, "but even his second best is very acceptable." Red Skelton and Lucille Ball did the Lahr and Merman roles in the MGM film, which used only three songs written by Cole for the show. (Burton Lane and E. Y. Harburg were among the other composers responsible for the other six songs.) Of course, the Production Code found many faults with the film. "There must be no single 'pansy' flavor to this . . . man described as 'slightly effeminate.' " Not even the word "jerk" was allowed. Page after page of the most puritanical objections made clear what Porter was up against in the war he subtly waged against censorship.

In January 1940 Cole and Linda sailed to the South Seas, via Cuba (a place Cole very much liked), the Panama Canal Zone, and Mexico, aboard the Swedish liner *Kungsholm*. Their party included Winsor French, Len Hanna, Roger Stearns, and Billy Powell. Jean Vanderbilt was also on board, along with her mother. During the cruise Jean celebrated her birthday and Cole wrote a song for her. He titled it "So Long, Samoa," a lamentation for their departure from that "lovely land." (In a version of the song seen only by his cronies, Cole rhymed "Iberia" with "gonorrhea"—a reference to the venereal disease Billy Powell caught on the cruise.) Porter recycled the music years later as "Farewell, Amanda" in the Katharine Hepburn–Spencer Tracy film *Adam's Rib*. Garson Kanin, who co-wrote the script, claims that Cole and he never met to discuss the song. The producers needed one for the film but were unable to locate a suitable composer. Hepburn suggested Porter and called him to ask if he would write something for the film. The heroine was originally named Madeline, after Robert Sherwood's wife. Cole had one stipulation when he talked to Hepburn: he could not write a song about "Madeline." Days later Kanin telephoned Cole and asked what name he could compose a song about. "Amanda," Cole replied—and so the character was renamed. (The royalties for "Farewell, Amanda" went entirely to the Damon Runyon Cancer Fund.)

Jean Vanderbilt observed that on the voyage Cole and Linda appeared devoted to each other and that Linda seemed "very motherly to all the men" in the Porter party. Linda was always beautifully turned out and "took a fancy" to Jean's mother. She observed too that the Porter party drank quite heavily. She considers this cruise to have been her "first exposure to dazzlingly sophisticated people."

A topic of conversation on the *Kungsholm* was Linda's desire to own a home in the country, where she could benefit in good weather from cleaner air. Writing to "dearest, dear" Bernard Berenson in April 1940, she complained of her "bronchial trouble," which sometimes made it difficult for her to breathe. "I cannot understand why, after all these months of rest, and have small faith in doctors." She looked forward to a life in the country when she could "walk and live in fresh air for a change . . . New York is no place to live." Winsor French suggested Williamstown in the Berkshire Hills, where he had relatives.

Back in the United States, Cole, who opposed Linda's plan, undertook a drive to Los Angeles via scenic sites, following a northern route which allowed him easily to cross over into Canada and pause at Banff and Lake Louise. Whether or not his displeasure with the plan was assuaged when he arrived in California in August of 1940 isn't known. One factor that discouraged him would have been the distance of the Berkshires from the scene he liked so well at Long Island's Lido Beach.

Meanwhile, Linda and French had traveled to Massachusetts in June 1940 to look at properties. Buxton Hill was what they found: a large fieldstone house on two hundred acres of land in Williamstown (or Billsville, as some called it). Perhaps in part because of Cole's resistance, Linda decided first to rent the house for a season before proceeding to purchase it. In September 1940 she wrote to Jean Howard: "This house is MINE—isn't that wonderful? I got it for nothing & pray God! I won't spend a fortune doing it over." Eventually Linda did buy Buxton Hill and redid the decor and much else within and without the house.

Brooke Marshall Astor had had occasion to admire Linda's gifts as a decorator when she and her husband, Buddy, dined at rue Monsieur. On that occasion she found Linda "beautiful and extremely *raffinée*. The house reflected her taste and she was able to make the eighteenth-century rooms comfortable and inviting without losing the original dignity of the eighteenth century and its architectural statement." Some time after Linda purchased Buxton Hill, Buddy and Brooke spent a weekend with the Porters in Williamstown. What she says about Buxton Hill reveals a lot about Linda's

Buxton Hill

taste and skills as a decorator. "On the outside there was an old-fashioned rough-stone monstrosity . . . but inside, with her extraordinary flair for decorating and assembling beautiful furniture and objects brought over from the Paris house, Linda had made it outstandingly attractive." She had wisely taken from rue Monsieur the precious Chinese wallpaper, which seemed, with its rare, colorful birds and forests of bamboo, perfectly placed in the enormous drawing room at Buxton Hill. She had also installed a swimming pool, which pleased Cole when he first came to see the place. But what most delighted him was the transformation of a carriage house on the property into a cottage where he could work at whatever hour of the day or night and where, with privacy, he could spend time with a lover or a friend. Whether it was at the Waldorf-Astoria, at Buxton Hill, or at some other residence, Cole almost always had a *garçonnière* which allowed him, although married, to enjoy a bachelor's privacy. Of course he also needed a place where he could work without noise or interruption of any kind. Cole called the cottage "No Trespassing." Ed Tauch was the architect who designed the changes Linda proposed, and of course that too pleased Cole. "Work must begin *at once*," Linda told Jean Howard, "so that my furniture can be moved from Beverly Hills." Cole, she reported, was "splendidly well" and "very busy. I have turned Buxton Hill over to Coley and he invites whom he pleases for weekends. Last week we were entirely alone as he wanted to work, but this Friday he is bringing Sturges & Ollie Jennings—and perhaps Kelly, if he can leave his job for that length of time." "Coley" was the name Cole's mother called him, and his liking Linda to call him that seems to situate her all the more *in loco parentis*.

"Sturge and I," Cole told Jean Howard in September 1944, "go every Friday to Williamstown and return [to New York City] every Tuesday." Occasionally, Sturges's loyalty flagged, wrote Cole, and Sturge failed to resist Newport society. In these war years Sturges was doing volunteer work mornings at a Red Cross canteen but rushing off to host "fashionable lunches" at the Colony. Apparently Buxton Hill was having the bracing effect on Linda's health that both she and Cole hoped for. "Linda is in wonderful form," wrote Cole, despite the departure of her butler, who left with these words: "I'm tired of the mountains and want to work on the seashore from now on for several months."

Jean Howard, with whom both Linda and Cole corresponded, was, after his mother and Linda, the woman foremost in Cole's affections from the time they met in 1931 until his death. Jean often went to Williamstown, where she stayed with Linda. "The Porters rather ruined my life," Jean Howard said wittily. "I thought theirs was the only way to live so I said goodbye to my husband Charlie Feldman. I do think it's a civilized way to live." In the decade left to Cole after Linda died, Jean became even dearer to him, and eventually they traveled together extensively, as she describes in her book *Travels with Cole Porter*. The letters the non-letter-writing Cole wrote to Jean Howard are often signed "Your slave," "A big kiss," "Your old sweetheart." There were also jokey references to Garbo, a friend of Jean's. Cole called her "that big Swede" and "that beautiful Swede."

As the 1940s advanced Porter could look back on a healthy number of musical scores of shows and films, many of which are now classics. (Cole claimed as the 1930s ended that he couldn't tell how many shows he had written, as he "hated statistics.") Even the shows that were never produced—*Star Dust*, for example—yielded songs that reappeared in subsequent shows and became great hits. Guy Bolton was to collaborate with Porter on a show to be called *Ever Yours*, which remained unproduced but had, among other numbers, "Miss Otis Regrets."

Miss Otis regrets she's unable to lunch today,
Madam,
Miss Otis regrets she's unable to lunch today.
She is sorry to be delayed,
But last evening down in lovers' lane she strayed,
Madam,
Miss Otis regrets she's unable to lunch today.
When she woke up and found
That her dream of love was gone,
Madam,
She ran to the man
Who had led her so far astray,
And from under her velvet gown
She drew a gun and shot her lover down,
Madam,
Miss Otis regrets she's unable to lunch today.

Several performers have claimed it as a number Porter wrote for them. Bricktop said that one evening in Paris Cole came to her club and said, "Brick, I've written a song for you." It was "Miss Otis Regrets." Cole claimed in a 1939 interview he didn't remember how the idea came to him except that leafing idly through the Social Register one day, he came upon the name "Otis." Since he wasn't in a mood to write about elevators, he thought he would write about a well-born young lady who had done wrong. Said Cole: "You haven't heard anything until you've heard Monty Woolley sing it. In fact he was the first one ever to sing it. I gave it to him and he did it at one of Elsa Maxwell's parties, and he was the life of the party for the evening thereafter." One American sleuth wondered whether or not Goethe's mother was Porter's source: in answer to an invitation she replied, "I must ask to be excused as I have to die."

When the mob came and got her
And dragged her from the jail,
Madam,
They strung her upon
The old willow across the way,
And the moment before she died
She lifted up her lovely head and cried,
Madam,
"Miss Otis regrets she's unable to lunch today."

Another newspaper cutting, unidentified but among Porter's papers, claimed "Miss Otis" was inspired by a bad cowboy lament he heard at a party at a private home. It sold 100,000 copies in Scandinavia and Hungary but did not do business to speak of outside of New York in this country.

Possibly also envisioned as a number for the Bolton/Porter effort was "Thank You So Much, Mrs. Lowsborough-Goodby," a tale of a hostess "who gives weekends" which are "not a success."

> For the clinging perfume
> And that damp little room,
> For those cocktails so hot
> And the bath that was not,
> For those guests so amusing and mentally bracing
> Who talked about racing and racing and racing,
> For the ptomaine I got from your famous tin salmon,
> For the fortune I lost when you taught me backgammon,
> . . . .
> Thank you so much, Mrs. Lowsborough-Goodby,
> Thank you, thank you so much.

Chapter 13

I'm in Love with
a Soldier Boy

The taste for Porter's songs seemed undiminished as the war in Europe escalated. Porter made a considerable contribution to his country in World War II. His patriotism was mixed with the epicureanism and wit that audiences continue to find so entertaining. Porter's patriotism has often been compared to Irving Berlin's, which Porter himself admired. Although Berlin was accused by the composer Harry Warren and others of exploiting the war and patriotic sentiments, Porter did not agree. He and Berlin had invented nicknames for each other: Porter was "Rat Porter"; Berlin, "the Little Gray Mouse." Impelled to defend Berlin against criticisms, Porter wrote affectionately to him:

> I can't understand all this resentment to my old friend, "The Little Gray Mouse." It seems to me that he has every right to go to the limits towards publishing the music of his Army show as every cent earned will help us win the war. If I had my way he would have been given the Congressional Medal because . . . he is the greatest song-writer of all time . . .
> Love—Rat Porter

Porter's contribution to patriotism in wartime was subtle and rather of the same stripe as what he offered to Americans in the depression-ridden 1930s. During the period from 1939 until 1944 Cole Porter had five hit shows on Broadway: *DuBarry Was a Lady, Panama Hattie, Let's Face It, Something for the Boys,* and *Mexican Hayride.* All ran for over four hundred performances. He also wrote the scores for five films. Neither the war nor his own physical distress slowed him down.

Porter's opening salvo in the 1940s was *Panama Hattie*—not exactly patriotic, although it did present men in sailor suits.

> *Boy, if you're a dancin' fool,*
> *Join the Navy.*
> *Don't waste time at dancin' school,*
> *Join the Navy.*
> *When you're dressed in Navy blue*
> *The hot totsies go for you,*
> *So join the Navy . . .*

Set in Panama City, which Cole had recently visited, the show, like *DuBarry,* had a book by Herbert Fields and Buddy De Sylva, was produced by the latter, and featured Ethel Merman as the eponymous heroine. In Boston the critics were, in retrospect, excessively enthusiastic, one naming *Hattie* "a better show than the vastly successful *DuBarry* . . . raucous and rowdy but less obvious." Another critic felt that any show combining Porter and Merman was "destined for success." *Variety* noted the "risque" and "rough spots." On October 30, 1940, *Panama Hattie* opened in New York and was, in Dorothy Kilgallen's opinion, "the scene of enough ermine to blanket Mt. Rainier." A preview had been given for "Society People," and De Sylva vowed "never again." Many of those invited arrived late, talked through the performance, rarely applauded, and left before the final curtain. The show ran for sixty-two weeks in New York.

What many found most memorable in this tale of a nightclub singer, Hattie Maloney, who is sometimes elated and other times in a funk, was the duet sung by Merman and eight-year-old Joan Carroll:

> *What say, let's be buddies,*
> *What say, let's be pals,*
> *What say, let's be buddies,*
> *And keep up each other's morales.*
> *I may never shout it,*
> *But many's the time I'm blue,*
> *What say, how's about it,*
> *Can't I be a buddy to you?*

Sturges and Ray Kelly were two such buddies of Cole's, boosting his morale when he was blue. No doubt Porter's melancholy was fed by the loneliness and isolation he suffered as a closeted homosexual. His close friends—his entourage, one might say—Sturges, Woolley, and the Duke of Verdura among them, were rarely lovers, but companions with whom he could share confidences about his passions, as he could not with Linda. "Let's Be Buddies" is another of those songs that allowed Porter to air his melancholy and articulate his search for loyal pals.

A friend Porter lost for the duration of the war was Paul Sylvain, his splendid Canadian valet, who enlisted in the Seabees. By this time Sylvain had married an elevator girl in the Waldorf, whom Porter liked despite his social snobbery. One of the Porters' dearest friends, Michael Pearman, agreed nonetheless that "Porter was a snob. Monty Woolley said Cole Porter was insecure about not coming from a good family." Of course one has to take "good family" as the code it often is for "upper class." Wilhelm replaced Paul: previously a waiter at the Waldorf-Astoria, he turned out to be intolerably tyrannical. Like many of the "rich rich," the Porters had servant problems during the war, although Cole's generosity helped keep most of the staff from straying. Katie thought her son was generous to a fault and sometimes on her visits to New York was so upset by what she considered his extravagances that she packed up and left the Waldorf to stay instead with friends in Englewood, New Jersey. She wasn't angry with her son, just uncomfortable with his largesse.

"I've Still Got My Health," another song from *Panama Hattie,* is less wish fulfillment on Cole's part (although there is an element of that) than it is a saucy send-up of the many substitutes that the composer had for health. The lyric is again a list and refers, for instance, to the Astors and the Vanderbilts and other swells: "When I give a tea, Lucius Beebe ain't there, / Well, I've still got my health, so what do I care!" The rhymes are mostly up to snuff: "Brewster body" / "Scheherazade"; "Jock Whitney" / "jitney." Some of the rhymes are adroitly internal: "I can't count my ribs, like his nibs Fred Astaire." "I'm Throwing a Ball Tonight" (from the same score) mentions friends of Porter's as well as persons familiar to the public. It tickled Porter to allude to friends in a way that was jokey but intimate too. Among those to whom the lyric alludes are Elsa Maxwell, Woolley, the Lunts, Bert Lahr, Gracie Allen, and Fanny Brice. Again, Porter the poet is practicing here a function as old as Homer when he fixes in a certain permanency the people whom he treasures. No matter how slick their veneer, Porter's songs almost always are centered in the sweetness and brevity of love and happiness.

Porter provided a patriotic touch with "Americans All Drink Coffee," celebrating the covenant between England and America. In each refrain he cites first the disparities, then the resemblance:

> *Americans all drink coffee,*
> *Englishmen all drink tea,*
> . . . .
> *Yet when some dictator threatens*
> *Johnny Bull or Uncle Sam,*
> *An American*
> *And an Englishman*
> *Both say "Scram!"*

Written for Arthur Treacher to sing, the song was never used in the show. Janis Carter was luckier than Treacher: she got to introduce "Who Would Have Dreamed?" Porter is said to have told Lew Kesler that if he'd been born a female, Janis Carter was the woman he'd like to have been.

In "Make It Another Old-Fashioned, Please," a song still in the repertoire of many contemporary chanteuses, one again encounters disillusionment:

> *Once I owned a treasure, so rare, so pure,*
> *The greatest of treasures, happiness safe and secure,*
> *But like ev'ry hope too rash,*
> *My treasure, I find, is trash,*
> *So make it another old-fashioned, please.*

In "God Bless the Women" Porter writes tongue-in-cheek about the "wonderful, terrible women" and asks God to "help the man." "You Said It," another number from *Panama Hattie*, illustrates the "naughtiness" that the public (mostly approvingly) took to be a hallmark of Cole Porter songs:

> *This is what I think of summer theayters!*
> *Actresses are made there, more and more,*
> *Still there's nothing new along that score,*
> *Girls have been made in barns before.*

And on another topic:

> *Winter cruises are, oh, so gay*
> *They never make your bed up night or day,*
> *But you meet such a lot of nice people that way.*

. . .

During April and May of 1941 Porter worked in Hollywood, composing five songs for the film *You'll Never Get Rich,* which starred Fred Astaire and Rita Hayworth. Of course on the West Coast he continued to host elegant parties—one of them to celebrate the recent wedding of Clark Gable and Carole Lombard. "Garbo-Peep," as he called her in a lyric he wrote that year, attended. Indeed, Porter's invitations were among the very few she accepted.

Two beautiful and highly successful songs he wrote for *You'll Never Get Rich* were romantic in different veins. "Dream Dancing" has a haunting melody, filled with a lover's longing for the world of dreams where a love impossible to attain in the real world becomes viable. Danced in the film by the two stars, lyrics deleted, "Dream Dancing" deserves to be ranked with "Night and Day" as top-drawer Porter. Astaire did get to sing a superior song from the score of *You'll Never Get Rich:* "So Near and Yet So Far." Again the lover dreams "we might make a team," and suggests that he and his beloved

> . . . *might find some isle*
> *Where lotuses smile*
> *And our time beguile*
> *Going native* . . .

But when he feels she is near, she turns out to be "oh, so far."

During March of 1941 Porter was occupied with the score for *Let's Face It,* a show that Walter Winchell called a "Danny Kaye-o." Sylvia Fine Kaye, Danny's wife and a composer especially equipped to write patter songs, contributed to the Porter score. With Max Liebman, she wrote "Melody in 4-F" and "Fairy Talk"—both successes. (The *Newsweek* critic thought them superior to Porter's songs, although he faulted Kaye for "a dangerous tendency to baby-talk and 'camp' [which] will have to go." Brooks Atkinson called Kaye's double-talk "Jabberwocky" and thought *Let's Face It* "a wonderfully joyous musical show." Danny Kaye performed "Melody in 4-F" again in the film *Up in Arms.* (In 1954 Mrs. Kaye wrote for a film a song called "All About You," which Porter judged "a perfect love song.") Danny Kaye is now written about as a homosexual and as Laurence Olivier's lover for ten years. His fame he owed to Moss Hart, who personally chose him for *Lady in the Dark.* In that show, he played a "nance" dressmaker. Like Porter, Kaye had an arrangement with his wife, and as Olivier's biographer puts it, "Kaye led a quite independent sexual life."

The first rehearsal of the show took place on September 9, and following a Boston tryout, which earned entirely praising reviews, it opened in New York at the Imperial Theatre on October 29. But Porter missed the opening, as he had again entered Doctors Hospital for surgery on his left leg on October 19, 1941. During his recuperation he learned that Fifi Laimbeer, a friend who performed in *Fifty Million Frenchmen,* was a patient on another floor and sent her a huge bouquet of red carnations. A few days later a nurse told Fifi that Porter's project for that day was to come to her room for a visit. She looked out to see Cole struggling down the hospital corridor, visibly in terrible pain, perspiration pouring down his face, but with a big smile and carrying a flower for his friend. Shortly after he left the hospital, the attack came on Pearl Harbor.

Set in the fictional Camp Roosevelt on Long Island, *Let's Face It* initiates the "soldier boy" motif that recurs in the musicals Porter wrote during the war years. In fact one song is titled "Jerry, My Soldier Boy" and it could be viewed as a cautionary tale that Porter addressed initially to himself:

> People tell me, "Never mold your
> Life around a soldier,
> Never let yourself get too warm
> And go loony for a uniform."

The title number is a patter song in which eight soldiers tell what their girls gave them: "the poems of Keats . . . crepe-de-chine sheets . . . A barrel of fun . . . And my girl gave me a little son of a gun." It ends with the line "Let's face it for Uncle Sam." The songs are replete with lists and allusions to personalities of the day: Billy Conn (the prizefighter, about whom rumors of an affair with Porter persist), Kit Cornell, Lady Mendl, Mae West, Monty Woolley, Fanny Brice, Elsa Maxwell (who "got well-goosed while dehorning her cattle"), George Raft (whose "cow has never calfed, / Georgie's bull is beautiful, but he's gay!"), and Liz Whitney (who "has on her bin of manure a / Chip designed by the Duke of Verdura"). For Porter it was obviously pleasure of a special kind to commemorate his pals in a public way. These songs demonstrate what one critic called his "genius for the topical and chatter chorus."

Let's Face It has, in sum, splendid songs of varying moods. Besides "Farming," there are other witty and upbeat numbers, including "A Lady Needs a Rest," "You Irritate Me So," "Let's Not Talk About Love," and "Ace in the Hole" (in which an allusion to Carole Lombard was deleted because of her death in an air crash not long after her marriage to Gable). Typical of

Porter's acidulous tone when he treats the outrage of the lady scorned are these lines from "I've Got Some Unfinished Business with You" (one can imagine the composer as the lady scorned):

> Before I crack up from black despair,
> Before I go mad and tear my hair,
> Before I break down and start to boohoo,
> I've got some unfinished business with you.
> Before I hang from the willow tree,
> Before I swallow some TNT,
> Before I leap in the deep ocean blue,
> I've got some unfinished business with you.
> I've got a certain job that must be done,
> So, little one,
> Wait til baby gets a gun,
> You'll be in heaven when once I get through
> That certain unfinished business with you.

In the way of wit, the show featured Danny Kaye and Eve Arden pattering about Marlene ("Let's praise the masculinity of Dietrich's new affinity"), Peggy Joyce (a favorite fixture of Porter's satire), Garbo ("Is it a fact the Navy's launched all her old shoes?"), and many others whom he saw socially in those years. Love/hate gets some attention in a number, now sweet, now acerbic, titled "I Hate You, Darling." Elsewhere, lines abound in an ambiguity crafted by Cole for himself and his friends: "Remember hell hath no fury / Like a queen who's been stood up." One duet in the score entitled "Ev'rything I Love" allowed the mood of the show to modulate from sass to ardor. The lover calls his air "a rondelay" (a simple song in which some phrase is continually repeated):

> You are to me ev'rything,
> My life-to-be, ev'rything,
> When in my sleep you appear,
> Fair skies of deep blue appear,
> Each time our lips touch again,
> I yearn for you, oh, so much again,
> You are my fav'rite star,
> My haven in heaven above,
> You are ev'rything I love.

Linking ardor to patriotism, Porter added the tag:

> And while I'm learnin'
> I'll keep the home fires burnin',
> You are ev'rything I love.

The English production of *Let's Face It* opened at the London Hippodrome on November 19, 1942, with an entirely different cast. W. A. Darlington deservedly dismissed the plot as "dull and bedraggled" but praised the performers and Porter's songs.

The dancer and choreographer Nelson Barclift remembered that it was when Porter was at work on *Something for the Boys* (1942) and also on a "dud film" (*Something to Shout About,* originally entitled *Through Thick and Thin*) that a romantic relationship developed between them. "You'd Be So Nice to Come Home To" (the only Porter song from that film still sung today) was "our song." Years later Barclift remembered with pleasure that this was the song that knocked Irving Berlin's "White Christmas" off the hit parade.

Barclift arrived in New York City in hope of finding an acting job. He had studied Denishawn dancing and knew of the pioneering work in dance being done by Doris Humphrey, Charles Weidman, and Martha Graham. He soon succeeded in landing a dancing role in *The Eternal Road,* a Max Reinhardt production with music by Kurt Weill. But the show was postponed until the next season because the distinguished stage designer Norman Bel Geddes, while erecting the replica of a mountain at the Manhattan Opera House, struck water under the stage, with unfortunate consequences.

Barclift betook himself to Bennington for the summer, where the modern dance festival was under way, and was able to study there with Humphrey, Weidman, and Graham. In the fall he returned to New York City and *The Eternal Road.* Later on, Barclift found work dancing in shows staged at the 1939 World's Fair in New York. That same year Barclift had his first solo dancing role in a Broadway show, Rodgers and Hart's *Too Many Girls;* he followed that, in January 1941, with a dancing role in the legendary Moss Hart–Kurt Weill–Ira Gershwin *Lady in the Dark.* The next year Barclift landed in the United States Army, stationed first at West Point and then at Fort Jay, New York where he functioned as a member of the Theatre Section. He co-choreographed Irving Berlin's all-soldier show *This Is the Army* and was the principal dancer in the production.

This Is the Army (or *TITA*, as it was affectionately called) opened on the Fourth of July, 1942, at the Broadway Theatre in New York City. It was a stupendous success and eventually was made into a popular film. The show toured America, North Africa, Europe, and the Pacific. The historian Allan Berube wrote that "*This Is the Army* did much to promote the wartime image of Army and Navy drag performers as normal, masculine, combat-ready soldiers," defining in his study the kinds of drag that were enacted in this and similar GI entertainments. He makes the point that the jokes, allusions, the boy-girl couples were all reassuring to men "for whom rigid gender roles and heterosexuality organized everyday life. But a gay spectator or actor—including those in the cast of *This Is the Army*—could read these same drag performances for their more implicit homosexual meanings. He could enjoy seeing—or being—the real man in the dress kissing, dancing with, or singing love songs to other men." Barclift was in a position as co-choreographer and participating dancer to enjoy both.

By July of 1942 Cole Porter was sending amorous telegrams to Barclift ("Thinking of you constantly. All Love, Cole"), who, one presumes, helped inspire the song Cole wrote for Betty Garrett which she was to introduce in *Something for the Boys:*

> *I'm in love with a soldier boy,*
> *So in love with a soldier boy,*
> *I'm in love with an Army man*
> *And can he send me? Yes, he certainly can.*

In fact, as Porter wrote in the title song of this show,

> *. . . Now my life's completely cluttered*
> *With soldiers,*
> *Sailors,*
> *Not to speak of those big marines,*
> *'Cause . . .*
> *I'm always doing something*
> *Something for the boys*
> *Or they're doing something for me.*

The lyrics Porter composed and sent to Barclift were done with professional skill and manifest Cole's impulse to give artful shape to his feelings even though these would only be read by one other person. "Barclift-Barclift," he wrote:

I just heard a meadow-lark lift
Her voice and sing a song in praise of thee
So Barclift-Barclift
I a glass of Cutty Sark lift
And drink to the Meadow Lark not thee. C.

On a photo he signed "Cole" and sent to Barclift he wrote "Puritan, awesome but beautiful. Cole." In telegrams (one of them addressed to "Edgar N. Barclift" at West Point) Cole thanks his soldier boy for phone calls and wishes him success in different theatrical appearances. And in a

Nelson Barclift

telegram dispatched to the stage door of the Broadway Theatre on September 14, 1942, Porter requests "Nelson" to "Come to 1-2-3 tonite." This intimate club opened in January 1942 at 123 East Fifty-fourth Street with the backing of Porter, Len Hanna, Dwight Wiman, Mrs. Paul Mellon, and other wealthy chums. Porter envisioned it as a luxurious lair where with some privacy he could rendezvous with friends. He also imagined it as a supper club where his homosexual friend (and, some say, lover) Roger Stearns would preside both as table-hopping host and performer.

Roger Stearns was part of Porter's entourage for many years. A student in New Haven a decade after Porter graduated, Stearns must have encountered Porter when Stearns worked with two other Yale alumni, Monty Woolley and Rudy Vallee, in *Out o' Luck*. Porter wrote three songs for that show, in which, incidentally, drag was an element. One of the performers recalled later that "Cole's songs were sandwiched into Act II, during an impromptu 'show' being put on by . . . soldiers dressed in spangled, chorus-girl 'tutus' (but still wearing their GI boots)." At a rehearsal one of the cast did falsetto burlesques of current divas for Porter, who reappeared a few days later with a song called "Opera Star," which proved to be very popular with the audience. It concluded with a couplet that echoes a complaint evident in Cole's letters to Barclift: "I'm a great success making love on the stage / But a terrible failure at home." As an artist Cole could cause characters to fall in love, but in his private life he failed to find an enduring romantic attachment. In another song from this show Porter seems to anticipate the theme of "I'm in Love with a Soldier Boy" when his character proclaims, "I'm in love with the nicest doughboy." The love he writes about here is a "*gentil*" (Porter's word) love, and so, perhaps significantly, he places it in Indiana with his reference to Kokomo (rhymed with "gonna go" and "bungalow").

Roger Stearns did not succeed as an actor, but he had considerable popularity as a pianist who suavely played the songs of the period. For some years his club was the rage. "The 1-2-3 Club," said *The New Yorker*, "is one of those places where friends gather . . . preferring a room that looks like the lounge of a movie theatre to the loathsome privacy of their own home." Porter and his companions persuaded Gertrude Lawrence, Clifton Webb, Danny Kaye, the Vincent Astors, Ethel Merman, and Ethel Barrymore to grace the opening. A month later the *New York Sun* reported that "the 1-2-3 [packs] them in for supper . . . Gin rummy is one of the major activities at the 1-2-3 in the shank of the evening." The crowds were so large that Wendell Willkie was turned away, and Tallulah Bankhead (greatly admired by gay GIs) and her party, which included Ruth Gordon and Lillian Gish, had to perch on beer cases. At the club Porter was able to mix with many friends, including Douglas Fairbanks Jr., Merle Oberon, Moss Hart, Princess Paley, Mona Williams, and Judith Anderson. But as the telegram to Barclift reveals, he could conveniently arrange late-night trysts there as well. A soldier who had a romantic meeting with Barclift when he came to Foggia, Italy, with *This Is the Army* recalls bumping into him at the 1-2-3 Club in the fall of 1945. Barclift was assisting Cole, who seemed in poor physical shape, and pretended that he didn't know the GI whom he'd romanced in Italy.

In his letters to Barclift, Cole writes intimately about his feelings. Often the letters were written late at night. At 2:30 a.m. Porter tells Barclift, "It's bedtime my C. [cute] L. [little] Nose so good night. I miss you like hell. Please don't forget me entirely. I realize I date. I know that my trimmings are tarnished [the lyricist is gaining ground here]. I admit that I'm poor. But be kind, Nelson, to someone who really is true-blue." Infatuation has not entirely nullified Porter's wit: "By the way," he asks, "what colour is true-blue?" He signs himself by his middle name, "Albert." Often affection and anger seemed to blend in his feelings for Barclift: "I actually miss you in spite of the fact that you are incapable of love, affection, loyalty, sentiment or friendship. Why should I suddenly throw away so much writing-paper? Could it be 'my cute little nose?' For Christ's sake don't have it altered . . . I enclose cash for candy. Forgive the dirty bills."

Sometimes his stance seems that of a solicitous uncle. "I beg you," he tells Barclift from Los Angeles, sounding a familiar Porter theme, "see every sight you can. It may be difficult now but do it. It will color your whole life & make you happier later on. If you have hardships & become homesick, think of one major hardship that people like myself have. I'm sick of having wonderful kids like yourself saying goodbye & disappearing for so long and feeling so damned inadequate to help get them back again to their families and their friends. Every Sunday lunch here now is as sad as Hell."

Porter sometimes projected his own promiscuity onto his lovers. And he anyway found male relationships, especially sexual ones, to be troubling. Perhaps his distrust arose from his early and enduring identification with his mother and a perception that men were antagonists. Of course, "I Hate Men" from the score of *Kiss Me, Kate* is a spoof, but its sentiment was at times predictable of Porter. At any rate, most of the males he formed firm friendships with were homosexual, and he rarely seemed sure of the affection of friends who were also lovers. As he wrote in what Barclift called "our song":

> ... Lothario, why not own up
> That you always chase
> After ev'ry new face
> in town?

At this time Cole was not without a large and glittering social circle in California. He describes to Nelson Barclift parties attended by Norma Shearer, Ann Warner, Fanny Brice, Reginald Gardiner, Howard Sturges, Bill Haines, Ernst Lubitsch, and Anita Loos. But none of this company dispelled his longings for Barclift. A chic circle of playmates did not obviate a need for companionship and romantic love, the lack of which Porter suffered for much of his life. His capacity for intimacy was slight except in the few love affairs where intoxication diminished his resistance to closeness. Intimacy he achieved with Sturges, Monty, and a few others. Having presented this roll call of Hollywood luminaries he plans to entertain (he humorously labels them "just us"), Cole says to Barclift, "I'm sorta depressed that Ma Honey won't be present to supervise ... But you will be next year."

The number of servicemen whom Porter befriended in these years was considerable. Robert Wheaton recalls that a person central to these liaisons was a Hollywood friend of Porter's called Sam Gertzen, who had changed his surname to Stark. The co-owner with a friend and lover, Allen Walker, of jewelry shops situated in the I. Magnin stores, he eventually married Harriette, daughter of the Mafia boss of Kansas City. She was considerably older than Stark and content, according to acquaintances, with a sympathetic traveling companion. Stark was an inveterate traveler, and Cole could usually count on him to take trips in these years. Once a month Stark journeyed to Kansas City, where his wife's money was stashed in local banks, and he would return to California flush with hundred-dollar bills. Stark was a theatre buff who amassed, for example, a huge collection of programs, which he kept in a beautifully furnished Hollywood apartment. How much Porter knew of Stark's somewhat raffish background is unclear. But they remained friends over the years. Sam being a person with whom he felt easy and secure.

In Hollywood Porter's spirits often were high. One evening, Cole and Sturge dined at Chasen's, where they ran into several other friends. Sylvia Ashley, married then to Douglas Fairbanks Sr., was at home with a cold, someone reported, whereupon the group drove to her home in Santa Monica and spent the evening lolling on her bed. Porter describes to Barclift the campy fun that followed:

Sturge found his way into Sylvia's fur safe & suddenly appeared with all of them on, including the god-damndest little muff you've ever seen. I examined Douglas's mink-lined coat on the Q.T. as Sylvia had mentioned it and (dare I say) with an idea of selling it. But it's a dud. The collar is Astrachan & the stuff of the coat is a restrained dark blue tweed but oh my God, that mink lining. It's lemon colored alley-cat so even if the whole ensemble (that's Jewish) were a foot & a half longer, I shouldn't allow you to be seen in it as it's Hollywood trash.

Therefore, my pretty, no mink-lined coat yet. Chin up but until I meet some rich widow, no mink coats at all.

The events of that evening bring to mind the parties that Lew Kesler hosted in New York City, where male guests would wade through trunks filled with women's clothes and disport themselves in drag. Porter seems to have found these parties fun, at the least.

Linda was dividing her time just then between Williamstown and New York. Despite the distance, Cole kept in contact with her by telephone. As was his habit, he encouraged his friends (including romantic ones) to become acquainted with Linda and to pay attention to her. "Please go out of your way," he writes to Barclift, "to be nice to Linda. She likes you an awful lot already & I want you to be friends, not only for her sake, but even more for yours."

The Porter marriage, in a few years to be so romanticized in the film *Night and Day,* had some stormy periods in the war years. Henry Hyde's mother, who had kept up with Linda after they both left Paris, went in 1942 to stay at Buxton Hill with Linda, who "took refuge in Williamstown during the War" in flight from Cole's "meanness." When she returned to New York, she told her son that Porter had "exiled" his wife to Williamstown and wasn't even telephoning her. This corresponds with the report of an actress daughter of Porter's old friend Dwight Wiman. While she was appearing at the Stockbridge summer theater, her mother stayed nearby at Buxton Hill. Sometimes, she reported to her daughter, Cole didn't treat Linda very well and tended to relegate her to the background. She linked this to his homosexuality and, as well, to his genius, which impelled him to take the spotlight.

Reports seem to vary a bit on the strains in the marriage. Saint Subber noticed that "Cole and Linda were often at very deep odds but they always maintained the deepest of friendships." Despite Linda's extraordinary tolerance of Cole's crushes and sexual wanderings, she must at times have felt hurt and angry. Then too, Porter probably resented her disapproval, if only implied, and the guilt it engendered. Earlier, in Paris and Venice particularly, Cole was able with his music to delight Linda and her friends. He charmed the elite society in which Linda moved and was sought after by the *monde*. No doubt Linda was pleased by Cole's social suitability. And she must have found the world of show business a fresh and fascinating one. Cole loved her tenderly, if not passionately, which seemed to satisfy her. But as the two aged and illnesses overtook them, Cole grew less guarded in his sexual pursuits and so jeopardized Linda's *amour-propre* with the gossip his behavior begot.

On the twentieth of March, 1942, Porter says he is writing to Barclift at 3 a.m., indicating that in Hollywood he kept to his habit of very late nights when he sometimes drank heavily and perhaps put aside inhibitions in song lyrics as well as letters. Ray Kelly remembered Porter working at songs into the late hours of the night and failing to note them down; often he was so drunk that next morning he could not recall the tunes. In about half the cases, Kelly could recreate the melody sufficiently for Porter to pick it up and work on it the next day. Over the years, Kelly guessed, he was responsible for the existence of a considerable number of Porter's songs and so perhaps felt that he earned part anyway of the monies that Porter lavishly bequeathed to him and his family.

Momentarily in the March 20 letter Porter is oddly *au fait* with the Church calendar, reminding Barclift that yesterday was the feast of St. Joseph and today, St. Cuthbert's Day. Rather cryptically Cole says he hasn't much use for St. Joseph as he [presumably Joseph] "resents being called the husband of the Virgin Mary & you know what she produced." Renovations were proceeding on "my hut," and the "nasty guest room" was to be ready for Barclift when he arrived. With his previous letter to Porter, Barclift had sent a photo of himself which led Cole wittily to opine that "you were that old Russian dike who used to sing in Paris with a guitar. Her name was I think—Stroeva. Ask Sturge." Porter also encouraged Barclift to ask Sturges to introduce him to Jean Howard, who was to be in New York City early the next week "on St. Victorian's Day. I've told her you're my Passing Fancy," he rather teasingly tells Barclift. Cole urges his friend not to miss meeting Jean Howard, whom he calls "one of America's Great Women."

Cole continued to keep in touch with Ben Baz and Ollie Jennings, still very much a loving couple. Porter seemed to admire them profoundly and told Barclift that they "are the only two people in N.Y.C. (excepting always Sturges) who are *good*." In California Porter got "that wicked city idea about New York & all those purlieus," by which he seemed to mean homosexual haunts. In a *faux naïf* voice he sometimes kept for boyfriends he asks Barclift, "Have you been in a purlieu tonight? Confess. Say Guilty." He continued to be troubled by jealousy, so that this query is darker than Porter pretends. But mixed with it are genuinely amatory feelings: "It would make me worry less about you if . . . you were in touch with [Baz and Jennings, who] for some intangible reason . . . cleanse the impurity out of all they touch." But concern yields to levity as Cole says of his two friends, "And they touch *plenty*." He wishes his "Puss . . . sweet dreams" and signs off, "Your chum and *still* Your Fan . . . Albert."

In one of his letters Porter tells Barclift that MGM wanted him to write new songs for the film to be made of *DuBarry*. They offered him a princely sum but refused his request that it be spread over several years. He feared that his income tax payment for 1942 would be "so big that I'd starve." He also complained that the "Ratoff job is so crazy that it has nearly got me down." This was the film originally titled *Wintergarden*, for which Porter had first contracted to write seven songs. On June 27, 1942, a new contract called for nine songs. Probably the added obligation vexed Porter. (Despite Gregory Ratoff's announcement that "music is the elixir of the soul. I luff [sic] it. In my pictures I have the very best I can buy," the actor-director-producer was difficult to collaborate with professionally.) In the letter of June 1, 1942, Porter apologizes for intruding business talk and says, "I'm much more interested in anything that concerns you," urging Barclift to telephone collect on Sunday around seven p.m. New York time. "You tell me you think of me a hundred times a day. I like that." Again Cole urges Barclift to ring up Linda in Williamstown, and "if you've got any spare days, ask her to ask you up. The reason I mention this is," he says feelingly, "because I love you so much and I know that the more you know her, the happier you will be . . . everything that you do is my twenty-four hour-a-day delight . . . Bless you for being alive." He signs jocularly, "Mrs. Harrington-Carrington." One wonders if Porter's motive in introducing his more accomplished boyfriends to Linda was a desire to lend respectability to his sex life.

Something to Shout About, which starred Don Ameche and Janet Blair, features the song Porter and Barclift thought of as "our song." Robert Kimball points out the various titles the song was given before it settled down to "You'd Be So Nice to Come Home To"; "Something to Keep Me Warm" is one. The song was completed in April of 1942 and was nominated for an Academy Award in 1943. It voices the sentiments of so many men and women separated by World War II. Of course Barclift was a soldier uprooted too by war. But as one reads these and other lyrics alongside Porter's letters to him, one sees that they are replete with biographical relevance. The song's persona confesses that he is "a worshipper / At your shrine," and complains quite as Porter did about what he took to be Barclift's inconstancy. So the tone of "our song" is in fact rather bittersweet.

When we read the love letters of persons who are wordsmiths by profession—poets even—we often come upon banal prose that we cannot reconcile with the shimmer and profundity of their verse. Cole Porter's letters to Kochno and to Barclift sound no more passionate or eloquent than those the average person composes. Paralyzed by passion, the lyricist cannot immediately summon words or images that are superior to the ordinary. Poetry, said Gerard Manley Hopkins, is "the common language heightened," and what distinguishes the poet is the power of art to heighten and allow language to leap to loftier perches. Porter, of course, had an additional language to rely on, and that was music. But the language of Porter's letters to his soldier boy in no way compares with the loving sentiments of "You'd Be So Nice to Come Home To"—the words and music of which convey not only Porter's love for Barclift but the feelings of all soldier boys for lovers from whom they were parted by war.

Porter's patriotism seems to spring from two sources: a deep decency and pride in his country, bred into him by his Indiana upbringing, and a concern for young servicemen that was rooted in romantic fantasies about sexually attractive, lonely young soldiers and sailors—another reflection, or so it seems, of Cole's craving for companionship and the way he fed it in fantasy. One man who had been a young naval officer in 1943 and whose father was a Yale friend of Porter's recalls being taken to dinner by Cole and Howard Sturges on the eve of his departure for a naval assignment. Porter and Sturges listened patiently while the young man—politically very to the left then—berated them for their self-indulgence. They waited until he finished, made no reply, and quietly paid the bill. Decades later the man couldn't imagine why the two had put up with him. "Don't forget," said his wife, "that you were a very handsome young naval man then." Charles was a young air corps man whom Cole met through Robert Wheaton. He found Cole "generous" in California, and even more so when Charles went overseas. Realizing how important mail was to servicemen, Cole sent news in several envelopes so that the young man would hear his name repeatedly announced.

Publisher Robert Giroux recalls it was during wartime (he was still in uniform) that a friend and he dropped in to the bar at the Waldorf-Astoria and saw Cole Porter, boutonniere in place, hosting seven or eight servicemen. Giroux was told that every day Porter was in New York City during the war, he hosted such groups. A bartender said, "If you want to meet Cole

Porter, he holds court here for members of the armed forces daily." No distinction was made between officers and GIs. In California soldiers were living in a kind of tent city, and in order to relieve overcrowding some of them found accommodations in private residences, including Porter's home in Brentwood.

Robert Wheaton met Cole in 1943 at the Cafe Gala, "the world's most interesting supper club," located then at the present site of Spago. The proprietor, Johnny Walsh, handsome, charming, and gay, was backed by Baroness Catherine d'Erlanger of the famous European banking family, who had long been a friend of Cole's and Linda's and had met John Walsh at the Lido in Venice. Cole visited the Cafe Gala several times a week when he was in California. Walsh had New York connections that allowed him access to the latest songs from Broadway musicals. Edie and Rack—perhaps the best two-piano team in supper club history—played the songs, and Johnny Walsh would sing them. Judy Garland, Lena Horne, and her husband, the film composer Lennie Hayton, were among the celebrities who sometimes had to queue up for inspection by the baroness before the red ropes were released and they were admitted. Cole always sat at a table, owing to his weak legs. A mutual acquaintance introduced Bob Wheaton to

Robert Wheaton, 1944

Cole, and after some amusing chat, Cole invited Bob, stationed then at San Diego and physically very much a type who would appeal to Cole, to the next Sunday pool party. The Cafe Gala, elegant and selective, ostensibly straight, had a strong gay undercurrent, everyone agrees.

Wheaton visited Porter once in the hospital in the war years and was shown a telescope through which Porter claimed to see ships arriving at and departing from the Brooklyn Navy Yard. According to Wheaton, Porter learned a lot about navy lore. He was clever at discovering military movements and used to circulate to servicemen of his acquaintance stationed abroad books that were coded to reveal the whereabouts of mutual friends—a cognate exercise to the construction of lyrics, perhaps.

> Glide, glider, glide
> 'Round the map
> Till we trap
> Ev'ry Jap—
> Anee . . .
> Till the skies of Deutschland we roam . . .

The song does indicate Porter's willingness to make a contribution to the war effort, although his enthusiasm abated when a snafu developed.

Published in January of 1943 was "Sailors of the Sky," which warned:

> So beware you Huns,
> Whether Japanese or German
> 'Cause we've got guns
> For exterminatin' vermin.

Porter must have found it ironic when a telegram arrived announcing that the "only factor preventing our exploitation of the song is Washington's frown on reference to girls in lyric."

Servicemen were not the only recipients of Cole's concern during those war years. While his friend Michael Pearman was in the army, Porter kept a careful eye on Michael's mother, who resided in Hollywood, while he was living nearby in the summer of 1942. Every second weekend or so he would send a car to fetch Mrs. Pearman and drive her to his home. Once he remarked regretfully, "I shan't see you for three weeks, as I'm going to Peru for the weekend." "Are you really going for just a weekend to Peru?" she asked. It's not, of course, surprising to discover that Porter had a penchant for older women. But he warmed to Mrs. Pearman in a special way: they

Michael Pearman with his Jack Russell terrier, Digby

were devoted to each other, and he often sent sumptuous gifts to "my dear Mrs. Pearman from your Cole." In her early eighties, Mrs. Pearman retired to a little hotel in Yorkshire, and Cole presented her with a chair operated by electricity. She took it to England but never used it. She had some of the independence if not the touchiness Cole exhibited when Michael Pearman would take his arm in an effort to help him. "I'm not blind, you know," Porter would object.

Porter's next show, *Something for the Boys,* had its tryout in Boston on December 18, 1942. The Boston critics applauded the welcome opulence. Although the critic Eliot Norton complained of the lame book, he called Cole Porter "the best of his kind among the musical show composers. A small, bespectacled man from Peru, Indiana, Mr. Porter is a semi-legendary figure whom the theatre's producers summon up from some gilded sanctuary . . . and who invariably delivers songs that are sung and hummed and whistled from East to West." But Norton had a caveat: "As is frequently the case, Mr. Porter is guilty again of offending good taste in his lyrics. But his melodies are marvelously tuneful and . . . there is compelling rhythm in all of them." Musically educated critics saw Porter's technical skills reflected in the felicity of tunes, harmony, and orchestration.

George Beisiwanger probably was the best of the many commentators on *Something for the Boys*. He wrote in *Theatre Arts* in April 1943:

An excellent musical comedy book such as Herbert and Dorothy Fields have put together for *Something for the Boys* has its wide open spaces through which a Gen. Grant tank can be driven or the wild horses of inspiration. That is the only word for the source of "By the Mississinewa," the song with which Ethel Merman and Paula Laurence bring down the house toward the end of the show. "It came to me on a gold platter," Cole Porter said. "We needed a comedy song—there has to be one in that spot. But what about? No one had an idea. That's when the going gets really tough. They ask you for a 'comedy song,' just that, nothing more. Someone suggested I use Miss Laurence's nightclub materials. But I didn't want to do that. Then, suddenly, the song was there. I don't know where it came from. Of course, the Mississinewa runs right past our front porch back in Indiana."

The New York opening (which Mike Todd managed to illumine even though it was wartime) was glamorous. One critic called it "the year's plushiest audience." Dietrich arrived with Jean Gabin. Grace Moore was there, along with military bigwigs in full fig. Many in the audience dined at what was then the traditional place, Jack and Charlie's, and afterwards repaired to the Stork Club, El Morocco, and the Copacabana. Elsa Maxwell was delighted to introduce Wendell Willkie ("another Hoosier") to Porter. On the day following the opening, people eager to see the show lined the sidewalk in front of the theatre for blocks. The play earned $20,655 from its first five performances, and the ticket price for Saturday night was hiked. 20th Century–Fox immediately bought the film rights as a vehicle for Betty Grable; the fee was $305,000—the highest ever paid for a Broadway show. The studio which already had invested $62,500 in the musical, offered $250,000 more for purchase of the rights, but Porter and the Fields thought the sum inadequate, and so the offer was augmented. Meanwhile, seizing the day, Mike Todd announced that *Fairytale for Adults* would be the next Porter/Fields show and would star Vera Zorina. Later the title was shifted to *Light Wines and Dancing*, and William Gaxton and Victor Moore were announced as Zorina's co-stars, but the show never materialized.

Todd, who produced *Something for the Boys*, is remembered now perhaps more for his marriage to Elizabeth Taylor and his death in an airplane crash than for his theatrical attainments. He came from a simple background: he shined shoes and sold newspapers in his youth, then worked as a butcher. In many ways his life was a Horatio Alger tale. He made money as an impresario at the Chicago World's Fair and far more at the World's Fair in New York; then he produced the show *Star and Garter*. When Porter and Vinton Freedley parted professional company, Cole remembered the success Todd had made out of *The Hot Mikado* and turned to Todd as a promising substitute.

Freedley had insisted on changes in *Something for the Boys* with which neither Cole nor the Fields agreed. Cole claimed that "all his suggestions were bad ideas" and judged that Freedley still considered him an amateur. So he decided to sever connections with Freedley.

All the more remarkable was it that Merman, who was back on the stage after having had a child, didn't see the script until two weeks before the show opened. While this sounds improbable, Merman explained this feat by saying: "I never had to memorize a song . . . I just run through it two or three times and it's in my head for keeps . . . The way I work on a song? Well I try it a few times with Lew Kesler. He's the man at the piano and he goes along with every Cole Porter show I'm in. Then I try it in the spot it's to go in the production, and maybe I add some little touch. You know, a finish with a little sort of a flick of the eye."

Despite Louis Kronenberger's opinion that the Porter score was "lacking in magic," and Wolcott Gibbs's comment that *Something for the Boys* featured "some of Cole Porter's second-best music" and that he missed in the songs the "eerie complexity of the old rhymes and even [felt] that the master is less inclined to be flippant about love than he was in the old days when he was writing hymns to the sex life of the bean and the cod," the public loved the show, and it was a hit still when it took to the road with Joan Blondell (Mike Todd's wife), not altogether earning the raves that Merman had.

The book describes the fortunes of a burlesque queen, a sidewalk vendor, and a female defense-plant worker who inherit a Texas ranch located near an Air Force base. They convert it to function as a residence for servicemen's wives, but an officer believes the three are running a bordello and tries to shut them down. The happy resolution comes about with the aid of a radio device doubling as a filling in a tooth. Despite the preposterous book (or perhaps because of the appeal silliness had to a war-weary public—Merman considered an easy-to-follow plot a plus), the show ran to 422 performances.

Porter was keen on the book. He considered the Fieldses ideal to work with because when he developed second-act trouble out of town they fished in their father's (Lew Fields, of the Weber and Fields comic team) trunk and immediately found some stage material that solved the problem. Merman contended that Cole and she "thought his score one of the best he had ever written for me." Examining it today, few (if any) would agree. Porter's diligent research did allow him to compose a song whose lyric affords a stunning list of Texas-born celebrities (titled "See That You're Born in Texas"):

> *You've got to give credit to Texas for startin'*
> *Gene Autry, Ken Maynard, and smart Mary Martin,*
> *Add Bebe Daniels, Peggy Fears, and Joanie Blondell,*
> *Texas Guinan, Jesse Jones, and Linda Darnell,*
> *And don't forget our Ginger Rogers, not to mention our*
> *Great heroes, Nimitz and Eisenhow'r.*

In another list song, "Hey, Good-Lookin'," Mrs. Browning gets a nod, so does Tallulah, and in the very same song Merman is described as "the missing link between Lily Pons and Mae West."

"By the Mississinewa" must have pleased Porter. The river runs near Westleigh Farms, and Porter romped in and near it for years. Merman and Paula Laurence dressed as Indian maidens. Laurence recalls that Porter first wrote the song as a solo for her, but when Merman heard it "she decided it would be a duet: and she was great in it." Merman wrote that the song

> provided us with a raucous show-stopper from its first performance. Part of the impact came from the song, part from the delivery, some from the staging. The outfits Paula and I wore were atrocious—funny, long Indian dresses, moccasins and braids. The visual impact broke up the audiences so completely that half the time their laughter drowned out the lyrics . . . Even though the jokes weren't some of Cole's wittiest, a lot of people still tell me it was the funniest number they ever saw in the theater . . .

After a few weeks, Merman feuded with Paula Laurence over stage bits that she claimed Laurence stole from her. Eventually, at the urging of Merman, Laurence was dropped from the show but went on to play an enviable role in *One Touch of Venus*.

In her autobiography Merman describes her practice of asking for a new song when the audience was unresponsive. And she describes very clearly how Cole wrote for her in this and earlier shows: "He studied my voice and decided A flat, B flat and C natural were my best notes. He saw to it that the key words coincided with one of those notes. It gave me my best shot and it helped put his songs across."

A few sentences that appeared in *Theatre Arts* magazine in April 1943 announced a view that was to gain support as *Oklahoma!* arrived and more demanding requirements were established for a credible book and an integration of songs and story. "The composer of a musical comedy score is not engaged in writing popular songs . . . His job is to provide the lyric fabric out of which an evening in the theatre of low comedy can be fashioned. His point of departure is not the song but the book." Porter, in one sense, had nearly always composed songs dictated by the plot and characterization. What is felt more to be a fault in these musicals of the twenties and thirties is the inanity of the plot, a judgment that would not have been understood by many on stage or in the audience in the years before Rodgers and Hammerstein (not to say Oscar Hammerstein II and Jerome Kern's *Show Boat*) demonstrated the reaches possible when song and story were wed.

Although it had been the site of Porter's tragic accident, Locust Valley and the Countess de Zoppola's estate in nearby Mill Neck (where the Duke and Duchess of Windsor sometimes stayed) was a place he still liked to visit on weekends in those years. Another was the country place in Jericho, Long Island, owned by Jimmy Donahue (Barbara Hutton's cousin and a Woolworth heir), who had purchased the mansion of Alfred Vanderbilt. According to Merman, Donahue sent limousines to town to fetch his guests and then to take them home in comfort. Merman, whose torrid tongue probably contributed to the louche conversation, repeats a story that Donahue's butler always engaged servants who were deaf, or nearly, so that they would not hear the racy exchanges of the guests. Horst remembers that at his parties "Jimmy Donahue used to lace the drinks with Benzedrine and worse."

Something for the Boys was Porter's last theatrical venture with Ethel Merman. He valued her greatly, as did Linda Porter, although offstage the inelegant Ethel seems not to have been Linda's style. Early in the autumn of 1943 Porter wrote from Williamstown to tell Merman that "my Linda has been seriously ill [with chronic lung disease] for eight months. But if anything can make her well again, it is your broadcast every Sunday night at 9:30. I always listen too. You are wonderful and I sit beside her and watch her revel in your excellence. You probably know after a few years on stage that no one can equal you." And he adds a poignant postscript: "If you have time, write Linda, tell her that you are happy to hear from me that she is better (she is not) . . . This will do her great good, which she needs." On October 24 Linda returned by ambulance from Buxton Hill to her Waldorf apartment, and shortly thereafter she tuned in to hear Merman dedicate "You're the Top" to her. Porter wrote to thank Merman and in his letter says that when Linda reached New York, "for the first time I felt that she had lost her morale due to exhaustion," Merman's words to her over the airwaves "brought back all of her bravery. You are a darling to have done this and I shall never forget it."

Sometime in the summer of 1943, while driving in the Berkshire Hills as he very much liked daily to do, himself at the wheel, from which he could operate manually all the controls, Porter discovered Grandma Moses and her primitive paintings at her home in the little town of Eagle Bridge, New York. This preceded her fame, but not by many years: by 1950 she was an American celebrity, and Cole mentioned her in a lyric from *Out of This World*: "Big dough pursues Grandma Moses, / But no one's pursuing me."

Paula Laurence and Ethel Merman in *Something for the Boys*, 1943

"Big dough" is not at all descriptive of the prices Cole paid for the pictures he purchased. Records of the distinguished Galerie St. Etienne in New York City, where she showed, indicate that on October 4, 1943, "Mr. and Mrs. Cole Porter" of Buxton Hill, Williamstown, Mass., bought five pictures. "By the Sea" sold for twelve dollars and "Old Oaken Bucket" for thirty; the cost of the other three pictures fell in between. This is surprising, as Anna Mary Robertson Moses (affectionately called "Grandma" in her neighborhood) had already had an exhibition in October 1940 at the Galerie St. Etienne titled "What a Farm Wife Painted." "She entered the New York art scene as one amongst a number of 'new' folk artists, whose work had become suddenly fashionable as a result of several landmark exhibitions at the Museum of Modern Art in the 1930's." When she died in 1961, aged 101, Grandma Moses was famous internationally.

A month and more later, in mid-November 1943, Porter again traveled to Eagle Bridge and Grandma Moses sold him five more paintings, all featuring turkeys; four of them he bought for four dollars each, and one for three dollars. The following summer he purchased two large pictures. Porter thought of Grandma Moses's pictures as an investment and hung several of them in his California home. One year he is said to have bought and given away twenty of them as Christmas gifts. Arthur Schwartz wrote late in December 1944 to thank Cole for "the wonderful gift you sent me for Christmas. Ever since I saw that Moses painting in your room, I have wanted to have one, and this is really a honey. It's already hanging in my home." Cole presented Michael Pearman's mother with two paintings by the artist and gave one to Ethel Merman. It depicted a farmyard with animals and colors that Merman thought clashed with the decor of her apartment, so she gave it away. Years later, she woke to her foolishness, but couldn't recall to whom she'd given the picture. Although Cole Porter disliked the work of American folk artists, he made an exception of Grandma Moses because her art was so unusual. "It just kind of pleased him that someone her age could take over and make something of herself," said his secretary, Madeline Smith.

Michael Pearman thought that Cole Porter had very few good pictures, except for a Picasso *Blue Boy* that Howard Sturges gave him. Ben Baz, a painter himself, thought that Porter "had a business person's" regard for art. "Painting," Baz said, "was not important to Cole." He did own two drawings by Lyonel Feininger, and in 1939 he acquired Paul Cadmus's picture of two muscular young men on bicycles and Grant Wood's sinister *Death on Hill Ridge Road*. The latter hung for many years in Porter's Waldorf apartment.

Little Houses in
Which Our Hearts
Once Lived

Early in 1943 Cole and Linda went
to California and rented for the first time the house at 416 North Rockingham, the street on which Garbo once lived. Porter was to return annually to
this house for the remainder of his life. It was owned by Bill Haines, who
until 1934 had successfully acted in films. (Some called him the Cary Grant
of his day.) Haines has been described as a "most outrageous personality."
Well known in Hollywood as a homosexual, he is said to have been George
Cukor's cicerone in the gay circles of the film colony. Some people supposed
that Porter and Haines were at one time lovers, but Robert Wheaton, who
was close to Cole at that time, thinks not.

Haines lived for many years with a man called Jimmie Shields. They
had a house near the ocean, and one day in June 1936 a family on El Portos
Beach discovered a child was missing. Someone pointed to the Haines
house and said they'd seen the child talking to someone who lived there.
When they investigated, the family found their child in the house, being fed
an ice cream by Shields (who was not a pederast, according to people who
knew him and were well aware of his homosexuality). The neighborhood
rose against Haines and Shields, although there was no indication that the
child had been molested. Haines and Shields felt they had no alternative
except to sell the beach house. William Randolph Hearst, who was a friend
of theirs, kept the story out of his papers for four days but finally called
Haines to say that as a competent journalist he could no longer ignore the

story, although he promised to downplay it. The studio tried to apply damage control, but to no avail. Haines got into other scrapes. MGM did nothing to bail him out or cover up the stories, with the consequence that he was no longer professionally bookable. He then turned to interior decoration, with great success, counting among his clients Walter Annenberg, who hired Haines to decorate the American embassy in London. Joan Crawford also helped him in his first efforts as a decorator.

This story ended sadly. Haines died of cancer in 1973 at the age of seventy-three, and Shields was inconsolable. Friends made a point of inviting him to parties. Ronald Reagan reportedly once took him aside at a party and gave him a pep talk. But a year later, in despair, Shields killed himself.

Porter's lease permitted him to make renovations with the proviso that when he vacated the premises he would restore the house, still standing in Brentwood today, to its original state. Michael Pearman was with Porter when he went to the house to inspect the newly installed swimming pool. Cole was furious to find that the diving board was inconveniently located

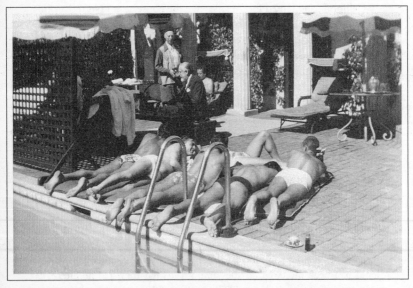

A Sunday afternoon pool party at Cole's, c. 1944. Seated in background is Monty Woolley; standing in background, Roger Davis; behind him Freddy Ney. Cole is seated on a chaise longue behind the trellis. The sunbathing young men include Jimmie Shields (right, with cigarette); Bob Raison (facing right); Bill Haines (with knee raised)

for pool parties. It must go at the other end, he insisted. And so the pool had to be completely rearranged, locating the deep end and the diving board exactly opposite to where they'd first been placed. He made other renovations, enclosing a rear porch to function as a dining room and erecting a Grecian gazebo. It was on the deck of the pool that Robert Wheaton several times saw Cole, stretched out in the sun, nude except for a small towel covering his genitals, looking a bit like a Buddha. Then his barber would arrive and not only cut Cole's hair but shave his entire body. "He had no hair anywhere on his body, except on his head," recalls Wheaton. Hair on his body, Cole said, made him feel "unclean." This was a weekly ritual.

Looking onto the pool were two rooms where Cole worked, ate, and entertained. *Vogue* described the house in these words:

> One room is really a garden *sous cloche*—the once open terrace glassed in, and strong with Mexican colours, raw pink and green. Thick green string rugs are planted like grass on the flagstone floor, philodendrum [*sic*] and pink orchids grow from beds of earth, and a grapevine spreads over the trellised glass ceiling. The second room is fresh as an outdoor pavillion, has fruit chintz, Chinese porcelains, a watery expanse of mirrored wall, a light-struck bar built across one window. Under the piano the rug is patched, worn thin by Porter's feet.

During the spring and summer of 1943 Porter worked on the score for a film that was never released, called *Mississippi Belle*. From the start this was a troubled project. The reader to whom Warners sent the script of *Mississippi Belle* for evaluation was almost entirely negative in her report. "In short," she wrote, "I'm not very enthusiastic about this as picture material. This story . . . has been done so often and so well that I think we would be hard put to it to do it better." *Gone With the Wind* was a recent film to which she felt *Belle* would be unfavorably compared. "I just can't quite believe," she concluded, "that anybody would be interested now in a story of the Mississippi River boats . . . It all seems very old-fashioned and remote." Nonetheless, Warner Bros. persisted with plans to make the film, although early on problems with it arose. As early as February 1943 an executive at Warners wrote to Cole: "I have the feeling that our plan for you and [writerdirector] Del Daves to work closely together, so that your lyrics and music may be interwoven in the script, is not panning out as well as we had hoped. I suggest another meeting." This project occupied him until 1944, when eventually it was abandoned.

> *Oh why, oh why,*
> *Mother, tell me why*
> *Did you ever let your goslin' go*
> *From the darlin' dell*
> *Where I used to dwell . . . ?*

These lines of a song from *Mississippi Belle* reveal the nostalgia into which Porter sometimes slipped. George Eells speaks of 1943–44 as a time during which Cole was suffering from deep depression attributable to no specific cause. Porter probably suffered much of his lifetime from moderate depression, which at times increased in intensity. His crippling wounds resulting from the riding accident and the medications he took for pain were in themselves sufficient to deepen his depression. These lyrics seem the lamentations of a lad for the lost world of his youth.

One curious case is "Don't Fence Me In." In *The Complete Lyrics of Cole Porter* Robert Kimball gives in a full way the provenance of "Don't Fence Me In." Kimball's careful scholarship should diminish the number of apocryphal stories that surround this song: e.g., Joan Fontaine's claim that once she was with Cole at a party in his Brentwood house when the telephone rang; it was Linda; they talked and suddenly Cole said to his wife, "Linda, please don't fence me in." Miss Fontaine took that to be an epiphanic moment when the idea for the song suddenly surfaced in the composer. "Sometime in the 1940s" was her approximation of the date when the telephone encounter took place, but in fact the song was composed a decade earlier.

Published in 1944, "Don't Fence Me In" reaches back to a contract Cole Porter signed in 1934 with 20th Century–Fox to do the film score for *Adios, Argentina*. Among his responsibilities was the composition of a song in which four cowboys, brought to the East by the turns of a typically witless plot, give voice to their loneliness. Lou Brock, the producer of *Adios, Argentina*, had a friend, Bob Fletcher, an engineer who compiled and sent to Brock a book of verse. Brock replied that he fancied for *Argentina* a song to be called "Don't Fence Me In." "If I use this, will probably have you write or collaborate on the lyrics for the tune, in which event I would want the chorus to start with the words 'Don't Fence Me In.'"

Fletcher wrote the song and, at Brock's request, mailed it to Cole Porter on November 24, 1934. It consisted of words and music for the refrain of "Don't Fence Me In" and some lyrics for a verse. A few days later Brock wired Fletcher with news that Porter wanted to buy the right to use the title and "some characteristic words and phrases from your lyrics." He suggested that $250 would be an appropriate fee for Fletcher to propose. Brock considered it unlikely that Cole would give credit in print to Fletcher, because Porter was widely known as a composer who invented both words and music. But Porter acquiesced to this arrangement, perhaps—Kimball hypothesizes— because he wanted to ingratiate himself with people powerful in Hollywood, which was rapidly replacing Broadway as the center of musical comedy. Cowboy songs were certainly not Porter's strength, and in fact "Don't Fence Me In" in no way has the signature of Porter anywhere in its measures, despite the fact that he did write all of the music. Here is Fletcher's version of the refrain:

> Don't fence me in.
> Give me land, lots of land,
> Stretching miles across the West,
> Don't fence me in.
> Let me ride where it's wide,
> For somehow I like it best.
> I want to see the stars,
> I want to feel the breeze,
> I want to smell the sage,
> And hear the cottonwood trees.
> Just turn me loose,
> Let me straddle my old saddle
> Where the shining mountains rise.
> On my cayuse
> I'll go siftin'; I'll go driftin'
> Underneath those Western skies.
> I've got to get where
> The West commences,
> I can't stand hobbles,
> I can't stand fences,
> Don't fence me in.

On January 7, 1935, Porter wrote to Fletcher and enclosed a copy of his own "Don't Fence Me In," asking him to "keep it carefully under your hat as the music will not be released until next autumn . . . I have given you credit under the title. Hope you will be pleased with it. Certainly, I am very grateful to you." Here is part of Porter's lyric:

Oh, give me land, lots of land under starry skies above,
Don't fence me in.
Let me ride through the wide-open country that I love,
Don't fence me in.
Let me be by myself in the evening breeze,
Listen to the murmur of the cottonwood trees,
Send me off forever, but I ask you, please,
Don't fence me in.
Just turn me loose,
Let me straddle my old saddle underneath the Western skies.
On my cayuse,
Let me wander over yonder till I see the mountains rise.
I want to ride to the ridge where the West commences,
Gaze at the moon till I lose my senses,
Can't look at hobbles and I can't stand fences,
Don't fence me in.

When *Adios, Argentina* was abandoned, Porter consigned "Don't Fence Me In" to the trunk. Ten years later, Warner Bros. resurrected the song for Roy Rogers to sing, as he did on horseback, in the film *Hollywood Canteen*. Many people heard the song for the first time when Kate Smith introduced it on her October 8, 1944 radio broadcast. Subsequently the song took off, and soon it soared to the top of the hit parade. The *Peru Tribune,* vigilant about the successes of the town's famous citizen, noted that "Don't Fence Me In" was "the top song of the 1944–45 season." The song "received a rating [source unprovided] indicating 700 million 'listenings' by way of the four major networks during the year." Many major artists recorded it, and sales of these recordings exceeded a million. (Ditto the sheet music, which did *not* acknowledge Fletcher. Porter claimed this was an oversight occasioned by his being in the hospital at the time.) What was it that gave this song such wide appeal? Even though it expresses the composer's lifelong predilection for the free and unfettered life, the song is scarcely one of Porter's more passionate statements of this yen. One story, which perhaps Linda sanctioned by placing it in a scrapbook, has it that in 1934 she had gone to a ranch in Arizona to rid herself of a persistent cold. She wrote letters to Cole filled with accounts of her delight in the bucolic life, and these are reputed to have motivated Cole to write "Don't Fence Me In" as a jokey gift for Linda.

Danton Walker reported in the *New York Daily News* that the song was "said to be one of F.D.R.'s favorites"—not surprising, as Roosevelt said on many occasions that the song he loved best was "Home on the Range," almost a companion piece to Porter's composition. Bob Hope joked that "Don't Fence Me In" was dedicated to Eleanor Roosevelt, whose peripatetic style had not hitherto been habitual with first ladies. Some commentators wrote very toney reflections on the song. In an unidentified newspaper clipping a critic found the song expressive of "man's insatiable longing for freedom of spirit," linking it to the legends of Prometheus, Icarus, and Ulysses as well as to Richard Lovelace ("Iron bars do not a prison make"), Rudyard Kipling, and William Ernest Henley. The same writer found in "Don't Fence Me In" resistance to "the Coalition of Evil . . . trying to fence in the whole world and to enslave its people . . . In the singing of this song, the bookkeeper tied to his desk, the clerk to his counter, the farmer to his plow may in spirit find release from the humdrum and ride to the ridge where the west commences." Maybe. One doubts that Porter would subscribe to such solemnity. When he was told that the song was to be used in *Hollywood Canteen,* he said, "Oh, that old thing."

Nonetheless its fame was international. The German general Karl von Rundstedt was said to have made a cash offer for a German version of "Don't Fence Me In" ("Lebensraum"—for which ostensibly Germany was waging World War II—might well be a translation of "Don't Fence Me In"). When Nelson Barclift wrote about the popularity of "Don't Fence Me In" with the troops, Porter said he was "delighted . . . but I resent getting words from a friend of mine that the Japs sing it too." No doubt part of its appeal in America was its implicit patriotism. In February 1945, when the liner *Gripsholm* landed in New York with twelve hundred wounded and disabled servicemen, they disembarked to Bing Crosby and the Andrews Sisters' recording of "Don't Fence Me In." In June 1945 the song was used in an advertising campaign for the New York Community Service Society's summer camps for children. Porter allowed the society to send its letter of appeal over his signature. "Whether you sing or not you can start a bunch of fenced-in city youngsters singing on their way to open country."

Appearing on the Kate Smith show, Porter was presented with a watch in recognition of his contribution to national morale in writing the song. Said Miss Smith, "['Don't Fence Me In'] reaches into the heart of the lad in the foxhole." Bob Fletcher heard the broadcast and wrote, Walter Winchell claimed, to Kate Smith identifying the part he played in the song's composition. He was said not to want any of the royalties, but he did covet the watch. When Porter's lawyers inquired around, Fletcher denied having written the letter, and finally the culprit was found to be an employee of United Artists who provided Winchell with gossip, much of it no doubt spurious, for the columnist to print.

However, in another quarter a more avaricious figure emerged. Late in December of 1944 Porter received a letter from a Warner Bros. attorney advising him that Ira Arnstein, "a constant litigant in the United States Courts," had written to Harry Warner and Arthur Schwartz claiming that several Cole Porter songs were plagiarisms of his compositions. "The letters," wrote the attorney, "are accompanied by various manuscripts and printed pages of Arnstein's music together with diagrams pointing out the claims of Arnstein." He thought the claims "absolutely ridiculous," but added ominously that "if Arnstein follows his usual course he can become an awful nuisance." A few days later Porter telephoned Warner Bros. and told them to "pay no attention." It was Arnstein's contention that Porter had pirated "Don't Fence Me In" from Arnstein's "A Modern Messiah"; "Night and Day" from "I Love You Madly"; and "My Heart Belongs to Daddy" from "A Mother's Prayer." This accusation from a man whose other compositions had such titles as "I Love You Molly" and "Sadness Overwhelms My Soul" was not convincing. Arnstein went further, charging that Porter never wrote original songs but lifted them all from his works. Dr. Sigmund Spaeth, for many years a member of an intermission panel on the Metropolitan Opera's Saturday matinee broadcasts, testified on Porter's behalf, as did Deems Taylor and Monty Woolley. A formidable tune detective, Spaeth had a piano brought into the courtroom and Arnstein's work played, followed by passages from Cole Porter's songs. The courtroom was the scene of unusual appointments in this trial. Huge sheets of music, photographically enlarged, were placed on a special easel and analyzed by the lawyers. Records were played on a phonograph so that the jury could make comparisons. "The jury came back from its deliberations and asked for the play of 'A Modern Messiah' by Arnstein and 'Don't Fence Me In' by Mr. Porter and after that it was only a short interval until their verdict for the defense was brought in." After they found him innocent of plagiarism, Porter shook hands with each member of the jury.

But this didn't end the matter. In February 1946 a higher court reversed the decision and reinstated the Arnstein suit against Cole Porter. (Arnstein did not include the Warner music companies in this suit, so Porter was left to defend himself.) Finally, in May the federal court ruled in Porter's favor, but the lawsuit must have been something of an ordeal for him.

Some blame friction between Porter and Arthur Schwartz for the disarray of *Mississippi Belle* and the eventual discarding of it. Criticism of Cole's score by another composer probably was galling to him, although the songs Porter wrote for the film are distinctly inferior. But just at this time Porter was in fact praising Schwartz to Barclift. Included in the general goodwill was "my producer . . . Arthur Schwartz & he's grand. He just finished *Cover Girl* & everybody went wild at its press preview." Schwartz had first come to Cole's attention as a gifted young composer. He was rung up by Porter, who telephoned to say how much he enjoyed some of Schwartz's songs. When eventually they met, Schwartz told Porter that he would soon be traveling to Europe, whereupon Cole gave him letters of introduction to friends in Paris, Cannes, Nice, and London. Schwartz considered Porter to have "a tremendous interest in young composers." His letters "worked like a charm" for Schwartz in Europe. To Schwartz, going into the project, Porter was "a great chap in addition to being just about the best there is among popular composers."

When Mike Todd and Porter worked together on *Something for the Boys,* Porter, so several friends say, considered Todd a virtual guru. His reverence for producers was religious—at least when the productions succeeded. Buoyed by their success in 1943, Cole promised Todd to do a new show next year. *Mexican Hayride* was the result of their collaboration. Again the book was written by Herbert and Dorothy Fields and the staging done by Hassard Short. Bobby Clark was the star, and June Havoc the female lead. Originally the show was written for Victor Moore and Billy Gaxton, but they were unavailable, so the book was reworked to fit the comic talents of Clark, whose trademarks were painted-on eyeglasses and a huge cigar. The first tryout was in Boston on December 29, 1943. "[Todd's] theory is that people escape from their troubles by [being offered] a feast for their eyes," wrote the *Boston Herald* critic the next day. He added that the "book was one of the least substantial articles of its kind ever turned out as the basis of so gorgeous a production." (While the show was still in Boston, Porter served as best man at the wedding of Sylvia Ashley to Lord Stanley. Mrs. William Randolph Hearst was matron of honor.) When *Mexican Hayride* opened in New York on January 28, 1944, at the Winter Garden Theater—the first non-Shubert show to play there—the show was the most sumptuous musical to be presented on Broadway since the Ziegfeld productions.

Mexican Hayride had a huge advance sale ($300,000) before it came into New York, having sold out until mid-March. "Porter has another hit," said one critic, and despite so many bad notices, a hit it was, registering 481 performances. Some attributed the eventual demise of the musical to June Havoc's announcement in July 1944 that she was injured during the show and couldn't continue. Miss Havoc maintains, "I left *Mexican Hayride* because of a broken leg, sustained when I was making an exit into a dark wing; I struck a cable, which knocked me down—and in the dark, the entire chorus of *Mexican Hayride* danced over me on their exit point. I was in a plaster cast from hip to toe, and much was made of it. I didn't return to *Hayride,* and that's why everyone was so angry. I had been in the show for, I think it was, a year." Porter believed that she left to play the title role in *Sadie Thompson,* a musical version of Somerset Maugham's *Rain.* He never forgave her. June Havoc's chief memory of the show is of Porter:

> struggling up and down the aisles during rehearsals on canes and crutches; he was in great pain, and hardly the strong, ebullient Cole Porter that so many other people knew. Rehearsing with him in his elaborate apartment in New York was such a pleasure . . . We worked very hard, and I suppose it was because I had two solo, show-stopping numbers which had, admittedly, come from the bottom of his trunk. Cole Porter sent me lavish gifts, among which were a few orchid trees. He was generous, amusing, and brilliant when he wasn't in pain. That pain was so worrisome to Mike Todd . . . Bobby Clark, and everyone in the company that, during a music rehearsal, a cello player (playing from a box because the orchestra was so huge, augmented by the strings, which, of course, Porter loved), crumpled over his instrument and fell. Only Mike Todd and I saw this—we rushed to the cellist's side as the music played on; he died in my arms, and when I asked Mike to stop the music, he replied, "This is the way he would have wanted it." There was little else to be done for the man but maybe Mike was right. There was beautiful music all around and we didn't tell Cole Porter until later, because he was suffering enough with his own pain.

The reviews were mixed. A critic in the *Daily News* wrote a rave notice and compared "I Love You" favorably with "Night and Day" and "Begin the Beguine." Others thought that Porter had mostly abandoned his languorous Latin songs in favor of those that allowed June Havoc and Bobby Clark to mug. "An undistinguished extravaganza," wrote another reviewer. Wolcott Gibbs in *The New Yorker* was more disturbing. "The great disappointment . . . is Cole Porter's music, which is not only derivative but at the moment as nonmemorable to me as the sounds that go with a hurdy-gurdy." Todd spent a quarter of a million dollars of his own money to mount *Mexican Hayride,* which was exotically set in a bullring, the bar at Ciro's, the palace at Chapultepec, and Xochimilco. Against this extravagant decor the actors told the lame tale of an American crook eluding the authorities by fleeing to Mexico, where he assumes various disguises.

These events have a rather surreal resemblance to events that befell the Porters when they traveled to Mexico earlier in the year. There they joined Mike Todd and other members of his staff. But not for long. Dysentery afflicted most of them, including Cole, whose osteomyelitis recurred and forced him, after two weeks, to return to New York and another operation at Doctors Hospital. Danton Walker wrote in his widely read column that Porter had been expelled from Mexico for scandalous behavior. Infuriated, Cole instructed his lawyer to insist that Walker recant, but no apology or retraction was printed. The columnist is reported to have asked, "If it isn't true, why is [Porter] upset?" Porter sometimes seemed to take private pleasure in thinking of himself as an outlaw, a fantasy his unacknowledged homosexuality and the secrecy it entailed no doubt generated. But he had no desire to be uncovered publicly and was probably frightened as well as angered by Walker's slander.

Notable in Porter's character was his refusal to be daunted: in August he and Sturges traveled again to Mexico. Linda reported on August 18 that both were in Buxton Hill for a long weekend after a "very exciting two weeks." Cole, she said, looked well, but tired after missing plane connections in Brownsville, Texas.

Of the songs he wrote for *Mexican Hayride,* Porter's favorite is said to have been "Sing to Me, Guitar," a lament of a lover separated from the beloved. There seems little in the lyric to account for Porter's enthusiasm: the rhyming of "roaming" with "gloaming" is particularly disappointing. Perhaps the feelings from which it sprang were dear to the composer. He and Barclift already had *their* song, but Porter referred in one letter to "the Barclift room" in the Brentwood house and continued to tell the young soldier how much he missed him. Then, some time in 1944, Porter met and fell in love with a marine from Montana (oddly enough, the name he gave to the female romantic lead in *Mexican Hayride*). "Sing to Me, Guitar" laments that "from my dearest of all / I am parted" and implores the guitar to "sing . . . of his lips pressed to mine / As we kissed and we kissed and we kissed."

"I Love You," the show's one hit, might have been inspired by Porter's passion for his marine, but the more immediate muse was Monty Woolley, who challenged Porter to write a song with so banal a title as "I Love You." (It was first called "It All Belongs to You and Me.") Robert Kimball refers to a telegram Mike Todd sent to Cole on February 4, 1944: "Dear Cole: Bing Crosby is recording 'I Love You' a week from today. I love you." By late April, Kimball points out, Bing Crosby's recording was the best-seller in America and the sheet music second in nationwide sales. "I Love You" was also the number-one song on radio's *Your Hit Parade.* Cole had easily won his bet with Monty. In the lyrics we have once again the plea of a lover:

> *If a love song I could only write,*
> *A song with words and music divine,*
> *I would serenade you ev'ry night*
> *Till you'd relent and consent to be mine.*

Sometime in the early months of 1944 Porter wrote to tell Barclift that "the Duchess of Peru," as he jestingly refers to himself, "has a new boy friend, a strapping Marine beauty from Montana called Bob Bray and is he swell." According to Jean Howard, Bray was "Cole Porter's last great love." If one puts the emphasis on "great," this may be true. Certainly he was not Porter's *last* love. Robert Wheaton remembers Bray as a lover of Nelson Barclift's, and such a liaison perhaps did come about. He recalled, too, that Barclift and Bray "were always high on marijuana" and that both came often to Cole's Brentwood home for lunch.

"California is wonderful," wrote Cole to his cousin Lou Bearrs in March. He speaks to her familiarly about Ed Tauch, with whom he was still in touch. Linda and her maid, Weston, would be arriving in California on March 27 to spend a month. Porter told Barclift with some relish the domestic arrangements that had been devised: Linda in the "Barclift room," Weston in Miss Mona's former room. He seemed amused when he wrote of the shock his secretary (Margaret Egan, familiarly called Tully) would have when she arrived on April 1 and discovered "she'd been moved downstairs to the Capehart room and she won't like it." His household staff again posed problems: " 'The Great Etienne' quit," he tells Barclift on March 14. "John has become so fresh that I have to fire him. This leaves me with Eric, a German Swiss . . . My cook is Jean Gabin's former valet. I have an old housemaid who replied when asked how she got her name, 'All I know is that *my* name is *Mishy* and my sister's name is *Tishy.*' "

On March 30 Cole wrote Barclift to say that Linda had arrived "and is living in your room. We . . . whipped up one of those dressing tables that ladies like, so she is in complete comfort." Etienne, he tells Barclift, "left giving me only one day's notice. He did not even say 'goodbye' to me. He has become a Captain in a restaurant where he makes fabulous money." Porter was not exempt from the problems that arose in wartime for the rich when servants left them for better-paying jobs in the commercial world. Of course for him the loss of trusted servants was especially threatening as he became less mobile in later life. He told Barclift that Paul Sylvain, his trusted valet, was still in the hospital suffering from severe headaches. Nonetheless, "Sunday lunches boom again," and he was brightened by the two blue jays that lingered near the pool. Sturge, who'd been staying with Cole in California, was just then at a dude ranch in Arizona and would soon go to live "in the [Roosevelt] hotel with the Beard [Monty Woolley]."

Cole continued to delight in gossip and dished out large portions of it in letters to Barclift: Jean Howard and her husband, Charlie Feldman, had gone to New York for the opening of Feldman's picture *Follow the Boys,* which Cole, especially attentive in these years to finances, predicted would make a lot of money despite it's being "*very bad.*" Cole in 1944 was interested in Moss Hart's wanting to do a musical with him "if he can get an idea." Porter was also waiting with some eagerness to see a story set in the 1890s which Herbert and Dorothy Fields had plans to send him.

The Hollywood party scene in spring 1944 was proceeding full tilt. Newlyweds Lady Ashley and Lord Stanley were visiting Norma Shearer, and what with parties for them and others for Linda, Cole's social calendar was packed. "Joan Fontaine," he told Barclift with traces of a conspiratorial tone, "and Brian Aherne are splitting up. Merle [Oberon] fell in love with her camera man and decided to throw Alex[ander Korda] out, but Alex was so kind about it that she is ticking. Kay [Francis?] is in the Aleutians drinking up all of the soldiers' whiskey rations." Porter had been to see the film *The Miracle of Morgan's Creek* and told his army friend, "Don't miss [it], it's the most brilliant picture I have seen in years." Signing himself "Your old pal, Cole," he tells Barclift (who seems to have attached himself by then to a new friend) that "we all miss you and Artie and love you dearly." Glamorous film stars do not appear to have supplanted in the deeper places of his affections this soldier, who remained dear to Cole. Barclift was just then stationed in Italy, and Cole continued to preach to him a favorite dictum: *carpe diem*—or, as he urged in a discard from *Mexican Hayride:*

> *You'll be safer if you squatta*
> *On the spotta that you gotta*
> *But if off you never trotta*
> *You will miss a lotta fun . . .*

"Don't fail to see Fulco [Duke of Verdura]'s ma . . . she is a great person . . . Try to go to Agrigenti [*sic*] and Syracusa. They are both fascinating and beautiful. Have you tried fried baby octopus yet? Delicious!" Porter concludes, in heartfelt but trite words, "Jesus but I miss y'all. We talk about you both all the time and the talk is all pretty. Goodbye and my blessings and love." Signed, "Yr. pal Cole."

Perhaps Porter's friendship with a dancer and choreographer led to the exceptional emphasis on dance in *Mexican Hayride.* Before rehearsals began, Mike Todd, Porter, and the choreographer, Paul Haakon, auditioned three hundred chorus girls for the show. Since the success of Agnes de Mille's choreography in *Oklahoma!* and *One Touch of Venus,* dancers had to be not only beautiful but accomplished in their art. "The production is the star," wrote one reviewer, and the dancing merited much of the praise the show received. *The New York Times* complained that the lyrics on the whole "do not have the usual convolution of tongue-twisting words." This judgment, while often true, is not everywhere applicable. June Havoc stopped the show with a list song titled "There Must Be Someone for Me":

> *Mister John L. Lewis I could not begin*
> *To imagine as my spouse,*
> *Yet a lot of girls would love to slumber in*
> *The bushes of his eyebrows.*

In this instance Porter linked his droll rhymes to a figure—Lewis, the labor leader and founder of the CIO—now forgotten by most. "Girls" ("Girls to the right of me, / Girls to the left of me") is a song that invokes the Follies and is still performed. Another number from *Mexican Hayride,* "It Must Be Fun to Be You," foreshadows Porter's very last song, "Wouldn't It Be Fun," although the tone differs dramatically. (Porter seems often to have had Errol Flynn on his mind while composing *Mexican Hayride:* he refers to the actor in three different songs.)

Cole was hoping, in fact, that Mike Todd would fail in his efforts to arrange a picture deal for *Mexican Hayride,* as he felt that the sale would make him so much poorer, owing to taxes. At the Winter Garden, *Hayride* was "roughing it" (as Porter described it to Barclift) on $46,000 per week, but meanwhile *Something for the Boys* was breaking records in Chicago. Porter was anxious to discover if the latter would survive Joan Blondell's departure from the cast and demonstrate that it was star-proof. He thought "it may still continue to draw as 'the sticks' are all so pleased about the production itself. Before it left for the road, Todd had completely new sets and costumes so it hadn't that bedraggled look of most road shows."

In June of 1944—a year that welcomed to Broadway such works as *Bloomer Girl, I Remember Mama, Dear Ruth, The Late George Apley, Harvey,* and *Song of Norway*—Dr. Sirmay wrote to tell Cole that the producer Billy Rose was eager to do a show with him. This project eventuated in the opening on December 7 of *Seven Lively Arts*. Cole wrote to Barclift:

> I leave [Hollywood] on June 30 to start work on the Billy Rose Revue, *The Seven Lively Arts,* which goes into rehearsal October 1st. He offered me that job last February but I threw it down as it included several ballets & a 20 minute Symphonic piece to be played on stage *plus* 10 songs. I would have leapt at it but he wouldn't give me six months to do it after this *Mississippi Belle* rewrite. I was practically set on a Bing Crosby job when Rose telephoned me last Friday and offered me the job again but without the ballets & symphonic bit. So I'm doing it . . . sounds very exciting & I need mental excitement . . . It will reopen the Ziegfeld Theatre in December. Bobby [Hassard] Short is staging it all . . . Aaron Copland or someone equally interesting will do the ballet & the on stage orchestral job.

Billy Rose and Mike Todd had been rivals since the 1939 World's Fair, when two of Todd's exhibits lost out to Rose's Aquacade. Perhaps it gave Porter some pleasure to quit Todd for Rose. According to Madeline Smith, Porter "didn't care . . . much for Mike Todd . . . He had [Todd] out to Williamstown, out to the country, and all. You know, Mr. Porter was very well brought up, a polite and gracious host, and he observed most of the amenities . . . But he thought that Mike Todd was a little too presumptuous and a little crude . . . He just didn't like him too much."

Whether Porter was any more charmed at first by Billy Rose—"the little Napoleon," as some redundantly called him—is questionable. By November 1944, though, Porter had been completely won over. "The show is wonderful," he wrote to Jean Howard, "and I have never had such a nice experience in the theater as with the curious little Billy Rose. He tops any producer that I have ever worked with." Persuaded by Rose's proposal, Porter agreed to do the score of a show that was to illustrate each of the "seven lively arts": theater, ballet, opera, concert, radio, painting, and music. Auditions were held to choose six unknown girls and one male youth who were to be matched by seven stars. Among the new talents chosen were several who went on to prominence in the musical theater: Dolores Gray (whom Rose had spotted in a show at the Copacabana), Helen Gallagher, and Bill Tabbert. The stars included Beatrice Lillie, Bert Lahr, the ballet stars Alicia Markova and Anton Dolin, and Benny Goodman and his Five—Teddy Wilson and Red Norvo among them. For the "Scènes de Ballet," Igor Stravinsky was to compose fifteen minutes of music (which turned out to be eighteen minutes). When Rose heard what Stravinsky had written, he found it too avant-garde and wired the great composer: YOUR MUSIC GREAT SUCCESS STOP COULD BE SENSATIONAL SUCCESS IF YOU WOULD AUTHORIZE ROBERT RUSSELL BENNETT RETOUCH ORCHESTRATION STOP BENNETT ORCHESTRATES EVEN THE WORKS OF COLE PORTER." Stravinsky replied at once: "SATISFIED WITH GREAT SUCCESS." (In another account of this story, Dolin is credited with sending the telegram.) William Schuman, who subsequently attained fame as a composer and arts administrator in New York, wrote "Sideshow for Music," an orchestral composition to illustrate the art of music. In retrospect, *Seven Lively Arts* seems to have been top-heavy with talent. The forty-piece orchestra was conducted by Maurice Abravanel, the chorus trained by Robert Shaw. Norman Bel Geddes did sets of such elaborate design that two carloads had to be left behind when the show was tried out in Philadelphia.

In the early autumn Porter went to Buxton Hill to work on the *Seven Lively Arts* score. While in Williamstown, Cole learned that Rose had jettisoned the original book and decided to convert the show into a satiric revue to be written by Moss Hart, George S. Kaufman, Robert Pirosh, Joseph Schrank, Charles Sherman, and Ben Hecht. Rose insisted that the show have little in the way of theme or point of view; he wanted it to be all veneer, in the manner of a Ziegfeld revue.

Some of the cast found Billy Rose tyrannical; and Hassard Short, the director, testy; but no one objected to Porter, who was elegant and a bit aloof—or so he seemed to some of the performers. Indeed, once while the show was in rehearsal, all the cast was invited to Billy Rose's swanky office and informed that Porter would arrive shortly to play the opening couplets describing what each character hoped to achieve in New York. Porter appeared, walking with difficulty and aided by two canes, but very merry and appealingly sweet. He played the couplets and gave each performer his or her own. A light supper followed, at which Porter said to Dolores Gray, "You made a wonderful impact at the Copa, Miss Gray. I was so happy to learn you were going to be in this show. How do you like the couplet I wrote for you?" "Just fine, thank you very much." He studied her for a few minutes and then said, "Dolores, I'd *really* like to know how you like your couplet." She stammered and fussed and finally said, "I have a powerful voice with unusual range, and I'm portraying a singer; but you've written my couplet all on one note." Porter stared momentarily, then said, "You're absolutely right. I'm going home and rewrite it completely." And he did.

Every seat had sold for the eight tryout performances in Philadelphia and the critic in the *Inquirer* had raved, especially about the Porter songs, which were "in his best vein." The advance sale for New York was half a million dollars. A soberer reviewer in the *Philadelphia Record* rightly regretted that *Seven Lively Arts* was "an as yet unfinished product, sprawling but elegant; lavish but smart . . . which will not emerge as one of this decade's great revues"—a judgment with which Bert Lahr agreed. Backstage in Philadelphia things had gone poorly. Lahr thought his material was unsuitable and that his protests about it to Rose were going unheeded. At the Philadelphia opening, when Rose came to Lahr's dressing room with a bouquet of flowers, Lahr angrily told him where he could put them. The great comic feared his return to Broadway after several years in Hollywood would prove ignominious. This anxiety made Lahr especially touchy, and he refused to sing one chorus of "Dainty, Quainty Me" which rhymed "cinema" with "inema." Cole Porter's efforts to circumvent this impasse were in vain, and the song was dropped, much to Porter's displeasure.

Lahr is said also to have been displeased by Dolores Gray's behavior in the show and complained that she took the attention of the audience away from him. Gray herself had decided to leave the show after Philadelphia, having concluded that it would be a mistake for her to debut on Broadway in so slight a part after her splashy Copa engagement. When Rose heard rumors of her quitting the show, he climbed five flights of stairs to her dressing room in Philadelphia. She later felt overtaken by guilt and telephoned Rose to ask if she could stay with the show until its third week in New York. They agreed to that, and after fulfilling her commitment Gray left for a three-month engagement at the Chez Paree in Chicago.

Opening night was a mess, according to Gray. The famous couturier Valentina had done gowns for certain numbers, and she came to the first night with several of her New York friends. "Is it the girl, or is it the gown?" sang Miss Gray; audience clapped riotously, and not a subsequent word of the song could be heard over the din.

According to George Eells, Porter felt the songs he'd done for the show were substandard except for a number he wrote for Lillie, "When I Was a Little Cuckoo." Porter's lifelong assertion that he tailored songs to the range of particular performers is patently evident in this comic song:

> *Last year down in dear Miami*
> *I picked up such a sweet Hindu swami,*

And as by the sea we'd gaily stroll
He'd talk of the transmigration of the soul.
I found since the world's beginning,
I've had many an outing and inning,
I'd been ev'ry sort of person and ev'ry kind of thing,
But my greatest success was as a bird on the wing.

When I was a little cuckoo
Was I full of mischief? Oh boy!
Flitting hither and thither
Far from mither and fither,
I lived in a dither
Of joy.

Cole's rhyming of "hither and thither" with "mither and fither" uniquely suited the comic style of Bea Lillie. Lillie was called "naughty but nice" by one critic, and "When I Was a Little Cuckoo" soon becomes a double-entendre-laden list song, with the singer naming the unlikely metamorphoses she underwent: "As a royal snake charmer I made Egypt gasp / When I struck Cleopatra for kicking my asp." And as a "little cuckoo" she knew

> *. . . Bob White, Tom-Tit, Cock Robin,*
> *And Bertie, what a dirty old jay!*
> *And if you think I was wrong*
> *To be had for a song,*
> *Just a little cuckoo was Ay.*

It was no doubt lyrics as clever as these linked, in this song and some others, to music less beguiling that led the critic of the *World Telegram* to write that "musically, though not lyrically, Cole Porter seems to have lost his inspiration."

Lillie disliked all the songs Porter had written for her and felt easy only with the sketches Moss Hart had done. One of these depicted her trying to buy a ticket to a ballet she thought was called "S. Hurok," in order to identify the work to the box-office clerk she danced her hilarious parody of *The Dying Swan. Variety* found her sketches especially funny but added that "the lyrics are . . . plenty blue."

A preview benefit performance was given the night before the show's opening in New York, but Bea Lillie did not appear; she was said to be ill. Her absence resulted from an impasse with Porter over the numbers he

Bert Lahr and Bea Lillie in *Seven Lively Arts*, 1944

wrote for her, one of which is said to have been his favorite in the show. Lillie refused to see the physician Billy Rose sent over to the Waldorf, where she was staying. According to her biographer, Rose next invoked Actors' Equity, but as late as five p.m. on the day of the opening both parties remained adamant in their demands. When the president of Equity called on Lillie, she promised to appear that night if she could sing one of her songs and the next night do the Porter number. Cole agreed to this, and the show went on with its reluctant star.

Billy Rose, who had invested heavily in the show, had feared the audience would think "arts" and forget "lively"; and so he had proclaimed that *Seven Lively Arts* was "the last word in complete escapism, a super Christmas Tree, a grabbag of fun." One New York reviewer agreed with him: "Last night . . . Billy Rose . . . turned back the clock and, abracadabra, there was no World War II." Rose had asked the opening-night audience to "please dress," but half the audience turned up in "civvies"—a signal of the postwar trend that augured ill for dressy nightlife in New York. Among the prominent people who attended were Judy Garland, Linda Darnell, Ethel Merman, Joe DiMaggio, Jesse Lasky, and Mike Todd. Present too were Lucius Beebe, the Gilbert Millers, the Bennett Cerfs, and the Oscar Hammersteins. Dorothy Hammerstein had supervised the redecoration of the Ziegfeld Theatre, and her daughter appeared in *Seven Lively Arts* as one of the "Ladies of Fashion." Before the curtain rose at the Ziegfeld, which Billy Rose had bought and was reopening that night, white-gloved waiters offered champagne to the audience; they appeared again at the intermission and as the last curtain fell. Three hundred cases in all were dispensed—a Billy Rose touch. In the lobby, drawings by Salvador Dalí of the seven arts were displayed. Afterward, Elsa Maxwell hosted a gala party at the Starlight Roof of the Waldorf. Cole sent Michael Pearman, on leave from the army just then, two tickets for the opening. Pearman took Irving Schneider, husband of George Kaufman's daughter Anne, with him. (Kaufman had been brought in to write a sketch that didn't succeed.) A man on the sidewalk offered Pearman one hundred dollars for the tickets—tempting him until he recalled that Porter would be sitting only a few rows away.

Little of this excitement at the opening night colored the review of the *New York Times* critic, who found that "the tunes definitely are not Cole Porter's best," or of Howard Barnes in the *Herald Tribune,* who also faulted Porter's music: "[It] does not come through with the melody and authority which might hold the show in a loose unity." He thought it little more than "a night club exhibit." Danton Walker, an old foe, accused Porter of pirating the show's single great number, "Ev'rytime We Say Goodbye," first from a French song called "Chanson de l'adieu" by Edmond d'Haraucourt and then from one written by Phil Ohman and Foster Carling and sung in a 1939 Hedy Lamar film called *Lady of the Tropics.*

Nothing developed from the charge that Porter had plagiarized "Ev'ry Time We Say Goodbye." The song, introduced by Nan Wynn in Act I and sung again by Dolores Gray in Act II (backed by Benny Goodman and his group), has continued to move audiences in the countless performances it has subsequently had. It echoes themes that throughout his life moved Porter to ardent utterances in both words and music. Departures and separation from the beloved characterized Cole's life in these war years, and his song articulated the sorrowful sentiments of millions around the world. Countless lovers felt Porter's words and music expressed their own sorrow in having to live separated from each other; and lovers ever since have embraced the song.

For a nonbeliever, Porter kept a keen eye on the "high gods." In "Ev'ry Time We Say Goodbye" he wonders

> *Why the gods above me*
> *Who must be in the know*
> *Think so little of me*
> *They allow you to go.*

Dr. Sirmay, whose opinion mattered so mightily to Porter, praised the song in a letter written (in rather Magyar English) the day before *Seven Lively Arts* opened.

> In your new show, you are giving again a most delightful evidence of your great talent. Instead of declining, your imagination, the freshness of your ideas and your skill both as a composer and lyricist are all on the increase. I myself have a personal affair with your song "Ev'ry Time." It chokes me whenever I hear it, it moves me to tears. This song is one of the greatest songs you ever wrote. It is dithyramb to love, a hymn to youth, a heavenly beautiful song. It is not less a gem than any immortal song of a Schubert or Schumann. Contemporaries usually fail to recognize real values. I don't care what critics may say, this song is a classic and will live forever as many others of your songs.

How right he was. Cole Porter's matching of words and music in this song is especially felicitous: the use of the repeated note (no matter how Dolores Gray disliked this device) is as successful here as it was in "Night and Day." The modulation from major to minor harmony just as the change "from major to minor" is remarked in the text is an effective musical gesture.

But this superb song is a rare exception to the otherwise mediocre material in the show, which Lillie took to calling *Seven Deadly Arts.* The distinguished Edwin Denby, then dance critic of the *Herald Tribune,* could not find anything to praise in the segment that was the yield of three such consummate artists as Stravinsky, Markova, and Dolin (who also choreographed the ballet). He called it "a pretentious fake" and insisted that "the notion of playing a serious Stravinsky in a show or of asking Markova to dance seriously in one is a mistake."

Like the ballet, virtually every other segment of this spectacle sooner or later proved problematic. The show closed on May 26, 1945, after 193 performances, its demise attributed by John Chapman not only to the ballet—both Stravinsky's score ("out of key and out of tempo with a revue") and

Dolin's choreography—but also to various other defects, such as Ben Hecht's monologues for Doc Rockwell. He thought the show was oversold at the beginning. He also blamed Billy Rose for selling tickets for the first twenty-three weeks only at the box office. Rose did manage to break even himself, but overall the show lost more than $150,000.

Lines that Ben Hecht wrote for *Seven Lively Arts* could apply only to "Ev'ry Time We Say Goodby." But if we think of Porter's entire output— "Night and Day," for instance—then what Hecht wrote seems poignantly true:

> Old Songs are more than tunes. They are little houses in which our hearts once lived. When we hear them we go visiting—we walk forgotten streets, we smile again at the skies of youth. Our town is full of old songs—for no town has ever had more troubadours serenading it. And one of the nicest of them is the human little music box who has written the songs for this show—the witty gentleman who has bidden us dance to tales of love and longing for twenty years. Here they are again—a parade of the ghost songs that will always haunt our hearts and the streets of our town.

Chapter 15

Night and Day

Irving Berlin suggested to Cole Porter that a film biography of Cole would be fitting. Berlin based his belief on the drama inherent in Porter's struggle with pain after his riding accident, and the inspiration his story would afford to wounded servicemen and veterans. Berlin then proposed the idea to Jack Warner. From the start Porter responded positively, although Linda had reservations and only agreed after being assured that both Cole and she approved the script. She hated Hollywood. Perhaps, too, she was discomfited or even felt threatened by the behavior of some lesbians in Hollywood. Ann Warner, whom the Porters often saw, was so aggressive that women were reluctant to use the powder room for fear of encountering her.

On Valentine's Day in 1943 Cole responded to Jack Warner's proposal that a film biography of Porter be made. "Your happy news arrived," he cabled. "I want to work for Warner Brothers." In May he cabled Warner about the "tough terms" (in Warner's phrase) that, Cole said, were the only terms to which he would agree. "I am extremely flattered that you are interested in such a proposition but at the same time I do not want to dispose of my life's work unless it can bring me at least the amount of security that is established in the deal [my agent] has submitted. I do not like to be in the position of putting a price on my head which says it is worth a figure which can be argued about." In December 1943 Warner Bros. agreed to pay Porter three hundred thousand dollars for "the right to select from his musical catalogue thirty-five musical compositions to be used in a motion picture based on the life of Cole Porter."

A number of screenwriters set about producing a script, but they lamented the lack in Porter's life of "struggle." Orson Welles asked: "What will they use for a climax? The only suspense is—will he or won't he accumulate ten million dollars?" Porter's homosexuality was by now common knowledge in Hollywood and elsewhere. How frustrated the screenwriters must have felt at the fact that they had to remain silent about all the conflict and drama inherent in Porter's private life and love affairs. No wonder he said after examining the script and giving his approval to it, "It was . . . as if I was reading about someone I know slightly." And elsewhere: "None of it's true."

Perhaps it was naiveté or perhaps dissimulation that led Arthur Schwartz later to write:

Musically (and financially) the film *Night and Day* was a great success, but the story suffered from insufficient dramatic incident and conflict. Apart from Cole's fabulous accomplishment, the only dramatic thing that ever happened to him was the horrible accident in which he was thrown from a horse.

He was phenomenally gifted, and very rich, he had an indescribably beautiful wife, his name was the proverbial household word and celebrated people the world over sought his companionship. He and I both knew that these were not quite elements of great story-making. But we also knew that fictionalizing was out of the question. Audiences wanted to meet the real Cole Porter. So we settled for the truth.

This posture differs from Schwartz's at the outset when he told a reporter that "there is enough substance to make a couple of great pictures."

Schwartz's memo to Jack Warner of April 13, 1944, is among the earliest documents concerning *Night and Day.* "Dear Boss," he began after having read the script, "so many ideas occurred to me for improvement as I went along that I could not believe anyone could regard this version as anything better than temporary." Among his suggestions was to introduce colorful personalities among Porter's friends. In this regard he urged that Monty Woolley be written into the script ("There has been an unbroken association between the two men since [Yale]"). Other "personalities" included Elsa Maxwell and Charles Cochran. Schwartz also submitted a list of stars associated with Cole's shows who should be invited to perform, including Fred Astaire, Jimmy Durante, Bob Hope, Ethel Merman, and Gertrude

Lawrence. He also cited the need to relieve "the terrible monotony of Cole Porter singing and playing at the piano." He thought the footage allotted to Porter in France should be diminished and more footage of Cole in London be featured. Finally, Schwartz lamented the dialogue and bad writing throughout.

On April 25, 1944, Schwartz told Porter that he "had started negotiations for Cary Grant," then forty-two and six foot two, to impersonate Cole, fifty-three, five-six, and balding. Cary Grant may have been introduced first to Cole Porter by Countess Dorothy di Frasso, an old friend of Cole's, who is said to have educated Gary Cooper in the elements of fine tailoring and who subsequently had an affair with Bugsy Siegel, one of the more raffish of the guests to visit the Porters.

One of the frequent guests at Porter's New York lunch parties, according to Cole's friend Colin Leslie Fox, was, Dorothy di Frasso. These lunches, Fox said, were "a wonderland of civilized, superficial fun, shallow talk, everyone beautifully dressed, all monitored by this benign person who wanted everyone to have a splendid time and who enjoyed so much having these people around. He himself was great fun, making little asides, almost coquettish with sly remarks and innuendos. You'd never know whom you'd meet and everyone was on!"

In August 1944, Schwartz wrote to Cole to say that for the film "we will probably have a great director, a great star, and a starting date in the Fall sometime." Cole had sent him for possible use in the film a song, "Annabelle Birby," written in his undergraduate years, and "I'm Dining with Elsa," his jokey anthem to Miss Maxwell. A week later Schwartz wrote again about lining up "some of the stars who introduced your famous songs" to appear in *Night and Day.* He asked Porter to make the initial request: "The many stars who are deeply indebted to you because of your great contribution to their success would surely be more receptive if approached by you."

Early in September 1944 Schwartz and Jack Warner came to New York to confer with Porter. "It will give us all the chance to get the ultimate out of a great story of what I consider a very important American guy," Jack Warner flatteringly wired. Porter replied, "Your swell wire received. I shall be here to cooperate in every way." They were eagerly attempting to secure Cary Grant and Monty Woolley for *Night and Day.* Mary Martin hoped to turn up for shooting in Hollywood the week between the close of *One Touch of Venus* in New York and its departure for the road. Schwartz urged Porter to send him a copy of an early, forgotten song called "I Never Realized," which the agent Louis Shurr was "crazy about," for possible use in the picture. He apologized for intruding, "knowing how engrossed you are in your job for Billy Barnum Rose."

Porter had sent to the studio the fifteen scrapbooks that Linda had by then so carefully put together documenting, mostly in reviews, Cole's career. Schwartz had set an associate, Herman Lissauer, to the task of searching through the scrapbooks, but in December Porter wrote to tell Schwartz that Lissauer "has not been thorough enough. I distinctly remember the Bob Benchley review in *The New Yorker,* in which he wondered why so great a production was built around such an inferior tune as 'Begin the Beguine' . . . also I remember reading a notice regarding 'Night and Day' as being an inferior attempt to copy 'What Is This Thing Called Love.' . . . Also there are many notices saying 'Cole Porter not up to his usual standard' which Mr. Lissauer has not found. Perhaps it would be better to give this job to some dirty lawyer."

Schwartz replied on December 27, 1944, advising Porter that he had gone himself to the research department at Warner Bros., where the scrapbooks were, but could find no evidence of the tin-eared reviews (Benchley's and others'). "It looks as if you are in the rather ironic position of a man disappointed by the lack of bad notices," he told Cole. In the same letter Schwartz advises Porter that early in January 1945 he will make a complete copy of the script of *Night and Day* for Cole. The starting date for shooting the film was announced as February 26. It is unlikely that Porter could have given much attention to a script that January; he was once again hospitalized, as he wrote irritatedly to Hedda Hopper: "Hedda dear, I am not out of the hospital. I am not going with Linda to our upstate home. I do not return to Hollywood in March. Jack Warner did not beg me to do another picture. I begged him. Love to you and your hat, through which you have been talking. Cole."

Tinkering with the script took more time than anyone expected. Jack Warner sent a telegram to Cole assuring him that Danton Walker was mistaken in his statement that *Night and Day* was to be abandoned because of the lack of drama in the story. "We [are] starting picture April 30 it will be in Technicolor and more enthused about it than ever. Mike Curtiz will direct." He signed it, "Love from Ann [and] myself." Michael Curtiz, the award-winning Hungarian, was indeed a coup, although this veteran of sixty-nine films would be driven to distraction by the demands of directing the picture, and particularly by the behavior of Cary Grant.

Porter had personal concerns and struggles just as the cameras were readying to roll. Late in March 1945 he wrote to give Barclift more advice about seeing sights in Europe and to ask that he look up "MT/Sgt. Robert

E. Bray (468915) Service Squadron 11, Marine Air Group 11, 4th Marine Air Wing and report to me about his health and general morale. He has been grounded since a long time from migraine. But for God's sake don't even hint at it, for he would never forgive me."

Only a little later in the spring he was describing his own ills to Barclift, in a manner that calls to mind the college boy Cole and the many pages he copied of his professor's lectures on physiology and anatomy:

On my left leg, Moorhead [his surgeon] first had to break both bones again, take out the jagged ends, splice the tendon of Achilles and then further up on the tibia cut eight inches of bone to take the marrow out and graft it over the fracture. He didn't want to do it as he was so afraid there were still streptococci in the fracture, but I insisted because I was so tired of hanging on to people. Luckily he didn't find streptococci but staphylococci, which are less dangerous germs. So I didn't die at all. Then he operated on the right heel in order to get the scar tissue out of it, so that I could once more, after seven and a half years, lie on a bed without putting my heel over the edge; it was so painful when it touched even a sheet, as the scar tissue pressed upon the heel bone. The first operation on this wasn't a success and he had to do it again. While this was going on I had two nervous breakdowns and lost 25 pounds which I am still regaining. I arrived here [California] more or less a wreck . . . I walk on crutches, short distances, but the wheel-chair is used a great deal. The pain in the left leg is hard to take, but it will gradually disappear within a year, he promises me . . . You ask how many more operations are necessary. I can't tell you yet as I am not at all sure that the last three are really successful . . . If this work doesn't have to be done again, I still have two operations ahead . . . in about two years.

"Why do you start me on stories about these legs?" he asks Barclift. "I have never talked so much about them in my life, as I am now. They don't depress me in the least, luckily"—which surely can not have been true.

Grant signed his contract in April 1945 and finally began work on *Night and Day* on June 14. Porter wrote exultantly to tell Barclift that: "I got everything I asked for including Cary Grant and technicolor. Last week I okayed Alexis Smith for the 'Linda' part . . . The last script that I saw was very good . . . It took any number of . . . scripts before I gave my okay, as there was [*sic*] too many gloomy moments. At present it is rather light except for the wonderful love story of Cole and Linda." The tone of this last remark is difficult to determine, but it seems ironic, addressed as it is to a homosexual lover. Cole was amused that the casting director had five possible mothers for him and fathers too. "I shall go to the Warner lot to take my pick."

Distanced to some degree from the fray, Cole particularly enjoyed the Sunday lunches around the pool where he flew a flag with the name Camp Porter. Leonard Goldstein, who as a young serviceman was stationed in California, came repeatedly to these parties and recalls that they usually began at two p.m. or so on Sunday afternoon and ended at seven-thirty or eight. Only males, predominantly servicemen, attended. "No ugly ducklings were welcome," said Mr. Goldstein. Porter discouraged any real friendship from forming. There was little overt sex: mostly, men met each other there and left together. "The sex took place later on." Camp Pendelton and the navy yard at San Diego were the principal sources of guests. Goldstein attended these parties in 1944 and 1945, although by then they were a longtime tradition. Some years later George Cukor wrote: "Dear Cole, I hope . . . that your life and your pool are full. I have a pretty good idea that they are." It was Porter's habit to isolate one or two of his guests and pay little attention to the others. Everyone drank heavily, although Goldstein remembers that "the booze was ordinary."

Linda had returned to the East Coast, but Sturges stayed on with Cole in California. Porter described in the letters he wrote regularly to Barclift how, as in the past at these lunches, Roger Stearns still sat at the end of the table, with a clown hat on, "and throws everyone into the aisles." Among the items Cole collected in California were flags of many nations and many state flags too. On Bastille Day, or if a French person was visiting, Porter flew the *tricolore*. But, said the songwriter and producer Saul Chaplin, if friends driving by saw a flag flying, they knew that Porter wanted his privacy.

Mel Wilson and Bill Holland, "kids twenty years old," were regulars at Porter's Sunday brunches around the pool. These boys had a woman friend, Audrey Aurette, who was a friend as well of Cole's chums Stanley Musgrove and Bobbie Raison. They often praised her entertaining ways to Cole. Mel and Bill began to be bored with the Sunday routine and thought to enliven it by hatching a plot with Audrey. On the appointed Sunday she drove to Cole's house with her girlfriend and pushed past the butler with a story about having left her bikini in Mel Wilson's car. They paraded through the house to the pool. "I'm Audrey," she told Cole, who had correctly risen to greet her. Her friend, very Brooklyn in her speech, asked if they might take a dip in the pool. Cole firmly refused her request. Then he apologized for not offering them brunch: "There's not enough for you to eat," he said stonily, surrounded by tables laden with food, as the girls were escorted off the property. Audrey Aurette remembered that Cole was "fierce" in protecting his Sunday brunch from female intrusion.

During the week the male houseguests dined with Porter at home:

We never go to restaurants. We never go to night clubs. For Saturday lunch there is a gang here always, a combination of the east and west, nicely mixed and then Sunday, the ole time stuff. My house will shock you. I rise at nine, breakfast by the pool at nine thirty. My trainer whom I brought west appears at eleven. There are infinite exercises and interminable massage. Freedom comes at three p.m. & a secretary at four who stays an hour.

He went on to tell Barclift about the anticipated return of Robert Bray for six months. "I hope awfully that he can spend most of his time in the house with me." Porter's gift as a raconteur and socialite seemed entirely intact as he moved about the Hollywood party circuit, albeit with sometimes exotic purpose. Writing to thank Gerald Murphy for an unusual gift, he said, "The belt made out of Lillian Russell's garters has completely re-established me socially in Hollywood. Everyone wants to see me simply in order to see the belt, and I am having a hell of a time."

Linda back in New York was less content, and this saddened Cole. The Williamstown house was ready for her, but she had to lie in bed for two weeks with a severe cold. "Poor darling—it is pitiful," wrote Cole, "the unending recurrence of these terrible colds." She was kept alive only because the sulfa drugs fought off the infections. "The scars in her lungs have gradually become bigger and it is practically impossible for her to throw off any infection." Cole urged his friends to write to Linda: "It would buck her up," he said.

On the sixty-ninth day of shooting *Night and Day* the unit manager wrote: "They do not know how the end of this picture is going to be done. They have been writing this story for two years and still it is not on paper."

Two or three times a day changes were made in the script, mostly at Grant's insistence. Many of Grant's complaints about the picture were valid: poor dialogue, little characterization. The disagreements between Grant and Curtiz escalated, and finally the director threatened to quit. Grant insisted that he be allowed to supervise the costumes of all the actors, male and female, complaining at one point that a quarter-inch of his shirt cuffs showed, whereas the proper cuff should show only an eighth. Alexis Smith chose to look on such demands as Grant's fastidiousness about his art. She tended to blame herself when things went wrong and shared Grant's judgment that the dialogue was badly written and meaningless.

It was the song lyrics that disturbed the Hays Office, and in particular Joseph Breen, the director of the Production Code Administration. Early in 1945 Breen wrote to Jack Warner requiring changes. "Now only use four-letter words" was unacceptable; neither "gigolos" nor "hell" could be used; "cocaine" could not be mentioned. In "Miss Otis Regrets," the phrases "she strayed" and "led her so far astray" had to be dropped. Of course, "Love for Sale" raised objections, as did "Me and Marie" and "My Heart Belongs to Daddy." Cole was in the hands of the Philistines again. "It is of great importance," Breen wrote, "that you make the eliminations suggested herein in as much as this material is almost certain to be eliminated by Censor Boards everywhere. If this is done, then there will be a *jump* in the sound track in the rendition of these songs."

The final script satisfied Breen and the board, but they had a few admonitions: Warner must be sure that the minister is depicted "in a virile and dignified manner"; the costumes for the girls must not allow unnecessary exposure, "especially in the breasts." The dialogue between Cole and Linda in one scene was judged to be "offensively sex suggestive." These and other objections of a similar kind all seem ludicrous today.

Then Monty Woolley, who lent the only touch of authenticity to the story, came down with a serious bladder infection and was kept going on drugs until he was rushed to the hospital for major surgery. (Charles Higham in his biography of Grant gives an enlightening account of the byzantine intrigues and complications that afflicted *Night and Day*.)

The filming finally was completed on November 20, 1945. Jack Warner wired Cole hyperbolically about "the most important musical ever written . . . Will take several weeks before scoring completed but when you see the film I know you are going to be extremely happy as I am. Everybody deserves plenty of kudos for the great work done." Cole distributed a few of these kudos himself, writing to tell Alexis Smith on May 6, 1946, that "what pleased us most was your wonderful performance as Linda. As my Linda said to me about your Linda, as we left the picture, 'How lucky I am to be shown on the screen as such an enchanting girl.' " And he wrote to Ginny Simms (or "Jinnie Sims"—Porter spelled badly), "I can never tell you how happy you made me by the way you sang my songs. Thank you, thank you, thank you." But Elsa Maxwell was not pleased by *Night and Day:* "I, of course, should be in this picture, for Cole and I have gone through Paris, London and Venice together . . . But Warners always has someone else to imitate me."

Reviews mostly fastened on the Porter songs: "The story is not important since it is so completely overshadowed by the songs," is a typical comment. *The New York Times* reviewer said, "*Night and Day* begs quick dismissal as an idealistic smattering of biography." And the *San Francisco News* reviewer called it "no more the story of Cole Porter's life than a two-cent stamp is of Washington." All the reviewers praised the cameo appearance of Mary Martin singing "My Heart Belongs to Daddy" and the tart performance of Monty Woolley. A review in *The New Yorker* underlined Cary Grant's failings in the role of Cole Porter:

Although he is getting on in years now, he is compelled by the script to depict the composer . . . as a Yale undergraduate . . . and to indulge in such painful juvenile activities as leading a chorus through that song about Eli Yale and a bulldog. Apart from having to attend college at an age when most Yale men would be working for the Luce publications, Mr. Grant is forced to break into song every now and then, which is rather too bad, since his voice, though resonant, is no more mellifluous than the average subway guard's.

No review was more savage than the piece that appeared in *Life* on August 5, with the subtitle, "Film About Composer Cole Porter Is an Exemplar of What's Wrong with Hollywood Musicals." It called the big musical numbers "tasteless"; the dialogue "an attempt to re-create the conversation of clever and intelligent people bravely made by a script writer who seems never to have associated with them"; the whole treatment "founded on weird distortions and timeworn tricks of plot." The reviewer refers to a preview of the film at the Yale Club in New York: "As the painful travesty came to an end with the Yale Glee Club singing 'Night and Day' [one] member was heard to mutter, 'Let's not have any more of these Warner Brothers pictures.' " Right after the *Life* article and one that took a similar tack in *Time,* Warner Bros. banned Henry Luce's correspondents from its studios.

Cole's home state, though, was certainly enthusiastic about *Night and Day.* When the film had its world premiere in Hollywood on August 1, the governor of Indiana asked Earl Warren, then California's governor, to proclaim the day "Cole Porter of Indiana Day." The Indiana State Society of Southern California, numbering eighteen thousand *dépaysé* Hoosiers, took a lively part in the arrangements for opening night: as a preliminary, its president called officially on Alexis Smith at the Warner studios and made her an honorary citizen of Indiana.

Night and Day is what the lingo of the trade calls a "biopic." Purging the plot of any semblance of the truth had inevitably produced a vapid film. It seems not to have been possible for Hollywood in the 1940s to produce a real biography of Cole Porter; at least the film that was made kept a revue of his songs before the public.

Orson Welles came prominently into Porter's life in 1945, when Cole agreed to collaborate with him. Welles had adapted a Jules Verne novel, *Around the World in Eighty Days,* for radio presentation by the Mercury Theater. "Cole Porter and I blocked out the plan for the script and music of the show last August [1945]." It was in that same month that Linda persuaded Williams College to part with a rare first edition of [Verne's] book. "Much of the scenery and costumes can be traced directly to the illustrations of that . . . first edition."

Around the World in Eighty Days represented to Cole an adventure into a new musical genre (or so he appears to have considered it). "Now I am planning to associate myself with the crazy and unusual production of the theater—the kind of thing one dreams about but never quite dares to attempt. I shall never follow a pattern again—which means I shan't write the kind of musical show I have been doing for so long. Frankly it's because I am bored. I want to do something 'different.' " Elsewhere, Porter said, "this is a drama with music too."

The show was presented in two acts with forty scenes, which led one critic to say, "the grandiose proportions of the show defeat the purpose . . . the elaborateness is precious, its complexity tiresome, its cleverness precocious." Elliot Norton, the prominent Boston critic, called the play "unusual" and indicated that *Around the World* "has everything from a cock fight . . . to a three-ring circus which nobody ever managed to get on a stage before." Norton noted that "this show shouldn't be reviewed. It is more suited to inventory than to criticism." Even after many props had been jettisoned, backstage "looked like Cain's Warehouse brought to life by a madman who ordered a circus and a barnyard." Forty-eight tons of sets, plus a sixteen-hundred-pound mechanized elephant, were among the detritus. The mechanisms that were retained often failed. One reviewer thought that *Around the World* was attempting to satirize the stagecraft of the Jules Verne period.

The tryout opened on April 28, 1946, in Boston, a day late. The lead had taken ill the day before and Orson Welles decided to play the part himself. As a consequence of this misfortune no dress rehearsal took place.

Faulty scene changes occurred and light cues were sometimes missed. Two stagehands suddenly became part of the performance when they soared to the ceiling along with the set. Porter admired Welles's way with the stagehands as much as he did his gifts as an actor and director. "Please, sweetheart, get that scenery up," Welles would say to them.

Nelson Barclift was choreographer of the show and mentioned by Porter as one of the "young hopefuls" to whom he was giving a chance. Barbette, the exquisite cabaret artist, arranged the first-act circus finale. Jack Cassidy, sometimes rumored to have become one of Porter's lovers, played a policeman.

After tryout in Boston, New Haven, and Philadelphia, *Around the World* opened in New York on May 31, 1946. A number of reviewers likened it to *Hellzapoppin'* (*Wellesapoppin'*, one wit dubbed it), that madcap farce devised in part by another Peru, Indiana, boy, Ole Olsen. Porter's score was said to be "ill-suited to the hyjinks of Mr. Welles." Today the songs are unknown. A number called "There He Goes, Mr. Phileas Fogg" demonstrates the persistence of the Gilbert and Sullivan influence.

After seventy-five performances, the show came to a dismal end. In *The New Yorker*, Wolcott Gibbs wrote: "If God will forgive me, Cole Porter's music and lyrics are hardly memorable at all." It's hard to believe that the felicities of *Kiss Me, Kate* were only two years away; and not difficult to understand the reluctance of backers to invest in *Kate*, Porter's next effort on Broadway.

Chapter 16

The Champ Is Back

After the openings of *Around the World* and *Night and Day,* Porter enjoyed considerable celebrity, but his professional reputation languished. In the mid-1940s there was a slowdown in his output, a series of flops and bad reviews. Then Bella Spewack reappeared with a libretto based loosely on Shakespeare's *Taming of the Shrew,* and Porter agreed to write the score for what became *Kiss Me, Kate.* Through it all Cole followed the advice he gave to Lisa Kirk (one of the featured players in *Kiss Me, Kate*): "Always want the best, always do the best you can, always aspire to have the best."

He had long depended on the secretarial skills of Margaret Moore, but in 1947 she suddenly sickened and died. Porter was deeply depressed by this loss, but eventually Madeline Smith came into his life. Mrs. Smith had formidable tutors. She had previously worked as a secretary for "Cissy" Patterson, the newspaper heiress, and for two other socialites, Mrs. William Rhinelander Stewart and Mrs. Lytle Hull. Before that she was employed by the Belgian embassy as personal and social secretary to the ambassador. She recalls being asked one day by Sylvia Ashley, another former employer, "to walk with her to the Pavillon Restaurant, where she was to meet her host for dinner. For once in her life she planned to be on time. 'I can't keep Cole Porter waiting,' she said. 'If I'm late I'll find him seated at the choicest table in the place beginning his dinner without me.' So, having arrived before Mr. Porter, she introduced us when he came in. That was my first meeting."

A few nights later, at ten p.m., Porter telephoned Mrs. Smith, asking her to come right over. She protested the lateness of the hour, but, as she sagely said, "it never occurred to him that anything he wanted or needed would not be forthcoming." Porter was stylishly attired in a white silk robe (both legs encased in casts), smiling and debonair. The letters he composed were brief, as was his custom, and he dictated as well some lyrics for *Kiss Me, Kate,* "on which he had just begun work." As the days passed, Porter continued to be pleased with Madeline Smith's performance. He found her even-tempered, and diplomatic with the rest of his staff. Friends all agreed that she became indispensable to Cole, and she functioned as his amanuensis until his death in 1964. In his late years he even orchestrated his social life, ringing up people he especially liked to see if they could come to dinner. (Even before his health declined, Porter never used engraved invitations, although his telephone invitations were always followed by engraved reminder cards.) "Formality was the word all through the years . . . I always addressed him as 'Mr. Porter' and he called me 'Mrs. Smith.' " (Despite her devotion, she was rewarded rather shabbily in Porter's will.)

"Almost no one became familiar with Cole Porter," said Madeline Smith, echoing an observation made by many, including some persons thought to be his intimates. "He was approached by the world at large with great deference, not only on account of his tremendous talent, but because that was the kind of man he was, always polite, somewhat distant, complex, sophisticated." Smith came to think of her position with the Porters to be the best she'd ever had.

When "the Great Katie" came to New York with Lou Bearss that winter, she invited Elise Smith, Madeline's daughter, to tea at the Waldorf. Elise was struck by the resemblance between mother and son: Katie was small and had the same jet-black eyes as her son. Elise found her "a very sweet lady but also a grande dame." Elise and her mother both loved Cole's dog, Pepi, and they sometimes looked after him in their flat if the Porters were away. The Duke of Verdura painted a very good likeness of Pepi which pleased Cole. Some months after this visit, Katie wrote to tell Cole she didn't think she could make it to New York next Christmas "because of her strength." In the end, Katie and Lou Bearss spent that Christmas and the month of January in their customary Waldorf suite.

Cole had only recently enjoyed a motor trip through the Southwest with Sam Stark, stopping in Las Vegas, where they went nightclubbing with Jean Howard (then divorcing Charlie Feldman) and with Michael Pearman. Sam and Cole traveled to Hoover Dam, the Grand Canyon, Phoenix and

Tombstone, Arizona. Eventually they visited San Antonio and the Alamo, which Porter found moving. After Houston they ended their journey in New Orleans, where both men lingered before Cole returned to New York.

On March 26, 1947, Cole indicated in a letter that he was planning shortly to fly to Hollywood for "the preparation of a new musical play in the films." This was *The Pirate,* which was based on an S. N. Behrman play which the Lunts had done on Broadway. Directed by Vincente Minnelli, the picture starred Judy Garland and Gene Kelly and featured Gladys Cooper and Walter Slezak, among others. The filming took from February 17 to November 18, 1947, although most of the Porter songs were written in 1946. Judy Garland was one source of the delay. She often canceled appointments with the costume office or failed to turn up on the set. Sometimes the reason given for her absence was "nervous exhaustion." The score has a passionate love song, "Love of My Life." The better-known "Be a Clown" is another Cole Porter song with its origins in his childhood delight in the circus:

> Be a clown, be a clown,
> All the world loves a clown.
> Act the fool, play the calf,
> And you'll always have the last laugh.

Gene Kelly had been sent by the producer to request a new number for the show. "What kind of a number do you need?" Porter inquired. Said Kelly: " 'Well, a gay number. I don't know.' Cole said, 'Well, what do you see?' I said, 'Something fast.' And he said, 'Well, how about a lot of lyrics?' And I said, 'That's good.' Anyway, the next afternoon he came in with three choruses of this song, 'Be a Clown,' and we used it as a reprise throughout the picture. Naturally, I think he's a genius."

Settling in Hollywood in 1947 wasn't quite as easy as in the past. Porter had had to bring a lawsuit against Bill Haines in order to continue residing at 416 North Rockingham. Porter asserted that Haines had agreed to let him renew the lease. Apparently the court decided in Cole's favor. After this dispute, Cole banned Bill Haines from the Sunday brunch parties. Otherwise for Cole, at age fifty-six, this was not an outwardly eventful year. In July he spent some time visiting his ailing mother in Peru.

Cole, Linda, and Sturge spent Christmas 1947 as they customarily did, in Peru, staying at Westleigh Farms with Cole's mother. "He used to go there every Christmas," said Madeline Smith, "Mr. and Mrs. Porter, and they'd usually take—Howard Sturges . . . And sometimes, Monty Woolley. And if they didn't go to Peru, Indiana, they would have a dinner in their apartment at the Waldorf and they'd invite Monty Woolley to come, and Mr. Porter's mother would come, and a Mrs. [Lou] Bearss who was sort of a distant relative by marriage, and always came with his mother from Peru . . . and spent a few weeks at the Waldorf." In the Westleigh Farms house with its polished floors and shelves of books the Porters and their guests relaxed. One of the Bearss family, Bearss Muhlfeld, recalls some of those Christmas Eves in Peru when Cole would sit at the piano pursuing all sorts of subjects with Peruvians, many of whom were now New York bankers, Washington lawyers, stockbrokers, and the like, but who returned to Peru for Christmas. Porter enjoyed all of this hugely, especially the moment when the Christmas tree, freshly cut in the graveyard jointly owned by the Bearss and Cole families, would be brought indoors and decorated.

Early in the new year Cole got started with the score of what was to be arguably his greatest hit, *Kiss Me, Kate.* (W. H. Auden even called *Kiss Me, Kate* a greater work than *The Taming of the Shrew.*) It had a disputatious beginning, largely because of the quarrels between the Spewacks (on the scene again after their earlier collaboration with Porter in *Leave It to Me*) and Arnold Saint Subber, the young coproducer. According to the latter, the idea of presenting Shakespeare's *Taming of the Shrew* in a modern version based on a production the Lunts had done was his. "Saint" had worked as an apprentice on that production and had observed the quarrels that sometimes ensued backstage between the two stars. Art and life seemed curiously, sometimes comically, blended in their behavior. Saint proposed a musical comedy based on the tale to his friend Thornton Wilder, who was too busy at the time to get involved. Burton Lane also declined to write the score.

Bella Spewack wrote that some time in late 1947 she was telephoned by Porter's agent, Richard Madden, who quickly gave the phone to the designer and producer Lemuel Ayers, an old friend of Bella's. Ayers proposed they meet on the next day. The agent attended the meeting, as did "a young man named Saint Souber [sic]," but Bella "hardly thought it was a Broadway show . . . not a commercial possibility." Questioned by Ayers and Saint Subber, she had to concede that she never had seen a production of *Shrew* and had not read it in many years. When she had read the play in high school, she didn't like it: she thought Shakespeare's comedies were weak and not very funny. She didn't think just setting *Shrew* to music would solve the problem. "Furthermore I was not a Shakespearean scholar and could not see myself tackling Shakespeare. Mr. Souber and Mr. Ayers thereupon pressed me to read the *Shrew* and Mr. Ayers bought me a copy to read. I thereupon read the *Shrew* and found myself rather attracted to the play as a musical possibility but not enough as a Broadway possibility." Bella queried Saint Subber, "as I had never heard of him and was not impressed with his credits which included work with George Kaufman on *Hollywood Pinafore* and *Firebrand,* both failures."

However, the three continued to meet over the next few weeks, Bella holding to her conviction not to do *Shrew* "as a musical alone but if I could think of a story to make it a possibility for Broadway, I would. I tried to bring the *Shrew* up to date to see if that would make it a commercial venture but decided against it." Finally she told the agent: "I had an idea for doing a musical but it could not be all *Shrew.* That notion was to write a personal story of people putting on the *Shrew* and it would be a play within a play." According to Bella, it was she who wanted Cole Porter to do the score, but Saint Subber and Ayers "thought it might be best to try someone else first." They considered Porter "washed up" and thought a young man who'd just done the Hasty Pudding Show at Harvard would be a better choice. Bella persisted, and finally, without either a lyricist or a composer, the two producers agreed to approach Porter. When they met with Cole, according to Bella, "I told him the idea of the backstage story and the acting couple putting on the musical version of the *Shrew.* I outlined some of the scenes and Mr. Porter said he would like to consider it but was not too sold on the idea of tackling Shakespeare."

Bella Spewack maintained that for a time Porter was adamant in refusing to do *Kate.* But the third time she visited him he suddenly said, "Draw the set."

I had brought titles and contents of songs that I had culled from the *Shrew.* "I've Come to Wive It Wealthily," "Where Is the Life That Late I Led?," "Were Thine That Special Face"—all in my final effort to show the lyric possibilities of the play within the play. [Saint Subber labeled this "a bare-faced lie."] I grew forensic about the similarities of show business in the 16th century and now; about a theatrical company that goes into rehearsal for three weeks and into limbo—not knowing or caring what is happening in the outside world. Out of that garrulous and lurid but fairly accurate description of our world today, came "Another Openin' Another Show." I remember Cole singing it to me at the piano for the first time and ignoring my ecstatic response.

Another op'nin', another show
In Philly, Boston or Baltimo',
A chance for stage folk to say hello,
Another op'nin' of another show.
. . . .
The overture is about to start,
You cross your fingers and hold your heart,
It's curtain time and away we go!
Another op'nin',
Just another op'nin' of another show.

"It's not what you wanted, Bella," Cole interrupted sadly, "but it's as close as I could get to it." She found Cole "as modest as his gift was large." However, when he asked her to draw the set she was flummoxed. Not only was she worn out by her efforts to persuade Cole but she had no gift for drawing at all. She made some feeble attempt at it, however. Cole looked it over and said, "Now tell me about the characters Lilli and Fred and Bill and Lois." Bella went home and wrote overnight the biographies of these four characters from the days of their birth until they appear in the play. Next day she delivered these to Cole, who, she felt, was beginning to waver. "Linda," he told Bella, "read some of *The Taming of the Shrew* to me . . . It's too big a challenge." Bella agreed that it was a tremendous challenge for all involved but that if they succeeded "it will live forever."

"Through my wild hyperbole I'd gotten no reaction but a well-bred, opaque stare. His velvety black eyes said nothing. Suddenly they smiled. 'Now tell me all about Gremio and Lucentio and all the rest of them. Linda said she couldn't read all that. It bored her.' "

Cole, Saint, and Bella met at subsequent intervals, although Bella refused to consider any of Saint Subber's suggestions, "as I did not regard him as my collaborator officially or unofficially and my regard for him was none too high." What Spewack did was write material for opera star Jarmila Novotna, who was then the front-runner for the title role. She and Alfred Drake tried out some of the material at Porter's apartment. Novotna liked the idea of the Shakespearean structure to the play and responded favorably, she said, when Saint Subber and Lem Ayers approached her about the part. In the play-within-a-play, they decided, she would impersonate an Austrian, so her (Czech) accent wouldn't obtrude. As Novotna remembered, it was she who first brought Saint and Ayers to Porter's apartment, as she knew Cole quite well. At their second meeting she brought a pianist friend with her, who played Viennese waltzes brilliantly. When he finished, to the praise of everyone, Jarmila said, "Isn't he wonderful? *Wunderbar*—he's *wunder-bar!*" She believes that thus Porter may have found his title for the show's bit of schmaltz-parodying-schmaltz. In the end Novotna did not sing *Kate,* because of her husband's need, just then, to return to Europe. Next, Porter wired Lily Pons in Cannes, but her health and other commitments prevented her.

Cole was sitting in his house in Hollywood glooming over the fact that there was no leading lady in sight when the show's director, John C. Wilson, arrived. The scion of a wealthy family and a graduate of Yale (ten years after Cole), Jack had been Noël Coward's longtime lover and still acted as his manager. "I've just heard . . . about a girl," Wilson said. "She plays bit parts in B and C pictures" . . . A little later Miss Morison arrived in an old jalopy driven by her father." (In Patricia Morison's memory, it was her agent who drove her to Rockingham.) To her this was not a serious audition, "as they already had an opera star in line for the role," but an opportunity to help her gain experience. "The moment I saw her," Cole said, "I thought this is it, if she can sing." She replied hesitantly that she used to sing, but Hollywood wouldn't let her. She purposefully sang a few Rodgers and Hammerstein songs. Cole gave her a few songs and told her to go home and learn them. Two weeks later she reappeared, looking ravishing, but Porter was dissatisfied with her voice. "Get someone to train your voice," Cole said, "and I'll get Constance Collier to give you lessons in reading Shakespeare." After a month's workout Cole thought she was perfect but said he needed the approval of Saint Subber and Ayers, who were in New York. Unable to afford a commercial flight, Morison suddenly was invited to perform in a USO show at Madison Square Garden, so she flew east. Saint and Ayers loved Morison, too, and she became their choice for the part. Early in 1948 Cole wrote to Bella Spewack that Pat Morison was studying the role of Kate with Collier. In June he tells "Bella, Bellissima" that two girls are contending for the Kate part: Ruth Warwick and Pat Morison. He doesn't believe Warwick has the voice for the part, and describes her as "a young, not too young Ruth Chatterton . . . Pat Morison is, to me, a much more interesting possibility. Apart from her voice which is a high mezzo, she looks like Lynn Fontanne & Kate [Hepburn] . . . I feel strongly that this is our girl. So much so that I believe we might, over night, create a great new star . . . this Morison is the one."

At this stage another opera star, Dorothy Kirsten, was also something of a contender, but Cole wrote to Bella Spewack that "she could never play the part." Anyhow, he added, only two songs interested her, "Were Thine That Special Face," which Alfred Drake sang in the show, and "I Am Ashamed."

Cole thought this sound judgment on Kirsten's part, "as the other Kate numbers are musical comedy despite some coloratura passages."

One night after a party in Hollywood, Porter asked Anita Colby if she was alone, and when she said yes, he asked her to follow him to his house, where he played her the score of *Kiss Me, Kate* on the piano. "Do you think Clark will object to this?" he asked, and played lines for "Always True to You in My Fashion":

> *Mister Gable, I mean Clark,*
> *Wants me on his boat to park,*
> *If the Gable boat*
> *Means a sable coat,*
> *Anchors Aweigh!*

At that time Gable was Anita's beau. She suggested Cole give a dinner party, invite them both, and have a musical evening. Gable was delighted. Clifton Webb was there, and after Patricia Morison left, Webb said, "That girl's voice won't carry in a large theatre." Porter became very nervous, and the next day he telephoned Anita, asking her to send him as a possible replacement for Pat Morison the rejects who had auditioned. Anita protested that Morison was marvelous, but Porter was unsure. So he rented the Wilshire Ebell, which was a sizeable theater. Just Cole, Pat, and her accompanist were there. She stood on the stage and sang while Cole climbed, with his injured leg, up to the last row in the top balcony, where he could hear her perfectly well. "They're crazy," he said, referring to the skeptics.

The war between Bella and Saint continued. When he and Ayers offered suggestions, "I finally had to rudely tell them that I liked to do my own writing," said Bella, and an agreement was reached that she would not see the producers again until she had completed the script to her satisfaction. Meanwhile, Jack Wilson was working out ideas for the direction. Hanya Holm, the choreographer, whom Saint Subber engaged, found Wilson "a difficult man who drank too much at the end." (Alcoholism seems to have been the cause of the bust-up of his affair with Coward.) However, Holm observed that Wilson was always searching for ways to help Porter. Saint Subber found him "a very mild man who would sometimes ask the performers in *Kate* what *they* thought was best." For two years or more Saint lived in Coward's New York apartment, thanks to Wilson's arrangings.

While she was wrestling with the task of composing the libretto, Bella was in a state of desperation, according to Saint Subber. Sam Spewack, her husband, had walked out on her and was living with a ballerina. Bella's literary attempts were "complete failures—draft after draft were terrible." Finally Sam was persuaded to contribute, and it was he who introduced the gangsters, whom Saint called "the backbone of the show." According to Saint (and others agree), "Bella gave [Sam] a share of her royalties, and what amount that was we never knew. She did not want Cole to write a song for the gangsters, because she wanted to hold some imaginary option that she could drop Sam's contribution if she wanted to." But apparently the situation was more complex than that. While Bella remained at her Fifth Avenue apartment, Sam was at the Hotel Tuscany, where in June 1948 Cole sent him a telegram: "Bella writes me that you don't want to take any credit for the book. I beg you to reconsider this due to all the contributions you have made . . . Will you do this great favor for me?" Sam never came to any interviews; his name didn't appear on the contract, only hers. "Sam Spewack was never officially an author of *Kiss Me, Kate*," Saint insisted. It was Alfred Drake and Saint Subber who "put Shakespeare into the play." But once the play was a success, Bella Spewack took all the credit for it. When Cole in correspondences addressed "Bellissima Carissima," Saint Subber claimed, he revealed that Sam was not in the picture. Cole wrote to tell Saint and Lem Ayers that "whenever I try to talk sense to Bella it is like

Arnold Saint Subber and Lemuel Ayers (standing), 1948

trying to talk sense to Russia." The feuds and counterclaims continued long after the show opened.

Saint Subber was a theater personality of exceptional gifts and warmth as well. Eells refers to him as "an eccentric young producer," which in some regards is accurate. He seemed pleased to report that a grandmother had a yacht on the Potomac. This news seemed to counter his more raffish pursuits: founding a gay bar in Manhattan, for example. He always insisted on emphasizing the love between his "complicated, educated" parents, whom he adored. He thought of himself as "more in love with [his] parents than loving them." They were the proprietors of Subbers' Ticket Office in New York City, second only to McBride's in success, which they'd been encouraged to establish by the Hammersteins and the Shuberts. Saint's father died early, and his mother continued to manage the business until she passed away. For many years Saint and his parents lived on Fifty-second Street, then lined with speakeasies (including the "21" Club), and he attended high school in Hell's Kitchen, where he was initiated into a gang of toughs. As his parents couldn't leave their office until nine p.m. and the boy was unsupervised, they sent him to boarding school in England to learn good manners. As a student he crossed the Atlantic thirty times until World War II began. He returned to America a street kid with elegant manners.

Saint Subber believes that Porter immediately detected the street kid beneath the manners and reveled in this, perhaps because to some extent, as a closeted homosexual, he identified with Saint's "deception." Anita Colby felt that Porter led a double life and dismissed people who tried to intrude on his private one. Early on in their relationship, Saint said, he and Cole let each other know they were homosexuals. "We had our own code. We had our private circle."

What touched off Porter's genius, wondered Saint, and kept it fresh? "Not the boys. Not the social life, which mattered no more to him than his memorizing the names of the governors of all the states"—which he once did. For ten years Porter seemed to Saint his surrogate father, "sweet, the top gentleman who could go further than Emily Post." In short, Saint thought Porter "the most unique character in his life, but far queerer than anyone else I knew." So it was surprising to hear from Ernest Martin, co-producer of *Can-Can* and *Silk Stockings,* that Cole once told him he never cared for Saint Subber! In regard to his "queerness," Saint also described Porter's infatuation with a dancer who went on to become a Broadway leading man. He had many such infatuations, and Saint was very pleased when later he learned of Porter's genuine love for a few men, most notably Ray Kelly.

"How wonderful to learn," he said, "that it wasn't only boys, boys, boys. I always suspected a great love, but all I heard about were the infatuations." Saint paraphrased Carson McCullers: "The beloved and the lover come from different countries: it's always a tragedy."

Saint was tone deaf, so he did only one piece of casting for the singing roles in *Kate:* notably, Alfred Drake. He also arranged for the dancer Harold Lang, one of his chums, to appear in the show, but was very disappointed in him. Lang angered Porter when he appeared onstage with an excessively large codpiece. When Cole told Saint Subber to remove it, Saint said he was leaving that to Porter. For Michael Pearman, this incident is an illustration of how "correct" Cole was. Hanya Holm found Harold Lang "difficult," and others called him "petulant." Lang was insisting that a song be added for himself, so Cole Porter obligingly wrote "Bianca." "He was kind of provoked, this young chap was," said Madeline Smith, "because he didn't have a big enough part in the play . . . so Mr. P. wrote that to please the young actor." Porter asked the cast for rhymes for "Bianca" and they shouted back "Sanka" and "Poppa spanka," which Cole then wove into the song.

> *Bianca, Bianca*
> *Oh, baby, will you be mine?*
> *Bianca, Bianca,*
> *You'd better answer yes or Poppa spanka.*
> *To win you, Bianca,*
> *There's nothing I would not do.*
> *I would gladly give up coffee for Sanka,*
> *Even Sanka, Bianca, for you.*

Pat Morison found Lang "a lovely artist, naughty but lovable." He drank heavily and rarely turned up on time for appointments, which must have irritated the punctual Porter.

All these efforts took place in the late winter and spring of 1948. Bella had noticed the growth in professionalism that Cole exhibited in the ten years since they had done *Leave It to Me.* "When *Kiss Me, Kate* went into rehearsal Cole attended practically all of the working sessions. He knew exactly how he wanted 'I Hate Men' staged. He was absorbed with every phase of the production. He was no longer the amused spectator of *Leave It to Me.*" Many people concerned with *Kate* thought "I Hate Men" was a mistake. Friends counseled Pat Morison to persuade Cole to remove it from the show; "It will embarrass you," they said. She grew unsure and went to see Porter about it. She already had talked with Wilson, who had told her at a rehearsal that went particularly badly that she wasn't succeeding in getting the effect he wanted. Cole recalled once seeing an operetta featuring a fellow who sang the line "I want what I want when I want it" and then slammed a table. Cole advised Pat to slam the tankard she carried on stage in just the same way. She did, and it was a great success.

> *I hate men.*
> *Their worth upon this earth I dinna ken.*
> *Avoid the trav'ling salesman though a tempting Tom he may be,*
> *From China he will bring you jade and perfume from Araby,*
> *But don't forget 'tis he who'll have the fun and thee the baby,*
> *Oh, I hate men.*

For work purposes, when they were preparing *Kate,* Lemuel Ayers, who five months into the production learned that he had leukemia, rented a room across from Saint Subber on Fifty-second Street. He refused to let his co-producer see the costume designs. When they were completed, he pinned them to the wall and invited Saint to view them, whereupon the latter tore a few down and showed Ayers that they were misconceived: they were modern, à la Matisse, and *Kate* required all period costumes. Within a few days Lem Ayers produced beautiful sketches which are works of art in themselves.

Often when Saint went to see Cole at the Waldorf, Cole would say, "Shall we let Linda know you're here?" Sometimes she would be wheeled in from her apartment across the hall in an iron lung. Saint Subber recalled being in Linda's rooms once when she was out of the iron lung and being fitted for clothes by Main Bocher. Both Linda and Cole continued to smoke heavily. "The two things you couldn't take away from Cole," said Saint, "were the cocktail in his hand and his cigarette."

All that spring Linda was "at a low ebb," as she wrote to Bernard Berenson, "having picked up a virus 'Flu' germ & I spent three weeks in bed. I am up for the first time today—a bit shaky." Next year, she told him, she planned to go to Paris to deal with the house on rue Monsieur, now occupied by a tenacious tutoring school which refused to vacate the premises. Meanwhile, Cole was hard at work with *Kate* and can't have had much time or emotional energy to devote to Linda. A number of her friends thought of her as neglected by Cole or, in the opinion of a few, sometimes coldly disregarded. In an August 1948 letter to Berenson, Linda sounds pitifully alone. "I have felt so tired I have ceased to cope with guests." She recalls a visit Berenson paid the Porters at the Palazzo Barbaro. "Life seemed so carefree and happy then," wrote Linda sadly. By October Cole was with Linda in Williamstown, and the two took long drives "over the Mohawk Trail which is at its peak of beauty now." But in two weeks all this was to end, and the Porters returned to the Waldorf and a New York from which Linda longed to escape. "New York is a nightmare," she wrote to Berenson. "It is over-crowded, noisy & hectic—everything & everybody in a rush."

Williamstown was sometimes conducive to creativity for Cole. In one four-day weekend he wrote for *Kate* "Another Op'nin', Another Show," "I've Come to Wive It Wealthily in Padua," and "Where Is the Life That Late I Led?" Many of the lyrics in *Kate* were more patently sexy than lyrics written by Larry Hart, opined Saint Subber. "Too Darn Hot," for instance:

> *According to the Kinsey Report*
> *Ev'ry average man you know*
> *Much prefers to play his favorite sport*
> *When the temperature is low,*
> *But when the thermometer goes 'way up*
> *And the weather is sizzlingly hot,*
> *Mr. Gob*
> *For his squab,*
> *A marine*
> *For his queen,*
> *A G.I.*
> *For his cutie-pie*
> *Is not,*
> *'Cause it's too, too,*
> *Too darn hot,*
> *It's too, too, too, too darn hot.*

And "Always True to You in My Fashion":

> *If a custom-tailored vet*
> *Asks me out for something wet,*
> *When the vet begins to pet, I cry "Hooray!"*
> *But I'm always true to you, darlin', in my fashion,*
> *Yes, I'm always true to you, darlin', in my way.*
> *I enjoy a tender pass*
> *By the boss of Boston, Mass.,*
> *Though his pass is middle-class and notta Backa Bay.*

. . . .

> *There's a madman known as Mack*
> *Who is planning to attack,*
> *If his mad attack means a Cadillac, okay!*
> . . . .
> *I could never curl my lip*
> *To a dazzlin' diamond clip,*
> *Though the clip meant "let'er rip," I'd not say "Nay!"*
> *But I'm always true to you, darlin', in my fashion,*
> *Yes, I'm always true to you, darlin', in my way.*

Perhaps this demonstrates what Saint Subber called Porter's ability to address himself in his songs. The lyric depicts in an antic way Cole's promiscuity but also his enduring link to Linda.

In "Brush Up Your Shakespeare" Cole claims alliance with the Bard's lightheartedness about sex:

> *Brush up your Shakespeare,*
> *Start quoting him now.*
> . . . .
> *Just recite an occasional sonnet*
> *And your lap'll have "Honey" upon it.*
> *When your baby is pleading for pleasure*
> *Let her sample your "Measure for Measure."*
> . . . .
> *If she then wants an all-by-herself night*
> *Let her rest ev'ry 'leventh or "Twelfth Night."*
> *If because of your heat she gets huffy*
> *Simply play on and "Lay on, MacDuffy!"*
> . . . .
> *Brush up your Shakespeare*
> *And they'll all kowtow.*

Porter had anticipated a Hungarian hassle when, in late summer of 1948, he sent the lyrics of "Brush Up Your Shakespeare" to Bella. "Bella will probably cut her throat when she gets this," he said. Writing later, she verified the agreement she had with Porter that there would be no songs for the gunmen, "but we realized," she wrote, "that . . . it was a 'boff' number—a show stopper." The lyrics of "Brush Up Your Shakespeare" are among Porter's most brilliant inventions and remain vivid in the repertoire of audiences who are familiar with the score of *Kate*:

Brush up your Shakespeare,
Start quoting him now.
Brush up your Shakespeare
And the women you will wow.
With the wife of the British embessida
Try a crack out of "Troilus and Cressida."
If she says she won't buy it or tike it
Make her tike it, what's more, "As You Like It."
If she says your behavior is heinous
Kick her right in the "Corialanus."
Brush up your Shakespeare
And they'll all kowtow.

So through the late winter and spring, Porter worked assiduously over the score of *Kate,* at the same time spending time and energy on attempts to raise money for the show. He had not had a hit in several years and was considered by some a back number. Porter's old friend Will Crocker came to his aid again, and Anita Colby "drummed up some friends to back the play." Howard Cullman's wife, Peggy, Saint said, was his principal backer, and he affectionately referred to her as "my angel." The sum of her investment was $25,000. Peggy Cullman remembers a party held at Lemuel Ayers's to gain backers for *Kate.* It was there she heard the score for the first time. The day after the party, she and her husband sailed to Europe; they returned a month later to discover that not even one other person had come forward to help fund the show. She proposed to Cole that she invite wealthy friends who loved the theater to dinner, and afterwards there'd be an audition. Everyone who came was delighted, and soon sufficient monies were collected to allow the producers to proceed. Other auditions were held, and finally seventy-two backers were found. Eventually they earned enormous returns on their investments.

In a photocopy of an analytic study of *Kate* which Saint Subber once annotated, Bella Spewack describes some of the working habits of Porter and the Spewacks (Saint contending that the designation should be singular, as Sam took so little part in the project). Porter asked questions about the characters: Lois Lane—was she a bad girl? What did Bella mean in calling Lois "unmoral" rather than immoral? The night that Porter received the Lois-Bill scenes, he telephoned the Spewacks at two a.m. and sang "Why Can't You Behave?" "One night . . . Porter asked if we knew who had written a poem with the line, 'I have been faithful to thee . . . Cynara! in my fashion,' we finished it for him." About a week later Porter sang and played for them "Always True to You in My Fashion," based on the Ernest Dowson poem:

> *And I was desolate and sick of an old passion,*
> *Yea, I was desolate and bowed my head:*
> *I have been faithful to thee, Cynara! in my fashion.*

Virtually all the songs in *Kate* were written in a time of "complete agony" for Cole, who suffered an ulcer and abscess due to a collision with his playful and much beloved schipperke, Pepin le Bref, or Pepi, a gift from Merle Oberon. He wrote to Sam Stark:

These [abscess and ulcer] appeared close together just over a nerve center. This started all the nerves in my leg raising terrific hell and the pain has been so great that the drugs have had practically no effect. Also due to the bump, part of my shinbone is exposed and the surface was scratched. The skin around the bone is gradually covering it and will within a few weeks cover it entirely . . . from now on I will always wear a guard on my right leg.

All this suffering Porter endured while writing such songs as "We Open in Venice," "Why Can't You Behave?," "We Shall Never Be Younger" (which was dropped, as it reduced the audience to tears), and "So in Love," which Porter played for Bella, saying he was going to put it in a film. "The hell you are," she told him. The next night (they often worked until two or three a.m.) Cole sang the lyrics he'd written for "So in Love." She insisted that the lyrics evolved from their discussions about *Kate* and that the song must go in the show. Porter did like to tease Bella, and this may have been a tease on his part. Charles Bowden, who was working as an assistant to Jack Wilson, recalled a dispute over another song, which Wilson favored but Hanya Holm disliked. Wilson wasn't as intelligent as Holm, Cole said, so eventually "Too Darn Hot" was substituted, and "Hanya seemed to choreograph it at once, and the alley scene with trunks was added as a setting for the song," Bowden said.

When Bella Spewack finished the book in the summer of 1948, she sent it to Porter, who was in Hollywood. He replied, "The best musical comedy book I have ever read arrived this morning. Congratulations." Porter felt Shakespeare's work was a subject he did know something about, according to Madeline Smith. (In another instance, she maintained, Porter turned down *My Fair Lady* because he felt he knew nothing about cockneys.)

Throughout the summer of 1948, Porter remained in California but kept in close touch with Bella, the producers, John Wilson, and the others shaping the show. One obvious problem was the excessive length of *Kate*. Bella felt ruthless about cutting her own lines but hesitated when it came to Shakespeare and Porter. In the rehearsals six songs were dropped, but seventeen remained. The only lyrics written by Shakespeare in the musical appear in Katherine's song "I Am Ashamed That Women Are So Simple," and in "I've Come to Wive It Wealthily in Padua."

Rehearsals for the show began on a rainy day in October 1948. One of the dancers recalls suddenly catching sight of Cole as he started down the center aisle, elegantly attired and carrying a gold-topped cane. He seated himself on a chair in the aisle near the tenth row. A second chair was placed ahead of him and he rested his leg on that. He wore a whistle around his neck and from time to time blew it to stop the rehearsals and suggest changes in the performance. Often he would shout, "I can't hear the lyrics, I can't hear the lyrics!" The cast, which was concentrating more on the production and the music, was astonished. "Come down front," continued Porter, "face out to the audience." This went on until he was satisfied. "The lyrics counted more to Mr. Porter," said one of the dancers, "than the dancing or anything else."

Perhaps this extraordinary concern was rooted in Porter's realization that the songs were more integrated with plot and character than had previously been true for his shows. Some felt these songs couldn't be hits if sung out of context. One critic wrote that "So in Love," that meltingly haunting love song from *Kate*, "is as neatly worked out as a lied: Far from being in the 32-bar mold that marks most 'hits,' its melody extends itself and glides to an end in a way only an artist could manage." Writing about his own composition, Porter remarked, "Look at my 'So in Love' . . . in that number the climax comes quite a while before the end of the song, a situation that would never have been accepted twenty years ago."

> So taunt me and hurt me,
> Deceive me, desert me,
> I'm yours 'til I die,
> So in love,
> So in love,
> So in love with you, my love, am I.

Readying for the Philadelphia opening, Cole wrote to Saint and Lem Ayers requesting seats for *Kate*, one pair for his agent, Richard Madden, one pair for Dr. Sirmay, and four seats for Howard Sturges. "This request . . . may seem excessive but . . . my producers have always granted this request . . . I am especially anxious that they be good because all of these people are dear friends of mine, to whom I *give* the seats." Among the personal belongings Cole took to Philadelphia with him to make his hotel suite more agreeable were five paintings, among them a large snowscape by Grandma Moses.

The show opened in Philadelphia on December 2, 1948, and underwent scarcely any revisions. Five minutes of the book were cut to make room for extra choruses of "Brush Up Your Shakespeare." "No rewriting of the libretto or songs; no songs added or dropped; no trying out of songs in different places . . . It is the only musical in the history of American musicals that can claim this heavenly distinction." Only two nights before the Philadelphia tryout the company had its first run-through at the New Amsterdam Roof. No costumes, no sets, no props or orchestra; only a rehearsal pianist. Then the book, music, and dances were blended in sequence. Saint and Ayers had secreted Moss Hart in the hall to secure his opinion of the show. It was entirely negative. Several other mandarins were of the same opinion, including Agnes de Mille. The success of the Philadelphia tryout proved how wrong they were. Pat Morison recalled that only in Philadelphia, when the cast heard the orchestrations of Robert Russell Bennett for the first time, did they realize what a brilliant show *Kate* was. Before that, they too speculated about whether or not the show would succeed.

In New York, the doubting Shuberts assigned the show to the inconveniently located New Century Theater on Seventh Avenue between Fifty-eighth and Fifty-ninth Streets, where it ran for two years before moving to the Shubert Theater. (As Bella cracked, they couldn't rely on an audience drifting in from Central Park.) December 30, the first night, was graced by Porter's party, which was made up of Linda, Ethel Borden, Howard Sturges, Elsa Maxwell, Sam Stark, the Lytle Hulls, and Bob Bray. Porter sent tickets to Moss Hart, George Abbott, Mrs. William Randolph Hearst, Countess di Zoppola, his former lover Ed Tauch, and Oliver Jennings, among others. Katie, Cole's mother, was escorted to the opening by Dr. Moorhead. She let pass many risqué lyrics, but when it came to "Othello's a helluva fella," she whispered to Moorhead, "Cole is a naughty boy."

From the theatre, where the audience reluctantly departed, filled with enthusiasm for a great new hit, Porter proceeded to the duplex of Sophie and Van Schley at 666 Park Avenue. (The Howard Cullmans were co-hosts.) Lisa Kirk once said that her most poignant memory was arriving

Katie Porter, c. 1935

at the Schleys' with Cole and being greeted by Saint Subber at the top of a
long stairway. He was waving a newspaper and announcing that the show
was a hit. "Cole threw his canes down and walked that whole flight of stairs,
unassisted. I just stood there crying," said Kirk. At the party, Pat Morison,
when asked to speak, said, "I feel Cole Porter is six feet tall, wears golden
armor, carries a sword instead of a cane, and has just lifted me out of my
pumpkin coach."

The show garnered rave reviews. At last the critics abandoned their
habitual comparing of Porter's current efforts with the peaks of his art in the
past. "Porter's score is . . . perhaps his best to date," said the *New York News,*
urging people to "rush to the box office immediately." Which they did. *Kate*
was a sellout and ran longer than any production of *Shrew* before or since.
The *Post* found the show "literate without being highbrow, sophisticated
without being smarty, seasoned without being soiled, and funny without
being vulgar."

The dances by Hanya Holm were praised as successful by virtually all
the critics. "Her numbers there," wrote the *New York Times* critic, "were . . .
unpretentious in the extreme, never stepping outside the structure of the
scene, never begging for applause, but invariably contributing charm and

value by heightening the motor rhythms of the situation and building them easily and ingratiatingly to a climax."

The Spewacks came off less successfully, which may explain the bitterness that developed between Bella and Cole later on. The reviewer for the *Hollywood Reporter* faulted the book for its corny jokes and lack of robust humor, as did others. But for Cole, *Kate* was a triumph. "King Cole has made a monkey out of the moaners. The champ is back again, and with the peerless Larry Hart gone for good, it's heart-warming to find Porter functioning at the old level."

A writer in *The New Yorker* thought that Porter and Shakespeare shared a penchant for outlandish and far-flung conceits. "Porter has been stimulated by a phrase, a couplet, or a situation in Shakespeare's text to run off a string of enchanting fantasies of his own. He has also attuned himself to a counter-melody of the play, the strain of gentle romance that underlies the boisterous comedy, and has produced a couple of unique and charming songs. 'I Am Ashamed That Women Are So Simple' . . . has been given lovely musical definition." Others expressed the same opinion. And the fact "Were Thine That Special Face" is written entirely in the subjunctive has not a little to do with its poignance:

> *Were thine that special face*
> *The face which fills my dreaming,*
> *Were thine the rhythm'd grace,*
> *Were thine the form so lithe and slender,*
> *Were thine the arms so warm, so tender,*
> *Were thine the kiss divine,*
> *Were thine the love for me,*
> *The love which fills my dreaming,*
> *When all these charms are thine*
> *Then you'll be mine, all mine.*

Kudos for *Kate* continued down the years and then the decades. "Who could have foreseen on the Lido in 1925 a Cole Porter *Kiss Me, Kate?!!*" wrote John Wilson to Linda. "Not Princess Jane, not even Elsa . . . Cole, aside from being a genius is the sweetest kindest person in show business." Earlier he had written to "dear, dear Cole" to thank him for his loyalty and affection. "All my career I wanted to do a show with you . . . working with you and for you is as warm, friendly, generous, efficient, amusing, and generally satisfying and exciting an experience as show business has to offer."

He seems always to have thought of his shows as gifts fashioned for his friends. Early in the new year he wrote to Liberty Music Shop asking that they send copies of the *Kate* original cast album to his mother, to Merle Oberon, and to such intimate friends as Sam Stark, Robert Raison, and Stanley Musgrove, and a card was to be included saying simply, "Love from Cole."

Chapter 17

Down in the Depths

In January 1949, the original cast recording of *Kiss Me, Kate* was made, and Cole attended the sessions. Then he went to California, where he wanted both to oversee the national company of *Kate* and to begin work on the show that was to become *Out of This World*.

Among all the anxieties that afflicted him at this time, paramount was worry over Linda, who had developed pleurisy as a result, it was thought, of the chill she suffered when the car in which they drove to Philadelphia for the tryout of *Kate* had a flat tire. Next day she was in bed with a fever, but she gallantly rose to attend the performance. Two days later she returned to New York while Cole stayed on. Back at the Waldorf, he found Linda gravely ill. In January 1949 he wrote to Bella Spewack, "Linda is still in the hospital but seems to be better. The terrible agony she went through spoiled all the joy [of *Kiss Me, Kate*]." After a week of vacillating health, she and a nurse traveled in a private railroad car to Phoenix, Arizona, where she was to spend the remainder of the winter. The journey nearly finished her, as there was an unexpected layover in Chicago and the heat turned off. In a panic the nurse caused such a stir that the railroad officials hooked the car to another engine and the heat resumed—but not in time to save Linda from suffering a relapse. Arrangements had been made for Linda to stay at a ranch, and Sturges joined her there. Cole stayed in California but kept in touch via letters, phone calls to Sturge, and occasional visits: in late February, for example, he flew to Arizona and spent four days visiting Linda. Subsequently he wrote to his mother to describe Linda's state of health. She could not tolerate the side effects of Aureomycin, with which her doctor was treating her, so that medication had to be abandoned. Coughing and the struggle for breath kept her awake all night. Yet she continued to smoke. (Robert Wheaton felt that he had earned Linda's friendship by passing on to her during his days in the service his allotment of cigarettes, which he as a nonsmoker did not consume.) Cole attempted to persuade her to spend a month near Palm Springs, where she would be not far from his residence in Brentwood. She chose, however, to return to the Berkshires.

Cole took some solo part in Hollywood social life that year. Katharine Hepburn, upon whom he seems not to have made a vivid impression, was one of his hostesses. He was invited to her home along with the cast and crew of *Adam's Rib,* for which he had transformed "So Long, Samoa" into "Farewell, Amanda." Cole wrote to Linda, "I think the nicest thing that happened to me this summer has been getting to know Kate much better. She has great quality and I am devoted to her." In heartfelt words he tells his wife, "I think of you constantly, darling, and can't wait to see you."

During much of 1949 Porter toiled at the task of writing the score for *Out of This World,* a musical version of the Amphitryon legend. *Amphitryon 38* was a work S. N. Behrman adapted from a Giraudoux play in which the Lunts had had a successful run in 1938. An earlier title, *Heaven on Earth,* describes in miniature the plot of the show. Jupiter, the supreme divinity, decides to woo an American mortal, Helen, and enlists Mercury, his son, to convey her to an Athenian inn, where Jupiter, disguised as her husband, makes love to her. Meanwhile his wife, Juno, pursues her unfaithful husband. But Helen solves everyone's problem when she recognizes Jupiter's trickery and embraces her mortal husband, declining Jupiter's offer of immortality.

Jupiter was George Jongeyans, a.k.a. George Gaynes, the son of Cole's longtime friend Lady Abdy. Juno was played by Charlotte Greenwood, an immense hit in the show, who was enticed out of retirement by a song Porter gave her to sing, "Nobody's Chasing Me":

> *Each night I get the mirror*
> *From off the shelf.*
> *Each night I'm getting queerer,*
> *Chasing myself.*
> *Ravel is chasing Debussy,*
> *The aphis chases the pea,*
> *The gander's chasing the goosey,*

But nobody's goosing me.
Nobody,
Nobody's chasing me.

According to Robert Kimball, Charlotte Greenwood told people she considered this to be the theme song of the show. Not surprisingly, the Boston censor demanded that "nobody's goosing me" be deleted.

The producers were, once more, Saint Subber and Lemuel Ayers; the direction was by Agnes de Mille, the first woman to direct completely a Broadway musical; the choreography was by Hanya Holm. The cast also included William Eythe, Priscilla Gillette, William Redfield, Barbara Ashley, and Janet Collins—a black dancer who famously starred in the *Aïda* ballet at the Metropolitan Opera, and danced "Night" in this show. (In reply to the question what he thought was the silliest moment in opera, Cole answered, "The children's ballet in *Aïda*.") Others who danced in the show were Glen Tetley, now internationally acclaimed as a choreographer, and Barton Mumaw, an American Indian who was a star of the Denishawn Ballet.

From the start *Out of This World* was troublesome to Cole. Dwight Taylor, son of Laurette Taylor, had not produced a functional book, and a collaborator had to be engaged. Betty Comden and Adolph Green were among those who tried to produce a workable libretto but failed. Finally Reginald Lawrence finished a book that suited the producers. "Cole's score was simply superimposed on [Lawrence's] book."

Quite in contrast to *Kate*, the producers had virtually no problems in raising money for *Out of This World*. People who had earned large sums of money from *Kate* were clamoring to invest in the new show. Nonetheless, Cole's enthusiasm for his new work was waning—perhaps the beginning of emotional troubles that threatened to engulf him before long, or perhaps his showman's instinct that the new work was a failure.

The Philadelphia tryout began on November 4, 1950. In preparation for Porter's *séjour,* Madeline Smith had written repeatedly to the concierge of the Barclay Hotel. A list of the foods Cole wanted in his pantry was forwarded. These included one box of ginger, one-half pound of white onions, cold cuts, sweet butter, and twenty-four cans of Pabst Blue Ribbon beer. She arranged rooms for Cole's chauffeur (appropriately called Bentley), his valet, and Dr. Sirmay, who required a double bed. Negotiations were also in motion with Steinway & Sons for a black baby grand piano, but instead a seven-foot parlor grand was offered, which delighted Cole: "Please order it for me," he wrote to the hotel manager.

Janet Collins and George Gaynes in *Out of This World*, 1950

In Philadelphia the weaknesses of *Out of This World* were confirmed, and George Abbott and F. Hugh Herbert were engaged to doctor the show as director and writer. Years later Cole Porter rejected the proposal that Jerome Robbins be invited to direct a musical comedy, saying that he had learned his lesson when he hired a choreographer to direct *Out of This World*. Although her name remained on the playbill as director, de Mille was in effect dismissed—by Porter, she believed, although Saint Subber claimed he and Ayers were responsible. "If you ask for my opinion of Cole Porter, I think he was a coward," she said.

De Mille had gone to Cole's suite for dinner on the eve of the Philadelphia opening. The rooms had been beautifully rearranged, she recalled, with some of Cole's pictures and objets. The bathroom had been virtually done over to accommodate Porter's disability: the bathtub, for example, was equipped with handles. De Mille noticed in a special way that evening "how really crippled Cole was." Two valets and a friend of Porter's age were in attendance. "You know, Cole, the show is in trouble. I want to talk to you about it," said de Mille. "Not now," Cole replied. "Tonight we're going to have a lovely, restful dinner." "Only later did I discover that Cole had already sent for George Abbott to replace me. I'd been fired. This is an illustration of Cole's cowardice." In December, before the show opened in New York, Cole told the *World Telegram and Sun,* whether out of guilt or not, "I must stress what Agnes de Mille did for this new show; she helped us such a great deal."

After the Philadelphia opening, the top personnel gathered with lawyers and discussed ways to rescue *Out of This World.* De Mille demanded to know what George Abbott was doing there. She insisted, "I am legally the director of this show," requesting that Abbott leave the room for this discussion, along with Hanya Holm, whom she described as delighted with the turn of events. Porter wanted de Mille to take over the dances. "I said, 'You have a choreographer.' 'She's not much good; I want you to take over the choreography.' " Abbott re-entered and de Mille again asserted that she was the director. He insisted that there couldn't be two directors. She agreed: "So I'll leave." Several of the dancers went to see her off at the train station.

Agnes de Mille felt that Hanya Holm was jealous of her as director of the show. Porter she found charming but not at all helpful to her. Once he gave her some wine at a meeting they had; she praised it, and he wrote something on a piece of paper. In a few days de Mille received a case of the wine. Undeniably, he did have charm and enjoyed making lavish gestures.

Hanya Holm (center) with dancers

There was disharmony among others in the show besides Holm and de Mille. Saint Subber and Ayers were often antagonists. De Mille thought that the show could be fashioned in mock-heroic style, and Saint Subber agreed with her; but Ayers disagreed.

"The book bogs down badly" was a typical comment of the critics at the tryout (and later). It is a judgment that in retrospect seems sound. One fault of the libretto was its lengthiness: in Philadelphia the show ran to eleven-thirty, so at least half an hour had to be cut. Despite the sumptuous sets some critics found the show "tedious." Plans for an aerial show had to be scrapped because of technical problems. Selma Tamber, the show's manager, remembered Porter coming to the theatre to see a new scene that had been written. A man came on stage with a machine gun and said to Jupiter, "Careful or there's going to be a navel disaster." "That's it," said Porter, who

Agnes de Mille, c. 1950

rose and left the theatre in disgust at the tastelessness of this scene. But Porter was usually sweet and generous to those with whom he worked in the theatre. Tamber recalled both his generosity and his elegant taste in sending everyone connected with *Out of This World* a small solid-gold flashlight from Cartier along with the advice that Cartier would replace the battery when it ran out.

Unlike *Kate,* the new show was far from frozen in Philadelphia, so on November 28 it went to Boston, where the producers kept it an extra week, ostensibly because of the demand for seats but in fact in order to make changes. The show sold out despite mixed reviews. Some critics complained about Hanya Holm's "pagan" dances: "One startling [dance brings the show] right down into the dirt." Perhaps this was the number that included Venus clad in nothing but a few doves. In fact, most of the critics' complaints (and, in New York, their praises as well) had to do with the exceptionally erotic choreography. A female censor in Boston issued a "de-sexing order" which stipulated in nine points the changes required for the show to continue. These included an objection to Janet Collins and Gisella Svetlik appearing only in bras and brief panties. The censor insisted that some songs be purged of words "not even heard in the better class of gin mills." The producers agreed to make these and other changes she required: the irreverent use of the word "god" was to be deleted; the sign of the cross was dropped; the Act I ballet was "modified"; Janet Collins was ordered to dance with "less abandon."

One of the unfortunate decisions George Abbott made was to drop one of Porter's best songs, "From This Moment On," although it later was used in the film of *Kate* and became a hit. A number of critics thought Porter was repeating or quoting himself in the score for *World*—attributable, *Variety* thought, to the paucity of first-rate singers in the cast. Selma Tamber thought this criticism was accurate when it came to William Eythe. It was her recollection that "From This Moment On" was dropped "because Billy Eythe couldn't sing it." Eythe had been hired by Cole, who spotted him on the street and found his looks appealing. But Tamber considered Eythe "a bad boy who chased [boys] too much." De Mille thought Porter often flamboyant with boyfriends. "Some of my young male dancers were seen having drinks with Cole. Absolutely out of order," she labeled this behavior. She recalled also that Baron Nicholas de Gunzburg and the Duke of Verdura spiked the drinks at their parties and behaved in a notorious way. In New York, William Eythe didn't return for an evening rehearsal, and it came out that he had gone directly from an afternoon rehearsal to a public toilet, where he was arrested for indecent conduct.

In Boston Herbert and Abbott performed major surgery on the show:
"Whole scenes were ripped apart, gags excised and new ones grafted into
the show." Radical changes were also made with the scenery.

The directors decided to confine the production to the size of the stage
where it was to play in New York. The scenery (said to be the second-
heaviest in Broadway history) was faulty: "Nothing went up or down and
confusion reigned. They finally got the flies straightened out and continued
to operate on the smaller stage in preparation for New York."

When *Out of This World* opened in New York on December 21, 1950, at
the New Century Theatre, it had an advance sale of half a million dollars.
Opening night was another glamorous evening for Cole, with a red carpet
stretched across the sidewalk on Seventh Avenue and women swathed in
ermine and sables on the cold winter night. Autograph seekers pursued the
fashionable first-nighters, who included the Duke and Duchess of Windsor.
The next day, Billy Rose wrote to Cole, "The critics must have been in one
theatre, I in another." Some of them had found the show offensive and
decried its blatant sexuality, much of it created through male nudity. Typical
are these comments: "The male dancing chorus is almost as unhampered by
godlike raiments as the customers in a steam bath. Hanya Holm has directed
them to create a kind of pagan innocence, which is not generally characteristic of the show's humor." "*Out of This World* [is] a modern Amphitryon
story with thread unravelled from golden G strings," wrote the *Herald Tribune* reviewer, one of the many who seemed to disregard some of the mar-
vels of the score to disapprove of the show's emphasis on sex. Brooks
Atkinson, then the doyen of New York City reviewers, complained that
World made sex "a tiresome subject" and blamed it on a book that sabotaged
moments of beauty with its "Night in Athens routines." How wearied Porter
must have been by the perdurance of such stern and censorious judgments.

But the dances and the dancers, so faulted for their eroticism, were
praised by ballet critics whose work we now think of as artful. Walter Terry
was one of these savants. Referring to "the Misses Greenwood, Collins, and
Holm" as "an incredible tango," Terry praised the choreography and the
dancers. And John Martin, the highly respected dance critic of the *Times,*
wrote that Hanya Holm surpassed in *World* her wonderful work in *Kate:*
"She has given us, indeed, just about as stunning a set of dances as a
Broadway show has boasted in . . . seasons." Martin called it "a dance
event."

The second-night audience, oblivious to most of the reviewers' nega-
tivism, cheered, stamped, and whistled for fifteen minutes. A large Christ-

mas party was held at the Century Theatre for the casts of *World* and *Kate,* and Porter attended: "I went home, thinking that the theatre was a good place in which to be," he said. By December 31, 1950, the sheet music for *World* was selling better than any Porter songs since *Anything Goes.*

Selma Tamber shepherded the show through 157 performances before it closed on May 19, 1951.

One of the loveliest songs from the show is "Use Your Imagination," which depicts a wise and happy persona quite in contrast to Cole in these months, when he was sinking deeper and deeper into depression.

> *Use your imagination,*
> *Just take this motto for your theme . . .*
> . . . .
> *Around you there lies*
> *Pure enchantment in disguise*
> *And endless joys you never knew.*

According to Eells, it was just prior to the opening of *World* that Cole's friends began noticing his symptoms, which included insomnia, loss of appetite, black moods, and fits of temper. Linked to these was sudden and unreasonable anxiety about his financial status. In December 1950 John Wharton, Cole's attorney, wrote to tell him that he ranked second in a survey of composers and lyricists and the monies ASCAP paid them. Cole was not encouraged by this, and in February 1951 he wrote to Wharton to protest his legal fees: "Do you feel you can shave the fee somewhat?" In May 1951 he resigned from the Players' Club, which he had joined in 1935. "I regret that I find it necessary to tender my resignation as a member of your Club," he wrote to the secretary. This was a further attempt on his part to lessen what he thought to be his financial peril. Concerned as he was about his popularity and income, he turned down a proposed radio program in March, "mainly because after arriving here [Brentwood] I suddenly realized how mentally tired I was and this mental fatigue continues."

In April 1951 Cole was approached about doing the score for a Broadway musical version of *The Shanghai Gesture,* for which the producers were seeking the services of Marlene Dietrich to play Mother Goddam, but Cole pleaded "previous engagements." He showed some interest in the old play *Berkeley Square,* brought to his attention by Frances Goldwyn, who thought it might have possibilities. In May 1951 Cole sent it to the Spewacks for their opinion but a month later wrote to tell them it "hadn't enough guts for the basis of a musical." Shortly after, he wrote to Bella to say he was excited by Sam's idea for a show to star Ray Bolger with a bevy of beautiful girls and a colorful set.

In June 1951 he flew east to spend the month with Linda, stopping on his way to visit Katie. "She booms," he wrote to Lou Bearss. On June 26, thousands were present at the Yale Bowl for a Cole Porter Night although, sadly, ill health caused Cole to cancel. This was the largest crowd ever to attend a popular musical event in the history of the Yale Bowl. Similar celebrations were staged in Seattle, Chicago (where fifty thousand attended), the Hollywood Bowl, and elsewhere in this year of his sixtieth birthday.

These had been difficult months for Linda. In February she had written to tell Bernard Berenson that for two years, really, she'd been ill. "Illness is so humiliating," she told him. Now she was able to take up life "in a restricted way." She attributed her renewal to air conditioning, which she had both at the Waldorf and in Williamstown, so she no longer had "to seek a climate." But her postscript to the letter is dour: "I don't like the world we are living in." Linda wrote to Berenson again from Williamstown on July 3; she hints at possessiveness and what must have been a rare happiness for her: Cole "has spent this month of June alone with me." Every day they took their customary drives in the countryside but that year in pouring rain or gloomy weather. Then Cole and Sturges flew off to the coast, where there was the life around the pool and the "boy parties" he continued to host.

Travel seemed not to allay Cole's anxieties and depressions. In Los Angeles guests at lunch were astonished when he quarreled with Sturges over a triviality. In August, at Cole's insistence, his accountant wrote to his lawyers: "Where will [Porter] get the money to run [the next four months] with the monies anticipated?" None of the lawyers' reassurances dispelled his fantasies. Nor does there seem any substance to his fear that were his "gossipy [California] secretary" to become aware of his impecuniousness, everyone would soon know of it. In fact the language of this handwritten letter sounds decidedly neurotic. He tells one of his lawyers that in his previous letter "I underplayed my gratitude to you for having hurried up those royalty checks." He calls his financial state "precarious" and foresees "disaster for 1952 . . . I am living in constant dread. Forgive me for not snapping out of this but I can't overcome it." Somewhere—probably in his unconscious—recurred the memory of his grandfather pointing out to him the Peru poorhouse and predicting Cole's confinement there.

People reminded Cole that in a recent survey five of his songs ranked among the thirty-five all-time American popular favorites, a figure that put him ahead of Jerome Kern, George Gershwin, and Richard Rodgers—only

Irving Berlin's record matched Cole's. Earlier in the year Cole's attorney John Wharton had written to allay his financial fears: "I do not believe you yet realize that you are no longer merely a talented composer depending on shows for his main income; you are one of the two or three really important figures in your field whose broad interests must be zealously guarded."

Three people to whom Cole especially turned at this time were his old pals Sam Stark, Stanley Musgrove, and Robert Raison. He had met Raison in the mid-forties, at the Cafe Gala, when Bob was a young serviceman. Probably they had an affair; and Cole eventually gave him the money to set up shop as an artists' agent. "An unsuccessful agent, a mean little boy" is the way Michael Pearman described Raison. Raison was not altogether a failure as an agent; among his clients were Dennis Hopper and Jane Wyman. A chapter in the autobiography Raison planned to write was to be called "The Night I Met Cole Porter." He had plans to write about his

Robert Raison

friendship with Wyman and write, too, about President and Mrs. Reagan. Jean Howard refused to see him when he asked for an interview. She and Pearman both thought that Raison was planning after Porter's death "to write an unpleasant book about Cole." But Raison himself died before he could write the book. Jack Coble had disliked Raison at once and described him as "a hustler type." Nonetheless, Cole leaned heavily on him in his distress. "Cheer me up," Cole would implore him. "I feel so low. So miserable. I'm depressed."

When Porter arrived in Williamstown at summer's end, Linda was shaken by his appearance. "Cole is here and he looks so thin, poor darling. And he worries about everything—having no money, having no show, and so forth, all of which is perfectly absurd . . . It is a new Cole. I have never seen him in such a state. However . . . I can straighten him out and get rid of his nightmarish ideas for he really has nothing to worry about." Linda's confidence seems ill-founded and naive as she continued to be alarmed by his state. Both Cole and Linda were scornful of psychiatry and considered therapy vulgar exhibitionism. He did consent to have a thorough physical examination, which revealed his only illness to be a hyperactive thyroid, which may have contributed to his insomnia and weight loss.

In 1950 Cole had told Berenson that "I haven't been [to Paris] since 1937 and I constantly pine for it." Late in September 1951 Cole and his valet, Paul Sylvain, flew to Paris for a six-week holiday, but returned after one week, Cole suffering from deep lethargy and delusions. Sylvain feared he might attempt suicide and looked after Cole vigilantly. The two returned to Boston, where Cole had another physical examination, and on October 5 he was admitted to Doctors Hospital in New York, but all news of this was kept from the papers. Two electric shock treatments were administered, and Cole improved so remarkably that Sylvain wrote to Sam Stark that in another week it was expected Mr. Porter would be his vivacious, charming, witty self again: "There is nothing to worry about anymore." Linda was still in Williamstown, and Paul telephoned her with daily reports. For a time visitors were prohibited. Dr. Moorhead, Cole's faithful physician, was then a patient in the same hospital but took a hand in Porter's care. Cole remained in the hospital until November 1 undergoing further shock treatments. His depression diminished, but he remained neurotically anxious about his finances. Paul described Cole's state of mind to Sam Stark: "His thinking is along these lines. I am so depressed about giving up 416 [Rockingham] and California altogether. The rent may be increased and I cannot afford living in California. What will I do with my beautiful things? Give them away? Store them? Ship them to New York? All my silver? Beautiful plates? What will I do with them? I love California so and because of my legs I cannot use a hotel swimming pool." He envisioned having to dismiss his servants in the Brentwood house and saying farewell to "all my friends [who] are there." "I always feel tops in the sunshine," Porter said.

Not surprisingly, Linda favored Cole's returning to year-round life in New York and concentrating on Broadway musicals rather than films, which he just then felt were neglecting him.

Porter remained in New York in order to take part in a two-hour Cole Porter salute Ed Sullivan planned for late February 1952. "To a person who has talent," said Cole on Sullivan's show, "and is willing to work hard, Broadway is as friendly as Main Street in Peru, Indiana." Several people close to Cole felt that this tribute buoyed him noticeably, and he returned to California on February 28.

A person who reappeared in Cole's life at this time was Alex Steinert, whom Linda and Cole knew in Paris in the 1920s when Steinert was a student, along with Cole, at the Schola Cantorum. Subsequently he worked with George Gershwin and then went to Hollywood to work on films. According to George Eells, they met again in 1948 and began to play two pianos. In February 1952 Cole wrote to ask Steinert, "Can you play two pianos with me beginning about March 2nd?" He then asks him to rent a good black baby grand and have it installed at 416 North Rockingham Road on February 27. All the plans were precise: the butler was to be informed and arrange for a tuner on the twenty-eighth. Cole tells Steinert, who was successor to Dr. Sirmay, "it looks as if I might be writing a show on the coast during my stay this time, in which case it might be charming if you could help me make those beautiful accompaniments! . . . please answer me at ze Waldorf."

July and August Cole spent as usual in California; and then in the fall he divided his time between the Waldorf Towers and Williamstown, working on the Spewacks' show for Ray Bolger, *Boy Meets Girl*. But by December he confessed that he could get nowhere. "I am afraid the reason is that the subject matter, even though it may be excellent, does not appeal to me, and I must withdraw from our possible collaboration on this show." He did so with regrets and hoped that maybe the Spewacks would come up with an idea more congenial to him. One of the scripts he declined at the time had been sent to him by a Jane Rubin, who perhaps knew of his long admiration for the Brownings. "Please tell Jane Rubin," he asked John Wharton, "that I should be very interested in working on a musical version of *The Barretts of Wimpole Street* if she can guarantee me a singing dog" (referring to Elizabeth Barrett Browning's beloved Flush).

Surprisingly, so many years after it was written, Cole's song "Down in the Depths" became a subject of discussion again. In 1951 there was considerable talk of revivals. *Jubilee* was being considered, but Cole wrote that "the lyrics are very topical and would have to be completely re-written to apply to any revival of the show today. This would be a major job, which I should find it impossible to do." For a new recording of "Down in the Depths" the lyrics had been "merely generalized so that they could be understood by anybody, whether he had ever been in New York or not. So," said Cole, "I see no harm done." He was not, though, renouncing all his resolves in this matter: "It does seem strange to me, however, that changes in my lyrics are often made, and even changes in the music, without anyone ever asking my permission." Goddard Lieberson was also considering Columbia's doing a recording of *Nymph Errant,* and Porter hoped they could secure Mary Martin for the lead. He began 1952 with some of his ebullience and charm restored, and they were to emerge entertainingly in the words and music he was to write for *Can-Can,* his next musical hit.

Chapter 18

Can-Can

Can-Can came along at a glorious time in the history of Broadway. *Guys and Dolls, South Pacific, The King and I, Wish You Were Here, Wonderful Town,* and a revival of *Porgy and Bess* were among the musicals in town. In his later years Cole Porter, besides his battle against ill health, continued to battle puritanism. *Can-Can* was in part another effort in that crusade. Cy Feuer, who with his business partner and friend, Ernest Martin, produced numerous musicals, had spent time in Paris as a GI and returned to the United States after World War II determined to do a show set in Montmartre in the 1890s. Martin concurred, as it suited his lifelong struggle with censors.

The two producers kept the prospect of *Can-Can* alive all the years they worked on *Where's Charley?* and *Guys and Dolls* with Frank Loesser. Their plan had always been to produce a show about Paris in the nineties, with the atmosphere of Toulouse-Lautrec and with his famous model La Goulue as its center. Feuer and Martin judged Cole Porter to be more likely than Loesser to do the music. They looked Porter up in the phone book, found his number, called him, identified themselves as the producers of *Guys and Dolls,* and soon they were at Cole's door. The subject appealed to Cole, and they quickly agreed that Abe Burrows, with whom they'd already done a show, should do the book, as comedy was to be its method as well as its weapon for attack on the censors. But when Feuer and Martin proposed to Cole that the three of them meet with Burrows, Cole rejected the plan, saying he knew nothing about librettos, that they were a weak spot with him. "Just tell me what you want and I'll write it," he told them. "Let me stick to what I can do."

Ultimately Burrows not only wrote the book but directed the show as well. When he got to work on the book, Burrows discovered that supposedly carefree Montmartre in 1890 was besieged by censorship troubles. The resident puritans were outraged by the new dance, the can-can. This led the producers to drop their earlier plot, the life and times of La Goulue. It was Ernie Martin who suggested naming the show after the dance. He also challenged Cole to write lyrics that avoided any mention of Paris: "Songs about Paris are so stale." Porter respected the musicianship of Cy Feuer, who was a Juilliard School graduate, and the two were artistically compatible. Feuer spent a good deal of time at Rockingham; Cole would telephone him and ask him to come over, and "often he played a song." Despite Martin's proscription, one of these was called "I Love Paris." "I jotted it down," Feuer recalled. "The fantastic thing to me was the transition in the release of the song, which went from minor to major and stays in the major—a big, bright splurge—until the return to the minor key." When Feuer began to play it later for his wife, she said, "For God's sake, it's a Jewish song." "Not in the middle," replied Feuer. Then he told Martin that Cole had written a Paris song. "Oh, Christ," said Martin, but Feuer said it was wonderful and warned him to behave himself until he heard it.

Porter worked hard on the show for reasons which Abe Burrows articulated:

> Shows [used to be] quicker to write than they are now . . . The songs didn't have to make sense, they didn't have to come out of the book as much as now. Really, until Rodgers and Hammerstein, if you had to change a scene, a girl could come out in front of the curtain and sing anything or dance anything . . . Porter created all of his songs to spring naturally out of the book. In his enthusiasm he composed ten songs more than could be used . . . To give a French quality to his music, Porter composed a good deal in a minor key which imparts a sense of sadness and longing to many of his melodies.

The plot Burrows devised was a simple one. Aristide Forestière is a puritanical judge whose plan is to shut down the city's dance halls. Pistache, owner of the club Bal du Paradis, opposes him. But then they fall in love and Forestière comes to see that "obscenity is in the eye of the beholder." All of this transpires in 1893 in Montmartre.

One day Cy Feuer had called Michael Kidd to say that he and Ernie Martin were preparing to do a show with Cole Porter. "We'll take you to Porter's house to hear the score." So they drove to Rockingham Road, where Porter was seated at the piano. Two valets were present but never spoke a word. They served drinks impeccably and Porter seemed to signal them in a silent way. Porter drank a martini and then played and sang "I Love Paris." Later Martin asked Feuer why Porter had played so slowly and softly and eventually drank so much. "He was in awe of Michael Kidd as a brilliant dancer and choreographer," said Feuer. Before the show closed Cole gave Michael a gold watch engraved, "To Michael, *Can-Can,* Cole."

Ernie Martin was amazed by the amount of time Cole devoted to society. Invitations to Rockingham Road usually entailed dinners and drinks elegantly presented to eight people. Martin recalls the ceramic nameplates and handwritten menus, the Baccarat crystal. The conversation was usually inconsequential showbiz talk. Martin remembers how Porter liked the pool and the little pool house, with its awning and always a flag flying. Every fifteen minutes or so Paul Sylvain would walk around the pool using a Flit gun.

That summer Cole had great trouble organizing a workable staff. Paul Sylvain was hospitalized for some time, so the butler had to assume his duties. Four cooks came and went. And Cole himself was suffering from violent headaches, ultimately attributed to a sinus infection. Then, on July 26, Katie, age ninety, suffered a cerebral hemorrhage and never regained consciousness. Cole had been notified of her failing health and hurried to Peru to be at her side. He was deeply involved in composing the score for *Can-Can* and readying it for production. So he found himself writing some of the uproarious music of the "Can-Can" number on the porch at Westleigh Farms as his mother lay dying in the house.

> *If in Deauville ev'ry swell can,*
> *It is so simple to do,*
> *If Debussy and Ravel can,*
> *'Twill be so easy for you.*
> *If the Louvre custodian can,*
> *If the Guard Republican can,*
> *If Van Gogh and Matisse and Cézanne can,*
> *Baby, you can can-can too.*

Katie's Miami Indian servants sat outside her door as if it were a church portal. After Katie died, on August 2, Cole gave each of the help six months' salary and persuaded his cousin James O. Cole, who retained two of the ser-

vants, to take over the house. Katie's estate amounted to $551,000, the bulk
of which, along with her property, she bequeathed to Cole. At least on the
surface Cole kept calm, seeming to accept with equanimity the death of his
mother after her long life. But the loss of this woman who for sixty-one
years had been the human being closest and dearest to him must have been
a profound and wrenching one. True to the stoic way she taught him, Cole
kept his sorrow carefully covered. Soon after Katie's death, Linda wrote to
Bernard Berenson and told him of their loss. "I was devoted to her, she was
so alive, so gay & endearing—& Cole adored her. They were very alike as a
matter of fact." Linda, in Massachusetts, with Cole in Hollywood, sounds
desolate in this letter written in August 1952. "The weather is gloomy. I am
alone which is not good for me—it wouldn't matter if I minded, but I
don't."

Cole drew even closer to his Peru cousins in the months following
Katie's death, thanking them for gifts and sending on to them books he
enjoyed: *Desiree* was "a wonderful bit of fiction history and the kind of book
you and Katie used to read aloud," he wrote to Lou Bearss, who had been
his mother's best friend. "I think of you so often." (He saved unusual
stamps for Lou's grandson.) *Brief Gaudy Hour* was another "fictionalized
history book" he read and passed on to Lou. He recommended it as "fascinating." His reading was certainly not highbrow.

Christmas 1952 was difficult for Cole. Lou sent him a carton of Chester-
fields—"my pet brand," as he called them—but did not come east. "We did
our best for Christmas dinner, but it was hardly a success," he wrote to her.
Sturge was to have been the host but was in the hospital "with a big abscess
on his behind." Linda and Cole transferred the party to their apartment and
invited a few friends, among them Monty Woolley, who, Cole told Lou,
arrived in tails but "roaring drunk, so the evening had nothing to do with
those wonderful evenings that we used to have with you and Katie."

"The Porters have started the New Year badly," Linda told Berenson as
1953 began. "Cole has some mysterious skin infection which itches constantly & almost drives him crazy . . . and I have been confined to my
apartment for days with bursitis in my right arm (a new disease for me) and
a rather alarming cough. I hope to get out for some air next week. I have so
few activities that I miss them terribly when they are taken away." Cole on
the other hand was extremely busy.

When it came to casting the show, Cole and the others auditioned
Allan Jones, who sang the song "I Am in Love." He first sang "For I am
madly [for 'wildly'] in love with you" and then "mildly in love with you."
There was no more talk of Jones, and Peter Cookson got the part, for which

he was adequate but no more. It was Cy Feuer who discovered Lilo, in Paris, where she was singing in a show at the legendary Théâtre du Châtelet called *Le Chanteur de Mexico*. Feuer liked her sass and discussed her with Porter before they called her to come to New York.

Porter spent quite a bit of time with Lilo, determining what her register was. She sang a few Piaf songs. Porter, whom she considered a poor pianist, did not accompany her at the audition. "I hope you will create a 'Begin the Beguine' for me," Cole said as the audition ended, and Lilo took this as a positive response. (Like Merman, Lilo had never had a voice lesson and possessed a gutsy voice, which Porter preferred to a sweet-voiced soprano. She had remarkably low notes in her range, which suited very well her role as Pistache.) She flew back to Paris that same night and returned to New York eight months later, a contract in her purse. Before she left Paris to do the show, Cole had telephoned her and said he'd written a song for her overnight. She listened as he sang and played "I Love Paris."

> *Ev'ry time I look down*
> *On this timeless town,*
> *Whether blue or gray be her skies,*
> *Whether loud be her cheers*
> *Or whether soft be her tears,*
> *More and more do I realize*
> . . . .
> *I love Paris ev'ry moment,*
> *Ev'ry moment of the year.*

She found Cole very nice to her but rude to some others. "He had a distinct sense of class," Lilo discovered. Born a German baroness, Liselotte Weil had come to live in Paris and work there in the theatre. Her father was deported to Germany and died in a concentration camp. Married to a French marquis, Lilo was always introduced by Cole as the Marquise de La Passardière. He was well aware that she had married into a very old and distinguished French family. Cole often took her to dinner at Millicent Hearst's or included her with the Windsors. "He adored that" and would begin their conversations always conducted in fluent French, addressing Lilo quite seriously as "ma chère marquise." Another place Lilo went with Porter was El Morocco, where he made scornful remarks about the potted palm trees.

Earlier in the day Porter would attend rehearsals, then retire to his apartment, dress, and reappear at the theatre with an entourage, to whom he would offer champagne (his butler and chauffeur being in attendance). He always invited Lilo to join his party but never offered any refreshment to Peter Cookson or Gwen Verdon. Lilo found this rude. Once, auditioning a possible understudy for Lilo, Cole and she sat down to listen to the girl. Porter, on a cane, sat in the fourth row center. (By the time *Can-Can* closed, his health had deteriorated and he was forced to use crutches.) After the girl sang one song, Porter ostentatiously rose and hobbled out of the theater, taking Lilo with him leaving the auditioning actress probably devastated. "It was very rude," said Lilo, who thought that Porter could be charming with his society friends but not generally to people in show business. Feuer found him otherwise: "not at all a snob."

The Porter party arrived at the Barclay Hotel for the Philadelphia try-out on March 17, 1953, having sent ahead long lists of items with which Cole required his suite be stocked. These included refreshments, standard kitchen items, "American Store Cheese—sharp, 1 can Water Chestnuts, 1 Smithfield Ham, 3 Lux toilet soap bars." Also listed were six cartons of Chesterfield cigarettes, three cartons of Camels, six cans of Pard dog food, and fruits of every variety. Few showmen can have prepared so royally for a tryout in a major city where such items weren't rare. Porter also made lists pages long of "Things to Take to Philadelphia," including music manuscript papers, paper clips, stamps, a pencil sharpener, a portable typewriter, a briefcase, a New York telephone book—about seventy-five items in all. A list called "To Be Put in Pantry of Cole Porter Suite" included one dinner table, one breakfast table, two dozen linen napkins, porcelain of every dimension for six, silver, crystal, and silver trays. These are referred to as "Mr. Porter's needs." Cole traveled to Philadelphia with Sturges by train and Paul Sylvain drove the car (presumably laden with Porter's impedimenta). The lists multiplied: "many wastebaskets," flower vases, card tables, an ironing board. A nearby pharmacy was apprised of items to be brought to Porter in the Barclay: twelve boxes of Kleenex (which Porter once discovered with delight, unaware that virtually everyone knew and used them), Carter's Little Liver Pills, pomade, milk of magnesia—twelve items in all.

Lilo was ambivalent about Porter's arranging for the rest of the company to stay in a less elegant hotel than his for the Philadelphia tryout, and then insisting that his "chère marquise" be in a suite adjoining his at the Barclay. Her reviews in Philadelphia were excellent: "Lilo is the most exciting discovery since Anna Held," wrote one captivated critic, invoking the legendary Ziegfeld star. And the show had the largest advance sale for Philadelphia—$195,000—and after a six-week run it had grossed over $300,000.

Many remember *Can-Can* as a very funny show. Hans Conried and Erik Rhodes contributed notably to the comedy, on- and offstage. The day the show arrived at the Shubert Theatre in Philadelphia the marquee read:

COLE PORTER'S *CAN-CAN*
Starring Lilo
Peter Cookson
Hans Conried

Gwen Verdon spotted Conried on a ladder, measuring with a ruler the size of the letters in his name compared with those of Lilo and Cookson. Verdon's own name had been cut by half. Verdon had begun her association with the show by performing with great success at her audition, where she danced, read, and sang "Pennies from Heaven." After she finished, Abe Burrows came onto the stage and called her "Claudine," the name of the character she auditioned to play. Her first sight of Cole Porter was bewildering: she thought his appearance in spats, a pearl vest, cane (which she took to be ornamental), and derby hat was comical—a costume which for some reason he had donned. Later she realized he regularly dressed this way.

Linda was too ill to attend the opening in New York. Cole dined before the performance with the Lytle Hulls, Millicent Hearst, the Countess di Zoppola, Elsa Maxwell, the Duke of Verdura, the Baron de Gunzburg, and the J. Omar Coles, his closest cousins. As the party prepared to leave for the theater, Cole donned a large homburg, which he said he was wearing "because I adore Eisenhower . . . I've never met our wonderful President, so the nearest thing I could do was to wear his hat." This must have been as close as Cole ever came to making a political gesture. Cole also had "Ike" cuff links made of diamonds, rubies, and emeralds—a gift of Elsa Maxwell. This was the last of Porter's openings at which Linda presented her husband with a cigarette case. Fashioned of fourteen-karat gold by Verdura, it bears the inscription "Can-Can, New York, May 7, 1953," the date of the New York opening.

Everyone agrees that the brilliant choreographer of *Guys and Dolls*, Michael Kidd, brought, in Lilo's words, "the most extraordinary gifts" to the show. A dancer of virtuosic attainment himself, he was able to invent steps for other dancers that showed them off in breathtaking exploits—none more than Gwen Verdon, who according to all observers "stopped the show totally." Even Lilo tells how "*jalouse*" she was on opening night when Verdon got all the applause. "The battle of Verdon," as Lilo called it, ensued. The leading lady should be the star, proclaimed Lilo, who attributed part of

Michael Kidd with Patricia Barker and Mary Heater,
backstage at Ballet Theatre

her trouble to her not knowing English. Lilo, who spoke no English and learned the lyrics phonetically, communicated with Burrows in Yiddish and German. When she asked Cole to help her with her lines, he said firmly that he never permitted himself any contact with the book. She thinks that her eventual mastery of English allowed her to become the star that some witnesses attest she was—that and costumes she held out for. According to Madeline Smith, Porter (although it's doubtful he was to blame) "had the star at the finale in an old calico dress. She said, 'A star shouldn't appear like that.' And she was right, because they finally made her a beautiful white evening gown, and she looked ever so much better in that . . . But sometimes the stars . . . get a little out of sorts . . . So [Porter] always tried to put them on an even keel again."

According to Gwen Verdon, her success was partly attributed to the rarity of her appearance onstage—a tactic devised by the Marquis de La Passardière, she thought, a broker who looked like a film star. This is the view of Verdon, although the book originally does not seem to have given her role much more exposure, and a number of people associated with the show recall that Verdon could be demanding. Gwen Verdon found that Porter was intent on writing every note himself, so Geneviève Pitot, the dance arranger, had no room to invent dance music from the Porter tunes. Neither Cole Porter nor the director made any move to rescue Verdon, who at one point was asked to duck behind a piece of furniture in order to make room for Lilo. "I just won't do that," she said, and exited the stage. The audience on opening night in New York caught on to what was happening and treated her like the underdog who more than deserved a bow. Verdon was changing in the dressing room and didn't hear any of this excitement until Michael Kidd burst in and said she must take a bow. She does remember walking onstage and seeing the four actors who followed her and whom

Gwen Verdon in the role of Claudine with Hans Conried in *C*

she'd never seen in their roles before. She didn't hear the applause but observed that everyone was standing and thought something must have gone wrong. When she left the theater on opening night she was mobbed by fans. Peter Cookson and his wife spirited Verdon into their East Side house. She was particularly frightened because the paparazzi had discovered her whereabouts and the street had to be blocked off to traffic.

Cole was properly congratulatory (he would be even more so when Verdon did *Damn Yankees*). As the ingenue in *Can-Can*, she had to sing songs high for her range (Cole's congratulatory note for *Damn Yankees* asked, "Where did you get that low voice?"). Verdon continued to feel uncomfortable and offered to resign. She did pay tribute to Lilo as "an extraordinary performer who made some mistakes on opening night." For one, she returned to the stage after her opening number and apologized for the quality of her singing, attributing it to nervousness. The song was "C'est Magnifique," which Lilo sang with Peter Cookson:

> When love comes in
> And takes you for a spin,
> Oo-la, lala, c'est magnifi-que.
> When, ev'ry night,
> Your loved one holds you tight,
> Oo-la, lala, c'est magnifi-que.
> But when, one day,
> Your loved one drifts away,
> Oo-la, lala, it is so tragi-que,
> But when, once more,
> He whispers, "Je t'adore,"
> C'est magnifi-que!

Porter never went backstage during the run of *Can-Can*. Gwen Verdon remembers that he would some...es attend rehearsals and she would see him grimace with pain. Insecure a... her own work, she would worry that he was wincing at her performa... til she realized that he was probably in agony with his diseased legs. ...odes told Verdon that at times Porter would take himself to Lenox H...bodes told Verdon would be suspended in a swinglike contraption, so pain...ital, where he to lie in bed.

But he remained active on the social front. Once he invited ... ...don and Garson Kanin to dinner. "Bring someone," he said, to th...

prise. "I'm terribly bored with all my friends and they with me. Can't you introduce me to new people?" Gordon proposed the Lee Shuberts. Kanin and his wife called the Shuberts, who were surprised, as they were dining with guests of their own. "It isn't tonight, is it?" In a few seconds Shubert dispensed with his guests—he met them later at "21"—and off they went to Cole's, who reminisced with his guests and then played the score for *Can-Can*." "They saw each other for a year," according to Gordon, "and then Cole dropped them."

Some view the score of *Can-Can* as second-rate. Kenneth Tynan wrote that "musically it is Mr. Cole Porter at half-pressure, a frail trellis for a multitude of internal rhymes, although two songs—'Live and Let Live' and 'It's All Right with Me'—have respectively his old buoyancy and his wan, bedside wit." He also praised Michael Kidd's choreography, although he thought that the whole conception of *Can-Can* was "an American's fantasy of Paris." This despite the fact that Porter immersed himself in the music played in French dance halls in the 1890s. People likened it to the film *Moulin Rouge,* perhaps because, in Ernie Martin's words, it was "a musical about some people Toulouse-Lautrec might have painted in Paris in the 1890s."

The sets and lighting were designed by Jo Mielziner; the costumes were by Motley. The lighting was especially effective, and Lilo recalls that Mielziner had a Japanese assistant who deserved much credit for the poetic effects the lighting achieved. Years later people remember a scene where Lilo entered a semidarkened stage, stretched and yawned as first she, then Paris awakened. The lights came up from below, gradually, revealing the rooftops. "Jo Mielziner has virtually brought Paris' Montmartre to the Shubert," wrote one Philadelphia critic.

"Live and Let Live," which Tynan admired, is another hurrah for tolerance, and it may have been one way Cole salved his wounds after the critics' objection to the sexy scenes in *Out of This World.*

> *Live and let live, be and let be,*
> *Hear and let hear, see and let see,*
> *Sing and let sing, dance and let dance.*
> *I like Offenbach, you do not,*
> *So what, so what, so what?*
>
> . . .
>
> *Live and let live and remember this line:*
> *"Your bus'ness is your bus'ness and my bus'ness is mine."*

"It's All Right With Me," Tynan's other preference, has become a standard. Cole rewrote it during the tryouts in Philadelphia, and Peter Cookson sang it cold.

You can't know how happy I am that we met,
I'm strangely attracted to you.
There's someone I'm trying so hard to forget,
Don't you want to forget someone too?
It's the wrong game with the wrong chips,
Though your lips are tempting, they're the wrong lips,
They're not her lips but they're such tempting lips
That if some night you're free,
Dear, it's all right,
It's all right
With me.

Everyone was filled with praise for the choreography and the dancers. Brooks Atkinson wrote in the *New York Times*: "Michael Kidd's . . . swift and tumultuous ballets dramatize the work more vividly than either the score or the book. And Gwen Verdon . . . is the practical star of the show." But he continued more negatively: "Cole Porter's score is not one of his best works . . . The lyrics are perfunctory, the sly obscenities Mr. Porter likes to slip into his lyrics are unrelieved by wit or humor . . . Both the music and the lyrics of 'Never, Never Be an Artist' would just about make the grade in a college show." Walter Kerr, another highly respected theatre critic, writing then in the *Herald-Tribune*, found the score less than distinguished and Porter "haggard about his lyrics." "When love comes in and takes you for a spin," he cited as banal rhyming, and he thought generally the production "slick" and "majestically commercial." "Don't look for inspiration this time round. Composer and librettist are in a hand-me-down mood." Monty Woolley wrote to Cole on May 9, 1953, to complain that "critics are truly abominable . . . the dirty introverts." He particularly harangued about Kerr, whom he called a "jealous idiot [who] has the nerve to say you were 'laggard' with your lyrics, and quotes one single line to substantiate his criticism, without reference to the hundreds of witty lines which he would be entirely incapable of writing, I know."

As for Cole, he told a *Times* reporter: "I hate to have the New York curtain go up. Then the show is on and the whole thing's over for me." The reporter describes Porter as "smiling a melancholy smile."

The first-night audience was glittering. Both Garbo and Dietrich attended, along with Gloria Swanson, Valentina, Harold Arlen, and Vera Zorina. A critic wrote: "As the overture played, I saw Cole Porter limping down a side aisle . . . he still uses a cane and walks painfully. But he's a debonair figure none-the-less, slender, impeccably groomed, a carnation in his lapel." Lilo was touched that Cole waited for her to change after the show and then escorted her on foot to Sardi's. He made other customarily gracious gestures, commissioning Vertès to sketch three of the Mielziner sets and presenting one each to Burrows, Feuer, and Martin. Burrows wrote to thank Cole: "When I think of the trouble you must have gone to in order to arrange it and the thought behind it that it took, I'm flabbergasted." On May 9 Cole flew off to California.

Later in May Cole appeared on *Jukebox Jury,* a popular TV show of the time, where in previous weeks six Porter songs from *Can-Can* were "judged" to be hits. In the script for this program Cole Porter describes what an inspiration it was for him to have Lilo "from the Paris music halls" to write songs for. He also rails against the "tone-deaf" critic George Jean Nathan, who had objected to the ball scene "with nearly nude girls and leopard-skin boys pinching each other's bottoms." The *Catholic News* deplored the scanty costumes of Gwen Verdon and thought that the replica of Sacré-Coeur in some sets "must to the discerning offer apt and eloquent comment on the rest of the proceedings." It must have cheered Cole considerably to receive in August of 1953 this letter from Irving Berlin:

Dear Cole:

Elizabeth (my youngest) and I went to see *Can-Can* last night and, along with a packed house of satisfied customers we loved it. It's a swell show and I still say, to paraphrase an old bar-room ballad, "anything I can do, you can do better."

Love, Irving

Kate reappeared in 1953 as MGM readied a screenplay of that show. Another project was *103 Lyrics of Cole Porter,* edited and introduced by Fred Lounsberry, president of a Buffalo, New York broadcasting corporation. Irving Lazar acted as Porter's agent in the film dealings with MGM. Porter probably profited from Lazar's acumen as an agent, but he disliked the man, telling Jean Howard that "Swifty" reminded him of "a nigger Baptist preacher."

Despite the bad notices *Can-Can* on the whole received, the public paid little attention to the critics. The show quickly sold out for months ahead.

As Sigmund Spaeth wrote in praise of the score: "Phonograph records have an embarrassing way of upsetting the dicta of drama and music critics." Nonetheless, Cole was said by friends to be himself disappointed with the show, and the reliable Dr. Sirmay reported that the disappointment had not a little to do with the failure of the French government to acknowledge the way in which Porter in *Can-Can*—and throughout his career—had invested his gifts in praise of Paris.

After 892 performances, the show closed. Subsequently Cole twice had Lilo and her husband to dinner in Brentwood. He took very little part in the conversation, and Lilo had the feeling that he wished they'd "get the hell out." After the second visit he asked them not to return. But devastated as he was by pain, Cole continued to play the *grand seigneur*. When they visited, he flew the French flag in their honor. Once he sent them the gift of an apple tree. His gestures continued to be munificent.

Chapter 19

The Dream Is Over

In July 1953 Cole told John Wharton to "keep it under your hat, but it looks as if I am going to do a new show for Feuer and Martin. They have come up with an excellent script." The show was *Silk Stockings,* based on the Garbo film *Ninotchka.*

Cole continued to receive scripts from an abundance of authors. One of them he characterized to Robert Montgomery as "beneath contempt." Montgomery in 1952 had begun more and more to be the lawyer (at Paul, Weiss, Wharton, Rifkind & Garrison) looking after Cole's affairs. Cole was in Los Angeles just then, working on a film, and Linda was in the Berkshires as summer began after "the usual virus infection and the usual cure with antibiotics which are enough to kill anyone."

Cole worked hard in Hollywood at composing the songs for *Silk Stockings,* to be directed by George S. Kaufman, with a book by Kaufman and his wife, Leueen MacGrath. The talent behind this version of *Ninotchka* was stunning: Jo Mielziner was to do the sets; Lucinda Ballard, the costumes; and Eugene Loring, the choreography. (Michael Kidd had turned down the offer because of the political sensitivities that existed just then in the United States, fanned by the witch hunt that Senator Joseph McCarthy conducted.)

Before she left the Berkshires in October, Linda received the devastating news of the Duke of Alba's death. To Berenson she wrote:

Darling B.B.

It was a dreadful shock to pick up the paper & read of Jimmy's death in Lausanne. What happened, I wonder? . . . I have been very sad and depressed ever since. We had been friends for so many years & I loved him dearly. You will miss him, B.B., as I do. There was no one remotely like him. This has been an unhappy summer. My niece, my sister's only child, died suddenly at the end of August— & now Jimmy. It is too much. Cole, who has been in Hollywood for four months, returns next Wednesday 7th—we will have a few weeks together here before I move back to N.Y. on the 22nd.

Christmas was no happier in 1953 for the Porters than it had been the year before, after Katie's death. Two days before the holiday, Cole wrote to Berenson:

The reason Linda hasn't answered you is because two days after she returned from the country in the middle of October, greatly improved, she dislocated a disc which, in turn, caused pressure on a nerve and she has been in great pain ever since. As if this were not enough, on top of her increasingly serious emphysema, which makes breathing most difficult for her, two days ago, due to a coughing spell, she broke a rib, which also is most painful. It is often difficult to understand why the gods above should decide to punish so violently someone so good. But this is what has happened and it is heartbreaking to see her suffer. I am afraid also that finally her morale has broken, and her moments of laughter become more and more rare . . . I wish I could send you a happier letter at Christmas time.

It was just as Porter was occupied with the score of *Silk Stockings* that a simmering feud erupted between him and the Spewacks. They had contracted with Knopf to publish the script of *Kiss Me, Kate,* incorporating the lyrics of Cole Porter's songs, and prefaced by an ample introduction written by Bella, titled either "How to Write Musical Comedy" or "Working with Shakespeare and Cole Porter." When Porter read this introduction, he objected to passages that presented him, he judged, as failing to appreciate Shakespeare's genius. He directed his lawyers to send a "threatening legal letter." The Spewacks responded: "We are distressed to hear that we have offended you . . . We have no desire to hurt you, even unwittingly." Porter accepted their word but still couldn't understand why they had not shown him the introduction before the book was published. "He assumes that

Knopf will publish no other edition of the book without his prior approval of it." The dispute seems to have begun in 1952 or earlier, when Bella wrote to advise her attorney, "Under no condition write to Cole about anything. It will just annoy Cole and why [Ben] Schankman [one of John Wharton's associates at Paul, Weiss, et al.] has asked you to write him, I cannot fathom. Unless Schankman is up to mischief . . . Cole doesn't want to be reminded of my help. Or anybody's. He's not well. In addition, his ego, with the aid of Schankman, is enlarged considerably." She says that in the future, Cole can call on Schankman to write his librettos.

Many legal matters occupied Cole in these months: films of earlier shows, stage and TV productions of others. The correspondence was oceanic and nearly submerged him, and he wrote in July to John Wharton that he understood none of it. "When you arrive here you will have to give me a little time and try to explain all of this . . . perhaps, also, I should take lessons when I get back to New York so that I won't be such an idiot regarding my own estate." He was ashamed when he remembered how Linda "knew exactly what she owned and why constant changes were made in her investments."

By early 1954 Linda's emphysema worsened and she mostly stayed in bed, struggling for breath. When Linda became too ill to move about much, Cole bought her a TV set, and she became quite addicted to it. "Oh Cole," she would say, "I wish you didn't have to go out to dinner and miss Groucho Marx." Cole had entertainments to which he was addicted, but these were radio serials. "I listen to *Stella Dallas* on the radio every afternoon— 4:30 p.m. here, 1:30 on the Coast. I have listened every afternoon I could for sixteen years. I once took a sixteen weeks' steamship trip and paid for a very expensive radio so that I could hear *Stella Dallas* . . . Also I've been told to look into another one of these things. 12:45 p.m. It's called *Our Gal Sunday* . . . I hear that's very fine too."

When Linda's maid had an afternoon off, Madeline Smith would go to Linda's apartment and sit with her. "They never wanted to leave her alone," said Smith. When Ray Kelly and his wife came to New York, Linda asked to see them. They arrived at the Waldorf but they hardly recognized her, so decimated was she by illness. At times Linda became irrational and suffered periods of unconsciousness. In May Cole left California to be at her bedside. According to one account, she whispered to him, "I want to die. I'm in so much pain." Her one regret was that she would soon be forgotten. "If only I was [important enough] so that a flower or something would be named for me." As soon as it could be done, Cole arranged that a "Linda Porter rose" be bred and officially so designated. (A tribute that may be more enduring is the melancholy fox-trot Poulenc wrote and dedicated to "Mme. Cole Porter." It's called "Carte Postale.")

Linda died on May 20, 1954, at her apartment in the Waldorf Towers. Despite her wish to be buried on a hillside in Williamstown, Cole arranged, after a brief funeral at Saint Bartholomew's Church, next door to the Waldorf, attended by only a handful of friends, to have her buried in the Cole plot at Mount Hope Cemetery in Peru. Bearss Muhlfield and his wife remember attending Linda's burial; he was a pallbearer. Cole sat in the car and didn't go to the grave. Mrs. Muhlfield remembers that as she went over to speak to him she felt it was "a very cold moment." Cole said after Linda's death, "I've had two great women in my life—my mother, who thought I had this talent, and my wife, who kept goading me along, in spite of that general feeling that I couldn't appeal to the general public." Now both had departed.

Asked by an interviewer if the Porters had "a good marriage," Madeline Smith replied "Well, I can't say that . . . Seemed to be."

People are often puzzled by the Porters' marriage. Certainly this was a marriage of convenience for both Cole and Linda, but it was much more than that. As a relative of Linda's wrote, "She had a very bad first marriage. It was always obvious to us why [Linda] married Cole Porter. She was so abused by a heterosexual she most probably would never have married again." The marriage of Cole and Linda was genuine and enduring, sexless as it was. Today such a marriage would be more difficult, because the press would not respect the privacy of a man as well known as Cole. "Linda Lee adored and inspired Cole Porter," maintains her cousin, "and he adored her . . . Linda Lee adored his sophistication, glamour, and he spoiled her more than she was." At the same time she was considerably older than he was, and both had needs that were met by what was virtually a mother-son relationship. With rare exceptions, Cole remained attentive to Linda, and she was happy to share a life with him.

The threat came when Cole began to be less guarded in his homosexual attachments and so seemed less concerned about causing embarrassment to Linda. Eells is direct in saying that just before the riding accident, Linda presented an ultimatum to Cole: either give up Hollywood or she would divorce him. Porter had needs he could not satisfy with Linda: not only sexual needs but social ones as well. He could not, for instance, discuss with her the beauty of young males. Nor could he lament to her about living without an intimate companion—a man with whom he might have shared a home. He had tried as a youth to fall in love with girls—Des Bearss, and others he met at preparatory school. But he could not. So he expressed his passions in his songs. He had to exercise great restraint because in his life-time the audience would have repudiated love songs written by a known homosexual.

Ellin Berlin wrote to convey the sorrow she and Irving felt about "our lovely Linda." She especially remembered Linda's "understanding and imaginative kindness to me when I was not a very happy child."

Linda left an estate of over one and a half million dollars in which Cole had a lifetime interest. Cole was given outright possession of the property in Williamstown as well as all Linda's personal belongings. He saw to it that friends received mementos that Linda had specified. Besides these he selected other items of her jewelry and presented them to friends: diamond and emerald clips to Jean Howard; two bracelets adorned with diamonds, emeralds, rubies, and sapphires to Natasha Wilson (Natalie Paley); and what was perhaps Linda's favorite bracelet to Anita Loos. On the surface Cole remained stoically unemotional, choosing not to indulge his grief in any public way.

Soon after the burial in Peru, Cole returned to California and immersed himself in work. It was his salvation but did not succeed entirely in vanquishing his sorrow. He asked George Eells, "How can one help not being depressed when all those you're closest to are dying?" Both in Hollywood and in New York he adhered even more rigidly to a schedule that left him almost never without company. According to Eells, whom Cole saw a lot of in these years, he met his guests in the lobby of the Waldorf Towers at exactly 8:15 p.m., whence they were driven to Le Pavillon, arriving at 8:20. They dined and departed the restaurant at 9:40 for a 10:01 screening of a film. An analogous exercise in precision took place in California, where, according to Saint Subber, Cole would drive to the home of someone he was to visit later in the day to determine the duration of the drive. Eells reports Mrs. Alex Steinert catching sight of Cole at four p.m. on a day he was due for dinner. He explained in the evening that he had been assuring himself of the route and the time the drive took.

Another friend who suddenly was felled by illness (a coronary) that year was Moss Hart. Cole wrote him a gossipy letter discussing the failure of Louella Parsons's facelift: "The neck which used to be rather full and nice, looks now like the Duchess of Windsor's . . . Irving Berlin called me up this morning and talked for half an hour, telling me how GREAT the pictures *White Christmas* and *No Business Like Show Business* are. His final line was 'Cole, I only called you to tell you I love you.'"

By the time Porter flew back to New York on September 6, 1954, he had completed the score for *Silk Stockings*, which was to go into rehearsal on

October 18. "*Silk Stockings* has a fine script and it seems to me that I have done a good job on the music and lyrics, although one never knows," he wrote to Hart. He labeled the exercise of composing the score "stimulating" and looked forward to "that strange existence that one leads in Philadelphia for a month after an opening."

Back in New York, Cole spent autumn weekends in Williamstown, working on refining the score of *Silk Stockings*. Often he would be accompanied by George Eells or Jack Coble. He preferred having only one guest, partly, Coble felt, because he had jealous feelings if a third party was present. Cole sat and worked in his favorite chair by the fireplace surrounded by his tools (pencils, dictionaries, etc.). He never visited the big house. Even when he wanted things from it, he would hand the housekeeper a list and wait outside while she fetched the items. No amount of urging would persuade him to enter the house, not even a cloudburst. Eventually he decided to give what had always been known as "Linda's house" to nearby Williams College. But this arrangement was canceled after a weekend during which Cole and Sturge and Baron de Gunzburg were plagued by the noise of visitors and their automobiles. The baron is credited with having convinced Cole to dynamite the big house and move the cottage onto its foundation, so that he would have the superior view of both the surrounding hills and the gardens. (In his will, Cole bequeathed the cottage and its 350 acres to Williams College, which has since sold it.)

Cole chose Jack Coble to effectuate this project. In October 1954 Coble wrote to Cole's attorney to describe in detail the work to be done at Buxton Hill. The cost was estimated at thirty-five thousand dollars. The furnishings from Linda's house (wallpaper from Knole, the Sackville-West house in England, for example) were to be moved into the much larger apartment Cole had decided to take in the Waldorf Towers. He wrote in November of 1954 to Robert Raison to say: "My new apartment at the Waldorf is going to be a dream of beauty. And my little cottage in Williamstown, moved to the site of the main house, will look so pretty. They start ripping the main house apart as soon as I have taken out of it whatever furniture I need for the New York Waldorf apartment. Everything else in it will be stored as I could never afford to buy what is there again."

Ray Kelly never could decide what Cole's motive was for dynamiting the main house at Williamstown. The cottage, formerly a carriage house, was a beautiful *garçonnière,* about five hundred yards from the main house. When the cottage was placed on the foundation of the mansion, the architects added a wing. This space served as Cole's bedroom–sitting room. The move was, in Kelly's opinion, an architectural feat. Even the phonograph records remained in their place. According to Jack Coble, it took about five days to move the cottage to its new site—a perilous venture that he remembers watching with a quickened heartbeat. But it all went off without any mishaps, and Linda's Scottish maid assumed the duties of housekeeper.

Sturges was due in New York on November 15, Cole told Raison, to accompany him to Philadelphia in order to "protect me from those awful weeks which I always have to face after an out of town Opening." Cole called Sturges "always a blessing to have along because he never talks show business. He only talks about nice, rich, fashionable people and it's such a lovely contrast." Ernie Martin thought of Sturges as an aesthete: "He knew special little inns, the best rooms to choose." Sturges claimed to be an anarchist and tried to convert Martin to this posture. "How is it you belong to the Travellers Club?" asked Martin. "That's not very anarchistic." "The only place that cashes checks on Sunday," Sturges sensibly replied.

In New York the rehearsals for *Silk Stockings* were not going well. "You hope," said Cole to Raison, "my show is going along beautifully. It is *not* going along beautifully. It looks disastrous; slow, gloomy, and most of the numbers very badly done."

Raison had become a prominent person in Porter's California life. Writing from New York to "Dear Bobbie" shortly before the Philadelphia opening of *Silk Stockings*, Cole told his friend that he wants to continue "to help you with my little contribution" until Raison had more success in his theatrical agency. Cole had given him, by some accounts, an impressive sum to inaugurate the agency. For a time Raison prospered financially, but he spent money extravagantly and had some bad luck when he lost a handsome home in a California mudslide. Cole did bequeath him the sum of ten thousand dollars in his will. According to several accounts, Raison was offended by this modest bequest. But to Raison's wish to stay at the Waldorf, Cole said an emphatic no. "You ask me what color is your room in my new apartment. As a matter of fact, I shall have a guest room, but I wouldn't ask you to stay in it for anything in the world because you bring strange people in and run up outlandish bills."

As he did with Saint Subber, Cole seems to have felt some kinship with the "outlaw" in Raison's makeup while at the same time being wary of it. Raison could be appallingly indiscreet. For a time he boarded with a male friend; his bedroom was next to the room of the friend's mother, who was gravely ill. Her nurses complained that Raison was bringing a succession of young men into the house and creating a disturbance. In time Raison abused cocaine, and that may have contributed to his recklessness. Of course Cole often enjoyed sharing in sexual hijinks. A friend who had been a young serviceman in those years recalled being put up by Cole overnight in the Brentwood house. He was shown to his room and only after he entered the darkened room was he aware that someone was sleeping in the bed. He seized the opportunity and had an unexpectedly amorous night. For his part Raison idolized Cole, and even married for a time in these years in an effort, many felt, to imitate Porter. His humor and camaraderie endeared him to Cole. But he lacked Cole's discipline. Drinking heavily and spending large sums on cocaine, he eventually mortgaged his other beautiful home in Beverly Hills and lost it to creditors.

In a letter to Raison, Cole mentions for the first time a man who became his good friend for some years: Colin Leslie Fox, whom he thought was "delightful. Everyone who knows him is devoted to him. This includes Merle Oberon." Tall, handsome Colin Fox had been the "Man in the Hathaway Shirt" and, among other achievements, had twice crossed the Atlantic solo in a sailboat. Porter and he shared a liking for opera. He became a part of Porter's entourage in the 1950s.

Although Don Ameche had begun his professional life as a crooner, *Silk Stockings* was his first Broadway musical show. The same was true for Hildegarde Knef, who played the Garbo role in this musical version of *Ninotchka.* (Her surname was changed to Neff for the American public.) Knef's reputation was made in films, at the outset German films, produced right after World War II. Handicapped in a musical by a strong but croaking voice, she nonetheless had great style and glamour. She played the role of a puritanical Soviet envoy sent to Paris to rehabilitate three commissars who have been corrupted by the delights of Paris. Predictably, love brings her to her senses and she becomes a convert to pleasure and the capitalist way. The plot is skeletally similar to *Can-Can*'s, and the theme the recurrent one of scorn for puritanism. In her memoir, *The Gift Horse,* Knef gives a detailed account of the long gestation of the musical and her impressions of the leading figures in the production. She describes Porter looking up at her at her audition in a darkened theatre "with slightly protruding eyes as big as fried eggs that express neither delight nor disappointment." Almost a year later "the Kraut," as Ameche and others called her, was at a pension in Schleswig-Holstein when a cable reached her from Porter and Kaufman inviting her to play the leading role in *Stockings.* Then the long ordeal of rehearsal and the road ensued.

When the tryout began in Philadelphia on November 26, most of the notices were enthusiastic. "Smash for Feuer and Martin, Kaufman and Porter, Neff and Ameche," raved one of the papers. Cole glanced at the headlines and said dryly, "Work can begin."

Knef gave the following description of Cole:

He sits small and delicate in his chair, straight and still as though awaiting reproof from his governess . . . Cole Porter is rich and successful. It
is sometimes hard to believe. He listens intently to every reservation
made by the producers, who are his juniors by many years, and fulfills
every demand. He works as though his daily bread were at stake, as
though he must still prove himself as a composer, lyricist, dependable
team worker . . . He disguises his preeminence so well that he has
apparently forgotten it himself.

In retrospect, the score does seem, with a few exceptions, dim. Porter's
favorite was a song sung by Hildegarde Knef titled "Without Love"—a song
whose sentiments many would find dated today:

> *Without love, what is a woman?*
> *A pleasure unemployed.*
> *Without love, what is a woman?*
> *A zero in the void.*
> *But with love, what is a woman?*
> *Serene contentment, the perfect wife,*
> *For a woman to a man is just a woman,*
> *But a man to a woman is her life.*

The Philadelphia tryout lasted three weeks, during which time Knef
contracted measles. Her illness was kept a secret from the rest of the cast and
she valiantly turned up for every performance. The show then went to
Boston for four weeks more. Critics in both cities had reservations about
the second act and felt the musical wasn't yet ready for New York, despite
Noël Coward's sweeping backstage in Philadelphia dressed in a black cape
and ordering the Kaufmans not to change a thing: "Best thing I ever saw."
Malevolently, or so Martin felt, Moss Hart did the same: "The book is wonderful but you need to get Cole to do something with the songs"—while to
Porter he said the opposite. Like Cole, the Kaufmans were disinclined to
rewrite. For a time many people tinkered with the book, trying to improve
the story and the dialogue. Everyone realized that the show needed more
radical alterations, and it eventually moved to Detroit for further doctoring.
Cole came to Detroit with Sturges. Ernie Martin remembers picking them
up at the airport. One sat on either side of Martin in the car, dressed in der-
bies and carrying canes "like two French dukes." Knef wrote: "Cole Porter

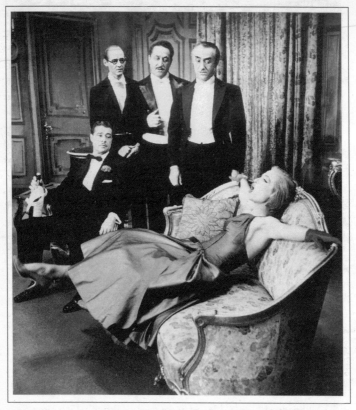

Don Ameche with Hildegarde Neff (and other members of the cast)
in *Silk Stockings*, 1955

observes each disfiguration of his work with the reserve of an English butler." Indeed, the producers infuriated Porter by their demand that he discard several of his songs, and he told George Eells that they underrated his
best numbers.

One night Feuer and Martin told the Kaufmans that they'd have to
bring someone in to assist with the revisions. They wanted the Kaufmans to
quit, but the two refused to do so. They refused as well to alter the show further, insisting that it hardly resembled their original conception of a glamorous romance with songs. Now, in their view, it had become a cliché. So
Martin fired MacGrath and Kaufman, who in his thirty-five years as a playwright had never been dismissed. His biographer called it "a blow to his
pride, and, perhaps worse, it was a blow to his health." Soon after the Kauf-

mans' dismissal, George Kaufman suffered a slight stroke. In the hospital Kaufman wept when he repeated to Lucinda Ballard Martin's description of how the cast had applauded when informed that Kaufman would no longer be rehearsing them. Abe Burrows was brought in, causing what the *Boston Herald* called "A theatrical earthquake of major proportions." Kaufman claimed he'd been fired, which Feuer and Martin denied. When the Kaufmans saw a new version of the show in Boston, they issued this statement: "It has been mutually decided that the areas of disagreement between ourselves and the producers (Cy Feuer and Ernest Martin) are too great to be bridged. Accordingly we have withdrawn and the show is now in the hands of Mr. Feuer as director, with Abe Burrows working on the book."

"Siberia" was a song Martin told Cole they needed, to show how bad that extremity of Russia could be. "What's so bad about Siberia?" queried Cole, whose knowledge of it was confined to conversations with relatives of the czar. He first had declined to write the score because he didn't know the political situation, although the cold war was then at its apex. There is evidence that Cole labored long over "Siberia." Kimball says that "this song troubled Porter enough for him to seek the help of his friend Noël Coward, who furnished some refrains." Once he called Cy Feuer from Williamstown at three a.m. and said, "I want you to help me with rhyme." (Cole would first write out the metrical rhythms of the verse and then search for the words.) "I need a rhyme for 'borealis,' " he said. "Just say 'It isn't as warm as a palace is,' " replied Feuer. "No," countered Cole, "palaces aren't warm; Linda and I had palaces in Venice." Nonetheless, he borrowed the suggestion:

> *When we're sent to dear Siberia,*
> *To Siberi—eri—a,*
> *Where they say all day the sun shines bright,*
> *And they also say that it shines all night,*
> *The aurora borealis is*
> *Not as heated as a palace is.*
> *If on heat you dote*
> *You can shoot a sable coat*
> *In cheery Siberi—a.*

Yvonne Adair, the original choice for the ingenue role, was ill during much of the rehearsal time. Gretchen Wyler, then a chorus girl, was invited to understudy the understudy, Sherry O'Neil. Twelve days before the Broadway opening, Yvonne Adair collapsed, and O'Neil couldn't be found. "We don't expect you to do anything but keep the curtain up," said the stage manager, who told Wyler the news. Her rendition stopped the show then, and tumultuous applause persisted throughout the run, rather to the displeasure of Ameche and Knef, who, Miss Wyler says, hated her. (Cy Feuer worked closely with the three but was unaware of animosity among them.) After the performance the producers, Burrows, and Cole came backstage and said, "You're opening the show in New York."

The number that brought Gretchen Wyler to fame and which saved the evening (and possibly the show) is called "Stereophonic Sound."

> *Today to get the public to attend a picture show,*
> *It's not enough to advertise a famous star they know.*
> *If you want to get the crowds to come around*
> *You've got to have glorious Technicolor,*
> *Breathtaking Cinemascope and*
> *Stereophonic sound.*

"Paris Loves Lovers" has a romantic air, but probably the most romantic of all the numbers in the show is "All of You":

> *I love the looks of you, the lure of you,*
> *I'd love to make a tour of you,*
> *The eyes, the arms, the mouth of you,*
> *The east, west, north, and the south of you.*
> *I'd love to gain complete control of you,*
> *And handle even the heart and soul of you,*
> *So love, at least, a small percent of me, do,*
> *For I love all of you.*

"Complete control," "handle," and "percent" point to Cole's effort to make the words underline the profession of Don Ameche's character, an agent. In 1956, when *Silk Stockings* was filmed, the Motion Picture Association, successor to the Hays Office, had reservations about "All of You"—especially references to making "a tour of you" and "the south of you." "Stereophonic Sound" they called "unacceptably vulgar," particularly the lines "There'd be no one in front / to look at Marilyn's behind" and "Unless her lips are scarlet / And her bosom's five feet wide." "Crum" was suggested as a replacement for "bum" in "Josephine." Cole's ancient enemies were at it again.

After a long out-of-town tryout, *Stockings* came into New York. Five days before the opening Cole went to Switzerland. He had made these travel arrangements well in advance, never dreaming that *Stockings* would be in rehearsal for fourteen rather than the customary four or five weeks. While the show was in Detroit, Cole asked Feuer if he'd mind his missing the New York opening. Some of his friends arranged for a cigarette case similar to those Linda gave him to be made to commemorate the opening. Two Russian coins were part of the ornamentation. Porter's cousin Louise Thwing described the opening for the *Orlando Evening Star* and pleased Cole very much with what she wrote, describing first-nighters like the Duchess of Windsor and Marlene Dietrich. She found Dietrich "breathtaking . . . ageless. Her skin is soft and youthful, her manner distinguished and gracious with no hint of movie-siren-type about her." The duchess fascinated Thwing with her "sparkle and chic. I found her jewels intriguing and spectacular. She wears them with a casual elegance that is arresting. Marilyn Monroe was there wearing the world's longest and largest ermine coat . . . Cole was very tired after much hard and difficult work on the show and he's left for St. Moritz where he will be riding around in a sleigh . . . Then he has been given a friend's yacht to cruise about leisurely and delightfully through the Greek islands before returning home early in June."

Jean Howard recounts in *Travels with Cole Porter* how Cole, planning their journey, sent out to her four tentative itineraries until finally they settled on one. They were very precise in detail, down to the hour at which they would arrive at various venues. The yacht, *Eros,* belonged to Stavros Niarchos, the Greek magnate, who had learned from Jean Howard of the journey she and Cole planned to take with Sturges and graciously offered the use of his ship. Sturge, Cole, and Paul Sylvain left New York on February 20 via Swiss Air for Zurich and immediately went on to the Palace Hotel in St. Moritz, where they remained until March 9.

Friends of Sturge and Cole were scheduled to meet them at certain points on the trip. Among them was the actor Robert Bray—"Cole's last intimate friend," according to Jean Howard, who identified him as "Lassie's master" and who resembled, according to Feuer, "a big motorcycle cop." Apparently Bray had attended rehearsals of *Silk Stockings* with Cole, because Cy Feuer was well aware that the two were an item.

Bray had a wife and children in California. According to Feuer, Cole paid for the education of these children, but apart from a few meetings with Bray, Feuer knew very little about him. "Cole kept his two lives—his homosexual world and the world of show business—quite separate." Several times Bray brought his children to visit Cole, who was not especially fond of children. From time to time on that European trip, Bray would fly off and then

Robert Bray

join up again with the party at a later date. Bray came to a sad end. Cole and he quarreled and parted. Years later, Bray was killed in what was labeled a hunting accident, although Jean Howard wondered if he hadn't shot himself.

Madeline Smith wrote to Louise Bearss about home-front conditions in the Waldorf, where she and the staff were occupied with shutting down Cole's old apartment, 41-C, and readying the new domicile, 33-A, "which is in the process of being overhauled and redecorated (it will be two months or so before it is finished). The decorator is trying madly to get one or two rooms in readiness, so the accountant and I can move down there—and put all the Porter possessions around us, to avoid paying rent in *two* apartments."

Cole's travels in Europe in 1955 on what he called "a dream-trip" were marred only by the press and "too many friends": "they interfere with sight-seeing in their different ways & I want to see everything," he said. Throughout this trip, Cole wrote frequently to George Eells—in February 1955, for example, from Zurich at two a.m. Sturges and Jean Howard had retired, Cole wrote, but he was sitting up "alone with a whisky & soda worrying about Richard," who for some time had been Cole's masseur back home, and often amusingly "unpresentable" to Cole's friends. He introduced him only to Eells and wrote often about him to George. "I don't mean the Richard I know and for whom I have a strange affection. I mean all the Richards all over the U.S.A., beautiful, sweet as hell but with, instead of schooling, television sets. It scares me . . . I'm sure the equivalent of the contemporary Richard was much better equipped for the future, before Noah's flood."

Porter seems to have been in an altruistic mood in Switzerland. The friends had dined in a little German restaurant "which no one but the old aristocracy knows" and spotted "a sad looking little man with very bad teeth & so lonely." After a few drinks they took pity on him and invited him to join them. He turned out to be Darryl Zanuck.

Back home, reviews were pouring in for *Stockings*. Dr. Sirmay wired Porter in St. Moritz: "Opening giant success. Brooks Atkinson raving especially about words and music. All other papers simply wonderful. Abe Burrows and Cy have achieved a theatrical miracle. Audience most elegant in years. Gretchen Wyler stopped show twice . . . You have every reason to be happy and proud. Love and kisses. Sirmay." Atkinson found *Stockings* had "the wittiest dialogue of recent years . . . one of Gotham's memorable shows, on a par with *Guys and Dolls*." He singled out for praise Ameche, Knef, and Wyler. "Mr. Porter [is] back in his best form . . . As in the most expert musical comedies, everything contributes to the vitality of everything else." Atkinson's applause for the integration Cole achieved must have pleased the composer greatly. In "Cole Porter Talks of His Musicals," published just as *Silk Stockings* opened, Porter spoke of the difficulties of writing a musical in the 1950s because of the heights that Rodgers and Hammerstein had attained.

> The integration of something like *South Pacific* is so complete that in today's musical everything has to be married to everything else . . . Take *Silk Stockings*. I've had to do a lot of rewriting because sometimes when the authors made changes in the play itself, my lyrics no longer applied. In the 30's you'd retain every song even if you had to make a wild digression to do it. And in my case this rewriting business is a chore . . . First it's done under gruelling pressure; but even more difficult is throwing out a song and then trying entirely to forget it . . . You must throw out the lyrics and keep the melody. Irving Berlin can do it. I can't . . . Since *Silk Stockings* went into rehearsal . . . I've thrown out six tunes and replaced them with others.

Porter discussed in this article the public's growing tolerance for "all kinds of advanced harmonies and idioms. The public buys Stravinsky records, listens devotedly to Bartók, Hindemith. Look at what Lennie Bernstein got away with in *Wonderful Town*. It's practically atonal. He starts numbers in one key and ends them in another. It's very effective and that's all that counts." Porter said he was interested in a song

only if it is effective on stage. I never sat down just to write a hit. How do you go about that anyhow? . . . I'm becoming less and less interested in tricky rhymes. I think I used to go overboard on them. In Yale, I was rhyme crazy. That was due to the fact that I was Gilbert and Sullivan crazy. They had a big influence on my life. My songs are easier than they used to be musically and lyrically. I've never been able to get complete simplicity the way Berlin does. I'll take twenty-five minutes to write a song, sometimes two days . . . Pretty often . . . you've got to have a bad line so that next one'll look good. It's planting, you know.

On another occasion Porter said he couldn't analyze his own music, although he could characterize others: "The word for Dick Rodgers' melodies, I think, is holy. For Jerome Kern, sentimental. For Irving Berlin, simplicity. For my own, I don't know."

There was talk about a third collaboration with Feuer and Martin, but when they presented Cole with the story he declined, saying he lacked the energy. The producers did not insist: they simply asked him to look it over when he was in a mood to do so. Feuer had grown up in Brooklyn, where he had a childhood friend called Baldassare. That was to be the title of the show they envisioned, the tale of a Sicilian family.

The trip took Cole and his party from St. Moritz to Milan. The manner of the tour, as usual with Cole, was stylish, with a new red-leather-lined Cadillac followed by a station wagon bearing the luggage. The chauffeur (who, Cole told Eells, looked like Jackie Gleason) was taken to a smart shop to be outfitted in the best livery. He assisted Bob Bray and Paul Sylvain in pushing and sometimes carrying Cole's collapsible wheelchair. Cole claimed he was always eager to prolong the sightseeing sprees, but the other men were exhausted from transporting him.

From Milan Cole wrote complainingly to Eells about "nine anonymous bitches" who sent him copies of a review that blasted *Silk Stockings*. In Monte Carlo he hoped to have news from Eells of Richard. (Eells deleted all references to Richard in quoting these letters in his own biogra-

phy of Cole.) "I have great affection for him," Cole wrote. "I also believe
he has exciting possibilities, but he's so . . . unequipped to buck this cruel
world. I'd like to help him but more money isn't the answer. He needs a
great nurse—a John Foster Dulles or perhaps a Marlene Dietrich to do
this. How can we save him? . . . I miss your companionship. One day we
should take a trip together and see beautiful things, inanimate and ani-
mate." Other references to Cole's puzzlement over Richard and his family
appear in his letters to Eells. Cole did spend money on Richard. He bought
his friend an overcoat, but Richard complained that it lacked a fur collar.
Eventually his mother, who once came to visit Cole, sewed a piece of fur
on the collar, giving the coat a cheap look. Cole was both entertained and
dismayed by such antics.

Jean called the trip in retrospect "the most exciting, frustrating, exhausting and memorable three months of my life." Later she told a friend that
Porter was not the ideal cicerone, as he plotted out every hour of the day and
robbed the journey of spontaneity.

When several of the party came down with influenza, Cole and Sturge
made a short visit to Paris. Returning to Milan, the reassembled party began
a drive to the French Riviera and up through Provence, stopping often for a
meal with friends such as Dickie Fellowes-Gordon. Spain and Portugal were
their next destinations. Jean Howard recalled that somewhere on the road
to Madrid, Cole hummed the tune of "True Love," which she praised
highly, although Cole dismissed her judgment. In Portugal the party mixed
with Eddie Fisher, Debbie Reynolds, and Umberto, the former king of Italy.
On one of the Parisian sorties, Jean saw Garbo, but Miss G declined to
acknowledge Cole; perhaps she was vexed by the parody of *Ninotchka* in
Silk Stockings. A friend Cole did see was Sir Charles Mendl. Cole felt "a
strange combination of joy and sadness" at the sight of friends who had
aged, and told Eells in a letter, "I dread old age."

Jean Howard did not always find Cole charming. When illness overtook her, for instance, she found that "Cole [became] ice . . . cold, cold ice!
True I didn't tell him until late, but it really couldn't have mattered that
much." "I don't mean to make Cole out to be inhuman," Jean wrote,
"although there were many times that I did think just that mostly he was
inhuman to himself. I watched him force himself to press on when it would
have been far wiser to stop and rest. I tried my utmost to make him do so,
but he would have none of it; he would shut me up with silence and that
blank stare. And as he wouldn't complain himself, he took a very dim view
of anyone else in the group who did."

Marti Stevens (left) and Jean Howard at the Wailing Wall, Jerusalem, 1958

The Mediterranean cruise began in May in Athens. As the ship sailed out of the harbor, Cole wrote: "At once a feeling of comfort and great taste." He loved the breakfast, served while he sat and looked up at the Temple of Poseidon. He noted that on some days the sea was turbulent, but seemed not to mind "rough weather." Jean Howard has detailed in her *Travels* mostly the conventional loci that travelers take in. Cole was amused by some of the Greeks the party encountered. One was "a former top whore" who was now a top bootblack. Cole described how he sat sidesaddle as his donkey meandered around a village. Despite his accident, he had no mis-

givings about riding on an animal. He also rode a donkey in Santorini. Cole
loved the white buildings there and wrote in his journal as the boat backed
off to give the passengers a better view of the volcanic island, "I felt the
beginnings of the earth and the terrors of hell." He described his visit to
the Valley of Butterflies, where he and his friends "had a long lunch on the
banks of a brook." They seemed to have visited virtually every museum,
Cole describing icons with considerable knowledge and enthusiasm. Posted
in his travel diary is a holy card depicting the Church of St. Peter the Apostle. Printed on it is a prayer for the conversion of sinners.

At Delphi they disembarked to enjoy the view. Cole noted in his journal the "hard donkey ride to the site of the Oracle." He was enthusiastic: "a
wonderful view, very melodramatic." Some of the art that Cole admired in
Greece included the friezes from the Temple of Apollo and a bronze chario-
teer. In Corinth he was particularly pleased by vases from the region. He
also mentioned the town high up in the mountains where "prostitutes lived
in the day of Corinth's glory." He wrote to Lou Bearss that he would
spend some time with Mona Williams—the Countess of Bismarck, as she
was then—who had invited Porter to visit on the Isle of Capri. Aly Khan
insisted that Porter occupy his lovely villa in Cannes. Cole wrote to Lou:
"You can see that, in spite of my old principle never to visit, I have completely broken down with these exciting invitations."

Eventually the yacht returned to Piraeus. On June 2 Cole wrote to Lou
that their sixteen-day cruise of the Greek Islands had ended—"sixteen days
of excitement, beauty, & fun on a lovely yacht . . . It was perfection." The
trip had also encouraged his muse. A section of his small notebooks is
labeled "Trip Abroad" and includes musical sketches. In Spain in March he
had been tinkering with lyrics linked to his temporary habitat:

> *I strolled the Costa Brava one evening by the shore*
> *And on the Costa Brava I found the one of all to adore.*
> *We dreamed on the Costa Brava a dream that could never be.*
> *But how I missed the Costa Brava and the lips I kissed by the sea.*

In Rome Cole sent word to Bricktop that he was coming to visit the
club she had opened there after World War II. Brick wrote in reply that she
would meet him at ten-thirty on the night he suggested. She arrived five
minutes late, only to see Cole's car pull away. Bricktop wrote an apologetic
note, to which Cole replied, "The sign read Bricktop's but I didn't see any
Brick." Over the years Bricktop made many telephone calls to Porter, but he
refused to reply. Cole had more than one personality, said a friend: he was

often immensely gracious and could make one feel special, but, as Michael Pearman saw, he had a mean streak which when provoked could be withering. Still, Cole wasn't misanthropic. "Please call me up," he wrote Eells from Athens after mentioning his anticipated return to New York City on June 7. "I pine for the prose that emanates from your entrails. Love and Kisses." He attempts to sign his name in classical Greek but gives it up: "Fuck it, it's Cole." The party lunched for the last time on deck and were toasted by the crew. Cole wrote in his diary, "The dream is over."

Chapter 20

After You, Who?

When the party returned to New York, "Cole with delight saw his newly-decorated apartment. He thanked Billy Baldwin, the noted interior decorator, who had been part of Linda's legacy to Cole." Everyone who visited Cole in the years following this move raved about the beauty of his surroundings and, in particular, the bookcases with brass piping and ebony shelves. "The book units give Mr. Porter's library . . . a cachet that decorators have been trying to emulate ever since," wrote a critic in *The New York Times*. None of these accounts mentioned that when Baldwin installed the bookshelves, one whole wall was mirror. A well-known phonograph maker insisted on giving Porter the latest in its line: a machine that, for example, shut off automatically if one picked up the telephone. It also captured high and low sounds that exceeded the ability of the human ear to hear—or so the advertising claimed. Soon after it was installed, Cole sat down to listen to a recording. He turned on the phonograph, and immediately the sound caused the wall mirror to split into hundreds of pieces. "Just the sort of thing that tickled Cole," said Michael Pearman, who recalled the occasion.

Vogue that year published photographs of the Porter apartment, and Baldwin's design was imitated by trendy types, who also tried to copy the dark walls of tortoiseshell designs done on the Chinese lacquered paper which Linda had brought from rue Monsieur. George Cukor came to visit Cole at the Waldorf in November and wrote to say, "I was *ébloui* by your apartment!"

Cole's apartment at the Waldorf Towers, 1955

After receiving an honorary doctorate of music from Williams College in mid-June, he flew to the West Coast, where he worked at writing the score for the film *High Society*. Based on Philip Barry's play *The Philadelphia Story*, the picture starred Bing Crosby, Grace Kelly, and Frank Sinatra, with the screenplay by John Patrick. Louis Armstrong and Celeste Holm were also in the cast. Armstrong and Ella Fitzgerald were among the few jazz artists Cole admired, although once he rather snobbishly doubted that Ella could make any sense of the allusions to the *monde* in his lyrics. For Armstrong and Crosby, Cole wrote "Now You Has Jazz." Anita Colby recalled Porter inviting her, Arlene Francis and her husband, Martin Gabel, and Bubbles Hornblow, wife of the producer Arthur, to come to his home, as he wanted to try out the song on them. The lyrics, addressed to "gentlefolk of Newport / Or should I say 'hats and cats,' " purport to teach the audience "precisely how / Jazz music is made." Seemingly Cole still had the wish to educate the elite in what was *à la page*, an impulse left over from the days when he hired Bricktop to teach his socialite friends the Charleston. Of course his customary irony was at play in these lyrics.

Frank Sinatra and Grace Kelly in *High Society*, 1956

Cole had first met Frank Sinatra in the early 1940s, when Sinatra was singing in a roadhouse called the Rustic Cabin in Englewood, New Jersey, just across the George Washington Bridge from New York City. It was a quiet Sunday evening with only a handful of patrons when Porter arrived with a party. Sinatra recognized Porter and revealed his identity to the audience, accenting Cole's greatness. Cole took a bow but "stared daggers" at Sinatra, who proceeded to sing "Let's Do It," forgetting most of the words. Porter left abruptly, obviously annoyed, said Sinatra, to be introduced to the audience in a shabby roadhouse. However, some years later, Cole said Sinatra "is the only person singing today with passion."

Saul Chaplin was the associate producer of *High Society*. He had supervised, together with André Previn, the music for the film of *Kiss Me, Kate*. When he first was given the script to read, the songs were not available, so he was sent to New York City to hear part of the score that was completed and to press Porter to finish it. "He's been at it for several months, and we've yet to receive anything from him," Chaplin was told by the producer. Cole received him warmly: "His friendly manner relaxed me," said Chaplin. "It was like checking up on what's new with an old friend." Chaplin remembers two grand pianos in the room. He was enchanted by Cole's beautiful apartment, where, according to him, only one picture hung, a portrait of Linda. Cole didn't speak of Linda; Chaplin noted that he "spoke either of the present or future, never the past." Cole moved to the piano to play a song he'd written for a particular scene in the film. "His method of demonstrating was interesting. He first played two choruses of the music alone. The third time he sang the lyrics. He maintained that it was unreasonable to expect anyone to listen to a new song and assimilate the words and music at the same time, so he first familiarized his listener with the tune, then sang the words."

Chaplin thought the song was "lovely" but not right for the dramatic situation. However, he was determined not to voice this view to a composer whom he'd idolized for much of his life. "Beautiful," murmured Chaplin, as Cole played the song over again. More praise from Chaplin, until Cole said, "I can tell from your reaction that you have certain reservations about the song." When Chaplin demurred, Cole said, "Now if we're going to work together, you must give me your honest opinion. If I think you're right, I'll either change the song or write a new one. If I don't agree, we'll use the song as I wrote it. Now what do you really think?" Chaplin believed the scene called for a simpler, more old-fashioned number. Cole agreed, and at their next meeting Cole played "True Love"—which Chaplin thought was perfect for the scene.

On the evenings he and Chaplin went to the theatre, Cole sat in his heated limousine until the crowd had entered. Then, with some support from Chaplin, they walked to third-row seats on the aisle. At intermissions they would return to the heated car. When the two went to see *Inherit the Wind,* Chaplin was amazed to learn that Cole had never heard of the Scopes trial. The next time Chaplin came to Cole's apartment he noticed two books on the Scopes trial and another on Darwin. This seems to support Ernie Martin's impression of Cole as more of a researcher than his colleagues were.

Cole's playing deteriorated to the degree that Chaplin could no longer judge the merits of new compositions. His piano playing in later life was scarcely adequate, and he generally declined any request that he play. Nor did he practice the piano or play classical music. He did sometimes play for Bobbie Raison, but he even disliked it when others played at his parties. Ray Kelly attributed this to his being terrified that he would get someone else's tunes stuck in his head. Often, though, on Sunday afternoons in

Williamstown, he would listen to classical recordings on an immense Cape-hart. He went to concerts, and when Ray Kelly expressed an interest in Gilbert and Sullivan, Cole took him to all the offerings of the D'Oyly Carte Company.

The task of scoring *High Society* took him from July until November. "I Love You, Samantha" was a favorite of Cole's, but he thought the public would delight more in "You're Sensational":

> *I've no proof*
> *When people say you're more or less aloof,*
> *But you're sensational.*
> *I don't care*
> *If you are called "The Fair Miss Frigid Air,"*
> *'Cause you're sensational.*
> *Making love is quite an art,*
> *What you require is the proper squire to fire your heart*
> *And if you say*
> *That one fine day you'll let me come to call,*
> *We'll have a ball,*
> *'Cause you're sensational,*
> *Sensational,*
> *That's all, that's all, that's all.*

These sophisticated lyrics, set to a glamorous tune, are an indication of the staying power Cole's songs still have.

Despite his sophistication, he had some simple pleasures. "I am in despair about Stella [Dallas] as I have been told," he wrote to Eells in September 1955, "that NBC is cutting out all of its soap operas . . . What does the future hold for me?"

Nonetheless, and as Porter often pointed out, writing hits is a completely unpredictable exercise. Cole himself was astonished when "True Love" took off.

> *I give to you and you give to me*
> *True love, true love.*
> *So on and on it will always be*
> *True love, true love.*
> *For you and I*
> *Have a guardian angel on high*

> *With nothing to do*
> *But to give to you and to give to me*
> *Love forever true.*

"Love forever true" was certainly what Cole sought all his life. He found it with his mother and Linda, but now both had died. "I was married 35 years to a wonderful woman," Cole told the *Chicago Tribune* in 1956, "who believed in me and my work. If it hadn't been for my wife, who died two years ago, and my mother, I would never have had the courage to continue my career through the nine years when I had nothing but flops." He was recalling the years from 1919 to 1928 when no one wanted to give him work because he was not a Tin Pan Alley type and lived far away in Paris. Whatever his preference among the songs in *High Society*, the public embraced "True Love." Max Dreyfus, an early rooter for Cole, wrote that in his sixty-year career "nothing has given me more personal pleasure and gratification than the extraordinary success of your 'True Love.' It is truly a simple, beautiful, tasteful composition worthy of a Franz Schubert." This is surely fulsome rhetoric for a song whose cadence and lyrics are often banal. However, many of Porter's fans felt otherwise. The point was made by several critics that only Cole Porter could have done the *High Society* score. One critic wrote with astonishment at the "infinite ease" with which Porter moved between the world of fashion and glitter and the world of the theatre. The public's admiration for "True Love" was contagious. Even Cole caught it and hired Stanley Musgrove to do publicity work that might result in Cole's being awarded an Oscar for the song.

Although it was not a hit, Porter and Chaplin both thought of "I Love You, Samantha" as their favorite number in the score. John Patrick remembered that one exchange he had with Cole when working on *High Society* concerned rhymes: "[Cole] said to me once, 'The leading lady's name is Samantha; what the hell rhymes with Samantha?' [Patrick] said, 'Lovely as a panther?' He said, 'Get out of my house.' "

> *I love you, Samantha,*
> *And my love will never die.*
> *Remember, Samantha,*
> *I'm a one-gal guy.*
> *Together, Samantha,*
> *We could ride a star and ride it high.*
> *Remember, Samantha,*
> *I'm a one-gal guy*

When Cole was all but finished with the score, the show needed one more number—a comic song for Crosby and Sinatra. Chaplin suddenly came upon a song that Porter used in *DuBarry:* "Well, Did You Evah?" which in most respects worked perfectly in the new film. Both agreed, though, that in a few places new lyrics would be preferable. Cole proposed that Chaplin write the new lyrics and was pleased with what he did. A letter Cole wrote to Chaplin late in 1955 demonstrates the care and musicianship he brought to the writing of his songs. "Please note that the first two measures are legato; the second two measures are staccato and hot; the third two, legato; the fourth two, staccato and hot; continuing until measure fourteen, when all the notes are staccato except for slurs. This should be observed not only instrumentally, but vocally." Nor was he any less attentive to the lyrics. "I am working hard on the double number [A duet entitled "So What?" which was dropped from the final score]," he wrote in fall of 1955, "but find that I have to invent all the nice sayings about women as, throughout history, practically all the quotations about women are anti." He kept near him a list of such quotations as he worked on the score for MGM. "A woman is a treasure hid" . . . "Woman, lovely is thy name" . . . "Woman must be loved by man": these are three of the thirteen axioms he kept in view. Asked in an interview who were the most glamorous women, Cole said, "The Italians are the most beautiful race, I think. The Spanish are high up on the list, but they tend to mature rather early. American women have the best cared for hair in the world. The English are pretty—so pretty that at one time a great number of the Folies-Bergère beauties were English instead of French, which is what *Les Girls,* the new film I'm working on is about. But the French—ah, the French have something."

During his 1955 California stay, Cole entertained in his usual style. Guests remembered his extraordinary graciousness as a host. A party that he gave in the garden at Rockingham consisted of two tables of ten guests each. Tony Curtis was present, and in the course of being shown a Baccarat glass, he dropped and broke it. Cole immediately broke his glass, laughed, and put Curtis totally at ease. Guests repeatedly invited by Porter to his California home that year included the Gary Coopers, Tony Curtis and Janet Leigh, Judy Garland, Frank Sinatra, and Kitty and Moss Hart. Sinatra, who was playing the Sands in Las Vegas, chartered a plane to bring Porter and other friends to a party Sinatra was giving for Lauren Bacall's birthday.

Porter never came to the set of the films that Chaplin worked on. Chaplin found Cole "aloof" rather than "snobbish." Later he came to feel that Porter was in a way just not there because he was so overtaken by pain. In fact the only time Cole was personal with Saul was when Porter was mildly drunk and described the pain from which he suffered. Otherwise he followed the legend embroidered, in French, on a pillow in his apartment: "Don't Explain; Don't Complain."

Cole did not even "complain" when he heard the terrible news of Sturges's sudden death from a heart attack in Paris that autumn—a death whose unexpectedness made it even more of a shock to Cole than Linda's passing or his mother's.

Cole said that making *High Society* was a pleasant experience for him, and Saul Chaplin concurred. In fact the picture earned Chaplin and Cole an Oscar nomination. Porter wrote to him in February 1956 in response to the recordings of the songs performed by the illustrious cast. Cole called the sound track "dreams of beauty, and throughout every number I feel your infinite care . . . even Louis Armstrong's diction is good. I don't see how you did it all."

In 1956, Porter told *Etude* magazine:

> I shall begin work on a new stage show for Feuer and Martin. The plot is based on one of Lubitsch's old Hollywood films, called *The Shop Around the Corner*. Here, the setting is Hungary, which offers me a pleasant novelty. I've never before written Hungarian music, and am studying all I can about it, notably the music of Liszt. He must have been a pretty wonderful person, when you consider his flexibility in turning from the classicism of his master, Czerny, and embracing the utterly new adventures of Berlioz and Wagner. What I shall do after that, I have no idea; but it'll be something interesting—working in music is always interesting!

On December 31, 1955, Cole had written to Irving Lazar about a new show Feuer and Martin wanted him to do. They were casting about for a book, "changing ideas every day about our new show." Lazar wrote about a film to be called *Les Girls,* which Porter was tempted to do so that he could make firm plans before he sailed off late in February on travels that would return him to New York on June 1. He expected to fly to California soon after arriving in America. "What you write about *Les Girls* sounds most interesting, and I do hope you can come up with more detailed news about this."

Others approached Cole about various projects. One company wanted Porter to record some of his songs, but he turned down this offer, his secretary saying that he "does not want to play and sing any of his songs, he says he 'does it too badly'." Bella Spewack wrote to see if they could collaborate again, but Cole replied, "I don't feel like working at the present moment on a show, but maybe later we could get together." He was pleased with the news that Yale was considering plans to confer on him an honorary degree. In preparation for that, Cole's attorney sent Dean Acheson a four-page biography (apparently Acheson was to write the citation) and suggested Alex Steinert write a brief statement about his music. Cole viewed all of this with his customary irony: "It all sounds a little bit cold-blooded."

On the Fourth of July 1955, Cole had seen Jean Howard at a party the actor Joseph Cotten hosted. Naturally they talked about their recent travels, and Cole suddenly said, "Let's do it again!" She replied, "Why not?" Marti Stevens was Jean's choice for a lively traveling partner, and Robert Bray was Cole's.

This journey began late in February of 1956. Starting out in Switzerland, the party flew in Niarchos's DC-3 to Madrid, where Cole noted in his handwritten travel diary (now domiciled at Yale) that spring had come to Iberia. In the cathedral in Seville, a concert of sacred and regional songs was presented by a choir of boys aged seven to fourteen in Cole's honor. "Expert singing & touching experience," noted Cole.

From Rome he wrote to George Eells: "Richard news is always interesting news to me. Oh how, oh how, can his life be saved? Why, instead of a second-hand Cadillac doesn't he buy a first-hand bicycle?" He complained of endless luncheons, dinners, and balls given by friends "who still think that the only song I ever wrote was 'Night & Day'!" Cole also complained about a letter from Bobbie Raison: "What a snob." He and his wife had moved to North Hollywood, where they were surrounded by peasants—far niftier in his final outlook than Cole in Brentwood with middle-class neighbors. The following day Cole wrote a jokey letter to Richard, urging him to discard the fading Cadillac and purchase a Vespa. "If you still have a complex about writing the English language, dictate to one of George's secretaries. Glad to leave Rome. My Italian masseur is much too violent."

For the most part this choice quartet worked magically well. But once, in Naples, Marti Stevens was late by ten minutes for a meeting with the others. Cole flew into a rage, pounding his cane on the floor and shouting at her: "You're *always* late . . . you destroy any trip!" No one, said Jean, appeared late for the remainder of the journey. Later that year Cole told an interviewer that "women who are late irritate me, and I'm also annoyed by the ones who are continually forgetting their gloves in theatres and restaurants."

Some of Cole's travels were strenuous. Journeying to Petra, the party had no alternative but to take to horseback, and Cole gamely mounted a mare whose colt ran alongside her. "It was an unforgettable sight to see Cole," wrote Jean Howard, "constantly poking with his cane, which he carried with him always, this little colt to keep him from coming too close to his leg."

Whether out of sadness at this trip coming to an end or what, Cole never bade Jean goodbye. Instead he left a note at their hotel for "Dear Jean": "Robert has to stand-by in Rome to find out when he must hit Hollywood & I'm going along for the ride. So goodbye, have fun & my love to you both."

Cole returned to New York in early June and then flew to Los Angeles, where he set about composing the score for *Les Girls*.

Cole's social schedule for the summer of 1956, when he turned sixty-five, was formidable. Every week he hosted one or two dinners for ten to twelve guests and one or more smaller dinners—three, four, or five guests—with more intimate friends. Then two dinners, usually, with Bob Bray alone. And perhaps two nights out. Cole's valet kept a list of the guests for the summers of 1956 and 1957 and the dates they visited. Bray tops the list with thirty-eight visits. Robert Raison paid thirty visits; Stanley Musgrove, twenty-three; George Eells, fourteen. Among the other guests were Fred Astaire (seven); George Cukor (five); Claudette Colbert and her husband (five); and Clifton Webb (seven). Single visits were paid by Frank Sinatra, Zsa Zsa Gabor, Noël Coward, Orson Welles, and many others.

Les Girls starred Gene Kelly, Mitzi Gaynor, Taina Elg, and Kay Kendall. Saul Chaplin, again the associate producer, found Cole frailer and usually needing two canes. "I was alarmed at how little he ate," said Chaplin. "He just picked at the minuscule portions that were set before him. Often it seemed he was just there to keep me company." He found Cole as witty as ever, however, eager to hear studio gossip and Chaplin's take on the musical theatre, which Cole attended less frequently than in the past.

Les Girls was directed by Cole's old friend George Cukor, with a screenplay by John Patrick. Among the successful numbers Cole wrote for it were "Ça, C'est l'Amour":

> *When suddenly you sight*
> *Someone for whom you yearn,*
> *Ça, c'est l'amour.*
> *And when to your delight*

> *She loves you in return,*
> *Ça, c'est l'amour.*

John Patrick and Porter never discussed the musical score; the songs were composed and slotted into place after the script was finished. *Les Girls* had considerable success and was praised by popular audiences and even by such a highbrow director as François Truffaut. Nonetheless, Porter wrote in 1957: "My job on *Les Girls* was hopelessly mangled, what with their cutting three numbers I wrote and then barely saving the ones which were left in the score. The fact is, they didn't need any music at all except the song to show the three girls doing their vaudeville act, so I was really lucky to get the job and I enjoyed the work."

Chapter 21

He Kept On Living

In January of 1957, Cole was hospitalized and underwent a partial gastrectomy. Following his hospitalization, he spent some time recuperating at the Montego Bay estate of the William Paleys. In the spring Cole toyed with a proposal that he write the score for a musical to be made of the film *All About Eve*. But finally he opted for a collaboration with S. J. Perelman on a production of the story of Aladdin's lamp. "Perelman is coming out here in about ten days," he wrote in July from California to his attorney, "with an outline, after which I could make up my mind. If I like the outline and decide to do it it does not mean a rush job and will be just the amount of work that I feel up to at the moment."

Richard Lewine, the producer, had overseen the television production of *Cinderella* with songs by Rodgers and Hammerstein, which recently had been a huge success, and he subsequently approached "Swifty" Lazar, Cole's agent, with the proposal that Porter compose a score for a musical version of the Aladdin tale. Perelman was Lewine's choice to do the book. But from the start they faced a structural problem: unlike *Cinderella*, *Aladdin* had no real story line, and so Perelman had to link a series of separate stories and make a whole cloth out of pieces. Nine months before the show was televised, Perelman and Lewine went to the coast and spent several days discussing ideas and casting with Porter. They found that he was "prompt, honored every promise—a delight to work with."

Throughout the summer Cole toiled over the *Aladdin* score and took pleasure in the success of the film of *Silk Stockings,* which was released in July. (In November *Les Girls* had its premiere.)

Of the several good numbers in *Aladdin,* one was a list that Porter compiled in late 1957 with some of his old élan. Cyril Ritchard sang it in the original, and Barbra Streisand later made a hit recording of it.

> *If you want to buy a kite*
> *Or a pup to keep you up at night*
> *Or a dwarf who used to know Snow White*
> *Or a frog who loves to sing,*
> *Come to the supermarket in old Peking.*

Here and there the lyrics have a touch of Porter sass: "Or in case you care to meet a maid / For a nice but naughty fling . . ."

This must be among the best-researched songs ever to have been composed. Lengthy notes in Porter's hand are visible on the manuscript regarding markets, gambling, and typical women's names in Peking. In August Lewine wrote to Porter, "I have sent the Osbert Sitwell book, *Escape With Me . . .* Only the second half of the book deals with Peking, but this half contains a lot of useful information about the market place . . . I will shortly be sending you further information as promised. This will include a description of the then known world for use in the Emperor's song; a list of the stars for the Astrologer; and as much detail as we can get about life at the Palace . . . The city, Peking, was called by this name, but [only] from 1421 onward." Further scholarship about Peking was sent by Lewine along with a list of one hundred or so items to be purchased at the Peking market. Porter's passion for accuracy persisted. He asked Lewine to take "Come to the Supermarket in Old Peking" to Dr. Sirmay and to play it for him, emphasizing the third beat in the left hand. "If he does not pay attention to this rhythmic detail, it will lay an old Chinese egg."

The moods of the songs vacillate between optimism and admonition. "Trust Your Destiny to Your Star":

> *When for someone's lips you have yearned and yearned*
> *But you live without hope so far,*
> *You will soon discover your love is returned*
> *If you trust,*
> *And you must*
> *Trust your destiny to your star.*

When Porter played this for Lewine, Cole commented, "Sounds like Noël, doesn't it?" (This marked a momentary return to the keyboard. Lewine, a trained pianist, thought Cole played accurately: "no flash—not much interest in playing—very literal at the piano.") In "Opportunity Knocks But Once" we are warned: "When for happiness someone hunts/Opportunity knocks but once—at thuh door."

On February 21, 1958, *Aladdin* was televised on CBS: ninety minutes of live TV featuring a cast of sixty (including an elephant) and an orchestra of thirty-five. The show's team boasted many gifted artists. Irene Sharaff did the costumes; Robert Russell Bennett, the orchestrations. Alex Steinert was the copyist. Cyril Ritchard and Dennis King starred, and the cast featured nineteen-year-old Sal Mineo, Anna Maria Alberghetti (who, after hours of skin-stretching, slanted her eyes and got the part), and Basil Rathbone. Nonetheless, the telecast was a failure. Lewine thought, looking back, that the casting was poor. CBS had pressed the producer to get famous players, but not all of them were successful. Ritchard and Mineo were fine, Lewine thinks, but others were less so. An attempt to engage Peter Lorre failed. Basil Rathbone, playing the Emperor, couldn't sing, but he was given the song "Wouldn't It Be Fun?" Porter never had a negative thing to say.

"Aladdin was saddnin" wrote the *New York Times* reviewer, paraphrasing one of Porter's lyrics, "a pretentious ordeal." He found that Porter was "uninspired. His score seldom was related to the narrative, and his individual numbers seemed inserted haphazardly . . . melodically the ear was seldom entranced."

Richard Lewine noticed how much more of a recluse Porter had become. Friends did their best to cheer him up. Right after the TV performance, Lazar wired him that "*Aladdin* was an absolute delight start to finish . . . A La La Palooza." Lewine sent word to Cole that the score was the best that ever had been written for a television show. He wired Porter with "warmest regards" and urged him to relax and not worry about the TV show: "Everything well in hand." But there were others, less generous, who felt the work was "a $50,000 flop" and that Porter was nearing the end of his career "on a sour note in a totally new medium."

On January 14, 1958, one month before *Aladdin* was shown, Porter had entered Columbia Presbyterian Hospital for further treatment of osteomyelitis. A physician attendant on him recalled him as "a very elegant, sweet man . . . quiet, meticulous . . . very polite to the nurses." His room at the Harkness Pavilion was filled with gifts and flowers. Many distinguished theatre friends visited him.

In February, although hospitalized, Porter hoped, as he had for so long, that medical science would soon find a cure for osteomyelitis and he would be all right. On February 27, Madeline Smith wrote Gerald Murphy that though Porter had been at Harkness for six weeks, he was responding to a new drug. It seemed effective "in lowering the leg pain and raising his spirits so we look forward to his home-coming before long." Alan Jay Lerner visited Porter at the time. As he reached the ninth floor, he was met by Cole's butler, who took him to a suite at the end of the corridor. Cole was in a corner with a cocktail shaker, cold hors d'oeuvres, and a small dish of fudge. The butler, in an adjoining room, concocted hot hors d'oeuvres, which he served. Lerner was quite astonished by this hospitality.

In April Cole's right leg was amputated mid-thigh. "I'm only half a man now," was his response to this loss, which for two decades he had been dreading. On the day of the operation Madeline Smith wrote to Louise Bearss:

> I was going to send you a "Happy Easter" card, but we don't feel the happiest this morning. I must tell you the latest development before the papers do:
>
> Another operation was scheduled early this morning for "The Little Boss" [as Sylvain and Smith affectionately referred to Cole when talking to each other], and they removed the right leg. It has given him so much pain and has refused to heal in all these many weeks, that the best medical men of the day came to this necessary decision—and they assure him that he will not be losing a leg so much as losing a baffling disease, and will be the better for it. He is assured his troubles will be over shortly, and he will be out of the hospital, back to normal, and into action again.
>
> We can't help feeling wretched about this—but we mustn't . . . Fortunately Mr. P. was reconciled to it, which was a great relief to all the rest of us.

"Osteomyelitis made the operation necessary," said the surgeon. "A bone disease brought on when Porter fell from a horse." He was fitted for a prosthesis and eventually put through rigorous exercise routines, all of which he dutifully did, but with an undercurrent of hopelessness.

Immediately after the surgery, only Paul Sylvain was permitted to visit Porter. His faithful valet was more and more indispensable to him, which made it an even greater blow when Paul himself entered the hospital a few months after Cole was discharged, for removal of a malignant tumor.

Noël Coward wrote of a visit to Cole:

> He has at last had his leg amputated and the lines of ceaseless pains have been wiped from his face. He is a bit fretful about having to manage his new leg but he will get over that. I think if I had to endure all these years of agony I would have had the damned thing off at the beginning, but it is a cruel decision to have to make and involves much sex vanity and many fears of being repellant. However, it is now done at last and I am convinced that his whole life will cheer up and that his work will profit accordingly.

"He was terribly uninterested," wrote Diana Vreeland. "He just couldn't get up the old interest to do anything . . . and then he stopped *speaking* . . . But he kept on living. He couldn't bear not being with people. He'd ask one or two of his friends up to see him for lunch or dinner in his beautiful apartment at the Waldorf. He had a lot of things offered to him. People would send him books they wanted turned into a play, or [they would] suggest something for him to do, but it all fell on infertile ground, because he never could do anything at all." Madeline Smith more and more piloted Cole's life.

Aladdin was Cole's only effort in television. As Smith said, "That was the very, very last thing he ever wrote, bar none. After . . . having his leg amputated in 1958, why, he never wrote another note." Nor did he read, although earlier in his life he'd been a voluminous reader, "read all the magazines, newspapers, and popular fiction" according to Smith. "He was just depressed." So she asked Porter if he'd like to be read to, and he said yes. This was a relief to her, as when they lunched together he rarely spoke. "It was rather a trial because he didn't put forth any effort in anyway." A book that he liked was *Aku-Aku,* about Easter Island. But as she read *Gone With the Wind* to Cole, she felt he lost interest in it. In her recollection Porter was never much of a conversationalist. Nor was he in a mood to speak on the telephone. He never answered the phone himself. Madeline Smith knew which people he would speak to, and "they were few." Katie and Linda had been correct in staving off the amputation, at least in their belief that the blow to Cole's psyche and *amour-propre* would finally be fatal. The last song Porter wrote, "Wouldn't It Be Fun," conveys his barely disguised desolation.

> *Wouldn't it be fun not to be known as an important V.I.P.*
> *Wouldn't it be fun to be nearly anyone*
> *Except me, mighty me!*

Ethel Merman dined with Cole from time to time when he was in New York. "It was sad seeing him so depressed, knowing in your heart that he no longer wanted to live." But even then the wit still occasionally surfaced. When Merman inquired about a mutual friend and how she looked, Cole replied, "She looked divine—except her pearls were too long." Richard Lewine recalled that he once asked Cole why he was going on a cruise. He replied, "It's my way of canceling February."

Henry Burke, Cole's new valet, made a detailed account of Cole's daily routine. Porter regularly rose at 11:00 a.m. His first act was to apply witch hazel to the skin around his eyes; he believed that it kept his skin youthful. He attended to some of his urinary needs and then was wheeled to the bathroom to wash and brush his teeth. (It seemed an ominous sign when in the last year of his life he neglected this ritual.) He had to be lifted onto a chair in the shower, washed, and then dried and dressed in a white cotton bathrobe before he did exercises and the masseur arrived. In Brentwood these activities took place alongside the pool. Richard, the masseur in New York, conducted his activities privately in Cole's bedroom. Porter's staff suspected that the sessions were in part sexual, especially when, besides a yearly salary, Cole continued to reward the man lavishly with gifts of money and even an automobile. Observers reported that when the masseur canceled his appointment, Cole would become noticeably more depressed. Colin Fox referred to Richard as "the outrageous masseur who catered to all sexual tastes." The masseur was followed by a barber, who daily trimmed and colored Cole's hair, then turned on a tanning machine. Burke recalled that in California the barber attended to Cole before dinner, and at midday Cole sunned himself around his pool. At lunch he drank Scotch, until Burke persuaded him to switch to gin or vodka so that Burke could disguise and diminish the quantity of liquor by adding extra tonic or tomato juice.

From 3:00 until 4:30 p.m. Cole napped in his room. Then his prosthesis was put in place and he would be dressed for a journey to the Institute for the Crippled and Disabled in New York and a program of physical therapy. His valet noted that Cole did very little exercising, preferring instead to chat up the staff as he smoked cigarettes. At 6:00 p.m. he was back home, where he read the evening papers, drank, and fed Pepi. At 7:00 p.m. Cole's assistant transported him to his room, his artificial limb was removed, and he rested until 8:00 p.m., when the leg was reattached and he was dressed, carnation and all, for dinner. He received his guests while reclining on a couch. In New York the food was prepared by the Waldorf-Astoria kitchen and the wines carefully chosen. Cole toyed with his food but drank wine steadily. Burke recalled that this sometimes led to distressing moments when the guests at the dinner table were asked to absent themselves briefly while Cole urinated. Of course there were embarrassing accidents; the consequent humiliation must have been a torment for someone as fastidious as Cole.

When the guests departed at midnight or so, Cole would watch television films and drink until 3:00 or 4:00 a.m. And so to bed. He had problems sleeping and regularly was given a single sleeping pill. When he asked for two, Burke would not oblige. Once, in a bizarre charade which Burke recounted to one of Porter's biographers, neither Cole nor Madeline Smith could find anyone to spend the weekend at Buxton Hill, so he designated Burke to be both servant and guest. Decorum had yielded to desperation.

> On the way to Williamstown Burke sat in the back of the car with Cole instead of sitting up front, as he normally would, with the chauffeur and Cole's dog, Pepi . . . Once at Williamstown Burke assumed the uneasy dual roles of employee and guest. Consequently, he would alternate between serving Cole his meals as an employee and then joining him at the dining table as his guest.

Friends invited to dinner in New York and weekends in the country regretted the invitations for many reasons. Cole's taciturnity was probably the most discouraging feature. And his ritualism became disturbingly rigid. Jack Coble and Michael Pearman are two of many who were frequently enlisted by Madeline Smith and who complained about Cole's compulsiveness. Coble remembers that Porter had an excellent cook in Williamstown but would not allow her any latitude in choosing the menu. This was all the odder in that Cole ate virtually nothing, and as a consequence his weight dropped to eighty pounds. Jean Howard thought Cole was enacting "the slowest suicide" she could imagine. According to Saint Subber, three or four years before he did die, Cole had repeatedly told him, "I want to die." "Won't you miss your other friends?" Saint asked Cole, although what he really wanted to say was, "Won't you miss me?" "Isn't there something you'd miss?" Saint persisted. "The last thing [Cole] said to me that day, after a thirty-second pause, was, 'Yes—my Queen Anne chairs.' "

Coble and George Eells, among others, recall that weekend after weekend the menu never varied. Cole greeted his guest at 12:15 p.m. and then boarded his automobile for the journey to Williamstown. Cole's Cadillac, his chauffeur at the wheel, was followed by a station wagon driven by a valet, which contained items that Porter considered indispensable for a comfortable weekend. The foulest weather failed to deter him. Coble remembers leaving the Waldorf in a blizzard that eventually found the cars in foot-deep snow on the Taconic Parkway. Unluckily, a tire went flat and had to be replaced in the driving storm. Cole remained unruffled.

When the car left the parkway, Cole always stopped at a diner, where he would sit and sample some of the food. "Hello, Mr. Porter," the locals would chorus. "Hello, boys," Cole would reply. Driving was always part of the weekend program. Each afternoon he would leave the house at 4:15 p.m. and drive on different roads through the Berkshires. Often his chauffeur or guests would point out that on autumn and winter days, darkness would obscure the views. But Cole kept to his schedule, sourly announcing that he loathed views.

Sometime after the amputation, Cole and George Eells went off to Williamstown. Cole slept poorly and repeatedly summoned his butler in the night. Next evening at dinner Cole and George dressed informally. Cole ate only one string bean and a quarter-inch piece of steak. When they finished, Cole rang for his butler, who reappeared with the serving dishes. Thinking the man must be exhausted with so little sleep, George said to him as he re-entered the room, "Thank you . . . but I won't have any more." When he exited, Cole turned on George: "Don't you ever do that again. Wait until he gets on your left side to tell him you don't want any more." George protested that the butler was tired. Cole replied, "No, servants prefer the ritual. They're the biggest snobs there are." George said, "I don't think Munden (the butler) likes it." Cole looked at George and said, "I wouldn't want to be a guest in any house you ran. The servants would soon be sticking their heads around the door saying 'You want a little more pie?' " Cole's wit endured.

Eells remembered that Cole departed for New York City at exactly 10:45 on Monday morning. Once, when everyone—Cole included—was ready to leave, a new servant naively asked at 10:30 if they should begin the journey. "What time is it?" Cole inquired. "Ten-thirty, sir." "Departure is set for ten-forty-five," said Cole. And so the staff and the guest lingered for fifteen minutes more.

Paul Sylvain died on July 21, 1959, an incalculable loss for Cole—he had been Cole's valet for twenty-two years. A few days later, Cole flew off to California, refusing an offer contrived by Bella Spewack to set the successful play *Tovarich* to music. In July Cole wrote to tell Robert Montgomery: "I should think it would be a good idea to have a one-shot television show covering my life as a composer but of course I could not be present."

Testimonials of various kinds were devised in Cole's honor in the last years of his life, even though he took little if any part in them. One project he did approve was *The Cole Porter Song Book* (a collection of Porter's songs arranged for solo voice and piano), for which Moss Hart had agreed to write an introduction at Cole's request. "I was surprised, flattered, and deeply pleased . . . that you had chosen me," wrote Moss to Cole. "I am unfitted, of course, to write a definitive piece on your musicianship, but perhaps I can catch a glimpse of the complex, perverse, and immensely arresting human being behind the music. It will be written, you may be sure, with admiration and affection." To read Hart's tribute to Cole is both a melancholic experience and an enlivening one. Hart was extremely successful in conveying the wit and the ardor of Cole's music as well as the glitter of his social life. Cole was pleased by what Moss had written and told him, "I couldn't like it more, although I find it perhaps too flattering."

In the early 1960s Cole phoned the Liberty Music shop on Madison Avenue requesting the services of someone to repair his phonograph. The young repairman, a resident of Queens called Walter Galeska, was touched and amused by Porter, who subsequently loosened tubes in the machine before telephoning Galeska and requesting him to make another professional visit. The impresario Ben Bagley, who lived near Galeska, remembers how jealous Porter was when Bagley mentioned Mrs. Galeska and her beauty. "Goodbye," Cole said to Bagley, "and say hello to the ugly Mrs. Galeska." It is doubtful that Cole was very active sexually by that time. Nonetheless, a friend speaks of Cole's being "desperate" for sexual partners in these later years. Four men with whom Cole had sex during this time threatened to blackmail him, but each was satisfied with a payment of five hundred dollars, and none of them returned to demand further payment.

On May 15, 1960, a "Salute to Cole Porter" took place at the Metropolitan Opera House, produced for the benefit of the Children's Asthma Research Institute by Jule Styne. Cole was unable to attend, but he told the press, "I have no plans at all at this time for writing movies or lyrics . . . and I have not played the piano for a long time." He was gratified by the tribute and pleased that Lilo, Beatrice Lillie, Billy Gaxton, Lisa Kirk, George Gaynes, and others sang his songs. For the finale, twelve composers gathered onstage, among them Harold Arlen, Vernon Duke, Burton Lane, Eubie Blake, Frederick Loewe, Harold Rome, Harry Warren, and Leroy Anderson. Richard Rodgers, conducting from the pit, led off with "Begin the Beguine." Each of the other composers then played one of his own best-known songs as a tribute. When asked why he chose "I'm in Love with a Wonderful Guy," Rodgers replied, "Because that's the way I feel about Cole." At a supper in Sherry's after the gala, Elsa Maxwell and Bricktop entertained.

On June 9, his sixty-ninth birthday, "a scaled-down academic delegation from Yale called upon Cole Porter in his library and awarded him the honorary degree of Doctor of Humane Letters." The provost, Norman S. Buck, a classmate of Cole's, in academic robes himself, decorated the academic gown in which Cole was attired with a blue velvet hood and read the citation:

> As an undergraduate, you first won acclaim for writing the words and music of two of Yale's perennial football songs. Since then, you have achieved reputation as a towering figure in the American musical theatre. Master of the deft phrase, the delectable rhymes, the distinctive melody, you are, in your own words and your own field, the top.
>
> Confident that your graceful, impudent, inimicable songs will be played and sung as long as footlights burn and curtains go up, your Alma Mater confers upon you the degree of Doctor of Humane Letters.

The conferral of an honorary degree in a private ceremony was unprecedented at Yale. It had been delayed by two board members who disapproved of Porter's lifestyle. Shortly after the ceremony Cole flew off to California.

Cole continued to give dinner parties. Janet Leigh and Tony Curtis were often invited. They revered Cole because their marriage was taken lightly by the press, but Cole, according to Curtis, "was one of the first who was kind to us and didn't kid us about the publicity, which speaks for his character."

As time passed, Porter became more taciturn. Anita Colby often went to dinner at the Waldorf in those years. She was aware that fewer and fewer people cared to do so because Porter was often deeply depressed and uncommunicative. Nonetheless, the carefully kept calendar of guests, the food and wines they were served, the porcelain on which the food appeared, points to what some might call an excess of entertaining. Seldom were there more than one or two guests at these dinners in the early 1960s, which often put the burden of initiating and sustaining conversation on Cole's dinner partner, as he was so laconic. Guests covered a broad range: one night the Duke of Verdura; another, Billy Baldwin and Kenneth Lane.

Sara and Gerald Murphy also kept in touch with Cole and sometimes dined with him. "It was a joy to see you both," he wrote to them. Moss Hart wrote touchingly to "dearest Cole" after Hart himself had been hospitalized in 1961 with a heart attack. "For some reason or other I am always quite shy in your presence, and I can never say quite what is in my heart. But on paper, at least, I can tell you how much I have admired the battle you have waged, and how gallantly you have fought it." Joshua Logan and his wife, Nedda, recall being invited by Cole to lunch "without any warning . . . and there was no one else there. Just the two of us. And almost immediately lunch was served, and the waiter put us in our seats. And Nedda and I talked and Cole never opened his mouth . . . We tried to be as funny and happy as possible. It was a very depressing thing to see, this marvelous looking man."

In November of 1960 Cole was again admitted to Columbia Presbyterian Hospital, and he remained there until July 4, 1961, "with chronic pneumonitis, emaciation, too much alcohol and a state of exhaustion and malnutrition which made the prognosis seem utterly bad." However, wrote a hospital official, "with nursing and constant care, he recovered, much to our surprise and we sent him home." He returned to the Waldorf, stayed only two nights, then flew to California, where he went afternoons to the UCLA walking clinic.

In 1961 Bella Spewack wrote to the American ambassador in Vienna saying she thought it terribly important that *Kiss Me, Kate* be staged in that city for a period including June 3 and 4, when President Kennedy and Nikita Khrushchev would be meeting there. "Something should be done at this time to further the cause of the West." She cited the countries in which *Kate* had played—Germany, Yugoslavia, Italy, Switzerland, Norway, Sweden, Denmark, Iceland, Israel, Mexico, Spain, Japan—all productions in the language of the country. "*Kate*," she wrote, "is the outstanding cultural export of the United States to the rest of the world. The musical is what we do best." But nothing seems to have come of her effort.

On his birthday in 1962—hailed as his seventieth but actually his seventy-first—a celebratory party took place at the Orpheum Theatre in New York, where a revival of *Anything Goes* was playing. But Porter remained in Williamstown. Elsa Maxwell was the *compère,* attired in a paneled, brocaded, and beaded evening gown. The celebration, she said, was just what Cole needed to dislodge his depression. "I'm the only one who sees him regularly, you know. He's been so depressed . . . and tires easily. But this will pull him out of it." The Murphys sent Cole flowers: "The beautiful peonies, together with the three red roses (so exquisite) are decorating my apartment, and I thank you both so much . . . Lots of love, Cole."

Depressed or not, Cole flew off to California on the fifteenth of June. Sometime during his stay there, he learned that Robert Bray was planning to leave his wife and children. He returned to New York in October and on November 28, 1962, Cole wrote Bray out of his will and bequeathed the half of his royalties (a sum larger than the estates many top composers realize, owing to Porter's authorship of lyrics as well as music), originally left Bray to Ray Kelly and his family. Porter valued loyalty and disapproved of Bray's decision to leave his family. On the other hand, he admired Kelly's fidelity over the years both to his family and to him. Since Kelly's death in 1992, his four children have become the recipients of Porter's bequest.

In January 1963 Robert Raison brought to dinner at Cole's Waldorf apartment a very handsome young man, John Cronin, with whom Cole soon fell in love. Cronin always insisted that he was not Porter's lover, although many said he was. In fact Cronin and Cole had met earlier, in 1962, but this visit was Cronin's first view of Cole's apartment. Cronin, the adopted son of a physician after whom a building at St. Vincent's Hospital in New York is named, and whose parents were a papal count and countess, was twenty-nine at the time. He had two ambitions. The first was to act in the theatre. As "Joe" Cronin, he had played the grown-up Patrick in a road company of *Auntie Mame,* and toured in *Bye-Bye Birdie* and *Wish You Were Here.* Raison functioned as Cronin's agent. Under contract to MGM, Cronin played in a number of films, including *Please Don't Eat the Daisies.* His credits also included television, where he often appeared on *The Perry Mason Show.* Cronin came to New York from California to play in a Broadway musical; but when the producers couldn't come up with the money, his reaction was to give up his ambitions for the theater and films, although a friend revealed, "He never quite got it out of his system." (The same was true with religion. Although in later life he was not a practicing Catholic, he always went to church when he was troubled, according to his companion.) When Raison brought Cronin to meet Porter, he must at least have known how pleased Cole would be. Subsequently Cronin dined weekly with Porter when both were in New York, and they talked by telephone every day. They had in common both the theater and their interest in art and antiques.

Cronin's second ambition was to work as a decorator. After a year at Fordham University, he attended the Parsons School of Design and eventually became a partner in a decorating and antiques business. Porter acknowledged Cronin's taste and his perhaps paternal affection for this handsome friend by bequeathing him the celebrated bookshelves that Billy Baldwin and Freddy Victoria had designed and executed. In addition, Cole left Cronin forty-two other items, which included furnishings, rock crystals, glass candlesticks, and outsize eighteenth-century glass rosary beads. Cronin called these "worry beads," and it seems established that they had belonged to Marie Antoinette. The eighteenth-century kidney-shaped tables which Anita Colby so admired were also given to Cronin. Many of the fine furnishings Linda acquired for the rue Monsieur house were part of the inheritance. Cronin thought it was his love for art that principally moti-vated Cole to bequeath him these treasures. Cronin had been apprised by Cole's lawyers in February 1964, months before he died, of Cole's instruc-tions "to send you directly from this office $250 a month, beginning with the month after his death . . . as long as you live. He has also made arrange-ments for you to receive . . . the bulk of his tangible personal belongings (i.e., furnishings, books, pictures, etc.; but not including his automobiles)." After two close relatives chose what personal possessions they wanted, John Cronin received the remainder. One late change Cole made in his will also concerned Cronin. A friend who was to have been given Porter's Swiss wristwatch received instead a statuette and Cronin was bequeathed the watch.

Cole certainly admired the vivacity, handsome looks, and charming personality of Cronin. Some of Cole's friends grew bored by his uninter-rupted praise of the young man. But virtually everyone agreed that Cronin was "a good boy who loved Cole deeply." John Cronin died in 1987 at age fifty-four. In his last years he became an alcoholic, and at age fifty he suf-

John Cronin in his late twenties

fered a heart attack. Then he developed throat cancer. According to his companion, he died of a massive stroke.

In May 1963 Monty Woolley died. Cole disapproved of Monty's having taken a black manservant as his lover and saw little of him in these late years. Once Ray Kelly was visiting Cole in Williamstown and Monty drove over from Saratoga. A snowstorm commenced and Monty asked Cole if he might spend the night, but Cole firmly refused.

From April into August 1963, Cole was again a patient in Harkness Pavilion in New York. He had been badly burned in Williamstown when he set his bedclothes afire while smoking. A negligent replacement for Henry Burke, who had gone on holiday to England, left his post at Cole's bed, which he'd been warned against doing while Porter smoked. He also mistakenly substituted Demerol for the sleeping pill that had been prescribed for Cole. Then, as the fire flared, the man fled in a panic to find Cole's chauffeur, who rushed over and extinguished the flames. Cole was transported by ambulance from Williamstown to Columbia Presbyterian Hospital, where medical records describe him as having suffered "2nd and probably some 3rd degree burns . . . His nutritional status is borderline at best."

In the days that followed he continued to be confused and incontinent, ate virtually nothing, and (over and over again the record reports) smoked incessantly. In May Cole suffered from severe headaches. In July he requested an air mattress but refused an air conditioner. He was being treated with many medications, including codeine, Demerol, atropine, and barbiturates. Dr. Dana W. Atchley, his physician, for whom a building at Columbia Presbyterian is now named, prolonged Cole's stay in the hospital, partly to allow for the skin graftings that were required. In late June he was "depressed, refuses all food." He cried out loudly in his sleep, complained of pain—some of it phantom pain. When calmer, he watched TV, often with Burke, who attended him in addition to the nurses. Richard Rodgers wrote to Cole on August 1, "Do you think you would like to see Dorothy and me? . . . We're available and would love to come." Porter replied, "I would like very much to see you, and hope to do so a bit later on when I will be feeling better."

Despite a bad night on August 2, during which he was confused, he was finally discharged on August 6. Cole and those around him were able to keep this latest hospitalization out of the newspapers. Upon his discharge he flew almost immediately to California. "When all is said and done," Dr. Atchley wrote to the California colleague who would be looking after Cole's health, "the saddest thing about him is his complete unwillingness to live and his deep depression, which is not too surprising in one sense. For a person of his fastidiousness to be bedeviled with amputations and incontinence and all of the unpleasantness of burns is almost too much to bear." Dr. Atchley expressed his hope that "you can take over this tough problem for he is a man who has made a great contribution to our musical world and is fundamentally a fine person, in spite of his present state."

For a time Cole reduced his alcohol intake, and he appeared brighter, even contemplating fashioning a show about Catherine the Great as a vehicle for Merman. Shortly, though, she became engaged and announced she was going to quit the stage, and Cole immediately abandoned the project. By August 17 he wrote to his cousin, James O. Cole, "I am spending most of each day by the pool and the progress is remarkable." And a few days later, "I feel better and hope never to go back to that dreadful hospital in New York." It may have been days like these that led Robert Raison to say that Cole had a great last summer in Hollywood, with film stars such as Rock Hudson among his visitors.

Friends who saw Cole in the winter of 1963–64 found him improved, but by spring he seemed again to be in decline. For his seventy-third birthday, on June 9, 1964, Cole invited only George Eells to dinner. Eells was shocked by Cole's appearance: disheveled, in a way Eells had never seen him, without his artificial leg, and wearing a dressing gown. He made little or no response to his guest's conversation. "Initially I assumed he was suffering from birthday blues, but gradually I realized that his body was periodically wracked by hiccoughs." That morning he had fallen off his chair and onto the stone bathroom floor and bruised the stump of his leg. On his way to the table, as Eells averted his eyes, Cole screamed with anguish, then apologized. He ate virtually nothing, then took a codeine pill and fell asleep.

Three days later Cole was back in Harkness Pavilion with a hip fracture, a bladder infection, and malnutrition. He was forbidden alcohol but managed to cadge cigarettes from visitors: "It's all I have left." He stayed in the hospital for ten days, and on the Fourth of July he flew to California. For a time he was cheerier, but then the phantom leg pain returned with greater intensity, and he had to be hospitalized at St. John's in Santa Monica for a bowel obstruction thought not to be dangerous. Vivien Leigh, Merle Oberon, George Cukor, and Julie Andrews were among the dinner invitees whom Cole asked Raison to reschedule without apprising them of the fact he was hospitalized. Bobbie Raison, the only person who knew of Cole's whereabouts, visited him daily. He entered into an exchange on the first day between Porter and a member of the staff who was filling out an admittance form: "Put down none," Cole said when asked about his religion. "Protestant?" asked the clerk. "Put down—none," Cole reiterated. Raison reminded Cole that he had been a Baptist: "Why not put down 'Protestant'?" But Cole was adamant. In 1946 or 1947, according to Sam Stark (himself a convert from Judaism to Catholicism), Cole had begun to take instruction in Catholicism, but he never finished. Stark discussed Cole's interest with Linda, who said she once had contemplated a conversion to Catholicism when it seemed likely that she would wed the Duke of Alba; but she lost interest when the marriage did not come about. Bearss Muhlfeld had heard that Porter was preparing in the 1940s to embrace Catholicism. He presumed that Cole needed the spiritual support a religion would offer.

Within a few days Cole's condition deteriorated. He developed pneumonia, lost the little appetite he'd had; a bladder infection flared up, and his whole body trembled. A kidney stone lodged in his ureter, threatening him with uremic poisoning and almost certain death. Surgery was decided on, and the medical opinion predicted a successful outcome. On October 13 the operation was performed, and Cole survived with no ill consequences except that the trembling returned. Perhaps realizing that death was near, he had told Raison before the surgery to rush to Rockingham and remove pornographic photos he had. Raison also took Cole's guest book with its schedule of dinner guests and menus.

Elsie Woodward, Cole's friend and neighbor in the Waldorf Towers, insisted to Gore Vidal that Cole had suffered delirium tremens and that deprivation of alcohol finally brought about his death. She claimed that Porter's regular physician was on vacation when the surgery took place. Afterwards the surgeon told Porter's physician that he ought to have told him that Cole was suffering from Parkinson's disease. Cole's doctor was astonished and asked the surgeon what he meant. He replied that he presumed from the shaking of Cole's body that he suffered from Parkinson's disease. "But didn't you know that Porter was an alcoholic?" asked Cole's doctor. In fact, maintained Woodward, Porter was suffering from delirium tremens, and had a doctor introduced a small quantity of alcohol into his body, he probably would have recovered from the surgery.

His heart stopped beating on the night of October 15, 1964. With Cole at the time of his death were Stanley Musgrove, his two valets, Burke and Eric Lindsay, and several nurses. "He was terribly alone at the end," said Madeline Smith. "He really didn't have anything or anyone he was close to."

Shortly thereafter, the Eikenberry Funeral Home in Peru received an "unusual" (in their word) telephone call from Pierce Brothers Mortuary in

Cole Porter, Mykonos, 1955

California, whose spokesman began by saying "We congratulate you. You are receiving the body of Cole Porter." The valets had accompanied Cole's body to Peru. The private graveside service was brief, as Cole had directed. His body was buried in Mount Hope Cemetery between those of his father and Linda (not, as often said, between Linda's and his mother's). The service was, as he requested, "conducted by the Pastor of the First Baptist Church in Peru, in the presence of my relatives and dear friends." At his request no eulogy was delivered and no service of any kind was conducted in New York City. Cole requested the following Gospel reading from John XI be recited: "I am the resurrection and the life; he that believeth in me, though he be dead, yet shall live; and whosoever liveth and believeth in me shall never die." Just after his mother died in 1952, Porter had directed Madeline Smith to look up the sources of these verses. "I think he had [religion] in the background, because every now and then he would refer to some biblical saying and ponder it," said Mrs. Smith. This psalm was followed, as he wished, by a recitation of the Lord's Prayer. (On October 16, Cole's cousin and heir James O. Cole lost his only son, aged twenty-two, in an auto accident.)

Had Cole Porter at the end made his peace with the "high gods," of whose behavior he had so often in his songs been scornful? There seems to have been détente, at least, in the end. Cole left the world with these words put shortly before his death to Robert Raison: "Bobbie, I don't know how I did it."

Notes

The following abbreviations are used in these notes: INT = *interview with author;* POR = *in possession of recipient. All lyrics quoted in the text have been taken from* The Complete Lyrics of Cole Porter, *edited by Robert Kimball (CLCP), unless otherwise indicated.*

People

AC	Anita Colby
ADM	Agnes de Mille
AH	Aurand Harris
BB	Ben Baz
BBag	Ben Bagley
BH	Bart Howard
BM	Bearss Muhlfeld
BV	Benay Venuta
CDR	Comtesse de Rochambeau
CF	Cy Feuer
CLF	Colin Leslie Fox
DG	Dolores Gray
DH	Dorothy Hirshon
ErM	Ernest Martin
EW	Elizabeth Welch
FL	(Prince) Faucigny-Lucinge
FS	Fifi Laimbeer Schiff
GarK	Garson Kanin
GM	George Melly
GoV	Gore Vidal
GV	Gwen Verdon
H	Horst
HaH	Hanya Holm
HB	Hazel Bowland
HD	Honoria Murphy Donnelly
HH	Henry B. Hyde
JC	Jack Coble
JH	Jean Howard
JoH	Jones Harris
JK	James Kingsland
JOC	James O. Cole
KCH	Kitty Carlisle Hart
L	Lilo (Marquise de La Passardière)

LT	Louise Thwing
MCR	Margaret Cole Richards
MJOB	Mrs. John Otter Briney
MP	Michael Pearman
MiP	Michelle Phillips
MS	Madeline Smith
PC	Peggy (Mrs. Howard) Cullman
PL	Paula Laurence
PMo	Patricia Morison
RG	Robert Giroux
RK	Ray Kelly
RL	Richard Lewine
RM	Robert Montgomery
RW	Robert Wheaton
SC	Saul Chaplin
StS	Arnold Saint Subber
TH	Tommy Hendricks

Books

ADF	Cooper, Duff and Diana. *A Durable Fire*. London: Collins, 1983.
ADL	Campbell, Nina, and Caroline Seebohm. *A Decorative Life*. New York: Panache Press, 1992.
ADLGC	McGilligan, Patrick. *A Double Life: George Cukor*. New York: St. Martin's Press, 1991.
AIP	Morton, Bryan. *Americans in Paris*. Ann Arbor, MI: Olivia and Hill Press, 1984.
ANYL	Gill, Brendan. *A New York Life: Of Friends and Others*. New York: Poseidon Press, 1990.
APS	Wilder, Alec. *American Popular Song*. New York: Oxford University Press, 1972.
B	Haskins, James. *Bricktop*. New York: Atheneum, 1983.
BP	Custen, George F. *Bio/Pics*. New Brunswick, NJ: Rutgers University Press, 1992.
C	Kimball, Robert. *Cole*. New York: Holt, Rinehart & Winston, 1971
CLCP	Kimball, Robert. *The Complete Lyrics of Cole Porter*. New York: Alfred A. Knopf, 1983.
COUF	Berube, Allan. *Coming Out Under Fire*. New York: Free Press, 1990.
CPB	Schwartz, Charles. *Cole Porter: A Biography*. New York: Dial Press, 1977.
CPOBM	London Sinfonietta Conducted by John McGlinn. *Cole Porter Overtures and Ballet Music*. EMI Records Ltd., 1991. Liner notes.
CPSB	Hart, Moss (foreword); Sirmay, Albert (arrangements). *The Cole Porter Song Book*. New York: Simon and Schuster, 1959.
CWME	Hadley, Bowes. *Conversation with My Elders*. New York: St. Martin's Press, 1986.
D	Buckle, Richard. *Diaghilev*. New York: Atheneum, 1979.
DABR	Kochno, Boris. *Diaghilev and the Ballets Russes*. New York: Harper & Row, 1970.
DV	Vreeland, Diana. *D.V.* New York: Alfred A. Knopf, 1984.
FP	Astor, Brooke. *Footprints*. Garden City, NY: Doubleday, 1986.
FR	Rosenberg, Geena. *Fascinating Rhythm: The Collaboration of George and Ira Gershwin*. New York: Dutton, 1991.

FRP   Graham, John A., and Omar Holman. *Five Rare Peru and Miami County, Indiana, Books.* Peru, IN: Peru Republican Printing Office, 1935.

GAMM   Chaplin, Saul. *The Golden Age of Movie Musicals.* Norman, OK: University of Oklahoma Press, 1994.

H   Lawford, Valentine. *Horst.* New York: Alfred A. Knopf, 1984.

HFH   Duberman, Martin, et al (editors). *Hidden From History.* New York: New American Library, 1989.

HLTH   de Acosta, Mercedes. *Here Lies the Heart.* London: Andre Deutsch, 1960.

IBB   Bergreen, Laurence. *As Thousands Cheer.* New York: Viking, 1990.

IH   James, Henry. *Italian Hours.* Boston: Houghton Mifflin, 1909.

LB   Secrest, Meryle. *Leonard Bernstein.* New York: Alfred A. Knopf, 1994.

LLL   Eells, George. *The Life That Late He Led.* New York: G. P. Putnam's Sons, 1967

LOAB   Spoto, Donald. *Laurence Olivier: A Biography.* New York: Harper Collins, 1992

LWIBR   Tomkins, Calvin. *Living Well Is The Best Revenge.* New York: Viking Press, 1962.

MAA   Merman, Ethel. *Merman.* New York: Simon and Schuster, 1978.

MISIA   Gold, Arthur, and Robert Fizdale. *Misia.* New York: Morrow Quill Paperbacks, 1981.

MMBC   Rubin, Joan Shelley. *The Making of Middlebrow Culture.* Chapel Hill, NC: University of North Carolina Press, 1992.

MS   Rodgers, Richard. *Musical Stages.* New York: Random House, 1975.

N&C   Citron, Stephen. *Noël and Cole.* London: Sinclair Stephenson, 1992.

NCAB   Hoare, Philip. *Noël Coward: A Biography.* New York: Simon and Schuster, 1995.

N&D   Hendricks, Tommy. *Night and Day: The Times of Cole Porter.* Peru, IN: *Peru Tribune,* 10/17/77 to 11/7/77.

NOACL   Lahr, John. *Notes on a Cowardly Lion.* New York: Alfred A. Knopf, 1970.

OK   Kerensky, Oleg. *The Guinness Guide to Ballet.* Enfield, Middlesex, England: Guinness Superlatives Limited, 1981.

PAP   Rubin, William. *Picasso and Portraiture.* New York: Museum of Modern Art, 1996.

PI   Coward, Noël. *Present Indicative.* Garden City, NY: Doubleday, 1947.

PM   Baer, Nancy Van Norman. *Paris Modern: The Swedish Ballet, 1920–1925.* San Francisco, CA.: Fine Arts Museums of San Francisco, 1995.

POGMH   Gardiner, W. H., and N. H. MacKenzie (editors). *The Poems of Gerard Manley Hopkins.* London: Oxford University Press, 1967.

RHR   Grafton, David. *Red Hot and Rich.* New York: Stein and Day, 1987.

RSVP   Maxwell, Elsa. *RSVP.* Boston: Little Brown, 1954.

SAY   Johnson, Owen. *Stover at Yale.* New York: Frederick A. Stokes, 1911.

TCPS   Hubler, Richard G. *The Cole Porter Story.* Cleveland, OH: World, 1965.

TDB   Grigoriev, S. L. *The Diaghilev Ballet, 1909–1929.* London: Penguin, 1960.

TFWW   Laffey, Bruce. *Beatrice Lillie: The Funniest Woman in the World.* New York: Wynewood Press, 1989.

TGBD   King, Ernest. *The Green Baize Door.* London: William Kimber, 1963.

TGH   Knef, Hildegard. *The Gift Horse.* New York: McGraw Hill, 1971.

TLH   Higham, Charles. *The Lonely Heart.* New York: Avon Publishing, 1960.

TMAL   Samuels, Ernest. *Bernard Berenson: The Making of a Legend.* Cambridge, MA: Harvard University Press, 1987.

TSD   Fairbanks, Douglas Jr. *The Salad Days.* New York: Doubleday, 1988.

TTUT   Harriman, Margaret Case. *Take Them Up Tenderly.* New York: Alfred A. Knopf, 1945

TWCP   Howard, Jean. *Travels with Cole Porter.* New York: Harry N. Abrams, Inc., 1991.

UF	Parsons, Schuyler Livingston. *Untold Friendships.* Boston: Houghton Mifflin Co., 1955.
UITOH	Mitchell, Joseph. *Up in the Old Hotel.* New York: Pantheon Press, 1992.
WOD	Percival, John. *The World of Diaghilev.* New York: Dutton, 1971.

Collections of Papers

A-MSS	Alegi, Peter C. *A History of Catholicism at Yale.* Senior Honors Paper, 1956. Yale University Archives.
ARIZ	Arizona State University at Tempe. Department of Special Collections. Collected Papers of George Eells.
CU-OH	Columbia University. Oral History. Reminiscences of: Pandro S. Berman, Oscar Ewing, Joshua Logan, Archibald MacLeish, Madeline Smith.
CU-SBSP	Columbia University. Sam and Bella Spewack Papers. Rare Book and Manuscript Library.
HAR	Harvard University Archives and Department of Special Collections. Collected Papers of George Eells.
I Tatti	I Tatti, Florence, Italy. Letters of Cole and Linda Porter to Bernard Berenson.
MCM	Miami County Museum, Peru, Indiana. Department of Special Collections.
MCNY	Museum of the City of New York.
MTAW	Hart, Moss. *My Trip Around the World* (unpublished mss.) State Historical Society of Wisconsin.
USC-CPC	University of Southern California, Los Angeles. Special Collections. Collected Papers of Cole Porter.
USC-E	University of Southern California, Los Angeles. Special Collections. Collected Papers of George Eells.
USC-FOTL	University of Southern California, Los Angeles. Special Collections, Friends of the Libraries Collection. *Cole Porter: The Life That Late He Led.* 2/12/67.
WAR	Worcester Academy Records. Worcester, Mass.
YAR	Yale University Archives and Department of Special Collections.

Periodicals

AD	*Architectural Digest*
AN	*Art News*
CHR	*The Catholic Historical Review,* Vol LXVIII No 3
CLEV	*Cleveland Press*
E	*Esquire*
ES	*Evening Sun*
EW	*Evening World*
F	*Fortune*
JA	*Journal American*
NHER	*New Haven Evening Register*
NHR	*New Haven Register*
NY	*New York* magazine
NYDN	*New York Daily News*
NYHT	*New York Herald Tribune*
NYP	*New York Post*
NYT	*New York Times*

PI	*Philadelphia Inquirer*
PR	*Peru Republican*
PT	*Peru Tribune*
SR	*Saturday Review*
T	*Traces of Indiana and Mid-Western History*
TA	*Theatre Arts*
TC	*Town and Country*
TNY	*The New Yorker*
V	*Vigornia,* Worcester Academy
VF	*Vanity Fair*
VOG	*Vogue*
WAB	*Worcester Academy Bulletin*
WT	*Worcester Telegram*
YAM	*Yale Alumni Magazine*

CHAPTER I

pg 3 In 1905 . . . boarded the train: LLL p. 25
his wealthy grandfather's demands: JOC INT
August of 1882 . . . "gave a reception": FRP p. 45
J.O.'s attitude: LLL p. 24
Cole's father took no part: LLL p. 15
J.O. presided over: T. Summer '89 pp. 41–42
"a couple of miles": LLL p. 21

4 Katie did not waver: LT INT
"Tyrant": USC-E
" 'too long dinners' ": USC-E
"dictatorial": LLL p. 15
his mother and grandfather refusing: LLL p. 24
visited Peru only rarely: LLL pp. 29, 30
A. A. Cole . . . came with his family: FRP p. 11
Albert Cole was a soldier: PR 2/7/23
A. A. wanted his son: LLL p. 12
J.O. resisted: LLL p. 12
"to furnish a thorough": MCM
By 1850, however: LLL p. 12
With six hundred dollars . . . San Francisco: PR 2/7/23

5 visits home in August: JOC INT
His first job was helping: PR 2/7/23
"It has always been my aim": MCM
Alphonso married . . . "Married life": MCM
In 1860 J.O. returned: PR 2/7/23
Two years later: MCM
In 1865 Rachel: MCM
J.O. finally sold: MCM
J.O. . . . cleverly invested: PR 2/7/23

6 J.O.'s son, Louis: MCM
"assisted in the management": MCM
Louis, Omar, Kate, and Samuel: MCM
Rumors reached Cole: MCR INT
Louis was an alcoholic: MCR INT
his untimely death in November 1903: MCM
"the gay season": MCM
"It's the best thing": USC-E
"As his family went regularly": TH in PT 10/18/77

pg 7 "These pages": MCM
In the summer of 1890 . . . Bessie LaBonte: FRP 2/9/23
On April 9, 1884: FRP 4/9/84
a captain in the War of 1812: CPB p. 7
Sam Porter gave the commencement oration: MCM
"a parvenu druggist": YAR; JH INT

8 "His business profited": PR 8/25/27
they named the latter: PR 8/25/27
the Cole Building: FRP II 8/21/1886
"he used his whiskers": FRP, V. II p. 29

9 "unconsciously J.O. probably preferred": George Melly—YAR; unidentified newspaper clipping
she was marrying down: HB INT
"rather dreamy": HB INT
protesting the "monopoly": LLL p. 14
"because I just love": BM INT
"he gave shows": PT 11/6/56
it had a population: FRP {pictures past and present}
As a boy, Cole sang: JOC INT
as did Emil Schramm: MCM
library, to which Andrew Carnegie: FRP p. 20
James O. Cole emphasizes: JOC INT

11 Cole was born on June 9: MCM
the deaths of their infant son . . . and . . . daughter: MCM
Cole read such childhood classics: LLL p. 22
Sam Porter liked to read poetry: LLL p. 20
"I suppose he started me": LLL p. 20
a Gypsy persuaded Katie . . . she added "Albert": JOC INT
"I thought that Sammy": JOC INT
Thomas Andrews Hendricks: T. Summer '81 p. 47
It was in July 1894: N&D p. 3
headquarters for the Hagenbeck and Wallace Circus: PR 11/24/11
"As a circus center, Peru": T. Summer '89 p. 42
a malicious keeper: NYP 10/31/46

12 Playing the steam calliope . . .: BM INT
"The lure and lore of the circus": T. Summer '89 p. 42
Tommy's father: N&D p. 7
Cole disclosed that his own: MCM
A clown suit: LLL p. 22
it took him only overnight: Gene Kelly INT

13 "How many elephants . . . ?": T. Summer '89 p. 43
The Wild Man of Borneo: N&D p. 9
The Fat Lady: LLL p. 23
" 'the Royal Repenskis' ": N&D p. 9
"learned the value of practice": N&D p. 9
"would dash in and out": N&D p. 10

14 they crashed through: N&D p. 10
the bedridden "Aunt May": N&D p. 12
"persons who are alive": N&D p. 12
"The Bobolink Waltz": N&D p. 12
The first work he composed: MCNY
Desdemona Bearss: MCM

15 Desdemona's mother read Shakespeare: LLL p. 21
Sometimes she took her daughter: BM INT
by the age of six: T. Fall '89 p. 40
studied at the Marion Conservatory: LLL p. 16

pg 15   "some of my lyrics owe": LLL p. 17
Cole's mother imported: LLL p. 17
In 1902 . . . "the elite of the city": MCM
sometimes supplied when films were shown: LLL p. 23
he climbed uninvited: LLL p. 23
learning to ride ponies: LLL p. 16
tutored in French: LLL p. 11
"Other children didn't mix": HB INT
Des and Cole met: N&D p. 5

16   peddling apples: LLL p. 21
"Des is the most beautifullest": N&D p. 5
he liked Des, "even loved her": LLL p. 22
"That was one thing": N&D p. 13
piano practice nearly ruined: T. Fall '89 p. 40
in a black jacket: T. Fall '89 p. 41
"the queen of our hearts": N&D p. 13
Lake Maxinkuckee: T. Fall '89 p. 42
Cole's parents built: MJOB INT
the steamer *Peerless*: T. Fall '89 p. 43

17   Cole was ruining the piano stool: T. Fall '89 p. 43
Captain Crook . . . tore after Cole: T. Fall '89 p. 43
"But when night came": T. Fall '89 p. 44
"Going to the dances": T. Fall '89 p. 44
"By that time not only": T. Fall '89 p. 44

18   "night after night": T. Fall '89 p. 43
Katie had two Indian maids: USC-E
"Katie Porter, you can't": USC-E
"Master Cole" performed: MCM
a school production of *Snow White*: PR 5/26/03
"The Wedding March was played": MCM
the Porters traveled there: LLL p. 23
soprano Emma Calvé: MCM
Worcester Academy records: WAR
at least three of the passports: MCM
the Worcester Academy . . . Founded in 1834: WAR

19   solid training in the classics: WAR
"at Worcester Academy": WAR
should be educated in Indiana: LLL p. 24
J.O. had scoffed: LLL p. 18
"Cole's grandfather wanted": HB INT
"It was always toward Des": T. Fall '89 p. 45
"Des knew Cole was": N&D p. 15
Des read a book: N&D p. 15
"lifted one trouser leg": N&D p. 15

20   Tommy attended Indiana schools: JOC INT
Des married Milton Edwards: PT 2/29/68
Her husband caught sleeping sickness . . . Years later: LT INT

CHAPTER 2

21   The school had 240 boys: WAR
On October 7, 1905: V 1/7/05
"after a hearty dinner": V 12/2/05
Porter tried out for the position: V 3/14/06

22   Faculty, and especially: LLL p. 25

pg 22   all remember the small youth: USC-E
"to convert middle-class": LLL p. 24
"Democracy is not a leveling down": LLL p. 24
"A gentleman never eats": LLL p. 24
"If Cole's father first": LLL p. 26
"there is always enough money": USC-E
he was asked to teas: LLL p. 25
didn't discuss his family: LLL p. 25
belief that Cole was an orphan: LLL p. 25
"neither to show weakness": LLL p. 25
Donald Baxter MacMillan: WAR
he had accompanied Admiral Peary: WAR

23   "Cole was a lonesome kind": LLL p. 27
received honors for the winter: WAR
Camp Wychmere: LLL p. 26

24   "put some iron in his spine": LLL p. 26
J.O. and Katie had reconciled: LLL p. 27
Cole was at this stage: WAR
In his junior year: WAR
"Cole Porter began": V 10/5/07
Sheridan's *The Rivals*: LLL p. 27
"Cole, as Bob Acres": V 4/10/08

25   dropped his interest in acting: LLL p. 28
he won the first prize: WAB 4/31
the boys clapped and whistled: LLL p. 28
the academy faculty on the whole: Harold G. (Dutch) Rader INT
"Porter was reprimanded": WT 7/22/83
In June 1908 Porter: WAR
"gave a reading": V 3/6/08
On March 13 he performed: WAR
In 1908 Cole took entrance exams: WAR

26   Cole wanted to work: LLL p. 29
"terrible new income tax": ARIZ
home again for only the second time: LLL p. 30
Des Bearss, whom he invited: N&D p. 15
"thrilled by the singing": LLL p. 31
Beulah Mae Singer . . . "fascinating": LLL p. 31
"stepped out of the shadows": LLL p. 31
"Cole talked all through": LLL p. 32
Eventually he left her: LLL p. 32
"Fi, Fi, Fifi": WT 7/22/83

27   He wrote as well the class song: WAR
he threatened Cole with expulsion: WT 7/22/83
"successfully argued": WAR
"Are You a Bromide?": N&D p. 15
announced to be salutatorian: WAB 4/31
"The Individuality of a School": WAB 4/31
"At the Crossroads": NYHT 10/27/64
"the beautifully decorated Gym": WAR

28   J.O. was pleased: PR 6/1/09
First he took again: WAR
he boarded with a middle-class: LLL p. 32
saw something of Switzerland: LLL p. 33
242 York Street: C p. 6
Garland's Rooming House: YAR
One of his housemates: C p. 7

pg 28 Howard Cullman, who reported: PC INT
       "were the uniform for Main Street": ARIZ
       "wore salmon-colored ties": LWIBR p. 21
       Auchincloss, Vanderbilt: YAR
       Owen Johnson's *Stover at Yale*: SAY
       "You might describe me": NYHT 1/21/51
       The first academic move: YAR

29   They were not permitted: ARIZ
       Nazimova when she came to New Haven: YAR
       By 1910, in the spring: CLCP p. 4
       a football song competition: C p. 9
       was copyrighted and published: CLCP p. 5
       Other football songs followed: CLCP p. 5

30   J.O. complained: LLL p. 37
       His allowance was said: LWIBR p. 22
       Len Hanna . . . the first Weimaraner dogs . . . bought an English castle: RK INT
       J.O. ordered his grandson: LLL p. 37
       Eventually a compromise: LLL p. 37
       No doubt he was busy: PR 6/10/10
       did not move to Westleigh Farms: JOC INT
       Back went Cole: YAR
       His courses were: YAR
       "A" indicated first-year level: YAR

31   Murphy was voted: ARIZ
       "There was this barbaric custom": LWIBR p. 21
       "Porter did not fit easily": LWIBR p. 21
       Murphy persuaded DKE: LWIBR p. 22
       In Porter's Yale years: YAR
       Harriman . . . never had a penny: RK INT

32   Johnfritz Achelis: ARIZ

33   the Whiffenpoofs: YAR
       he took only four courses: YAR
       "I won't ask you": SAY p. 327

34   Henry Humphrey Parsons: *Yale Alumni Magazine* 11/92
       Cole had often visited: ARIZ
       English was his major: YAR
       William Lyon Phelps: YAR
       the Pundits, whose ten members: YAR
       "A large amount of difficult reading": YAR
       "In the mid-30's": MMBC p. 281
       Lucius Beebe proclaimed: MMBC p. 281
       "Nobody has ever said it": MMBC p. 282

35   joined with the composer Sigmund Romberg: MMBC p. 283
       drew 16 percent: MMBC p. 283

36   went to no church: ARIZ
       "fire, fancy, and faith": YAR
       Porter was in frantic flight: AC INT; JH INT

37   the many Omars: MCM
       "majored in outside work": LLL p. 40
       He belonged to the Mince Pie Club: YAR
       he composed more than one hundred songs: YAR

38   "Look, Mr. Woolley": JA 5/21/49
       "one of my finest experiences": LLL p. 39
       His Riggs grandfather: CHR p. 452
       Lawrason's father: A-MSS

39   named for St. Thomas Aquinas: A-MSS

pg 39 the elegant Westminster School: A-MSS
        As a senior at Yale: A-MSS
  40   "his refusal to pander": YAR
        In his junior year: YAR
  41   "Everybody else": USC-FOTL
        "the growth of democracy": ARIZ
        Cole, whose academic achievement: YAR
  42   "the hot-cha baby": N&D p. 22
        "ran hellbent for the bastille": N&D p. 22
        "Cole Porter was definitely": N&D p. 24
        "Mr. Porter's work": NHR 11/12/11
        Porter's first musical comedy: CLCP p. 9
        Whitridge also recalled: CLCP p. 9
  43   "the event of the midwinter": N&D p. 24
        "The star of this": N&D p. 24
  44   In April 1912: CLCP p. 10
        "Much might be written": ARIZ
  45   "Tell me whom you select": C p. 17
        And so *The Pot of Gold*: CLCP p. 13
        Four letters from Cole: C pp. 17, 18
        "the splendor of Wagner": LLL p. 43
        "Out in Peru": YAR
  46   *The Pot of Gold* was performed: CLCP p. 13
        "I Want to Be Married": CLCP p. 16
        he found him fast asleep: ARIZ
        Their Christmas trip: MCM
        "The average student": MCM
        "But the glittering star": MCM
  47   traveling in a luxury train: MCM
        "snap and dash": MCM
        "the singing of Cole Porter": MCM
        "a pleasing feature": MCM
        "featured Mr. Cole Porter": MCM
        "Mr. Cole Porter . . . appeared": MCM
        Other, anonymous newspaper cuttings: MCM
        Porter's last show: CLCP p. 19
  48   "As I Love You" was: CLCP p. 21
        In 1915 Sigmund Romberg: CLCP p. 21
        "every serious man": YAR
        On June 14 he appeared: YAR
        "I have the clearest memory": ARIZ
        a work called "Bright College Years": YAR

CHAPTER 3

  50   In the summer of 1913: MCM
        "to recite a particular": Oscar Ewing CU-OH
        At 404 Craigie Hall: HAR
        Later in life Acheson: David Acheson INT
  51   "One day I was at a party": NYDN 11/4/39
        "I'm used to being sat on": YAR
        He had received the equivalent: HAR
        "the Gilbert and Sullivan": YAR
        both Porter and Riggs: A-MSS

pg 52   *Paranoia . . . opened:* CLCP p. 23
      "We had such fun": YAR
      We're All Dressed Up . . . : CLCP p. 27
      "first class accommodations": YAR
      For this show Cole wrote: C pp. 26, 27
      Its final performance: YAR
      In April 1915 Cole: ARIZ
      "Tell grandad": C p. 31
      Elizabeth Marbury, very rich: A-MSS
      She was Oscar Wilde's: NHER 6/8/15
      "I am convinced": NHER 6/8/15
      a diva called Madame Edvina: MCM

  53   "He has written an operetta": MCM
      "Everything going beautifully": C p. 32
      "who refused to enter": YAR
      the then unknown Clifton Webb: C p. 34

  54   "an achievement that college boys": EW 3/29/16

  55   "Dooks for Dollars": CDR INT
      Dorothie Bigelow: NYHT 3/29/16
      "inevitable that he and I": C p. 34
      "project her personality": EW 3/29/16
      "worst musical comedy": ES 3/29/16

  56   closed after fifteen performances: LLL p 52
      "I'll never forget that night": NYDN 11/8/53
      "For years New York critics": YAR
      "I've got an awful lot": CLCP p. 34
      So Cole resumed: LLL p. 52
      "I spent the fall": ARIZ
      Riggs had invested: A-MSS
      Riggs completed his M.A.: A-MSS

  57   appointed Yale's first Catholic chaplain: CHR p 460
      Among his admirable attainments: CHR pp. 463, 466
      In the summer of 1917: C p. 38
      "In form it looked like": C p. 39
      "A great many Americans": NYT 5/3/53
      A Paris partner: UF pp. 74–77
      "inducted into the Foreign Legion": UF pp. 74–77

  58   An acquaintance recalls: LLL p. 52
      "as Cole had done": LLL p. 52
      "not the Red Cross": RW INT

  59   "Katie of the Y.M.C.A.": YAR
      "I went to a little office": C p. 59
      "Cole was with the French": NYHT 5/3/53
      "is a case for Scotland Yard": LLL p. 53
      "Porter," says Wooley: LLL p. 53
      Eells has checked: LLL p. 54
      "I met Cole": YAR

  61   "quite arrogant": USC-E
      It was in Paris: CU-OH
      "Cole . . . seemed to me": CU-OH
      Cole first met Maxwell: *American Weekly* 3/16/58
      "one of Europe's *femmes fatales*": RSVP p. 18
      "I never had a sexual experience": RSVP p. 18
      "There is something in you": RSVP p. 45
      " 'Are you paging me?' ": RSVP p. 120

  62   "example of how far you can get": YAR

pg 62   "because she was so outrageous": RK INT
         "before the days when she became": PI pp. 155, 156

CHAPTER 4

63   according to his friend Marthe Hyde: HH INT
      "Every morning at half-past seven": LLL p. 69
      his French was fluent but: MP INT
      his meeting Linda Lee Thomas: C p. 40
      Linda was a descendant: CLEV 10/17/64
65   "the most beautiful woman": RW and FS INT
      Tall and blond: LLL p. 59
      When Mrs. James Borden Harriman came: LLL p. 60
      So Linda came to meet Edward R. Thomas: LLL p. 60
      resided in a variety of houses: LLL p. 60
      Her favorite department store: STS INT
      "You look very lindaporterish": TTUT p. 144
      Linda often wore white kid gloves: MJOB letter in possession
      The lives of the Thomases darkened: MJOB INT
      the first American to kill someone: LLL p. 61
      in 1912 they divorced. Linda received: LLL p. 62
      Frank Crowninshield . . . wrote: C p. 40
      Linda . . . had gone: C p. 42
66   "a social powerhouse": TC 10/53
      Her reputation was made: TC 10/53
      "foinish," as she always: ADL p. 29
      "something else": DV p. 161
      Sutton Place: C p. 42
      "She stood on her head": ADL (Intro)
      "For all I know": ADL (Intro)
67   "Elsie deWolfe": Mrs. Samuel Dushkin INT
      "to stamp out the stuffy": ADL p. 1
      "The gloom of interiors": ADL p. 40
      she did extensive relief work: *Louisville Courier Journal* 10/16/54
      Elsie had served courageously: ADL p. 82
      "enchanting, rather negroid": TMAL p. 235
      "the meeting with the composer": TMAL p. 235
      the Duke of Alba, or Jimmy: LLL p. 63
      "listened to Cole Porter": TMAL p. 246
69   "had the most faultless": LLL p. 59
      "Until she is sold": RK INT
      "Linda Thomas called me": UF p. 83
70   "Linda was the air": STS INT
      "Tired of Living Alone": CLCP p. 48
      On December 6, 1918, J. O.: MCM
      "heard Porter moodily playing": TTUT p. 141
      On the strength of the several: TTUT p. 142
      "When the musical theatre started": USC-FOTL
      Hitchy-Koo opened: CLCP p. 44
71   The couplet is proof: OK p. 54
      "Old-Fashioned Garden" is the song: CLCP p. 45
      "I suppose the biggest song hit": LLL p. 66
      "Cole must have written this": ARIZ
      Certainly in "Another Sentimental Song": CLCP p. 46
72   a set of dazzling floral costumes: LLL p. 65

pg 72   Another amusing story: C p. 47
       "J.O. pounded the arm": GM in SR

73   "It was not for her money": SR 2/23/91
       Cole and Linda were married: C p. 47
       "Les Colporteurs": C p. 53
       "the Beauty of the Peace Conference": Letter in possession HD
       "The 1920's was a period of license": David Ewen in TA 6/55

74   "Suppose I had to settle": TTUT p. 143
       they went to live: YAR
       At that time Cole listed: YAR
       Early in 1920, Porter: TTUT p. 183
       founded by Vincent d'Indy: Schola registrar INT

75   "Between 1916 and 1928": NYP 6/7/91
       "with all his success": C p. 64
       Linda, eager to do her part: NYP 6/7/91
       "when he found the influence": TTUT p. 142
       "craftsmanlike problem-solving": NY 10/14/91

76   "The stylistic overview": NY 10/14/91
       "I had not previously": SR 12/25/71
       "My accompaniments are usually": MCM
       Linda sold it and purchased: VOG 8/25

77   the Porters' garden backed up: DH INT
       Thirteen rue Monsieur was described: VOG 8/25

78   "Although it sounds garish": Stephen Citron in AD 12/92
       "one of those rounded eighteenth-century": DV p. 218
       "Here's Diana": DV p. 218
       "she had imported and planted": Stephen Citron in AD 12/92
       Sturges, a native of: RK INT
       Sturges attended Groton and Yale: YAR
       he owned a black bear: RK INT

79   Horst photographed: H INT
       Sturges took a one-room apartment: RW INT
       "Sturges sometimes made": CLF INT
       In these years Sturge: TWCP p. 13
       "Once I went through two": TWCP p. 13
       "Linda gave considerable time": JH INT
       Once Sturge disappeared: JH INT

80   "If ever you go off": GoV INT
       Every year, on the anniversary: GoV INT
       "was always very, very smart": JH INT
       "I can always buy": JH INT
       "easier [for Cole]": GoV INT
       The Sturges family deny: John Sturges (nephew HS) INT
       "terribly funny": JH INT
       one bedroom in Westleigh: JOC INT

81   The Porters chartered: C p. 50
       "The only thing they've got": C p. 50
       Mayfair and Montmartre: CLCP p. 93
       "among the half-dozen best": E 4/35
       The song was inspired: C p. 57

82   Gerald, meanwhile, had married: LWIBR p. 24
       Gerald studied landscape architecture: LWIBR p. 25
       began to study painting: LWIBR p. 29
       the Murphys met Picasso: AN 5/94
       The art critic Michael Kimmelman: NYT 4/21/94
       "Picasso's Aborted Love Song": AN 5/94

pg 82   "Gerald Murphy was on his way": TNY 7/22/96
    83   "We rented the Château": YAR
           Pictures survive: YAR
           "Cole always had": LWIBR p. 36
    84   Eventually the Murphys decided: LWIBR p. 49
           On February 3, 1923: LLL p. 75
           "Distinguished Citizen of Peru": PR 2/9/23
    85   He left, as well: LLL p. 75
           "True to his word": Eleanor Harris in *Park East* 10/52

CHAPTER 5

    86   "Elsa led, of course": PI p. 159
           In 1923 she was engaged: CPB p. 63
           "Her international reputation": F 91 7/34
    87   "a large number of men": F 91 7/34
           Anthony Heilbut notes: Anthony Heilbut, *Thomas Mann: Eros and Literature*
           (New York: Knopf, 1996), p. 437
           "collect all the Venetian socialites": F p. 91 7/34
           Elsa donned an 1890s bathing costume: F p. 91 7/34
           "These Lido boys": F p. 91 7/34
           "the world capital of diversion": F p. 91 7/34
           Once, one of the clues: F p. 91 7/34
           the premiere of Stravinsky's ballet *Les Noces:* OK p. 189
    88   Darius Milhaud was at that time: PM p. 27
           Swedish dancers and staff: PM np. (foreword)
           "Porter had not yet": TTUT p. 41
    89   Milhaud, who at the suggestion: C p. 65
           In 1923 the Porters: LLL p. 75
           They journeyed that summer: TTUT p. 144
           Within the Quota . . . "a lively thirty-minute": LWIBR p. 41
           "a pantomime ballet": PM p. 28
    90   "Porter used the musical scale": YAR
           "It included an ocean liner": LWIBR p. 41
           "the first jazz ballet": PM p. 28
    91   *Le Figaro* labeled *Quota:* C p. 67
           "comprised some very good": YAR
           "The original music sheets": NYT 5/5/70
           "Lieber & Co. have just framed": MCM
           Diana Vreeland, who described: DV p. 218
           "Scions of proud old Italian": NYT 8/29/26
    92   "Titles in those days": DH INT
           "I am sure of Gershwin": *Dial* 8/23/23
           Hitchy-Koo of 1922: CLCP p. 5
    93   Monty Woolley . . . rank of lecturer: YAR
           "in 1923 Monty Woolley and I": NYHT 1/21/51
           In the summer of 1924: D p. 459
           According to Kochno: D p. 459
    94   "How dare they give presents": D p. 459
           "a first-class scandal": D p. 457
           Diaghilev brought the company to Paris: DABR p. 12
           "I am first a great charlatan": WOD p. 7
           people dressed differently: WOD pp. 7, 8
           Léonide Massine, whom he had recently: D p. 371

pg 94   "a handsome seventeen-year-old": Gold, Arthur and Robert Fizdale, *Misia* (New York: Knopf, 1980), p. 236

95   "a well-educated and intelligent": TDB p. 190
"Cole is writing a ballet": DABR p. 222
"a friend of Cole Porter": DABR p. 222
"outraged by the jazz invasion": DABR p. 222
In 1924, while still in Venice: LLL p. 75
Anderson found his stride later: LLL p. 87
The show opened in New York: CLCP p. 61
Anderson sensed: TTUT pp. 144, 145

96   "Cole Porter's passion": KCH INT
"Mr. Porter's best song": E 4/35
In 1927 Porter wrote: C p. 70
"I went to the band leader": C p. 70
a series of undated love letters: YAR
In 1920 Porter had problems: Interviewee requests anonymity
"such a prima donna": YAR

97   "You made a great friend today": YAR
"As for your departure": YAR

98   "is the only thing in the world": YAR
Linda had long been known: LLL p. 71
"When will I find you again?": YAR
"You write to me like": YAR

99   "After lunch, I come back": YAR
"If you aren't familiar": YAR

100   "Leaving this evening": YAR
"This is just a word": YAR

101   "done something stupid": YAR
Rubinstein, "who, as always": YAR
"there was a sense": YAR
"I don't feel too inspired": DABR p. 247
the last ballet in which Balanchine danced: DABR p. 247
In one letter Kochno is informed: YAR

102   And Guaranty Trust: YAR
"I have to see you": YAR
"Even before daring": YAR
"Linda's condition": YAR
Horst recalled: H INT
"realized Porter was gay": GM in SR 2/23/91
"great beauties don't want sex": JoH INT
"Linda became Cole's best friend": CDR INT

103   "It was always obvious": MJOB INT
Linda was lesbian: Mrs. Gary Cooper INT
"tolerated [Cole's] homosexual affairs": IBB p. 417
"not at all lesbian": BB INT
"old-fashioned": FS INT
"She didn't know how": ARIZ
He always rose: MP INT
"big sex scandal": MP INT
"The Young Oak": TDB p. 247
"Diaghilev est mort": TDB p. 264
they rented for $4,000: LLL p. 77

104   "transcends description": IH p. 57
"Noël was in Venice": MS p. 87

105   "As soon as he touched": MS p. 88
"Dinner at the Coles' last night": ADF letter 8/12/25

pg 105   "withdrawn and aloof": DH INT
"cold, indifferent, rude": B p. 101; RSVP p. 112

106   "interested in me as a person": B p. 112
"If you were going to be pushy": B p. 105
"He could have told off": B p. 101
"on an oriental scale": YAR
the notorious *galleggiante:* C p. 75
"a large barge": C p. 75
The "arca di Noe" made only one: YAR
"The whole of Venice": C p. 75
"It is always strange": Letter 9/24/55, Cole Porter Trust

107   The musicologist Ernest Newman: ARIZ
Beecham privately printed: C p. 75
"Tho' perhaps you be a scorner": C p. 75
"We gave an Eighteenth century ball": YAR

108   "My greatest claim to Fame": B p. 98
"a slight, immaculately dressed man": B p. 100
"Everyone in Paris knew": B 101
"I was about to become the dance teacher": B 102
"I could have had romantic involvements": B 153

109   Aspiring as a youth: *London Times* 8/19/69
"I am a gentleman": *Evening Standard* 8/18/69

110   "an arrangement": CDR INT
"not a funny man": CDR INT
"I remember [Porter's] cigarette case": TGBD p. 48

111   "seated at the piano": TGBD pp. 48, 49
"in the doldrums" . . . "of Cole's despondency": C p. 72

112   "Looked at in the cold light": C p. 71
"during an impromptu 'show' ": C p. 71

114   "Royalty and gangsters": LLL p. 82
"whom we grew to know very well" . . . "That was the reason": CLCP p. 98
"Weren't We Fools": CLCP p. 99

115   Coward's parodic powers: "Weren't We Fools": LLL p. 99
"a jazz revue which for swing": B p. 110
"At least something has impressed Brick": B p. 111
"I recall a tight rope dancer": p. FL INT

116   In August of 1927: Peru courthouse death certificate
The *Peru Republican* praised: PR 8/21/27

117   According to Lew Kesler: BB INT
"kicked us around": YAR

CHAPTER 6

118   At a party given: Frances Gershwin Godowsky INT
In the spring of 1928: AIP p. 117

119   "few hand-picked men": UF p. 144
"will be the great rendezvous": PI 4/8/28

120   Goetz . . . was determined to stage: LLL p 91

121   the show opened in New York: CLCP p. 72
The New Yorker declared: TNY 10/20/28
"the absent Mr. Cole Porter": NYHT 10/9/28
"this joyously tuned and worded": *Chicago Herald* 10/22/29
Everyone knows what "it" means: Peter Murphy INT
"Porter discovered the facts": E 4/35

122   "You've ideas inside your head": YAR

pg 123   Cochran described the origins: *Star* (London) 3/27/29
         Later *Wake Up and Dream*: CLCP p. 77
124   The *Sunday Pictorial* urged: *Sunday Pictorial* (London) 3/31/29
         The London *Sunday Express*: 3/31/29
125   When Walter Winchell heard: YAR undated, unidentified news clipping
         in 1945 it was listed: YAR
         "wailing, moaning": YAR
         The whole song was the work: *Newark Star Eagle* 10/14/35
126   "This cast a slight gloom": YAR
         "the expatriate": YAR undated, unidentified news clipping
         called the revue "flat": *NY Evening Post* 12/31/29
         "Porter is a young American": *Kent Echo* 3/28/29
127   "No sooner am I engaged": *NY Dispatch* 1/27/30
         Fifty Million Frenchmen opened: CLCP p. 84
         "The words and music leap": NYT 1/5/30
         "Cole Porter was the greatest": ADM INT
         "a great man of the theatre": Carmen Capalbo INT
         "The best musical comedy": IBB p. 284
129   "Why do you think T. S. Eliot": CWME p. 95
         Beaton's words in interviews: H INT
         "Harlem was regarded": RHR p. 107
         "Moore had a fondness for celebrities": HFH p. 323
         Porter always paid for sex: StS INT
130   "*Frenchman*'s most famous": CLCP p 84
132   "as near to a perfect": *Evening Graphic* 12/29/29
         "among the Elegansia": NYHT 12/16/27
         "I love animals": *NY Telegram* 12/16/67
133   In an interview published: NYHT 12/8/29
         "We need two minutes": FS INT
         "Writing for musical comedy": LB p. 130
134   "Broadway pleased [Porter] so little": NYHT 12/8/29
         "[Life] would get pretty dull": MCM
         "What they don't understand": LLL p. 73

CHAPTER 7

135   "All these [songs offer]": NYT 12/9/73
136   "Cole Porter started around": NYT 12/14/30
         "Mr. Porter . . . killed some time": NYT 12/14/30
         Mrs. Joshua Cosden, "well known": *Morning Telegraph* 3/16/31
         an ardent fan of Dick Tracy: RK INT
137   "filthy": NYHT 12/9/30
         "colored girl": CLCP p. 102
         "I like it best": PR 8/28/53
138   Other songs for *The New Yorker*: CLCP pp. 101–103
         prisoners wrote from Sing Sing: *Radio Guide* 10/19/35
139   "mean" and "a travesty": *Daily Mirror* 2/4/31
         an *après* theatre party: *Philadelphia Record* 12/14/30
         "Mr. Porter, the guest of honor": *Philadelphia Record* 12/14/30
140   " 'Take me back to Manhattan' ": 12/26/30
         "I'll write Jewish tunes": MS p. 88
         "My ears tell me": N&C p. 102
         On January 18, 1931: NYT 1/19/31
         "He is wholly unable": VF 2/31
142   "It is well for all to know": C p. 108

pg 142 "The U.S.A. to all good Americans": C p. 108
Marquis de Talleyrand, "who has arranged": C p. 108
"one of the various homeland": C p. 109

143 both Walter Winchell and "Cholly Knickerbocker": CLCP p. 109
"she had an arrangement": CLCP p. 109
"He had me screaming": YAR

144 Baron Nicholas de Gunzburg . . . joined with Elsa: RSVP p. 155
Serge Lifar, who arrived: RSVP p. 155
"Cole and Linda were great friends": Letter in possession of A
"no gentleman wears a brown suit": H INT
The walls were lined . . . "lit them": B p. 158

145 "Because I had plenty": NYHT 1/21/51
It was in 1932: RK INT
Marthe Hyde and her son: HH INT

146 "came to be known as the 'Night and Day' show": USC-FOTL
Cole sat down at the piano: CLCP p. 107

147 " 'Night and Day' has a long range": USC-FOTL
"I wrote 'Night and Day' ": *NY World Telegram* 11/26/38
"I put the tune together": *NY World Telegram* 11/26/38

148 "I must have that eave mended": LLL p. 99
"I don't know what this is": *NY World Telegram* 11/26/38
"A crazy business": *NY World Telegram* 11/26/38
he heard a Mohammedan: C p. 110
the title changed to suit: CU-OH-PB
"I could blow a better": CU-OH-PB
"the most brilliant gathering": JA 12/4/32

149 "the international society pet": *Buffalo News* 12/6/32
"We had a rather rocky": USC-FOTL
"Cole Porter has done": NYDN 12/4/32
"Mr. Cole Porter . . . shares the mantle": TNY (undated), YAR
"suggestiveness and dirt": JA 7/5/33
"Dear Cole, I am mad about": C p. 110

150 He telephoned Max: RM INT
"An outrageous arrangement": RM INT
Cole's lawyers founded . . . Buxton Hill: RM INT

151 "His loyalty was great": RK INT
"You know, Cole was": LLL p. 193
it was Dr. Sirmay, some say: Al Cendry INT
when Frank Sinatra sang: LLL p. 127; letter in CP Trust
"The Doc doesn't like it": LLL p. 200

152 the practice, which Sirmay encouraged: Al Cendry INT
"Let's call Sirmay": RM INT
"It gives me great satisfaction": Letter in CP Trust
"the greatest surprise I ever had": NYT 2/20/55
"an utterly sophisticated farce": *Birmingham Gazette* 10/23/33

153 "Fred Astaire and Claire Luce": *Daily Telegraph* (undated), YAR
"Everybody loves dear Coalie": *Bystander* (undated), YAR
"it was no good": BBag INT
"What a dwedful": HH INT

154 They went for six weeks: MP INT
"Weston, where did you get": MP INT
"She will return to us": JA 4/16/34
"When Cole sailed for London": Letter Linda Porter to Bernard Berenson, I Tatti
"The great love of Cole Porter's life": MP INT
Porter's intimates were: JC INT

155 In pictures taken: YAR

pg 155 "He was a crazy boy": MP INT
he was shocked to discover: MP INT
"Porter's great friend": H INT
But another of Porter's pals: JC INT
Variety announced that Porter: 6/13/33

156 he and Brent met in Paris: LLL p. 103
"Nothing of the bitch": LLL p. 103
"Cole was a first-rate": LLL p. 104
In order not to make: LLL p. 104

157 "a pantomime for highbrows": 9/17/33
"the most daring ever seen": *Paris Herald* (undated), YAR
"the big time": Anne Edwards, *The De Milles* (New York: Abrams, 1988), p. 129
"I want to express to you": YAR
"had a big, ballyhooed preview": TSD p. 234
One of the dances de Mille created: ADM INT
"Tell me about your score": YAR

158 "the most elegant-looking": TSD p. 234
Elizabeth Welch, a featured singer: EW INT
"the Duke of Verdura": *Tatler* 10/7/33
"the best the stage has known": YAR

161 "He had a terrible voice": EW INT
"Irving Berlin wrote for": EW INT

162 "I have no objection": Cole Porter Trust
"eliminating the bores": JA 11/1/33
"Exclusive Gathering Includes": JA 11/1/33
"Cole Porter seems to have edged": JA 11/19/34

CHAPTER 8

163 "Sing 'Listen to the German Band' ": Hildegarde INT
"kind, gentle, very elegant": Hildegarde INT
"the leader of the habits-of-rabbits school.": E 4/35

164 "The Town's Topnotch Tunester Today": YAR, undated, unidentified publication
Freedley paid Charles Cochran: LLL p. 110
fire aboard the U.S.S. *Morro Castle:* NYT 9/9/34
In a story Ethel Merman: MAA p. 70
Lindsay and Crouse famously co-authored: CLCP p. 118

165 "Oh, but you can do that": *Hollywood Reporter* 3/9/54
"Mr. Porter was equal to all": *Hollywood Reporter* 3/9/54
"Such works of art": YAR
"Cole and I liked each other": MAA p. 72
"a stage bully": RK INT

166 "the vocabulary of a longshoreman": USC-FOTL
He said he'd rather write: MAA p. 9
"I never change a word": MAA p. 9
Anything Goes opened in New York: CLCP p. 118
"My favorite tune in *Anything Goes*": *Boston Traveller* 11/6/34

167 "any substitutes for": CLCP p. 118
"so Porter removed the reference": CLCP p. 118
"Cole substituted that for some lines": MAA p. 73
"I got a letter": YAR, unidentified news clipping
"Of course, the line": USC-FOTL

168 "Naturally I knew what type": NYHT 8/19/34
"Many gorgeous girls": NYDN 3/23/34
"Cole Porter has written": NYT 3/22/34

pg 168   "Mr. Porter is the bold, bad": *NY World Telegram* 3/22/34
            "No less a minstrel": NYHT 3/22/34
            "Kaufman and Gershwin led off": *NY World Telegram* 9/27/35

169   the government brought some pressure: George Murphy INT
            Whatever the White House's sentiments: NYT 12/29/34
            "during a supper at Boeuf": TTUT p. 139
            "just a trick": *Hollywood Reporter* 3/9/54

170   "An Ascot Bonnet": NYHT 6/23/35
            Daniel Klein was among the many: *Hollywood Reporter* 3/9/54
            Mr. Al Stillman was paid: Cole Porter Trust
            parodies were "dirty": USC-FOTL
            "Why was it necessary": JA 11/25/35
            "a fine ribald version": RM INT
            the mention of Mussolini: RM INT
            "Cole would get stuck": RHR p. 68

171   "I have engaged Ted Fetter": YAR
            "what Cole had done": MAA p. 72
            "the famous parody": Robert Kimball INT
            Garson Kanin was once present: GarK INT

172   "The complexity of Porter's best work": VF 11/83
            "Cole had a worldwide": MAA p. 74
            "We'd like you to take over": BV INT
            "He couldn't play his own songs": BV INT
            "Cole would be a little bombed": BV INT
            "In those days people": BV INT
            "How right you were": BV INT
            "composing and writing his glossy tunes": YAR, undated news unidentified

173   "after midnight in a lengthy": YAR
            "and his dress and manners": JA 1/3/34
            "clings to the background": JA 1/3/34
            "daily redecorated": YAR NYHT, undated
            he had acoustical "mud" installed: CPB p. 170
            "I never stop thinking": JA 8/18/35
            "Wears black tie": JA 8/18/35

174   Cole had two cats: MP INT
            The opening of *Anything Goes:* CLCP p. 119
            "In those days there was no more horrible": YAR
            he described to Gerald Murphy: HD INT
            "one afternoon a Metro story editor": HLTH p. 70

175   Another big bash: *Family Circle* 1/18/35
            Brian Friel's play *Dancing at Lughnasa: Dancing at Lughnasa* (London: Faber &
            Faber, 1990), pp. 63–65

CHAPTER 9

176   On January 12, 1935, Cole: NYHT 1/12/35
            Moss Hart first met Cole: CPSB p. 1
            the Left Bar was called: N&C p. 54
            "Cole Porter, looking like": N&C p. 54

177   "He introduced me": Thomas Beer letter to Ernest Boyd 5/15/28, Aldeman Library,
            University of Virginia
            "were aware that a new": CPSB p. 2
            "Gaiety," "impishness": CPSB p. 2

178   he pestered Porter to use the name: MP INT
            Powell's first coup: MP INT

pg *178* "When Messrs. Porter and Hart": NYHT 1/12/35
"heir apparent to the throne": NYHT 1/12/35
"an ugly carved statue": LLL p. 119
Linda . . . gathered up all his clothing: LLL p. 120

179 she had never been told this tale: KCH INT
"Every new sight excites in me": MTAW p. 1
"I knew instinctively": MTAW p. 1
"New York sliding off": MTAW p. 3
"one of the most acclaimed songs": CLCP p. 131

180 Madame Piaget, who met: MTAW p. 10
"Cole Porter 'worker' ": CPSB p. 5
"He used work as a weapon": CPSB p. 5
"thoroughly exhausting days": MTAW p. 12

181 he fired off a telegram: MTAW p. 12
Cole adopted a routine: YAR
"magnificent specimens": MTAW p. 25
"two pretty strange places": MTAW p. 34
In Zanzibar Cole and Moss: YAR

182 "It was dawn": Cole Porter Trust
"I took a world tour": CPB p. 94
"You know, that Mrs. Porter": LLL p. 123

183 a bright red airplane: CLEV 8/14/35
It was there at the farm: CPSB p. 7
Ed immediately suggested "gossamer": LLL p. 128
"very much the sort of idea": *Brooklyn Eagle* 10/27/35
"Get off the stage!": MP INT

184 Troubles began when members of: LLL p. 126
Mary Boland slowly succumbed: LLL p. 127
the mothers of Mary Boland, Max Gordon: *NY Telegraph* 11/25/35
Later, in New York: LLL p. 129
"There'll be no war": *Boston Herald* 9/23/35
"*Jubilee* is definitely one": NY 10/14/91

186 *Jubilee* opened in Boston: CLCP p. 130
"Not since *Show Boat*": *NY Inquirer* 10/13/35
Another located *Jubilee:* NYHT 10/19/35
"a brilliant musical play": *Boston Herald* 9/23/35
"unquestionably a hit": *Variety* 9/23/35
Ned Saltonstall . . . threw: UF p. 201
"not since 1929": *Durham Times* 10/22/35
Linda wore a new: *NY Evening Post* 10/17/35
People were offering: MP INT

187 "*Jubilee* is a tapestry": NYT 10/14/35
"gay, noisy, truthful": NYDN 10/14/35
"much more than just": 10/20/35
"distinctly a South Sea melody": *Sunday Mirror* 10/13/35

188 "the Black Martiniquois": Letter to Frank O. Colby 3/23/45, Cole Porter Trust
"The beguine is the popular dance": Cole Porter Trust
"a latin beat to a swing time": VF 11/83

189 Recently, Sam Kusumoto: *Pinnacle* magazine, undated, p. 10
"the lyricist of the boulevard": YAR

CHAPTER 10

190 "likes to do shows": MCM
"It's like living on the moon": C p. 139

pg 190   "Porter's homosexuality, fed by opportunity: GM in SR 3/23/91
191   "He would rather compose": *NY Evening Journal* 12/12/36
            "Cole liked rather boisterous": ARIZ
            busy with *Red, Hot and Blue!*: CLCP p. 145
            "I think a lot of the time": MCM, undated, unidentified news clipping
192   "sweet little grey-haired woman": MCM, undated, unidentified news clipping
193   The *New York Evening Journal*: 5/21/36
            "Of course it's something": NYT 5/22/36
194   "looking more dead than alive": LLL pp. 150, 151
            "Now Sam this material": LLL p. 151
            "to turn out 'ditties' ": *NY Evening Herald* 6/19/36
            "[Eddy] Tauch soon became": JC INT
            became an intimate of Horst and of the Duke: H INT
195   "a good man": JC INT
            "she was friendly about it": JC INT
            "It is hard, at this distance": Horst, *Salute to the Thirties* (New York: Viking, 1971),
            p. 38
            In November, according to: YAR
            "I asked Cole Porter": YAR
            "So sweet to awaken": YAR
            "How can you 'stop' ": NYT 3/30/37
196   *Variety* listed three: *Variety* 12/23/36
            alluding not only to sex: Earl Blackwell INT
            "There is a story": *Economist* 6/15/91
            "Upbeat," "positive": *Economist* 6/15/91
            "There aren't so many torches": YAR, Dorothy Kilgallen in *NY Evening Journal,*
            undated
197   "It is such a struggle": YAR, Dorothy Kilgallen in *NY Evening Journal,* undated
            "Cole Porter gets his inspiration": NYHT 12/20/36
            "forced me to learn": NYHT 12/20/36
            "the newest wisecracks": NYHT 12/20/36
            "Porter 'retired' at 10": CLEV 12/1/36
            "From this title I work out": NYHT 12/20/36
            Very often, remarked a critic: *Indianapolis Times* 12/11/36
198   "Motion pictures are more difficult": *Indianapolis Times,* 12/11/36
            "It's fascinating work": YAR unidentified news clipping, 11/16/36
            stages were two hundred feet long: *Brooklyn Eagle* 12/13/36
            he solicited the help of the U.S. Navy: *Louisville Times* 12/8/36
199   Greta Garbo would sing: YAR
            Beneath the gardenia: YAR
            "Your score applauded": YAR
            "The Cole Porter music": *Hollywood* 11/14/36
200   "I've worked like a dog": CLEV 12/30/36
            "Sophisticated allusions": CLCP p. 145
            Red, Hot and Blue! tried out: CLCP p. 145
            Horst, who was so beguiled: H INT
201   Freedley, late in 1935, hired: MAA p. 79
            "was doing the show": ARIZ
            "I've never worked on a play": *Boston Traveller* 10/7/36
            One critic suggested: *Boston Traveller* 10/7/36
            "Wait till you see Jimmy": *Boston Traveller* 10/7/36
            "overboard on plot": *Christian Science Monitor* 10/13/36
            "we all decided another song": YAR
            The next lines were inspired: BBag INT
202   Radio once found the reference: BBag INT
            Crouse presumed: LLL p. 156

pg 202 "I'd think I was talking": ARIZ
"One thinks of these things": NYT 11/8/36
"Every night the performance": ARIZ
203 "a dream": MAA p. 83
"was too ill to be at hand": YAR
"Merle wants everything!": AC INT
"The morning after": NYT 11/8/36
204 "of the second magnitude": *Time* 11/9/36
206 "liked everything in the score": C p. 147
207 "Never hate a song": C p. 147
Mayer, who is said to have burst: C p. 147
209 Linda appears in some photos: YAR
From Denmark the three: YAR
One photo features many: YAR
On October 4, 1937, he boarded: YAR

CHAPTER 11

210 "If Cole were warned": MP INT
Once in World War II: BH INT
211 a gentleman never depresses: YAR
as he lay with his crushed legs: C p. 180
"a symbol of the invincible youth": LLL p. 164
Cole had the initial surgery: NYHT 2/3/38
Linda wrote to Bernard Berenson: YAR
212 "It's too heartbreaking": LLL p. 173
For some time before the accident . . . Linda: LLL p. 173; RK INT
"It just goes to show": LLL p. 165
Kelly was employed: RK INT
213 Bart Howard remembered: BH INT
assigning a personality to each leg: LLL p. 167
"There are about a thousand": LLL p. 167
"14 different kinds": ARIZ
"Because it bruises": AH INT
"practically an extension": JC INT
214 "a tough little cookie": RK INT
"lumbering" and "dull": *NY World Telegram* 12/31/37
"tuneful but not exceptional": *N.Y. World Telegram* 12/31/37
"a simple little Ruritanian story": *Times* (London) 1/24/38
215 *You Never Know* is . . . Produced by: CLCP p. 159
"Little song and not much beauty": NHER 3/4/38
("uneven," . . . "skirts the edge": *Boston Post* 3/8/38
"The premiere of Cole Porter's": *Variety* 3/9/38
"Mme. Tarzan": *Washington News* 3/22/38
"this has been a dreadful winter": YAR
216 "Nothing in the Broadway year": NYHT 3/23/38
217 *You Never Know* was performed in Indianapolis: *Indianapolis Star* 5/24/38
"This was a premiere": *Chicago Tribune* 5/2/38
"tawdry vulgarities": *Hartford Times* 9/17/38
"Lacking in electricity": *NY Sun* 9/22/38
Walter Winchell knocked: *NY Daily Mirror* 9/22/38
as did Brooks Atkinson: NYT 9/22/38
Richard Watts assessed: NY *Inquirer* 10/9/38
"Why anyone ever dug up": LLL p. 169
Inside was one dead lily: RK INT

pg 218 In 1938 Cole's friend Ollie Jennings: JC INT
"one summer he and his wife": TNY 11/23/40
"the Long Beach Lido": TTUT p. 149
"a house which I believe [he] used": JC INT
"Ray Kelly, the great love": JC INT
One army veteran stationed: Charles Reilly INT

219 "It was a drinking-and-sex party": Charles Reilly INT
Harriman reports that neighbors: TTUT p. 149
This show gave him the most satisfaction: *NY Sunday Mirror* 5/20/56
"a sparkling and enormously talented": *NY Sunday Mirror* 5/20/56
"small, dapper": CUSBSP

220 "I would suggest": CUSBSP
"the show belongs to Mr. Porter": *NY Daily Mirror* 11/10/38
"he did a magnificent job": NYP 11/12/38
"the pride I felt": USC-FOTL
"at the top of his form": NYT 11/20/38
"despite a moment when Victor Moore": NYHT 11/26/38
"Cole Porter has provided": NYP 11/12/38

221 "You'll never hear it": YAR, undated, unidentified news clipping
"Mary Martin, you know": NYHT 1/21/51
The rumor was that finally: MP INT

222 "We got along with him": CU-SBSP

223 "You must never even hint": YAR, undated, unidentified news clipping
"My great professional tragedy": NYHT 4/2/39
In April 1939, Lucius Beebe: NYHT 4/2/39
"One really big hit": NYHT 4/2/39
"and are bored or disappointed": NYHT 4/2/39

224 wasn't at first famous: NYHT 4/2/39
"As long as there is that much": NYHT 4/2/39
Leave It to Me gave 307 performances: CLCP p. 168
"back in stride": *Variety* 11/10/38

CHAPTER 12

225 "The wise lived yesterday": TTUT p. 135
Although the house: MP INT
Ray Kelly claimed that Cole: ARIZ

226 "It was completely primitive": RK INT
"One washed outdoors": ARIZ
the score for *Broadway Melody of 1939*: CLCP p. 178

228 "ensconced in [the] cottage": *NY Daily Mirror* 6/2/39
"It was a way Cole had": JC INT
a musical to star Mae West: *Time* 4/2/39
"When Lahr first heard": NOACL p. 204
"Cole was a horrible piano player": NOACL p. 204

230 "You'll break down all discipline": ARIZ
"Linda, I'm so sorry": ARIZ
"She could freeze people": ARIZ
"to write a Noël Coward–type song": CLCP p. 196
This was Lady Olga: UITOH p. 94
"I and you and Mr. Woolley": UITOH p. 98
"There were more than a hundred": UITOH p. 99
"Some of the better class": UITOH p. 99

231 *DuBarry Was a Lady* had its first: CLCP p. 181
"This girl has a sugar grand-daddy": *Boston Advertisor* 11/13/39

pg 231   "on the crude, even the lewd": *Yale Daily News* 11/10/39
        Lahr's son tells us: NOACL p. 203
        "it was dirt": NOACL p. 205
        "a sophisticated song of seduction": NOACL p. 205

232   "saw little to blue pencil": *Boston Post* 11/14/39
        He tempted the girl: BBag INT
        "What can I do?": BBag INT
        Grable detested Merman: BBag INT

233   "Porter feels that syllables": TTUT p. 138
        Joyce asked, "For ninstance, whom?": TTUT p. 138
        "Porter's trick of tossing": TTUT p. 148

234   an hour after the first curtain: *Boston American* 11/14/39
        Betty Grable and Charles Walters sang: CLCP p. 185
        According to Porter's pal: JC INT
        "Friendship" was another: CLCP p. 188
        In Boston, Lahr came down: *Meriden (Conn.) News* 11/10/39
        his father got on famously: NOACL p. 207
        "whose talent he admired": NOACL p. 208

235   "Bert Lahr knows all there is": *Boston Morning Globe* 11/14/39
        "helped audiences to forget": *Indianapolis Star* 12/13/40
        "Lahr is equally at home": *Chicago Daily News* 12/23/40
        "but even his second best": YAR, undated, unidentified news clipping
        "There must be no single 'pansy' ": USC Archives, addressed to Louis B. Mayer, undated
        In January 1940 Cole and Linda: NYHT 1/20/40
        "So Long, Samoa": CLCP p. 284
        Cole rhymed "Iberia" with "gonorrhea": MP INT
        "Farewell, Amanda": CLCP p. 284
        Hepburn suggested Porter: Katharine Hepburn INT
        The royalties for "Farewell, Amanda": LLL p. 259

236   "very motherly to all": Jean Vanderbilt INT
        "dearest, dear" Bernard Berenson: I Tatti
        "This house is MINE": TWCP p. 16
        "beautiful and extremely *raffinée*": FP p. 128

237   "On the outside there was": FP p. 184
        Ed Tauch was the architect: H INT
        "Work must begin *at once*": TWCP p. 16

238   "I have turned Buxton Hill over": TWCP p. 18
        "Sturge and I go every Friday": TWCP p. 19
        "Linda is in wonderful form": TWCP p. 18
        "I'm tired of the mountains": TWCP p. 19
        "The Porters rather ruined": JH INT
        jokey references . . . "that big Swede": TWCP p. 19

239   "Brick, I've written": Bricktop INT
        "You haven't heard anything": NYDN 11/4/39
        One American sleuth: Jane Wise of New Rochelle, YAR, undated, unidentified news clipping

CHAPTER 13

241   Although Berlin was accused: IBB p. 418
        He and Berlin had invented: IBB p. 417
        "I can't understand": IBB p. 418

242   "a better show": *Boston Transcript* 10/9/40
        "destined for success": *Boston Daily Record* 10/10/40

pg 242 "risque" and "rough spots": *Variety* 10/9/40
On October 30, 1940: CLCP p. 199
"the scene of enough ermine": YAR, undated
"Society People" . . . "never again": JA 11/4/40
243 "Porter was a snob": MP INT
Katie thought her son: BM INT
244 "Who Would Have Dreamed?": CLCP p. 203
Porter is said to have told: B.Bag INT
245 "Garbo-Peep": "Farming," refrain 3, CLCP p. 214
"Dream Dancing": CLCP p. 209
The *Newsweek* critic: YAR, undated
"Jabberwocky": NYT 10/30/41
"a perfect love song": NYT 10/29/91
Danny Kaye is now written about: LOAB p. 228
"Kaye led a quite independent": LOAB p. 229
246 it opened in New York . . . on October 29: CLCP p. 212
he had entered Doctors Hospital: *Variety* 10/29/41
he learned that Fifi Laimbeer: FS INT
Let's Face It has, in sum: CLCP pp. 212–20
247 "I Hate You, Darling": CLCP p. 219
"Remember hell hath no fury": CLCP p. 218
248 Nelson Barclift remembered: YAR
249 *This Is the Army* (or TITA): COUF p. 70
"*This Is the Army* did much": COUF p. 70
"for whom rigid gender roles": COUF p. 72
By July of 1942 Cole: YAR
"Barclift-Barclift": YAR
250 On a photo he signed "Cole": YAR
251 "Come to 1-2-3 tonite": YAR
Porter envisioned it: *NY Sun* 2/13/42
"Cole's songs were sandwiched": CLCP p. 94
a "*gentil*" . . . love: CLCP p. 95
"The 1-2-3 Club is one of those": TNY 6/13/42
"the 1-2-3 [packs] them in": *NY Sun* 2/13/42
252 A soldier who had a romantic meeting: Interviewee requests anonymity
"It's bedtime": YAR
"I actually miss you": YAR
"I beg you": YAR
"I Hate Men": CLCP p. 276
253 "I'm sorta depressed": YAR
Robert Wheaton recalls: RW INT
he eventually married Harriette: MP INT
254 "Sturge found his way": YAR
parties that Lew Kesler hosted: BBag INT
"Please go out of your way": YAR
"took refuge in Williamstown": HH INT
Sometimes, she reported: Nancy Gardener INT
"Cole and Linda were often": StS INT
255 often he was so drunk: RK INT
he hasn't much use for St. Joseph: YAR
"are the only two people in N.Y.C.": YAR
"that wicked city idea": YAR
256 "so big that I'd starve": YAR
"music is the elixir": YAR
"You tell me you think of me": YAR
Something to Shout About . . . Robert Kimball points out: CLCP p. 222

pg 257 Poetry, said Gerard Manley Hopkins: POGMH p. xxxiii
        One man who had been a young: JK INT
        Cole sent news in several: RW INT
        Publisher Robert Giroux recalls: RG INT
258   Robert Wheaton met Cole: RW INT
259   "Glide, glider, glide": Cole Porter Trust
        "only factor preventing": CLCP p. 284
        Porter kept a careful eye: MP INT
260   "I'm not blind, you know: MP INT
        Something for the Boys: CLCP 227
        "the best of his kind": *Boston Post* 12/19/42
261   "the year's plushiest audience": NYHT 1/16/43
        The play earned: NYT 1/12/43
        the fee was . . . the highest ever paid: NYHT 1/13/43
262   "all his suggestions": LLL p. 205
        "I never had to memorize": YAR
        "lacking in magic": *Morning Telegraph* 3/8/43
        "some of Cole Porter's second-best": YAR, TNY, undated
263   He considered the Fieldses ideal: MAA p. 127
        "thought his score one of the best": MAA p. 128
        "she decided it would be a duet": PL INT
        "provided us with a raucous": MAA p. 129
        Merman feuded with Paula Laurence: MAA pp. 129, 130
264   "He studied my voice": MAA p. 136
        Donahue's butler always engaged: MAA p. 172
        "Jimmy Donahue used to lace": H INT
        "My Linda has been seriously ill": MAA p. 153
265   "for the first time I felt": MAA p. 154
        Porter discovered Grandma Moses: LLL p. 199
266   "She entered the New York art scene": Galerie St. Etienne, NYC
        "the wonderful gift you sent": Cole Porter Trust 12/27/44
        Merman thought the decor clashed with: LLL p. 199
        "It just kind of pleased him": CU-OH MS
        Porter had very few good pictures: MP INT
        "had a business person's" regard: BB INT

CHAPTER 14

267   Early in 1943 Cole and Linda: LLL p. 207
        "most outrageous personality": ADLGC p. 117
        George Cukor's cicerone: RW INT
        in June 1936 a family: RW INT
        Shields (who was not a pederast): RW INT
        Hearst . . . kept the story out: RW INT
268   He then turned to interior decoration: RW INT
        Ronald Reagan reportedly: RW INT
        in despair, Shields killed himself: RW INT
269   And so the pool had to be: MP INT
        "He had no hair anywhere": RW INT
        "One room is really a garden": VOG 9/1/45
        a film . . . called *Mississippi Belle:* CLCP p. 238
        "In short, I'm not very enthusiastic": Cole Porter Trust
        "I have the feeling": Cole Porter Trust
270   George Eells speaks of 1943–44: LLL pp. 202–204
        Kimball gives in a full way: CLCP pp. 126, 127

pg 270   Joan Fontaine's claim: Joan Fontaine INT
           "If I use this, will probably have": CLCP p. 126
           Porter wanted to buy the right: CLCP p. 126

271   But Porter acquiesced: CLCP p. 126
           Fletcher's version of the refrain: CLCP p. 127
           "keep it carefully under your hat": CLCP p. 126

272   when Kate Smith introduced it: YAR
           "the top song of the 1944–45 season": PT 7/11/45
           "said to be one of F.D.R.'s favorites": YAR, NYDN, undated

273   Bob Hope joked: YAR
           "man's insatiable longing": YAR
           "Oh, that old thing.": YAR
           The German general: YAR
           "delighted . . . but I resent": YAR
           In February 1945, when the liner: NYT 2/22/45
           "Whether you sing or not": Cole Porter Trust
           "['Don't Fence Me In'] reaches": YAR
           Bob Fletcher heard: YAR

274   Late in December: Cole Porter Trust
           Dr. Sigmund Spaeth . . . testified: LLL p. 219
           "The jury came back": PT 6/7/46

275   "my producer . . . Arthur Schwartz": YAR
           "a tremendous interest": YAR
           "a great chap": YAR
           considered Todd a virtual guru: ARIZ
           "[Todd's] theory": *Boston Herald* 12/30/43
           Porter served as best man: *Variety* 1/5/44
           When *Mexican Hayride* opened: CLCP p. 244
           "Porter has another hit": *NY Mirror* 1/29/44
           "I left *Mexican Hayride*": JH letter to A, 8/22/96

276   Porter believed that she left: LLL p. 212
           Porter "struggling up and down": JH letter to A, 8/22/96
           A critic in the *Daily News:* NYDN 1/29/44
           Porter had mostly abandoned: *NY Sun* 1/29/44
           "An undistinguished extravaganza": NYHT 1/29/44
           "The great disappointment": TNY 2/5/44

278   osteomyelitis recurred: LLL pp. 209, 210
           Danton Walker wrote: LLL p. 210
           "If it isn't true": LLL p. 210
           Linda reported on August 18: TWCP p. 18
           Porter's favorite is said to have been: LLL p. 212
           "I Love You," the show's one hit: CLCP p. 245
           Monty Woolley, who challenged Porter: LLL p. 212
           Robert Kimball refers: CLCP p. 245

279   "the Duchess of Peru": YAR
           "Cole Porter's last great love": JH INT
           "California is wonderful": YAR, dated 3/24/44
           the domestic arrangements: YAR
           "and is living in your room": YAR
           Mike Todd, Porter, and . . . Paul Haakon auditioned: *Collier's* 2/5/44
           "The production is the star": *Christian Science Monitor* 12/30/43
           "do not have the usual convolution": NYT 1/29/44

280   June Havoc stopped the show: *Boston Post* 12/30/43
           "it may still continue to draw": YAR

281   "I leave [Hollywood]": YAR
           "didn't care . . . much for Mike Todd": CO-OH MS

pg 281 "The show is wonderful": TWCP p. 19
282 "Your music great success": CPAB p. 217
In the early autumn Porter went: LLL pp. 214, 215
"You made a wonderful impact": DG INT
283 "in his best vein": *Philadelphia Inquirer* 11/25/44
"an as yet unfinished product": *Philadelphia Record* 11/25/44
he refused to sing one chorus: NOACL pp. 229, 230
When Rose heard rumors: DG INT
284 "musically, though not lyrically": NYWT 12/8/44
"The lyrics are . . . plenty blue": *Variety* 11/25/44
285 Rose next invoked Actors' Equity: TFWW p. 134
"the last word in complete escapism": NYHT 12/3/44
"Last night . . . Billy Rose": NYP 12/8/44
286 A man on the sidewalk: MP INT
"the tunes definitely are not": NYT 12/8/44
"[It] does not come through": NYHT 2/8/44
Danton Walker, an old foe, accused: NYDN 12/9/44
287 "In your new show, you": YAR
"a pretentious fake": NYHT 12/24/44
"out of key and out of tempo": NYDN 5/26/44
288 "Old Songs are more than tunes": YAR

CHAPTER 15

289 Irving Berlin suggested: LLL p. 220
Ann Warner . . . was so aggressive: DH INT
"Your happy news arrived": Cole Porter Trust
"I am extremely flattered": Cole Porter Trust
Warner Bros. agreed to pay Porter: Cole Porter Trust
290 "What will they use": LLL p. 220
"It was . . . as if": LLL p. 221
"None of it's true.": PR 2/11/49
"Musically (and financially) the film": TCPS p. xi
"there is enough substance": MCM, undated, unidentified news clipping
"Dear Boss": USC, Motion Picture Academy Collection
291 "had started negotiations for Cary Grant": Cole Porter Trust
Countess Dorothy di Frasso . . . educated Gary Cooper: DH INT
had an affair with Bugsy Siegel: DH INT
These lunches: CLF INT
"we will probably have": Cole Porter Trust
"some of the stars who introduced": Cole Porter Trust
"It will give us all the chance": Cole Porter Trust
"Your swell wire received": Cole Porter Trust
Louis Shurr was "crazy about": Cole Porter Trust
292 "has not been thorough enough": Cole Porter Trust
"It looks as if you are": Cole Porter Trust
"Hedda dear": *Hollywood Reporter*, 1/19/45
"We [are] starting picture": Cole Porter Trust
Late in March 1945 he wrote: YAR
293 "On my left leg, Moorhead": YAR
"I got everything I asked for": YAR
294 Leonard Goldstein, who as a young: Leonard Goldstein INT
"Dear Cole, I hope": USC, Motion Picture Academy Collection letter dated 7/14/48
"kids twenty years old": Audrey Aurette INT

pg 294 she drove to Cole's house: Audrey Aurette INT
295 "We never go to restaurants": YAR
"the belt made out of Lillian Russell's garters": Letter in possession of HD
"Poor darling—it is pitiful": YAR
"They do not know how the end": TLH p. 183
Grant insisted that he be allowed: TLH p. 184
Alexis Smith chose to look on such demands: TLH p. 184
296 Breen wrote to Jack Warner: USC Motion Picture Academy Collection
Charles Higham in his biography: TLH pp. 183–87
"the most important musical": Cole Porter Trust
"what pleased us most": MCM
"I can never tell you": MCM
"I, of course, should be": NYP 12/24/45
297 "The story is not important": NYP 7/26/46
"*Night and Day* begs quick dismissal": NYT 7/26/46
"no more the story": San Francisco News 7/28/46
"Although he is getting on in years": TNY 7/27/46
Warner Bros. banned Henry Luce's correspondents: NYDN 8/16/46
The governor of Indiana asked: MCM
called officially on Alexis Smith: MCM
298 "Cole Porter and I": NYHT 6/16/46
"Now I am planning": *Boston Sunday Globe* 4/28/46
"the grandiose proportions": *Variety* 5/1/46
"has everything from": YAR *Boston Post* undated clipping
299 "Please sweetheart": *Boston Globe* 4/28/46
likened it to *Hellzapoppin*: *Newsweek* 6/10/46
"If God will forgive me": TNY 6/8/46

CHAPTER 16

300 "Always want the best": *Celebrating Cole Porter,* Symphony Space, NYC, 1991 (tape copy in possession of A)
Margaret Moore . . . in 1947 . . . died.: LLL p. 243
"to walk with her to the Pavillon": RHR p. 160
301 "it never occurred to him": RHR p. 160
"Formality was the word": RHR p. 160
"Almost no one became familiar": RHR p. 160
"He was approached": RHR p. 160
"a very sweet lady": Elise Smith INT
Cole had only recently enjoyed: LLL pp. 228–230
302 "the preparation of a new musical": Lincoln Center Music Collection, letter to Mrs. Arthur Reis, Executive Chair, League of Composers, 3/26/47
The Pirate: CLCP p. 269
"What kind of a number": USC-FOTL
Porter had had to bring a lawsuit: PR 1/25/47
"He used to go there": CU-OH MS
303 W. H. Auden even called: TNY 8/17/92
According to the latter, the idea: StS INT
Burton Lane also declined: Burton Lane INT
"a young man named Saint Souber": CU-SBSP
she had to concede: CU-SBSP
304 "Furthermore I was not": CU-SBSP
"as I had never heard": CU-SBSP
"as a musical alone": CU-SBSP

pg 304   "I had an idea for doing": CU-SBSP
it was she who wanted Cole: CU-SBSP
"washed up": CU-SBSP
"I told [him] the idea": CU-SBSP
"I had brought titles and contents": CU-SBSP

305   "It's not what you wanted": CU-SBSP
"Now tell me about the characters": CU-SBSP
"Linda read some of *The Taming*": CU-SBSP
"it will live forever": CU-SBSP
"Through my wild hyperbole": CU-SBSP
"as I did not regard him": CU-SBSP
As Novotna remembered: Jarmila Novotna INT

306   Jack had been Noël Coward's lover: StS INT
"I've just heard . . . about a girl": YAR, NYP undated
"as they already had an opera star": PMo INT
"The moment I saw her": YAR
"Get someone to train your voice": YAR
"Bella Bellissima": CU-SBSP
"she could never play the part": CU-SBSP
"Were Thine That Special Face": CLCP p. 276
"I Am Ashamed": CLCP p. 280

307   he played her the score: AC INT
"That girl's voice won't carry": AC INT
She stood on the stage and sang: PMo INT
"They're crazy," he said: AC INT
"I finally had to rudely tell them": CU-SBSP
"a difficult man": HaH INT
"a very mild man": StS INT
Sam Spewack . . . had walked out: StS INT

308   "complete failures": StS INT
"Bella gave [Sam] a share": StS INT
"Bella writes me": Cole Porter Trust
It was Alfred Drake and Saint Subber: StS INT
"whenever I try to talk sense": StS INT

309   "an eccentric young producer": LLL p. 238
"complicated, educated": StS INT
"more in love with his parents": StS INT
Porter immediately detected the street kid: StS INT
"Not the boys.": StS INT
it was surprising to hear: ErM INT

310   "How wonderful to learn": StS INT
Lang angered Porter: MP INT
"difficult" . . . "petulant": HaH INT
"He was kind of provoked": *NY Sunday News* 10/24/71
Porter asked the cast: *NY Sunday News* 10/24/71
"a lovely artist": PMo INT
He drank heavily and rarely: PMo INT
"When *Kiss Me, Kate* went": CU-SBSP

311   Cole advised Pat to slam: PMo INT
Lemuel Ayers . . . learned that he had leukemia: StS INT
Ayers produced beautiful sketches: StS INT
Sometimes she would be wheeled: StS INT
"The two things you couldn't take": StS INT
"at a low ebb": I Tatti 4/5/48
A number of her friends thought: HH INT; Eleanor Childs INT

pg 311 "I have felt so tired": I Tatti 8/23/48
312 "New York is a nightmare": I Tatti 10/9/48
In one four-day weekend: StS INT
313 "Bella will probably cut": StS INT
she verified the agreement . . . "but we realized": CU-SBSP
314 Howard Cullman's wife: StS INT
Peggy Cullman remembers: PC INT
Porter asked questions: CU-SBSP
"One night . . . Porter asked": CU-SBSP
315 "These [abscess and ulcer] appeared": LLL p. 243
which was dropped, as it reduced: LLL p. 244
"The best musical comedy book": CU-SBSP
Porter turned down *My Fair Lady:* CU-OH-MS
316 One of the dancers recalls: Ingrid Edwards INT
"The lyrics counted more": Ingrid Edwards INT
"is as neatly worked out": *Chicago News* 10/9/49
"Look at my 'So in Love' ": NYHT 2/20/55
317 "This request . . . may seem excessive": Cole Porter Trust
Among the personal belongings Cole took: *Time* 1/31/49
The show opened in Philadelphia: CLCP p. 274
"No rewriting of the libretto": CU-SBSP
Saint and Ayers had secreted: StS INT
Pat Morison recalled: PMo INT
she whispered to Moorhead: USC-E
318 "Cole threw his canes down": NYDN 10/31/89
"I feel Cole Porter": PMo INT
"Porter's score is . . . perhaps his best": *NY News* 12/31/48
"literate without being highbrow": NYP 12/31/48
"Her numbers there": NYT 1/14/51
319 the *Hollywood Reporter* faulted the book: *Hollywood Reporter* 12/31/48
"King Cole has made a monkey": *Hollywood Reporter* 12/31/48
"Porter has been stimulated": TNY 4/2/49
"Who could have foreseen": YAR undated
"All my career I wanted": TNY 4/2/49

CHAPTER 17

321 paramount was worry over Linda: LLL p. 249
"Linda is still in the hospital": CU-SBSP
The journey nearly finished her: LLL p. 250
322 "I think the nicest thing": LLL p. 259
323 the Boston censor demanded: YAR, letter, 11/29/50
the silliest moment in opera: CLF INT
"Cole's score was simply superimposed": LLL p. 265
The Philadelphia tryout began: CLCP p. 287
Madeline Smith had written repeatedly: CU-OH MS
324 by Porter, she believed: ADM INT
Saint Subber claimed he and Ayers: StS INT
"If you ask for my opinion": ADM INT
"how really crippled Cole was": ADM INT
"You know, Cole": ADM INT
325 "I must stress what Agnes de Mille": *World Telegram and Sun* 12/19/50
"I am legally the director": ADM INT
Once he gave her some wine: ADM INT
326 Saint Subber and Ayers were often: ADM INT

pg 326   "The book bogs down": *Philadelphia Daily News* 11/6/50
Selma Tamber . . . remembered: ST INT

327   Tamber recalled both his generosity: ST INT
on November 28 it went to Boston: CLCP p. 287
"One startling [dance]": *Boston Post* 11/29/50
"de-sexing order": YAR, letter from Beatrice Welton, 11/29/50
One of the unfortunate decisions: LLL p. 266
Selma Tamber thought . . . "because Billy Eythe": ST INT
Eythe had been hired: StS INT
"a bad boy who chased [boys]": ST INT
"Some of my young male dancers": ADM INT
In New York, William Eythe: Charles Bowden INT

328   "Whole scenes were ripped": NYHT 12/17/50
"Nothing went up or down": NYHT 12/17/50
When *Out of This World* opened: CLCP p. 287
"The critics must have been": YAR
"The male dancing chorus": *NY World Telegram and Sun* 12/22/50
"*Out of This World* [is] a modern": NYHT 12/22/50
"a tiresome subject": NYT 12/22/50
Terry praised the choreography: NYHT 12/31/50
"She has given us, indeed": NYT 1/14/51

329   "I went home thinking": YAR, *NY Mirror,* undated
Cole's friends began noticing: LLL p. 268
In December 1950 John Wharton: Cole Porter Trust
"I regret that I find": Cole Porter Trust
"mainly because after": Cole Porter Trust
"previous engagements": YAR
"hadn't enough guts": CU-SBSP

330   Shortly after, he wrote: CU-SBSP
"She booms": Postcard in possession of Louise Thwing, 6/9/51
thousands were: *New Haven Journal Courier* 6/27/51
"Illness is so humiliating": I Tatti
In Los Angeles guests at lunch: LLL p. 269
"Where will [Porter] get": Cole Porter Trust
"gossipy secretary": Cole Porter Trust 8/4/51
"I underplayed my gratitude": Cole Porter Trust 8/4/51

331   "I do not believe you yet realize": Cole Porter Trust
"An unsuccessful agent": MP INT
among his clients were: MP INT
A chapter in the autobiography: MP INT
He had plans to write: MP INT

332   Jean Howard refused: JH INT
"a hustler type": JC INT
"Cheer me up": MP INT
"Cole is here": I Tatti
"I haven't been [to Paris]": I Tatti
Sylvain feared he might: LLL p. 270
on October 5 he was admitted: LLL p 271
"There is nothing to worry about": LLL p 271
"His thinking is along these lines": LLL p 272

333   "To a person who has talent": *Toast of the Town,* CBS-TV, 2/24/52
"Can you play two pianos": Lincoln Center Music Collection, letter dated 2/9/52
"I am afraid the reason": Cole Porter Trust
"Please tell Jane Rubin": Cole Porter Trust

334   "the lyrics are very topical": Cole Porter Trust
"merely generalized": Cole Porter Trust

CHAPTER 18

pg 336   "Just tell me what you want: CF INT
He also challenged Cole: NYHT 5/3/53
"often he played" . . . "jotted": NYHT 5/3/53
when Feuer began to play it: CF INT
"Shows [used to be] quicker": NYT 5/3/53

337   "He was in awe of Michael Kidd": CF INT
Every fifteen minutes or so: ErM INT
on July 26, Katie: PR 8/8/52
Katie's Miami Indian servants sat: LLL p. 276
After Katie died: JOC INT

338   "I was devoted to her": I Tatti 8/16/52
"a wonderful bit of fiction": Letter in possession of Louise Thwing
"We did our best for Christmas": Copy of letter dated 12/26/52, in possession of author
Monty Woolley, who arrived . . . "roaring drunk": Copy of letter dated 12/26/52, in possession of author
"The Porters have started": I Tatti 1/5/53
Allan Jones, who first sang: ErM INT

339   It was Cy Feuer who discovered: *NY World Telegram and Sun* 5/12/53
"I hope you will create": L INT
Like Merman, Lilo had never had: L INT
"He had a distinct sense": L INT
Lilo was always introduced: L INT
"He adored that": L INT

340   Once, auditioning a possible understudy: L INT
"not at all a snob": CF INT
The Porter party . . . sent ahead: Cole Porter Trust
"Lilo is the most exciting": *Evening Bulletin* 3/24/53

341   Gwen Verdon spotted Conried: GV INT
Her first sight of Cole Porter: GV INT
"because I adore Eisenhower": JA 5/23/53
"the most extraordinary gifts": L INT
Even Lilo tells how "*jalouse*": L INT

342   "had the star at the finale": CU-OH MS

343   Geneviève Pitot, the dance arranger: GV INT
"I just won't do that": GV INT
Michael Kidd burst in: GV INT

344   "Where did you get that low voice?": RHR p. 186
"an extraordinary performer": GV INT
Porter would take himself to Lenox Hill: GV INT
"Bring someone": GarK INT

345   "musically it is Mr. Cole Porter": YAR, *Observer*, undated
"a musical about some people": *Philadelphia Inquirer* 3/22/53
"J. Mielziner has virtually": *Evening Bulletin* 3/24/53

346   "Michael Kidd's . . . swift and tumultuous": NYT 5/17/53
"haggard about his lyrics": NYHT 5/3/53
"critics are truly abominable": YAR
"I hate to have the New York curtain": NYT 5/3/53

347   "As the overture played": *Indianapolis News* 4/25/53
Lilo was touched: L INT
"When I think of the trouble": YAR, letter dated 6/6/53
what an inspiration it was for him: YAR
"with nearly nude girls": JA 5/24/53
"must to the discerning offer": *Catholic News* 5/16/53
"Dear Cole": YAR

pg 347 "a nigger Baptist preacher": JH INT
348 "Phonograph records have": LLL p. 282
Dr. Sirmay reported that the disappointment: LLL p. 283
Lilo had the feeling: L INT

CHAPTER 19

349 "keep it under your hat": Cole Porter Trust, letter dated 7/9/53
"beneath contempt": RM INT
"the usual virus infection": I Tatti 7/24/53
Michael Kidd had turned down: Michael Kidd INT
350 "Darling B.B.": I Tatti 10/53
"The reason Linda hasn't answered": Cole Porter Trust, letter dated 12/23/53
They had contracted with Knopf: CU-SBSP, letter dated 9/3/52
he objected to passages: Cole Porter Trust, letter dated 11/13/53
"threatening legal letter": Cole Porter Trust, letter dated 11/13/53
"We are distressed to hear": Cole Porter Trust, letter dated 11/18/53
"He assumes that Knopf": Cole Porter Trust, letter dated 11/23/53
351 "Under no condition write to Cole": CU-SBSP, letter dated 2/11/52
"When you arrive here": Cole Porter Trust, letter dated 7/6/54
"I wish you didn't have to go": CU-OH MS
"I listen to *Stella Dallas*": NYT 2/20/55
they hardly recognized her: RK INT
"I want to die": LLL p. 285
"If only I was [important enough]": RK INT
Cole arranged that a "Linda Porter rose": NYT 8/28/55
352 the melancholy fox-trot: *MISIA* p. 308
Linda died on May 20, 1954: NYT 5/21/54
"a very cold moment": MRS. BM INT
"I've had two great women": NYT 2/20/55
Asked . . . if the Porters had "a good marriage": CU-OH MS
"She had a very bad": MJOB INT
"Linda Lee adored": MJOB INT
either give up Hollywood: LLL p. 287
353 "our lovely Linda": LLL p. 286
Linda left an estate: LLL p. 287
"How can one help not being": LLL p. 287
Eells reports Mrs. Alex Steinert: LLL p. 287
"The neck which used to be": Cole Porter Trust, letter dated 8/25/54
354 "*Silk Stockings* has a fine script": Cole Porter Trust, letter dated 8/25/54
But this arrangement was canceled: LLL p. 290
In his will, Cole bequeathed: LLL p. 290
"My new apartment at the Waldorf": Cole Porter Trust, letter dated 11/9/54
355 it took about five days: JC INT
"protect me from those awful weeks": Cole Porter Trust, letter dated 11/9/54
"He knew special little inns": ErM INT
"You hope my show is going": Cole Porter Trust, letter dated 11/9/54
"Dear Bobbie" . . . "to help you": Cole Porter Trust, letter dated 11/15/54
"You ask me what color": Cole Porter Trust, letter dated 11/15/54
Raison could be . . . For a time: RW INT
In time Raison abused: MP INT
A friend who had been: RW INT
356 he eventually mortgaged: MP INT
"delightful. Everyone": Cole Porter Trust, letter dated 11/9/54
Her surname was changed: TGH pp. 180, 254

pg 356 "with slightly protruding eyes": TGH p. 283
"the Kraut," as Ameche: TGH p. 288
when the tryout began: CLCP p. 311
"Smash for Feuer and Martin": TGH p. 299

357 "He sits small and delicate": TGH p. 299
Noël Coward's sweeping backstage: ErM INT
"The book is wonderful": ErM INT
Ernie Martin remembers: ErM INT
"Cole Porter observes each": TGH p. 312

358 So Martin fired Kaufman . . . "a blow to his pride" . . . In the hospital Kaufman:
Malcolm Goldstein, *George S. Kaufman: His Life, His Theater* (NY: Oxford University Press, 1979), p. 444

359 Abe Burrows was brought in: *Boston Herald* 1/26/55
"It has been mutually decided": YAR
"What's so bad about Siberia?": ErM INT
"this song troubled Porter": CLCP p. 315
"I want you to help me": CF INT
"We don't expect you": Gretchen Wyler INT

360 the Motion Picture Association: USC Special Collections, Arthur Freed Collection

361 Louise Thwing described the opening: *Orlando Evening Star* 2/28/55
The yacht, *Eros:* LLL p. 296
Sturge, Cole, and Paul Sylvain left: YAR
"Cole's last intimate friend": TWCP p. 27
Cy Feuer was well aware: CF INT
"Cole kept his two lives": CF INT

362 Years later, Bray was killed: JH INT
"which is in the process": CU-OH MS Letter, Madeline Smith to Lou Bearss, 2/25/55
"a dream-trip": CU-OH MS Letter, Cole Porter to Lou Bearss, 4/12/55
"alone with a whisky & soda": YAR, letter, Cole Porter to George Eells, 2/24/55

363 "a sad looking little man": LLL p. 295
"Opening giant success": C p. 246
"the wittiest dialogue": NYT 2/25/55
"Cole Porter Talks of His Musicals": NYHT 2/20/55

364 "the word for Dick Rodgers' melodies": YAR
"nine anonymous bitches": YAR, letter, Cole Porter to George Eells, 3/15/55

365 Jean Howard recalled that somewhere: TWCP p. 36
"a strange combination of joy": LLL p. 296
"Cole [became] ice": TWCP p. 51

366 "At once a feeling of comfort": YAR

367 "I felt the beginnings": YAR
"You can see that, in spite": Letter, Cole Porter to Louise Thwing, POR
A section of his small notebooks . . . "I strolled": YAR
In Rome Cole sent word: RHR p. 199

368 he had a mean streak: MP INT
"I pine for the prose": YAR, letter, Cole Porter to George Eells, 5/11/55
"The dream is over": YAR

CHAPTER 20

369 "Cole with delight saw": CU-OH MS
"The book units give": NYT 3/1/67
one whole wall was mirror . . . the sound caused the wall mirror: MP INT
Vogue that year: VOG 11/55
"I was *ébloui*": YAR

pg 370   After receiving an honorary doctorate: LLL p. 299
         Armstrong and Ella Fitzgerald were among: *Downbeat* 9/4/58
   371   Cole had first met Frank Sinatra: USC-FOTL
         Sinatra "is the only person singing: Mrs. Arthur Hornblow INT
         "He's been at it for several": GAMM p. 153
         "His friendly manner relaxed me": GAMM p. 154
   372   "His method of demonstrating": GAMM p. 154
         "I can tell from your reaction": GAMM p. 154
         Chaplin was amazed: GAMM p. 157
         Ernie Martin's impression of Cole: ErM INT
   373   when Ray Kelly expressed an interest: RK INT
         "I Love You, Samantha" was a favorite: LLL p. 300
         "I am in despair about Stella": YAR, letter, Cole Porter to George Eells, 9/10/55
   374   "I was married 35 years: *Chicago Tribune* 10/1/56
         "nothing has given me more": Cole Porter Trust, letter, Max Dreyfus to Cole
         Porter, 11/12/56
         hired Stanley Musgrove: LLL p. 304
         "[Cole] said to me once": USC-E
   375   "Well, Did You Evah?": CLCP p. 186
         "Please note that the first two": Cole Porter Trust, letter, Cole Porter to Saul Chap-
         lin, 11/10/55
         "I am working hard": Cole Porter Trust, letter, Cole Porter to Saul Chaplin, 11/3/55
         He kept near him a list: CU-OH MS
         "The Italians are the most": *Chicago Tribune* 10/1/56
         Tony Curtis was present: Leonard Gershe INT
         Chaplin found Cole "aloof": SC INT
   376   the terrible news of Sturges's: TWCP p. 111
         "dreams of beauty": Cole Porter Trust, letter, Cole Porter to Saul Chaplin, 2/1/56
         "I shall begin work": *Etude* 9/56
         "changing ideas every day": Cole Porter Trust 12/31/55
         "does not want to play": Cole Porter Trust 12/18/54
   377   "I don't feel like working": CU-SBSP, letter dated 6/25/55
         Cole's attorney sent Dean Acheson: Cole Porter Trust, letter dated 9/12/55
         On the Fourth of July 1955: TWCP p. 111
         This journey began late in February: TWCP p. 112
         "Richard news is always interesting": Cole Porter Trust, letter dated 4/19/56
         "if you still have a complex": YAR
         "You're *always* late": TWCP p. 151
         "women who are late": *Chicago Tribune* 10/1/56
   378   "It was an unforgettable sight": TWCP p. 181
         "Robert has to stand-by": TWCP p. 209
         Cole's valet kept a list: Richard Kamror INT
         "I was alarmed at how little": GAMM p. 165
   379   "My job": Cole Porter Trust, 10/5/57

CHAPTER 21

   380   In January of 1957, Cole: Letter from Dana Atchley, M.D., to William Smith,
         M.D., dated 8/10/63, copy in possession of A
         he spent some time recuperating: DH INT
         "Perelman is coming out here": Cole Porter Trust, letter dated 7/27/57
         "prompt, honored every promise": RHR p. 202
   381   "I have sent the Osbert Sitwell": YAR, letter, Richard Lewine to Cole Porter, 8/57
         "If he does not pay attention": RL INT
   382   "Sounds like Noël, doesn't it?": RL INT

pg 382   "no flash—not much interest": RL INT
          On February 21, 1958, *Aladdin:* CLCP p. 332
          Alberghetti (who after hours): RL INT
          "*Aladdin* was saddnin'": NYT 2/28/58
          "*Aladdin* was an absolute delight": YAR, letter, Irving Lazar to Cole Porter, 2/24/58
          "a $50,000 flop": YAR, unidentified, undated news clipping
          "a very elegant, sweet man": Leonard Brand, M.D. INT

383   On February 27, Madeline Smith: Letter in possession of HD
          Alan Jay Lerner visited Porter: USC-CPC
          "I'm only half a man": RHR p. 203
          "I was going to send you": Cole Porter Trust, letter, Madeline Smith to Louise
          Bearss, 4/13/58
          "Osteomyelitis made the operation": JA 4/4/58

384   "He has at last had his leg": Graham Payn and Morley Sheridan (editors), *The Noël
          Coward Diaries* (Boston: Little, Brown, 1982), p. 379
          "He was terribly uninterested": DV pp. 219, 220
          "That was the very, very last": CU-OH MS

385   "It was sad seeing him": LLL p. 314
          Henry Burke, Cole's valet, made: Cole Porter Trust
          Cole continued to reward the man: CPB p. 265
          "the outrageous masseur": CLF INT
          Burke persuaded him to switch: CPB p. 265

386   "On the way to Williamstown": CPB p. 267
          "the slowest suicide": JH INT
          "I want to die": StS INT

387   Thinking the man must be exhausted: Aurand Harris INT
          a new servant naively asked: LLL p. 315
          Paul Sylvain died on July 21: LLL p. 313
          "I should think it would be": Cole Porter Trust, letter dated 7/25/59

388   "I was surprised, flattered": YAR, undated letter, Moss Hart to Cole Porter
          "I couldn't like it more": Cole Porter Trust, letter dated 4/23/59
          The young repairman . . . was touched: BBag INT
          Four men with whom Cole: The impeccable source requests anonymity
          "I have no plans at all": NYHT 5/16/60
          "Because that's the way I feel": *Variety* 5/18/60

389   On June 9, his sixty-ninth birthday: NYT 6/10/60
          "As an undergraduate": *Variety* 6/10/60
          "was the first who was kind": *Peru Tribune* 9/29/61
          "For some reason or other": Cole Porter Trust, letter dated 2/28/61

390   "without any warning": CU-OH-JL
          In November of 1960 Cole: Dana Atchley, M.D., to William Smith, M.D., letter
          dated 8/10/63, copy in possession of A
          In 1961 Bella Spewack wrote: CU-SBSP, letter dated 5/20/61
          "I'm the only one who sees him": NYP 6/10/62
          "The beautiful peonies": Letter in possession of HD
          on November 28, 1962: Cole Porter Trust

391   In January 1963 Robert Raison brought: Stephen Stempler INT
          "He never quite got it out": Stephen Stempler INT
          Porter acknowledged Cronin's taste: NYT 3/1/67

392   Cronin had been apprised: Cole Porter Trust, letter dated 2/64
          "a good boy who loved Cole deeply": BBag INT
          John Cronin died . . . In his last: Stephen Stempler INT

393   Cole disapproved of Monty's having taken: CPB p. 267
          He had been badly burned: LLL p. 318
          "Do you think you would like to see": Cole Porter Trust, letter dated 8/1/63

pg 393   "When all is said and done": Dana Atchley, M.D., to William Smith, M.D., letter
         dated 8/10/63, copy in possession of author
    394   "I am spending most of each day": Letter to JOC dated 8/17/63
         Eells was shocked: LLL p. 320
         "It's all I have left": LLL p. 321
    395   "Put down none": LLL p. 323
         Cole had begun to take instruction: StS INT
         Bearss Muhlfeld had heard: BM INT
         he had told Raison before the surgery: RW INT
         Elsie Woodward . . . insisted: GoV INT
         "He was terribly alone": CU-OH MS
    396   "We congratulate you": Leon Allen Eikenberry Funeral Service, Peru, Indiana, INT
         His body was buried: JOC INT
    397   "I think he had [religion]": CU-OH MS
         On October 16, Cole's cousin: JOC INT
         "Bobby, I don't know how": MiP INT

Index

Page numbers in *italics* indicate illustrations.

PERMISSIONS ACKNOWLEDGMENTS

Grateful acknowledgment is made to the following for permission to reprint previously published material:

Robert Cornfield Literary Agency: Excerpt from *Cole* by Robert Kimball, copyright © 1971 by Robert Kimball. Reprinted by permission of the Robert Cornfield Literary Agency.

DaCapo Press: Excerpts from *D.V.* by Diana Vreeland (New York: DaCapo Press, 1997). Reprinted courtesy of DaCapo Press.

Scott Meredith Literary Agency, L.P.: Excerpt from *The Life That Late He Led* by George Eells, copyright © 1967 by George Eells, copyright renewed 1995. Reprinted by permission of the author's estate and its agents, Scott Meredith Literary Agency, L.P.

Peru Tribune: Excerpts from two articles "Night and Day" and "The Times of Cole Porter" by Tommy Hendricks (10/17/77 to 11/7/77). Reprinted courtesy of the *Peru Tribune.*

The Rodgers and Hammerstein Organization: Excerpts from *Musical Stages* by Richard Rodgers, copyright © 1975 Richard Rodgers. All rights reserved. Reprinted by permission of The Rodgers and Hammerstein Organization.

Calvin Tomkins: Excerpts from *Living Well Is the Best Revenge* by Calvin Tomkins (New York: Viking Press, 1962). Reprinted by permission of Calvin Tomkins.

University of Oklahoma Press: Excerpts from *The Golden Age of Movie Musicals and Me* by Saul Chaplin, copyright © 1994 by Saul Chaplin. Reprinted by permission of the publisher, the University of Oklahoma Press.

ILLUSTRATION CREDITS

Stanley Kubrick

A Biography

John Baxter

'In this superbly readable biography, John Baxter traces Kubrick's career from the day this spoilt Jewish boy from the Bronx was given a camera for his thirteenth birthday to his present situation as an eccentric hiding away in a remote Hertfordshire mansion.'

GERALD KAUFMAN, *Sunday Telegraph*

'John Baxter's highly readable biography makes Kubrick maddening, endearing and paranoid in equal proportions . . . Many of the stories are riveting.'

NIGEL ANDREWS, *Financial Times*

'Judicious and well-researched.'   PHILLIP FRENCH, *Observer*

'John Baxter's superb biography sets out with enormous relish to unravel this mystery [of Kubrick's reclusiveness]. His earlier biographies, of Buñuel, Fellini, Ken Russell and Spielberg, are among the best in their field, and his account of Kubrick's somewhat tortured soul is written in the same vivid prose.'

J.G. BALLARD, *New Statesman*

'*Stanley Kubrick* is the sharpest book on cinema since Jake Eberts and Terry Ilott's *My Indecision Is Final*, the history of Goldcrest Films.'   BRIAN ALDISS, *Daily Telegraph*

ISBN: 0 00 638445 5

Leading Minds
An Anatomy of Leadership

Howard Gardner
with the collaboration of Emma Laskin

A UNIQUE EXAMINATION OF
THE CONCEPT OF LEADERSHIP

Howard Gardner, one of the world's most accomplished psychologists, identifies the features, trends and paradoxes that characterize leadership today. While there have been many previous studies of leadership, Howard Gardner's is the first to concentrate on the crucial component of leadership – the human mind. In illuminating portraits of a wide range of leaders – including J. Robert Oppenheimer, Martin Luther King, Jr, Margaret Thatcher, Pope John XXIII, Eleanor Roosevelt and Mahatma Gandhi – he explores the complex, dynamic relationship between the mind of the leader and that of his or her followers.

Drawing a distinction between direct and indirect leaders – the former, politicians, military men and business gurus who seek to exercise power and influence people, and the latter, scientists, novelists, painters who do so through the creation of symbolic products – Gardner reveals the key to leadership: the ability to create a story that affects the thoughts, feelings, and actions of other individuals. In addition, at a time of uncertainty in world leadership, Howard Gardner addresses a range of issues which must be resolved for future leadership to be effective.

Leading Minds provides a significant and original contribution to our understanding of the challenges faced by leaders of organizations and nations.

'Gardner has written another enthralling book'

ANTHONY STORR

'This book should become required reading not simply for leaders and aspiring leaders but for everyone who seeks clearer insights into leaders' roles'   SIR DOUGLAS HAGUE, *Templeton College, Oxford*

0 00 638123 5

Dorothy Rowe's Guide to Life

'Dorothy Rowe is full of robust good sense, rare intuitive wisdom and unhurried sensitivity . . . she is a giver of courage'

NIGELLA LAWSON, *The Times*

The central theme of all Dorothy Rowe's work is that, while the world and ourselves might *seem* to be solid and real, the way in which we are constituted means that we can never know reality directly, only the meanings we have created about reality.

It is when we don't understand this, when we mistakenly think that we, our life and the world are fixed, unalterable parts of reality which we have to put up with and cope with as best we can, that we find we can't handle life's problems – we make mistakes, feel trapped, and often despair.

When we do understand it, we realize that we are free to change.

Dorothy Rowe has helped tens of thousands of people reach this understanding through her books on fear, depression and unhappiness. She has shown how, by understanding our nature, we can end our suffering. Her *Guide to Life* is a summation of this wisdom but with more besides, for there is no end to self-understanding. Like all her books, it is clear and compassionate, witty and wise.

ISBN 0 00 638422 6